The GRE® CAT For Du

Success on the Verbal Sections

General Tips

- Use roots, prefixes, and suffixes to determine the gist of an unfamiliar word.
- Guess quickly if you are stumped. The computer won't let you go on until you've made a guess; answering a few questions incorrectly hurts your score less than not finishing a section.

Antonym Tips

- Create an approximate definition of the word in your mind.
- Predict the obvious opposite.
- Remember that words have more than one meaning.

Reading Comprehension Tips

- Choose positive or neutral answers to the Reading Comprehension questions, not negative ones.
- Roman numeral and negative/exception questions are often tricky and time-consuming; guess quickly on them and go on.
- Don't choose an answer simply because it's true; make certain that it answers the question correctly.

Analogy Tips

- Create a sentence that shows the relationship between the two words, then use that sentence on each answer choice.
- Use roots, prefixes, and suffixes to help define unfamiliar words.
- Beware of answers with inverse relationships (for example, part to whole when the question was whole to part).

Sentence Completion Tips

- Read the entire sentence to get its gist before looking at the individual blanks.
- Search for key connector words (such as *because, although, however*) that may change the meaning of the sentence from what you'd expect.
- Predict whether the blanks need positive or negative words.

This test is rated PG — Proctor Guarded.

Proctors have been genetically altered to have eyes in the backs of their heads; they'll catch you if you peek at this cheat sheet during the GRE. Learn it, and then burn it.

The GRE® CAT For Dummies®

Tips for Success on the Math Sections

General tips

- Lose the calculator (not allowed); scratch paper will be provided by the proctor.
- The GRE tests algebra, geometry, and arithmetic, not calculus or trigonometry.
- Memorize formulas before you take the test. The GRE doesn't provide them.

Quantitative Comparison tips

- Triple-check your answer before hitting the CONFIRM button, as the QC questions are often not the obvious, first-response answer.
- Remember that the answer choices are the same for every question. Choose A if Column A is greater than Column B; B if Column B is greater; C if the two columns are equal; and D if insufficient information is given. E is not a choice.
- If the columns seem to be equal, do the required calculations to *prove* that they are.
- Play the *what-if* game by plugging in 1, then 2, 0, –1, –2, and 1/2. If the answer *depends* on what you plug in for the variable, choose D.

Problem solving tips

- Note what the question specifically asks for: perimeter, area, length, degree, fraction, percentage, and so on.
- Before you begin working on the problem, read the answer choices. You may be able to estimate and answer without working out the solution.
- Plug answer choices into the question to see which one works. Do the easy choices first; you may not have to do the hard ones.

Tips for Success on the Analytical Ability Sections*

Logical Reasoning tips

- Determine the style of the questions (strengthens/weakens, draws conclusion, parallel reasons, and so on) and first complete the ones you do best.
- Guess quickly on questions that are long, tortuous and convoluted; these can be real time-wasters that must be read over and over and over again to be comprehended.

Analytical Reasoning tips

- On the scratch paper the proctor gives you, jot down a list of the people or items involved in the question.
- Be prepared to make more than one diagram when new information is introduced.
- Don't use information given in one question as you answer another question.

*Some schools don't use the Analytical Ability section score. Don't use the Analytical Ability section score. Check with each school individually to find out its policy.

Tips for GRE CBT Success

- The first five or so questions in each section are critical; take your time to answer those correctly.
- You cannot skip and go back to a question, but guess quickly and go on when you are stumped; you benefit from answering every question more than you lose by missing a few.
- Keep an eye on the clock and sprint to the end, being sure to fill in something for every answer before time runs out.

For Dummies™: Bestselling Book Series for Beginners

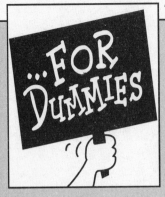

TM

BESTSELLING BOOK SERIES

References for the Rest of Us!™

Do you find that traditional reference books are overloaded with technical details and advice you'll never use? Do you postpone important life decisions because you just don't want to deal with them? Then our *...For Dummies*® business and general reference book series is for you.

...For Dummies business and general reference books are written for those frustrated and hard-working souls who know they aren't dumb, but find that the myriad of personal and business issues and the accompanying horror stories make them feel helpless. *...For Dummies* books use a lighthearted approach, a down-to-earth style, and even cartoons and humorous icons to dispel fears and build confidence. Lighthearted but not lightweight, these books are perfect survival guides to solve your everyday personal and business problems.

> *"More than a publishing phenomenon, 'Dummies' is a sign of the times."*
>
> — The New York Times

> *"...you won't go wrong buying them."*
>
> — Walter Mossberg, Wall Street Journal, on IDG Books' ...For Dummies books

> *"A world of detailed and authoritative information is packed into them..."*
>
> — U.S. News and World Report

Already, millions of satisfied readers agree. They have made *...For Dummies* the #1 introductory level computer book series and a best-selling business book series. They have written asking for more. So, if you're looking for the best and easiest way to learn about business and other general reference topics, look to *...For Dummies* to give you a helping hand.

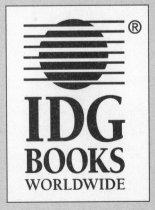

1/99

The
GRE® CAT
FOR
DUMMIES®

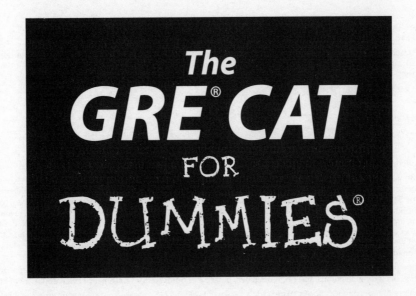

The GRE® CAT
FOR
DUMMIES®

by Suzee Vlk

IDG Books Worldwide, Inc.
An International Data Group Company

Foster City, CA ◆ Chicago, IL ◆ Indianapolis, IN ◆ New York, NY

The GRE® CAT For Dummies®

Published by
IDG Books Worldwide, Inc.
An International Data Group Company
919 E. Hillsdale Blvd.
Suite 400
Foster City, CA 94404
www.idgbooks.com (IDG Books Worldwide Web site)
www.dummies.com (Dummies Press Web site)

Library of Congress Catalog Card No.: 99-00092

ISBN: 0-7645-5252-X

Printed in the United States of America

10 9 8 7 6 5 4 3 2

1B/RQ/VQ/QQ/IN

Distributed in the United States by IDG Books Worldwide, Inc.

Distributed by CDG Books Canada Inc. for Canada; by Transworld Publishers Limited in the United Kingdom; by IDG Norge Books for Norway; by IDG Sweden Books for Sweden; by IDG Books Australia Publishing Corporation Pty. Ltd. for Australia and New Zealand; by TransQuest Publishers Pte Ltd. for Singapore, Malaysia, Thailand, Indonesia, and Hong Kong; by Gotop Information Inc. for Taiwan; by ICG Muse, Inc. for Japan; by Intersoft for South Africa; by Eyrolles for France; by International Thomson Publishing for Germany, Austria and Switzerland; by Distribuidora Cuspide for Argentina; by LR International for Brazil; by Galileo Libros for Chile; by Ediciones ZETA S.C.R. Ltda. for Peru; by WS Computer Publishing Corporation, Inc., for the Philippines; by Contemporanea de Ediciones for Venezuela; by Express Computer Distributors for the Caribbean and West Indies; by Micronesia Media Distributor, Inc. for Micronesia; by Chips Computadoras S.A. de C.V. for Mexico; by Editorial Norma de Panama S.A. for Panama; by American Bookshops for Finland.

For general information on IDG Books Worldwide's books in the U.S., please call our Consumer Customer Service department at 800-762-2974. For reseller information, including discounts and premium sales, please call our Reseller Customer Service department at 800-434-3422.

For information on where to purchase IDG Books Worldwide's books outside the U.S., please contact our International Sales department at 317-596-5530 or fax 317-572-4002.

For consumer information on foreign language translations, please contact our Customer Service department at 1-800-434-3422, fax 317-572-4002, or e-mail rights@idgbooks.com.

For information on licensing foreign or domestic rights, please phone +1-650-653-7098.

For sales inquiries and special prices for bulk quantities, please contact our Order Services department at 800-434-3422 or write to the address above.

For information on using IDG Books Worldwide's books in the classroom or for ordering examination copies, please contact our Educational Sales department at 800-434-2086 or fax 317-572-4005.

For press review copies, author interviews, or other publicity information, please contact our Public Relations department at 650-653-7000 or fax 650-653-7500.

For authorization to photocopy items for corporate, personal, or educational use, please contact Copyright Clearance Center, 222 Rosewood Drive, Danvers, MA 01923, or fax 978-750-4470.

About the Author

Suzee Vlk

"I'm not a complete idiot. Parts of me are missing."

Although more likely to admit to being a mortician, used-car salesperson, or guinea pig for Army experiments, Suzee Vlk has been a test-prep specialist since 1975, working her way through graduate business school and law school by teaching courses in GMAT, GRE, LSAT, SAT, and ACT preparation. She found the paranoia and take-no-prisoners mind-set required for doing well on the GMAT a big help in developing cutthroat tactics to use in the board-room or courtroom.

Today Suzee is president of Suzee Vlk Test Prep (no ego involved in *that* company name!) and has taught thousands of students in dozens of courses at universities and private corporations, including "mature" adults who have been out of school for a decade (or two or three) and international students from countries all over the world. (All victims have, so far, survived.) She has written material used in GMAT and SAT preparation software and videos (starring in one set of videos when she was younger and blonder). Her prep books for the GMAT and other standardized exams have been published worldwide.

Suzee currently specialized in one-on-one tutorials and teaches GMAT prep tricks and traps to all levels of students from those who are struggling to remember the basics ("Let's see: A triangle has three sides, or is it four?") to whiz kids who will probably be her boss one day. Her students have not only been accepted at graduate business progams in colleges and universities nationwide, including such dream schools as Harvard and Stanford, but they also have done well enough on their GMATs to be awarded scholarships (to the unbounded joy of their parents, who can now spend what's left of their kids' education funds on sail-boats, flashy sports cars, and other midlife crisis toys).

Suzee lives by the following motto, which she is delighted to share with you:

"Madness takes its toll. Please have exact change ready."

ABOUT IDG BOOKS WORLDWIDE

Welcome to the world of IDG Books Worldwide.

IDG Books Worldwide, Inc., is a subsidiary of International Data Group, the world's largest publisher of computer-related information and the leading global provider of information services on information technology. IDG was founded more than 30 years ago by Patrick J. McGovern and now employs more than 9,000 people worldwide. IDG publishes more than 290 computer publications in over 75 countries. More than 90 million people read one or more IDG publications each month.

Launched in 1990, IDG Books Worldwide is today the #1 publisher of best-selling computer books in the United States. We are proud to have received eight awards from the Computer Press Association in recognition of editorial excellence and three from Computer Currents' First Annual Readers' Choice Awards. Our best-selling ...*For Dummies*® series has more than 50 million copies in print with translations in 31 languages. IDG Books Worldwide, through a joint venture with IDG's Hi-Tech Beijing, became the first U.S. publisher to publish a computer book in the People's Republic of China. In record time, IDG Books Worldwide has become the first choice for millions of readers around the world who want to learn how to better manage their businesses.

Our mission is simple: Every one of our books is designed to bring extra value and skill-building instructions to the reader. Our books are written by experts who understand and care about our readers. The knowledge base of our editorial staff comes from years of experience in publishing, education, and journalism — experience we use to produce books to carry us into the new millennium. In short, we care about books, so we attract the best people. We devote special attention to details such as audience, interior design, use of icons, and illustrations. And because we use an efficient process of authoring, editing, and desktop publishing our books electronically, we can spend more time ensuring superior content and less time on the technicalities of making books.

You can count on our commitment to deliver high-quality books at competitive prices on topics you want to read about. At IDG Books Worldwide, we continue in the IDG tradition of delivering quality for more than 30 years. You'll find no better book on a subject than one from IDG Books Worldwide.

John Kilcullen
Chairman and CEO
IDG Books Worldwide, Inc.

Eighth Annual Computer Press Awards ≷1992

Ninth Annual Computer Press Awards ≷1993

Tenth Annual Computer Press Awards ≷1994

Eleventh Annual Computer Press Awards ≷1995

IDG is the world's leading IT media, research and exposition company. Founded in 1964, IDG had 1997 revenues of $2.05 billion and has more than 9,000 employees worldwide. IDG offers the widest range of media options that reach IT buyers in 75 countries representing 95% of worldwide IT spending. IDG's diverse product and services portfolio spans six key areas including print publishing, online publishing, expositions and conferences, market research, education and training, and global marketing services. More than 90 million people read one or more of IDG's 290 magazines and newspapers, including IDG's leading global brands — Computerworld, PC World, Network World, Macworld and the Channel World family of publications. IDG Books Worldwide is one of the fastest-growing computer book publishers in the world, with more than 700 titles in 36 languages. The "...For Dummies®" series alone has more than 50 million copies in print. IDG offers online users the largest network of technology-specific Web sites around the world through IDG.net (http://www.idg.net), which comprises more than 225 targeted Web sites in 55 countries worldwide. International Data Corporation (IDC) is the world's largest provider of information technology data, analysis and consulting, with research centers in over 41 countries and more than 400 research analysts worldwide. IDG World Expo is a leading producer of more than 168 globally branded conferences and expositions in 35 countries including E3 (Electronic Entertainment Expo), Macworld Expo, ComNet, Windows World Expo, ICE (Internet Commerce Expo), Agenda, DEMO, and Spotlight. IDG's training subsidiary, ExecuTrain, is the world's largest computer training company, with more than 230 locations worldwide and 785 training courses. IDG Marketing Services helps industry-leading IT companies build international brand recognition by developing global integrated marketing programs via IDG's print, online and exposition products worldwide. Further information about the company can be found at www.idg.com. 1/24/99

Dedication

This book is dedicated to Dr. Regis Weiss, my oncologist, who will be in my thank-you prayers every night for the rest of my long, long, loooooonnng life.

Author's Acknowledgments

After years of having California students groan at my puns, make rude hand gestures in response to my scintillatingly clever quips, and threaten to storm out of the classroom if I tell my geometry jokes one more time, it's wonderful to get the chance to inflict my dysfunctional humor on a worldwide, unsuspecting audience. The decline of civilization begins here.

Thanks to my agents, Bill Gladstone and Matt Wagner of Waterside Productions in Cardiff, California, for getting me this opportunity. A panegyric and paean for my project editor, Sherri Fugit, my associate acquisitions editor, Karen Hansen, and copy editor Donna Frederick, not only for their erudition but also for their effervescence and ebullience that didn't flag even under deadlines. Special thanks to Barb Terry for the iron fist in a velvet glove (and for laughing at most of my jokes). Many thanks also go to Kristin Cocks, Jennifer Ehrlich, as well as all past editors of previous editions.

Thanks to independent college counselor Jill Q. Porter of La Jola, California, for her up-to-the-minute insights about what college and university programs seek.

And thanks as always to my students over the years, those wonderful young and not-so-young adults who have had enough faith in me to use my tricks and tips and enough kindness to let me share their joy in the good scores that result. You all keep this fun.

Publisher's Acknowledgments

We're proud of this book; please register your comments through our IDG Books Worldwide Online Registration Form located at http://my2cents.dummies.com.

Some of the people who helped bring this book to market include the following:

Acquisitions, Editorial, and Media Development

Project Editor: Sherri Fugit
  Previous Edition: Colleen Rainsberger, Barb Terry, Jennifer Ehrlich

Associate Acquisitions Editor: Karen H. Hansen
  Previous Edition: Mark Butler

Copy Editor: Donna Frederick
  Previous Edition: Linda S. Stark

Acquisitions Coordinator: Jill Alexander

Technical Editor: Marcy Denmark Manning

Editorial Manager: Jennifer Ehrlich, Kristin Cocks

Editorial Assistant: Laura Jefferson

Production

Project Coordinator: E. Shawn Aylsworth

Layout and Graphics: Mary Jo Richards, Brent Savage, Jacque Schneider, Janet Seib

Proofreaders: Corey Bowen, Jennifer Mahern, Charles Spencer

Indexer: Richard Shrout

Special Help
  Kathleen Dobie, Carol Strickland, Janet Withers

General and Administrative

IDG Books Worldwide, Inc.: John Kilcullen, CEO

IDG Books Technology Publishing Group: Richard Swadley, Senior Vice President and Publisher; Walter R. Bruce III, Vice President and Publisher; Joseph Wikert, Vice President and Publisher; Mary Bednarek, Vice President and Director, Product Development; Andy Cummings, Publishing Director, General User Group; Mary C. Corder, Editorial Director; Barry Pruett, Publishing Director

IDG Books Consumer Publishing Group: Roland Elgey, Senior Vice President and Publisher; Kathleen A. Welton, Vice President and Publisher; Kevin Thornton, Acquisitions Manager; Kristin A. Cocks, Editorial Director

IDG Books Internet Publishing Group: Brenda McLaughlin, Senior Vice President and Publisher; Sofia Marchant, Online Marketing Manager

IDG Books Production for Dummies Press: Debbie Stailey, Director of Production; Cindy L. Phipps, Manager of Project Coordination, Production Proofreading, and Indexing; Tony Augsburger, Manager of Prepress, Reprints, and Systems; Laura Carpenter, Production Control Manager; Shelley Lea, Supervisor of Graphics and Design; Debbie J. Gates, Production Systems Specialist; Robert Springer, Supervisor of Proofreading; Kathie Schutte, Production Supervisor

Dummies Packaging and Book Design: Patty Page, Manager, Promotions Marketing

◆

The publisher would like to give special thanks to Patrick J. McGovern, without whom this book would not have been possible.

◆

Contents at a Glance

Cartoons at a Glance

By Rich Tennant

"Okay - now that the paramedic is here with the defibrillator and smelling salts, prepare to open your test booklets..."

page 5

page 73

page 163

"Let's see - your listed salad dressings are 'Vinaigrette', 'Creamy Garlic', and 'Hydrochloric Acid'. Hmm - I think I'll go with the 'Hydrochloric Acid'."

page 17

page 177

page 283

"For the next month, instead of practicing on a baseball diamond, we'll be practicing on a baseball trapezoid. At least until everyone passes the geometry section of the GRE test."

page 135

Fax: 978-546-7747
E-mail: richtennant@the5thwave.com
World Wide Web: www.the5thwave.com

Table of Contents

Introduction

Welcome to *The GRE CAT For Dummies*. Don't take the title personally. You're no dummy; you're just normal. Unfortunately, the GRE is anything *but* normal. As I've learned in more than two decades of fighting the GRE wars, the GRE has no connection to the Real World. When you were given the dire news that you had to take the GRE to get into graduate school, you probably flashed back to the SAT (lovingly known as Sadists Against Teenagers) that you had to take to get into college. Although there are some similarities (both exams are the leading causes of ulcers, migraines, and decisions to become a Bora Bora beachcomber), there are even more dissimilarities.

The primary dissimilarity has to do with your familiarity with the material. In high school, instructors often "teach to the test." They know that their students are going to take the SAT, know the kids themselves, and teach them what will be on the test and how to take the exam. In college, you're on your own. Your professors may not have any idea who you are ("The kid in the *I'm only here for the beer* T-shirt who sits in the upper row of the lecture hall? In my mind I call him Bud, but I don't know him at all"), and they almost certainly are not going to take time away from class to discuss the tricks and traps on the GRE. In addition, you have spent the last few years of college working on the courses specific to your major: invertebrate biology, lifestyles of the upper Botswana natives, sociological and psychological implications of domestic dissonance. It's been a long, long time since you've taken basic algebra, geometry, and arithmetic (found in the math portions of the exam), or vocabulary and logic (found in the verbal and analytical portions of the exam). And what about those of you who are no longer in college? I, for one, entered college in the days of parchment and quills but didn't get around to taking the GRE until the era of laptops and battery packs. No doubt about it; you need some help. And the skills you need are best provided by a specialist. Think of this book as a SWAT team that you can call in when the situation gets desperate.

Like a SWAT team, this book aims to deal with the crisis efficiently, do the job, save the day, and get you out as quickly as possible. I know that you have a life you'd like to get back to. The goal of this book is to help you to learn what you need and can use on the GRE — period. No extra garbage is thrown in to impress you with esoteric facts; no filler is added to make this book the fattest one on the market. If you need a doorstop, go pick up the New York City telephone directory. If you need a quick 'n' easy guide to surviving the GRE, you're in the right place.

Why You Need This Book

It's Us versus Them. Who are They? The creators of the GRE, those gnomes in green eyeshades. The next time you're trying to get away from a *soporific dolt* (sleep-inducing dummy) at a party, answer the question, "So, what do you do for a living?" with the response, "I create questions for the GRE." That conversation stopper is guaranteed to send any *paramour manqué* (would-be sweetie) running and screaming into the night.

In *The GRE CAT For Dummies*, I show you how to approach each type of question, recognize the traps that are built into the questions, and master the tricks that help you to avoid those traps. The book is full of Gotchas! that I (a test prep tutor since the Dawn of Time) have seen students fall for repeatedly. In this book, you learn to think the GRE way (don't worry; it's not permanent) to identify the point behind the various styles and types of questions and what each is trying to test. This book also gives you a review of the basics (math formulas and common roots, prefixes, and suffixes useful for improving your vocabulary), along with a laugh or two to make learning the material as painless as possible.

Note to nontraditional students: As I mentioned before, I'm aware of the fact that some of you are not 21-year-old college seniors taking this exam to go into graduate school right after college. You may have been out of college so long that your *children* are 21-year-old seniors! Maybe you've just decided to go back to grad school after a long career or after raising a family, and you need help getting back into math and verbal stuff that you had in what seems like another lifetime. I sympathize with you; it's tough to deal with nonagons, quadratic equations, and analogies again. Don't despair; you can get outside help, especially in math, which is one of the first things to fade when people get away from school. Call a community college (or even a high school; the math on this exam doesn't exceed what is taught in upper-division high school math classes, depressing as that may seem to you as you're sweating through it). Ask for help in finding a tutor or for suggestions on finding a quick review course in your area. You also can call your local library for assistance.

How to Get Your Money's Worth Out of This Book

If you use this book just to prop open a window or as a booster seat for a toddler, you won't get the best out of it. I suggest two alternatives:

- ✔ **Fine-tune your skills.** Turn to specific sections for specific information and help. The organization of the book makes it very easy to find the type of math question you always have trouble with, suggestions for answering reading questions without having finished the passage, and tricks for guessing. If you are in college classes or in a career in which you use this jazz every day (maybe you're a math major at school or teach high school English classes) and need just a nudge in one or two areas, you can work through those sections only.

- ✔ **Start from scratch.** Read through the whole book. Actually, this is what I'd like you to do. No matter how well you do on a section, you can improve. It's a common mistake to believe that you should work on your weakest sections only. The 50 points you gain in your mediocre section by skimming through the suggestions in this book are just as worthwhile as the 50 points you get by grunting, groaning, and sweating through the most difficult portions. If you have the time, do yourself a favor and read the book from cover to cover. Besides, you don't want to miss any of my jokes, now do you?

The GRE CAT For Dummies, is simple and straightforward enough for first-time GRE victims, er, students that they can understand the entire exam and do well right out of the starting gate. But it's also detailed and sophisticated enough that veterans — those of you who have taken the exam once or twice before but aren't resting on your laurels (sounds painful, anyway) — can learn the more complicated information you need to get those truly excellent scores.

To help you to get through this book more quickly, I include some icons that flag the particularly important stuff. If you need to work on your vocabulary, for example, flip through the book to find the Vocabulary icons and then make a list of the accompanying words and their meanings. The icons look like this.

This icon points out the big words (useless in the Real World and therefore almost inevitably tested on the GRE) that you may not know. (Let's face it: Some of the vocab words on the GRE are so tough that you practically have to be constipated to pronounce them!) Learning those words and their definitions is sure to help you on the GRE. The words themselves are in a special typeface — *like this* — and their meanings appear next to them. (You'll fix these words even more in your memory if you try to use them in your real life. Call your roommate or your children *indolent, lethargic,* and *listless* when they don't jump up to do the dishes right after dinner; promise your professor you will be *diligent, meticulous,* and *painstaking* in your lab assignment.)

This icon marks sample problems that appear in the lectures.

This icon directs you to tips that should make taking the GRE go much more smoothly. These tips alone are worth the price of this book. Trust me.

The test makers throw in some nasty traps that may get you if you don't think about the questions carefully. Learn the tricks marked by this icon, and you'll be amazed at how easily you can outsmart the GRE.

Be wary of the important stuff that this icon points out to you. If you skip these sections, I claim no responsibility for what may happen to you.

This icon points out information pertaining to international students and suggestions that can make life easier for those of you for whom English is a second or third language. International students, please see welcoming comments to you in Chapter 1.

Pardon Me for Having a Life: Who Has Time for This?

You have school or work, sports or other hobbies, family responsibilities and, oh yes, something that vaguely resembles a social life. How on earth are you going to fit in studying for the GRE?

Time required to go through the GRE lectures

Buying this book was brilliant. (Okay, so your roommate, your spouse, or some significant other bought it and tossed it at you with the snide comment, "Hey, you can sure use all the help you can get." Whatever.) How much time should you take to go through this book? I suggest 28 hours.

Each subject (antonyms, analogies, sentence completions, reading comprehension, quantitative comparisons, problem solving, analytical reasoning, logical reasoning, and analysis of explanations) includes a chapter on the format, approach, and tricks and traps for that particular type of question. A quiz chapter featuring a sampling of questions that test what you learned in the lecture follows each lecture. The detailed answer explanations point out the traps you may have fallen for and the tips that you should have used to avoid the traps. You learn which questions to skip (as either too hard or too time-consuming) and which to double-check. You should spend about two hours per lecture, including the quiz. The book also includes a three-part math review; each section (geometry, algebra, and arithmetic) should take roughly one hour, for a total of three hours.

Time required to go through the practice GREs

At the end of the book are two full-length GREs. Each exam takes two and a fourth hours to complete and about another hour to review. My thinking you should take an hour to review the exam does not reflect a lack of confidence in your *erudition* and *sagacity* (knowledge and wisdom). I'm not saying that you're so *inept* and *bungling* (unskilled) that you're going to miss a *plethora* (abundance) of questions. My suggestion is that you review *all* the answer explanations, even those for the questions you answer correctly. You'll learn some good stuff there; you'll review formulas, find shortcuts, and see more tricks and traps. I'll exaggerate and say that the whole test and review should take you three and a half hours. The following table gives you what I think is a reasonable timetable.

Activity	*Time*
9 lectures at 2 hours per lecture	18 hours
2 exams at 3½ hours per exam (including review)	7 hours
3 math review chapters at 1 hour per chapter	3 hours
Time spent laughing hysterically at author's jokes	5 minutes
Time spent composing letter complaining about author's crummy jokes	5 minutes
TOTAL	28 hours, 10 minutes

No one expects you to read this book for 28 hours straight. Each unit is self-contained. The answer explanations may remind you of things from other units because repetition aids learning and memorizing, but you can read through each unit separately.

Are you ready? Stupid question. Are you resigned? Have you accepted your fate that you're going to take the GRE no matter what and you may as well have fun studying for it? Take a deep breath, turn the page, and go for it. Here's hoping that, for you, GRE comes to stand for Genius Rocks Exam!

Part I

An Aerial View: Putting the GRE into Perspective

The 5th Wave   By Rich Tennant

"Okay — now that the paramedic is here with the defibrillator and smelling salts, prepare to open your test booklets..."

In this part . . .

I know, I know — the only aerial view you'd like to have of the GRE is the one you see from 10,000 feet up as a jet takes you far, far away from this exam. Use the info in this book correctly and you can ace the GRE, go to a top grad school, get a great job — and then buy your own private jet and buzz the office of that college guidance counselor who told you your best chance at a good life would be to marry rich. Hey, it's something to aim for (the goal, not the college counselor!).

You're probably eager to get right into studying for the GRE (or maybe not), but take a few minutes to go through this introductory material. It's good strategy to find out everything you can about your enemy before going into battle.

Chapter 1

Know Your Enemy: What the GRE Looks Like

*U*nlike traditional standardized paper and pencil tests, which feature a roomful of test-takers sweating and fretting together in a lecture hall, the GRE is computer-based. No, you don't get to take the test on your home computer with a dictionary in one hand and a tropical drink with a paper umbrella in the other (sorry if I got your hopes up only to dash them cruelly). The GRE Computer Based Test (CBT) is offered at designated technology centers (many of them are Sylvan) throughout the world on most days of the year during most business hours. This means that if you are not a morning person, you don't have to worry about getting up at the crack of dawn and trudging across town to attempt to make your lethargic brain cells function at 8:00 a.m. You can take the test at any hour you personally consider civilized, such as later in the afternoon or even in the evening. For information on signing up for the GRE, see the current GRE Registration Bulletin. (You can pick up this bulletin at a college admissions office, request one from 1-800-537-3160, or download it from the web at www.gre.org)

Table 1-1 provides a quick overview of what the GRE is all about, how many questions it torments and delights you with, and how much time you get to complete each section. The sections of the test may be arranged in any order.

Table 1-1	GRE Breakdown by Section	
Section	*Number of Questions*	*Time Allotted*
Verbal	30	30 minutes
Math	28	45 minutes
Analytical	35	60 minutes
*Unidentified unscored	28 to 35	30 to 60 minutes
*Identified unscored	Test-maker's surprise	

Not always given, but be prepared for the worst.

Table 1-2 shows another way to look at the GRE: by the approximate number of each type of question.

Table 1-2	GRE Breakdown by Question Style (Not Including the Unscored Section)
Type of Question	*Number of Questions*
Antonyms	9
Analogies	7
Sentence Completions	6
Reading Comprehension	8
Quantitative Comparisons	14
Problem Solving	9
Data Interpretation	5
Analytical Reasoning (Logic Games)	25
Logical Reasoning	10

These different question types are mixed throughout the section in which they belong. For example, you may get two analogies, two sentence completions, and two antonyms to start off your verbal section. Next, you may see some reading comprehension questions, then more analogies, and so on. The math section could feature three quantitative comparisons, two problem solving questions, two data interpretation questions, four more quantitative comparisons, and so on.

So what's the story with these "unscored" sections? (Some people refer to them as *experimental* or *equating* sections.) Why does the GRE often feature sections that don't count? With the one that will not be identified as an unscored section, the test-makers are using you as a guinea pig, trying out new questions on you, double-checking that all questions on the GRE are fair. You are an unwilling — and unwitting — participant. You're obviously unwilling — who would want to prolong this agony? You're unwitting, because you don't know which section is experimental. (The test-makers wouldn't find out too much about their new questions if you could sit back and refuse to do your best, knowing that your unwillingness will not hurt your score.)

The experimental, or uncounted, section can be verbal, math, or analytical, and you will have absolutely no idea which section is uncounted. Well, you may have *some* idea: If the test has two verbal sections, you can deduce that one of them is an experimental section — but which one? Don't try to outsmart the test-makers. The GRE has rooms full of men and women whose only task in life is to create these mind-warping questions. You, as a normal person, don't stand a chance of outsmarting them; why even try? Just do your best on every section.

If you want to give your brain a break, you may be able to do so on an "identified experimental section." As mentioned previously, the GRE sometimes tells you about an experimental section, which you do not need to take, at the end of the test. If you feel like playing with the computer and helping out ETS (Educational Testing Service), you can go ahead and answer the questions, but you have no obligation to do so.

Add it all up, and you realize that the part of the test that determines your future takes two hours and fifteen minutes. (That's right. Two hours and fifteen minutes of this test may be roughly as important as four years of college.) You may spend up to approximately three and a half hours dealing with test material, depending on how many experimental sections you get. Keep in mind, though, that you will probably be at the testing center for approximately four and a half hours. You get some breaks (discussed in the next section) and will have to go through some procedures (such as getting comfortable with the computer via a tutorial, receiving scratch paper, finding out your score) before and after the test. In other words, kiss an entire morning or afternoon good-bye.

Gimme a Break! The GRE Intermissions

You have the option of taking a ten-minute break between the second and third sections of the GRE. Depending on whether your bladder is the size of Rhode Island or Texas, you may or may not spend most of your break in the bathroom. Do yourself a favor: Don't drink more than a mouthful or eat much during the break. There's nothing worse than sitting there crossing and uncrossing your legs during the test, feeling your eyeballs slowly turn yellow.

Between other sections of the test, you get a one-minute break — just enough time to stand up and stretch a bit. You don't have time to leave your seat and come back before the test resumes. If you absolutely, positively have to go to the restroom, and leave the computer during the test, the clock keeps ticking.

You may want to take some munchies to eat and water to drink at the big break, but make sure that the snacks are light and nutritious. Sugar makes you high for a few minutes and then brings you way down. You don't need to crash right in the middle of a quadratic equation ("Twinkies Trauma: Film at 11:00 . . ."). Take a handful of peanuts, some trail mix, or anything light that won't send all the blood from your brain down to your stomach for digestion. Life's hard enough without trying to figure out how to find the interior angles of a nonagon using your stomach instead of your brain.

The Computer-Based Test (CBT)

Good news: You have a choice. No, you don't get to choose whether to take the GRE or not (sorry if I got your hopes up only to dash them cruelly); you do get to choose whether to take the pencil-and-paper GRE or the new Computer Based Test (the GRE on computer).

On the Computer Based Test, the level of questions is tailored to your abilities. You have a *bespoke* (custom-tailored) exam. Each section of the exam begins with a question of average difficulty (500 level). If you answer this question correctly, the computer elevates you to the 600 level or so and gives you a question more difficult than the first. If you answer this second question correctly, the computer places you over 650, and you get a question commensurate with that ability level. As long as you keep answering questions correctly, your score goes up, and you get more difficult questions. Later questions don't cause as dramatic a jump in your score as the first few do. When you miss a question, your score goes down, and you get an easier question. Eventually, you get to a level at which you are answering about half of the questions correctly, and the computer adjusts your score by only about ten points at a time. (Test-takers scoring at or near 800 may never get to the point where they miss half the questions, while those scoring at or near 200 may never achieve a level at which half of their answers are correct.)

The CBT consists of three scored sections: one 30-minute verbal, one 45-minute quantitative (math), and one 60-minute analytical. Typically, you get 30 verbal questions, 28 quantitative questions, and 35 analytical questions, with the number of each question type (such as Analogies, Quantitative Comparisons, or Logical Reasoning) proportional to what appeared on the old pencil-and-paper version of the test. Remember, however, that the order of these different types of questions may differ from that of the pencil-and-paper test. For example, you may get two analogies, two sentence completions, and two antonyms to start off your verbal section and get some more of these short-verbal questions in between some reading comprehension questions and then get some more short verbal at the end.

Because you cannot go back and change your answers, you are given more time per question on the CBT than you were on the pencil-and-paper test. Be sure to use this time wisely. Because you cannot go back and change your answers, you must be as accurate as possible on the first five questions of average difficulty to ensure that you get harder questions for the rest of the exam! Sound bizarre? Strange, but true. You *want* harder questions because your score is determined by the level of difficulty you reach. If you slip up and miss one early question, you can still reel off a series of correct answers, show that your mistake was a fluke, and get to the harder questions. However, if you miss a handful of early questions, the computer determines that these questions are too difficult for you and gives you easy questions. You may answer all these easy questions correctly, but your test will be over by the time the computer raises the difficulty level to the high-score range.

The first five questions of the CBT are the most important. You get a much higher score if you answer the first five questions correctly and miss all the rest than if you miss the first five questions and answer all the others correctly.

When you finish the test, you have the option of seeing your score or canceling it. You cannot, however, decide to cancel your score after you see it, so think carefully about how you feel you've done. Finding out your score at the end of the testing session is one of the things students like about the computerized testing. Instead of waiting two to four weeks to get scores in the mail, you can get your good news immediately! Schools still have to wait a little while, generally receiving the scores within 15 days, much less time than it takes to get the pencil-and-paper test scores out. Other benefits of the CBT include being able to sign up just a few days before, flexible scheduling (great if you're not worth much on a Saturday morning), and a quieter testing environment.

Although taking the CBT version has many advantages, it does have some disadvantages:

- ✔ **You can't do scratch work on the computer screen the way you can in the pencil-and-paper test booklet.** (For many test-takers, this is the greatest drawback to taking the CBT.) You are given blank scrap paper for scratch work, but some students have difficulty focusing when they have to go back and forth between the screen and the scrap paper.

- ✔ **The lack of a test booklet forces you to scroll through reading comprehension and analytical reasoning (logic games) questions.** Some stressed-out students find it particularly annoying to scroll through the passage or game as they read it and then answer the questions.

- ✔ **You can't cross off answers you know are incorrect.**

  One way to mitigate this disadvantage is to write a series of columns, numbered one through five (to correspond to the choices on the CBT, which are just ovals without the letters A through E). Do this while you read the general instructions for the exam because this part of the CBT does not count toward your testing time. When you get to a question in which it would help to cross off incorrect answer choices, simply go to one of your unused columns and cross off the choices there.

Beat the Clock: Timing Tips

The computer provides you with a stopwatch — an on-screen clock — to time each section. (One of my students told me that with that image of the clock ticking away, she kept looking for Mike Wallace and Morley Safer!) You have the option of removing the clock from the screen. If that ticker makes you nervous, by all means, get it out of sight (the computer tutorial at the beginning of the session tells you how to do so).

Professionally, I definitely recommend that you hide the clock when you begin the section. Why? You should do whatever it takes to get the first five questions right (I talk about the importance of those first five questions in the previous section). Bring the clock back when you finish the first several questions, or at least check the clock every fifteen minutes or so. Because the early questions count more than later ones , if you've answered fewer than half the questions when half of your time has expired, you're still doing okay. *Note*: The clock comes on and stays on during the last five minutes; you can't banish it from that point on. This clock serves to remind you that you may have to sprint to the finish soon.

Answer ALL the questions, even if you have to make wild guesses to do so. When it comes to scoring your test, you're not penalized for wrong answers.

Scratch work

You are not allowed to bring in a grease pencil and do scratch work on the computer screen! (Don't laugh! I've had more than one student ask me about doing so!) You are given blank scratch paper (you cannot bring in your own) before the test begins. Of course, it's clear to all test-takers that they should use this paper for such traditional scratch work as mathematical calculations and logic-game diagrams, you can use this paper another key way: Use the general instruction time (this time does not count against you) to write down any key strategies and formulas that will help you get through the exam. You may not bring such memory aids into the testing center, but you may certainly write them down just before you start tackling the questions.

What to Take to the GRE

Take your brain down from the shelf, dust it off, and take it to the exam with you. In addition, take along a few more items:

- ✔ **Authorization voucher from ETS:** You can request that a voucher be mailed to you when you register for the test. Some testing sites may send you notices in the mail; others may simply give you a confirmation number which you must mention when you show up for the exam. Have the information with you.

- ✔ **Map or directions:** Be sure that you know in advance how to get to the testing site. Drive there a few days prior to your test and check out how long the drive takes you, where to park, and so on. One of my students took the test at a center in the middle of a downtown area, couldn't find any parking, and was totally stressed out before she got to the testing site. The last thing you need the day of the test is something more to worry about.

- ✔ **Photo ID:** You must have identification with three key elements:

  - A recognizable photo (something that shows you as the haggard, sleep-deprived person you are after studying for this test, not as the perky, cheerful person you vaguely remember having been a month or so ago).

  - The name you registered under (if your driver's license lists you as Steven Boyd Brown, don't sign up under your nickname of "Boatman" or "Bubbles" or whatever your friends call you).

  - Your signature.

  Usually, a driver's license, passport, employee ID, or military ID is acceptable. A student ID alone is usually not enough, although it is acceptable as a second form of ID, in case there is some confusion with the first form. Note that a social security card or a credit card is not acceptable identification.

✔ **Clothes:** You signed up for the special Nude GRE, you say? Well, everyone else should remember to take a few extra layers. Testing centers may be boiling hot or freezing cold. It's the pits to sit there for hours, either shivering with hands so cold they can't hit the computer keys, or sweating all over your keyboard from the heat. Dress in layers and be prepared for anything.

What Not to Take to the GRE

Besides your dreams, hopes, goals, and aspirations, leave these other things at the door of the GRE testing room:

✔ **Books and notes:** Forget about last-minute studying. You aren't allowed to take books or notes into the room. If you don't know the material by that time, you never will. (One student asked me whether he could take in a dictionary. You gotta give the guy credit for hope, but somehow I think he missed the point of the verbal questions.)

✔ **Scratch paper:** You are not allowed to bring in your own scratch paper (with handy notes prepared ahead of time). You will be given scratch paper at the computer center. (If you run low, request some more from the proctor during the one-minute breaks between sections.) You'll have plenty of room to do calculations and scribbling. (I understand, however, that ETS owns the copyright to all last will and testaments written during the exam.)

✔ **Calculator:** You are not allowed to use a calculator during the exam. Those of you who grew up before calculators were common and learned your times tables have a definite advantage here over those young whippersnappers who can't add 2 + 2 without dragging out the calculator. Don't think that because your watch has a calculator, you can bend this rule — NO mechanical or digital calculating devices are allowed.

✔ **Test aids:** You may not bring in a radio, cassette or CD player with headphones, cell phone, personal computer (like a laptop or a PalmPilot). In other words, leave the electronics at home. The most you can bring is that good, old-fashioned #2 pencil.

Isn't That Special? Unusual Circumstances

Dare to be different. If you have a special circumstance, those GRE testers are usually willing to accommodate you. For example, if you have a learning disability (no, that doesn't include being bored and frustrated), you may be able to get additional testing time. Following is a brief list of special circumstances and what to do about them.

✔ **Learning disabilities:** These can range from attention deficit disorder to dyslexia and all sorts of other things. To find out whether you qualify for a disabilities waiver of any sort, contact the Office of Disability Policy of the Educational Testing Service Corporate Headquarters, Educational Testing Service, Rosedale Road, Princeton, NJ 08541; phone 609-921-9000; fax 609-734-5410; e-mail etsinfo@ets.org; Web site www.ets.org.

✔ **Physical disabilities:** Pay attention: I'm about to say something nice about ETS here, a once-in-a-googolplex occurrence for me. ETS tries very hard to accommodate everyone. Those who need them can get braille or large-print exams, can have test readers or recorders, can work with interpreters, and so on. You can get the information about what are considered disabilities and how they can change your taking the GRE in the GRE Information and Registration Bulletin.

✔ **Financial difficulties:** Until you ace the GRE, get into a top-notch graduate school and come out with a smokin' brain ready to make your first million before your 30th (40th? 50th?) birthday, you may have a rough time paying the GRE fees. Fee waivers are available. Note that this waiver applies only to the actual GRE fee, not to miscellaneous fees, such as those for the test disclosure service, hand-grading service, and so on. Your college counselor can help you to obtain and fill out the appropriate request forms. (If you're not currently in college, a counselor or financial aid specialist at the closest college or university may still be glad to help you. Just call for an appointment.) The GRE is inflicted upon rich and poor alike.

Everyone Wants to Score

You don't have the Ferrari yet (if you do, and you are a single, eligible male, please write to me care of the publisher . . .). You don't have the six-digit paycheck yet (if you do, please see the previous parenthetical comment). It's rough being 21 (or 25 or 30). You need something to boast about. How about your GRE scores? GRE scores are to would-be graduate students what salaries are to people in the Real World. Students brag about them, exaggerate them, or try to impress others with them. How are your scores determined?

How scores are determined

With the GRE, you don't get one "combined" score, you get three separate scores: verbal, math, and analytical. So, unlike after the SAT test of your youth, for which you added the verbal and math scores and spoke of one combined score, you won't be boasting to your buddies, "Yeah, I got an 1800 on my GRE." Every score is separate:

✔ **Verbal score:** The verbal score (called verbal ability) ranges from 200 to 800. You get 200 points for showing up at the technology center and staring at the computer.

✔ **Math score:** The math score also ranges from 200 to 800.

✔ **Analytical score:** Take a wild guess . . . you got it. The analytical score ranges from 200 to 800 as well.

Not every graduate school looks at every score. In my experience, one of the three scores counts much more than the other two, depending on the program to which you are applying. For example, if you apply to an engineering program, your math score is more closely scrutinized than are your verbal and analytical scores. Students going to grad school in journalism can expect their verbal score to be the most important. *Many schools don't obsess over your analytical score. Before* you go through this book, *before* you begin sweating out the lectures, *before* you spend the time and destroy brain cells learning the two types of analytical questions, find out from the grad schools in which you are interested whether they even care about the analytical score. And get that information in writing. You want an official letter on letterhead stationery telling you that analytical scores aren't considered.

One final point on analytical ability scores: A student of mine told me she had a discussion with a graduate school counselor who mentioned something interesting. The counselor said that even if the school doesn't count analytical scores, it may not be the best idea to blow the section off completely on the day of the test. A 650 verbal, 700 math may look very impressive, but if those scores appear with a 200 analytical, the school may not like your attitude. Something to think about.

For each section of the GRE, the difficulty level of the questions is tailored to your abilities. You have a *bespoke* (custom-tailored) exam. Each section of the exam begins with a question of average difficulty (500 level). If you answer this question correctly, the computer elevates you to the 580 level or so and gives you a question more difficult than the first. If you answer this second question correctly, the computer will place you at about 640, and you will get a question commensurate with that ability level. As long as you keep answering questions correctly, your score will go up, and you will get more difficult questions. Later questions will not cause as dramatic a jump in your score as the first few will. When you miss a question, your score will go down, and you will get an easier question. Eventually, you will get to a level at which you are answering about half of the questions correctly, and the computer will be adjusting your score by only about ten points at a time. (Test-takers scoring at or near 800 may never get to the point at which they are missing half the questions, while those scoring at or near 200 may never achieve a level at which half of their answers are correct.)

What is a good score?

On a recent GRE, the averages (that is, half the students taking the exam were above these scores, half were below these scores) were as follows: verbal 480, math 570, analytical 550. Averages change according to the administration. Your individual goals should depend on which grad schools you are applying to and what GPA (grade-point average) you have. There is no such thing as a passing or failing score — only what you need to get accepted to the program that you have your heart set on.

Should I guess?

You have no choice but to guess. The computer doesn't budge until you choose an answer. Unlike paper-and-pencil tests, on which you can move around and choose questions more to your liking, the CBT requires you to mark an answer before you go on to the next question. So, if you are completely stuck, don't waste time agonizing. Guess quickly and move on. Which oval should you fill in? Any. There is no truth to the *scurrilous* (obscenely abusive) rumors that the exam has more of the first oval or second oval or third or fourth ovals (remember that on the computer screen, the ovals are not marked A,B,C, D and E; they are left blank). Every answer has the same probability. It doesn't matter which oval you choose.

Be sure to answer all the questions. You are penalized more for an unanswered question than for a wrong answer, so make sure that you get to the end, even if it means guessing wildly in the last minute or so.

Number of correct answers you need for specific scores

Here are rough estimates of how many questions you must answer correctly to get certain scores on each section. Keep in mind that these numbers change from exam to exam.

Verbal scores
To get a 400, you need 14 out of 30 questions correct (about 47 percent).
To get a 500, you need 18 out of 30 questions correct (about 60 percent).
To get a 600, you need 22 out of 30 questions correct (about 73 percent).
To get a 700, you need 25 out of 30 questions correct (about 84 percent).

Math scores
To get a 400, you need 11 out of 28 questions correct (about 38 percent).
To get a 500, you need 15 out of 28 questions correct (about 51 percent).
To get a 600, you need 19 out of 28 questions correct (about 66 percent).
To get a 700, you need 23 out of 28 questions correct (about 81 percent).

Analytical scores

To get a 400, you need 14 out of 35 questions correct (40 percent).
To get a 500, you need 18 out of 35 questions correct (52 percent).
To get a 600, you need 23 out of 35 questions correct (66 percent).
To get a 700, you need 29 out of 35 questions correct (82 percent).

Déjà Vu All Over Again: Repeating the Test

Should you repeat the test? Before you make that decision, ask yourself the following questions:

- ✔ **Am I repeating the test to get a certain minimum qualifying score or just to satisfy my ego?** If you have your heart set on a particular graduate school that requires a minimum GRE score, you may want to take the test again and again and again until you get that score. If you're taking the test only because your ego was demolished when you didn't score as well as your friends, you should probably think twice before putting yourself through all that trauma again.

- ✔ **Am I willing to study twice as hard, or am I already burned out?** If you put your heart and soul into studying for the exam the first time, you may be too pooped to pop (*enervated,* as we didactic dames like to say) for the second exam. Scores don't magically go up on their own; you have to put in a lot of effort.

- ✔ **What types of mistakes did I make on the first test?** If you made mistakes because of a lack of familiarity with either the test format (you didn't understand what to do when faced with a Quantitative Comparison question) or substance (you didn't know the vocabulary words or were baffled by the geometry problems), you're a good candidate for repeating the test. If you know what you did wrong, you can fix it and improve your score.

  However, if your mistakes were due to carelessness or a lack of concentration, you are very likely to make those same types of mistakes again. If you truly, honestly, sincerely, without *dissembling* (lying) feel that you can sit in the test room and stay focused this time and not make the same stupid mistakes, go for it. But chances are, if you're the type who either always makes a lot of careless mistakes or rarely makes them, you're not going to change your whole test-taking style overnight.

- ✔ **Were there extenuating circumstances beyond my control?** Maybe your nerves were acting up on the first exam, you were feeling ill, or you didn't get enough sleep the night before. In that case, by all means, repeat the exam. You're bound to feel better the next time.

- ✔ **Did I not finish?** If you did not reach a lot of questions, take the test again (you may take the test only once during each calendar month, but a smart test-taker can schedule her testing so that she takes the exam on, say, October 31 and then again on November 1) and fill in something for every question. Remember that you lose more points for not reaching a question than you do for answering the question incorrectly.

Can repeating the exam hurt you? Not really. Most schools look only at your highest score. Find out from the individual schools you're interested in whether this is their policy; it isn't for every school. If you are borderline, or if several students are vying for one spot, sometimes having taken the exam repeatedly can hurt you (especially if your most recent score took a nosedive). On the other hand, an admissions counselor who sees several exams with ascending scores may be impressed that you stuck to it and kept trying, even if your score went up only a little bit. In general, if you're willing to take the time to study and take the repeat seriously, go for it.

GRE score reporting is cumulative; that is, all the scores you obtain for five years are sent to the schools you designate. You cannot, I repeat, CANNOT send scores from only one exam date. For example, if you do great in October, take the exam again in April and blow it big time, you cannot tell ETS to ignore the April *debacle* (a sudden collapse, a rout) and send just the October scores. All scores are part of your permanent record.

Can You Use Older Scores?

What if you took the GRE years and years ago when you thought you were going to go to grad school and then elected to take a job or start a family instead? Between October 1, 1974, and September 30, 1985, ETS promised students that scores would be valid for 20 years. Never one to go back on its word, ETS (noted for its *veracity,* or truthfulness) agrees to send those scores out if you so desire . . . but will do so with a note to the schools to be extra careful in looking at such old scores. But the good news is, if you liked your scores from as long ago as two decades, you may be able to get away with sending those and not taking the exam again at all. If that's so and you're waving me good-bye at this point, adios and good luck to you. For the rest of you who can't escape my company so quickly, read on.

I wish it were all Greek to me: A welcome to international students

Students the from all over the world take the GRE to attend American graduate schools. I've taught GRE prep courses to students from Brazil, Taiwan, the Ivory Coast, Egypt, Japan — all over the globe. When I got my own graduate degree, my courses were enriched by the contributions of students from Korea, Hong Kong, Saudi Arabia, the Netherlands, China, and Mexico. To all of you readers from other nations, welcome!

As international students, you have strengths and weaknesses that are different from those of American students; therefore, the focus of your study should be different as well. Here are my suggestions to help you to get the most out of this book and to help you do your best on the actual GRE:

1. Concentrate on the questions that test vocabulary in the Antonyms and the Analogies sections. You probably have an advantage over American students on these questions, believe it or not — especially if your native tongue is a Romance language, such as Spanish or French. Romance languages are Latin-based and commonly use words that are uncommon in English. Take, for example, *bibliophile*. A Spanish speaker knows *biblio* means book (*biblioteca* means library) and can figure out this "hard" word pretty easily. (A bibliophile is a book-lover.)

One more thing: Because you've studied English, you're used to memorizing vocabulary tests (unlike American students who haven't taken vocabulary tests since junior high school). Although you probably can't dramatically change your basic reading comprehension level in a few hours, you *can* dramatically add to your vocabulary. You, more than American students, need to keep and learn the vocabulary lists suggested throughout this book.

2. Forget about the Reading Comprehension section. The reading passages in the GRE are long, hard, and booooring. They are difficult enough to understand for people who grew up speaking and reading English and are totally demoralizing for people who didn't. My suggestion is that you not take reading comprehension too seriously. Take your time on the first passage, reading it slowly and carefully. Then scroll through the passage thoroughly to answer the questions. It's probably a good idea to make quick guesses when you get to the other passages.

3. Concentrate on the math, especially geometry. Although you do get separate verbal and math scores, some colleges concentrate on your overall or combined score. Doing extremely well on math can compensate for weaker verbal skills. I suggest that you pay particular attention to the geometry problems. They rarely are "word problems" — questions that require a lot of reading. Geometry problems usually feature figures that you can easily understand and use to answer the questions even if English is not your strong suit.

4. Go, Go, Go! I've said it before and I'll say it again: The GRE penalizes you more for unanswered questions than for wrong answers. Be sure to fill in an answer for every question, even if you have to guess wildly. You must finish the exam.

Part II
A Word to the Wise: Verbal Questions

The 5th Wave   By Rich Tennant

REAL LIFE APPLICATION OF CORRECT ANTONYM IDENTIFICATION

"Let's see – your listed salad dressings are 'Vinaigrette', 'Creamy Garlic', and 'Hydrochloric Acid'. Hmm – I think I'll go with the 'Hydrochloric Acid'."

In this part . . .

One of the sections on the computer-based GRE is verbal, with 30 questions. The verbal questions come in four styles: Antonyms (finding words that are opposites), Analogies (far and away the easiest for most people), Sentence Completions (good ol' fill-in-the-blanks, the same stuff you've been doing since kindergarten), and Reading Comprehension (dull and deadly). Each question style has a chapter of its own in this part. You learn the format of the question (what it looks like), an approach to the question (where to begin, an organized plan of attack), and the various tricks and traps built into the questions (with, of course, suggestions for recognizing and avoiding such traps). Vocabulary-building material features roots, prefixes, and suffixes. Following each lecture chapter is a chapter that includes particularly wicked practice questions followed by detailed answer explanations that show you what you should have done, how to make the best use of your time, and what you should have guessed at randomly. *Remember:* On the computer-based test, never leave any bubbles blank. On the computer-based test, you must answer a question before the computer lets you go on to the next question. Because you can't go back and change your answers once you've hit the Confirm button, you want to be sure of each answer, but you also need to work quickly enough to get through all the questions.

Chapter 2

Starting with the Easy Stuff: Analogies

In This Chapter
▶ Understanding the format of an analogy
▶ Building your vocabulary with prefixes and suffixes
▶ Answering an analogy question with the correct two-step approach
▶ Recognizing the nasty and vile traps built into analogies
▶ Identifying and avoiding dumb (trap) answers

ANSWER: The shiny red bike you got for your 10th birthday. Your first kiss from someone who wasn't related to you. Analogies.

QUESTION: Name three of the best gifts you've ever received.

Analogies are a gift. Manna from heaven. Freebies. For most students, analogies are the place to rack up the points big time. The number of analogies on the computer-based GRE can vary, but you almost certainly have at least seven.

The great thing about analogies is that they are doable. Some of the Reading Comprehension passages are ridiculously hard. Some of the Sentence Completion questions are so long you may be tempted to take a snooze in the middle of them. But analogies are great. You read 12 words, apply a few tricks, and you're outta there. Here's an example of what you see. (***Note:*** This book uses the paper-based version of questions. The computer-based test has the same format, but the ovals have no A, B, C, D, E in them.)

If Only All Relationships Were This Easy: The Format

Some people look at analogies and wonder, "Where's the question?" Even though analogies can be quite simple (with practice), the format is bizarre. Here's an example of what you see:

PIG : STY ::

(A) teenager : rubble

(B) roommate : bathroom

(C) bird : nest

(D) swine : house

(E) barnacle : barn

You see two words in uppercase letters. The five answer choices consist of two words in lowercase letters. Not a lot of reading here. When you get good at analogies, you can zoom through them faster than you can finish a pint of ice cream.

Your job is to identify the *relationship* between the question words and then choose a pair of answer words that expresses the *same* relationship.

Approaching Perfection

When you see an Analogy question, you should take this very straightforward two-step approach:

1. **Use both words in a *descriptive* sentence.**

   Make a sentence using the words. Avoid something vague and useless such as "has." For example, do *not* say, "A pig *has* a sty." That tells you nothing. From the sentence, you have no idea what the relationship between a pig and a sty is. Pretend that a Bulgarian exchange student comes up to you and says, "Excuse me, please. What is the connection between a pig and a sty?" If you answer that a pig *has* a sty, the Bulgarian may go away thinking that a sty is a curly tail, a snout, or a big stink. But if you say, "A pig *lives in* a sty," your Bulgarian now understands the relationship. A good sentence paints a mental picture: You can actually see the scene in your mind.

2. **Apply the *exact* same sentence to each answer choice.**

   Go through each of the answer choices using your sentence.

   (A) *A teenager lives in rubble.*

   Maybe you flash back to your teenage years and recall having to wade through the *detritus* (trash, rubble) of your bedroom to get to the door, but this is the GRE. The test-makers assume that all of you were sweet little kids who obeyed your parents, respected traffic signals, and didn't ever use the middle finger of your hand for pointing or otherwise gesticulating. By the way, *rubble* is the ruined remains of a building, such as knocked-down bricks and junk. If you forget this word, think of Barney Rubble from the Flintstones. He's short, like a knocked-down pile.

   (B) A roommate lives in the bathroom.

   It may seem like it sometimes, but it ain't so. Any answer that is funny, witty, or charming is almost certainly the wrong answer. (The GRE has nooooooo sense of humor; count on it.) If you think that an answer is funny — or desperately *trying* to be funny — you can be sure that it's wrong.

   (C) *A bird lives in a nest.*

   Sounds pretty good, but you have to go through all the answer choices, just in case. Just like not marrying the first person you kiss, don't immediately choose the first answer that looks good. There may be something later that makes you happier.

   (D) *A swine lives in a house.*

   If you choose this answer, remind me not to come to your home! The trap here is that a pig (from the question) and a swine are much the same. Be careful: Just because words are connected in *meaning* does not mean that the answer is right. The *relationship* between the words is being tested. For example, the question may be about perfume, and the correct answer may involve sweatsocks. No connection.

   (E) A barnacle lives in a barn.

   If you don't know what a barnacle is, you may be tempted to choose E, but C is the right answer. A *barnacle* is a creature that lives in the water (not in a barn) and often attaches itself to the bottoms of ships. You scrape the barnacles off the ship periodically to clean the ship's hull. *Correct Answer:* C.

Just Because You're Paranoid Doesn't Mean They're Not Out to Get You: Traps, Tricks, and Tips

Face it — this is why you really bought this book. You want to know about those little traps built into the questions, sitting there waiting to pounce on unsuspecting victims. What time bombs have the test makers created, ready to go off in your face? Here are a few, with suggestions for how to deal with them.

Turn a verb into an infinitive

No, an infinitive is not the latest Japanese import car. An infinitive is the "to" form of any verb: to drink, to burp, to party. When an analogy features a verb, turn it into an infinitive and the sentence practically writes itself.

GIGGLE : LAUGH ::

To giggle is *to laugh* a little bit.

YELL : TALK ::

To yell is *to talk* loudly.

RUN : WALK ::

To run is *to walk* rapidly.

Notice that I'm adding another word on the end, usually an adverb to answer the "How?" question. How do you laugh when you giggle? A little bit. How do you talk when you yell? Loudly. How do you walk when you run? Rapidly. It's not enough to say, "To giggle is to laugh." You want to fine-tune the sentence, tweak it a little bit to clarify the relationship between the words. Remember: That Bulgarian exchange student is counting on you.

Identify the part of speech of the question word

Sometimes your sentence is easier to write if you know which part of speech — noun, verb, or adjective — a difficult word is. You find out by looking at its counterparts in the answer choices. That is, if you want to know which part of speech the first word in the question is, look at the first words in the answers. If you want to know which part of speech the second word in the question is, look at the second word in the answer choices.

DASHIKI : TAILOR ::

(A) shovel : professor

(B) table : singer

(C) garment : jock

(D) cake : baker

(E) book : poseur

Don't know what the word *dashiki* means? You're not alone; it's a pretty hard word. Not to worry. You know by looking at the first words in the answer choices — shovel, table, garment, cake, and book — that *dashiki* must be a noun and is a thing. (Remember that nouns are persons, places, or things.) Your very simple sentence should be: "A dashiki is a thing of a tailor." That's all you can do for now. Go through each answer choice.

(A) shovel : professor — Although it can get deep in the classroom sometimes, a shovel is not standard equipment for a professor.

(B) table : singer — A singer may stretch herself out on a table during a Las Vegas lounge act, doing a sexy, sultry number, but a table is not normally associated with a singer.

(C) garment : jock — This is a trap answer. You may be tempted to choose it because a tailor (from the question) deals with garments. However, you've already learned that the meanings of the question words are not necessarily related to the answer; the *relationship* between the pairs of words is important. Had the question said GARMENT : SEAMSTRESS or even GARMENT : MODEL, it would have been a good choice. But a garment is not necessarily a thing of a jock.

(D) cake : baker — A cake is a thing of a baker. Yeah, this answer sounds pretty good. There is a logical connection. Try the next one to be sure, but D is probably right.

(E) book : poseur — This answer is put here to trap students who immediately assume that the hardest word in a question or any word they themselves don't know must be the correct answer. A poseur is someone with an attitude, a person who adopts an affected style. People who go around using words like poseur are often poseurs themselves.

The right answer is D. A *dashiki*, by the way, is a type of shirt, and a tailor creates a dashiki just as a baker creates a cake. You can get the question right without knowing what the word means. *Correct Answer:* D.

Look for the salient features of a word

The *salient* feature is what makes something stand out. The salient feature of a basketball player is his or her height. The salient feature of a genius is his or her intelligence.

MINNOW : FISH ::

(A) elephant : animal

(B) recluse : shy

(C) gnat : insect

(D) giraffe : quadruped

(E) votary : peremptory

The salient feature of a minnow is that it is a *small* fish. Although most of the answers are or may be synonyms (an elephant *is* an animal; a recluse *may be* shy), only C gives the salient or outstanding feature. A gnat is a *small* insect. Choice E features antonyms. A *votary* is a devoted follower (think of a votary as an elegant, grown-up groupie!). *Peremptory* means absolute, imperative, allowing no disagreement. The boss may be peremptory; the votary would more likely be *docile* (easily swayed; compliant). *Correct Answer:* C.

Back into it

QUESTION: Is it okay to make the sentence by using the words backward?

ANSWER: Sure, as long as you remember to use the answer choices backward as well. That is, don't say, "A tailor makes a dashiki," and then say, "A cake makes a baker."

Identify common relationships

Certain standard relationships are often found in the analogies. There are a *plethora* (a lot) of them; here are ten of the more useful ones.

1. **Opposites**
   BIG : LITTLE
   PULCHRITUDINOUS : UGLY

2. **Synonyms**
   HAPPY : GLAD
   PUSILLANIMOUS : COWARDLY

3. **Cause and effect**
   TICKLE : LAUGHTER
   OSSIFY : BONE

4. **Part to whole**
   TOES : FOOT
   TALON : EAGLE

5. **Position**
   FRAME : PICTURE (a frame goes *around* a picture)
   SHOULDER : ROAD (a shoulder is to *the side of* a road).

6. **Greater to lesser**
   OVERJOYED : HAPPY
   CATACLYSMIC : UNFORTUNATE

7. **Location**
   PIG : STY
   RABBIT : WARREN

8. **Purpose or function**
   PILOT : FLY
   PUGILIST : BOX

9. **Characteristic**
   BLEAT : SHEEP (a bleat is the sound a sheep makes)
   POD : WHALES (a pod is a group of whales)

10. **Member to group (or specific to general)**
    FORK : UTENSIL
    ISLANDS : ARCHIPELAGO (an archipelago is *a group* of islands)

Use roots, prefixes, and suffixes

My three favorite words. . . . Other women like "I love you," but I live for "roots, prefixes, and suffixes." These three words can bump up your score significantly. If you know just a few basic roots, prefixes, and suffixes, you can write magnificent analogy sentences and avoid falling into traps.

Suppose that the question is

IMPECUNIOUS : MONEY ::

If you don't know *impecunious,* you may be tempted to make the words synonyms and simply say, "Impecunious *is* money." A tempting and logical answer may be reservoir : water, for example. Alas, once again you pay the price for giving in to temptation.

If you know that *-ous* means full of and *im-* means not, you can make a good sentence: "Impecunious is *not full of* money." That changes the whole picture. Now the right answer may be, for example, vacuum : air. A *vacuum* is *not full of* air. Note that a *reservoir* in fact *is* full of water; this is just the opposite of your relationship sentence.

Although you can learn hundreds of prefixes and suffixes, I realize that you have a limited number of brain cells that you're willing to devote to this subject. Therefore, here is a list of ten commonly used prefixes and eight commonly used suffixes, with examples of each. Memorize them. Burn them in your brain. I get to some of the more common roots later on in Chapter 6. I don't want you to get overexcited by this stuff all at once.

Prefixes

1. *a-* = **not or without:** Someone *amoral* is without morals, like the sadist who designed this test. Someone *atypical* is not typical, like the students who wear pocket protectors and love to take tests. Someone *apathetic* is without feeling, uncaring, like most students by the time they finish the test and are leaving the exam room. ("The world is going to end tomorrow? Fine; that means I can get some sleep tonight.")

2. *an-* = **not or without:** An *anaerobic* environment is without oxygen (like the test room feels when a killer question leaves you gasping for air). *Anarchy* is without rule or government (like a classroom when a substitute teacher is in for the day).

3. *eu-* = **good:** A *eulogy* is a good speech, usually given for the dearly departed at a funeral. A *euphemism* is a good way of saying something or a polite expression, like saying that someone has passed away instead of calling her "worm meat."

4. *ben-/bon-* = **good:** A *benefit* is something that has a good result, an advantage. Someone *benevolent* is good and kind; when you have a date, a benevolent father lets you take his new car rather than your old junker. *Bon voyage* means have a good voyage; a *bon vivant* is a person who lives the good life.

5. *caco-* = **bad:** Something *cacophonous* is bad-sounding, such as nails on a chalkboard.

6. *ne-/mal-* = **bad:** Something *negative* is bad, like a negative attitude. Someone *nefarious* is "full of bad," or wicked and evil, such as a nefarious wizard in a fantasy novel. Something *malicious* also is "full of bad," or wicked and harmful, such as a malicious rumor that you are really a 30-year-old undercover narc.

7. *im-* = **not:** Something *impossible* is not possible. Someone *immortal* is not going to die but will live forever. Someone *implacable* is not able to be calmed down, she's stubborn. Notice that im- can also mean inside (*immerse* means to put into), but that meaning is not as common on the GRE. First, think of im- as meaning not; if that doesn't seem appropriate, switch to Plan B and see whether the im- can mean inside in the context of the question.

8. *in-* = **not:** Something *inappropriate* is not appropriate, such as the language people may use in front of small children when studying for the GRE. Someone *inept* is not adept, not skillful. (Can you sue an inept surgeon who amputates the wrong leg? Nah, you wouldn't have a leg to stand on!) Someone *insolvent* has no money, is bankrupt, like most students after four years of college. *In-* can also mean inside (*innate* means something born inside of you) or beginning (the *initial* letters of your name are the beginning letters). However, its most common meaning is *not*. Think of that one first; if it doesn't seem to work, try the others.

9. *ante-* = **before:** When the clock tells you that it's 5 a.m., the a.m. stands for *ante meridian*, which means before the middle, or the first half of the day. *Antebellum* means before the war. Tara in *Gone with the Wind* was an antebellum mansion, built before the Civil War. *Antediluvian* literally means before the flood, before Noah's deluge. Figuratively, it means very old; if you call your mother antediluvian, you mean that she's been around since before the flood. It's a great word to use as an insult because almost no one knows what it means and you can get away with it.

10. *post-* = **after:** When the clock tells you that it's 5 p.m., the p.m. stands for *post meridian*. It means after the middle, or the second half of the day. Something *postmortem* occurs after death. A postmortem exam is an autopsy.

Suffixes

1. *-ette* = **little:** A *cigarette* is a little cigar. A *dinette* table is a little dining table. A *coquette* is a little flirt (literally, a little chicken).

2. *-illo* = **little:** An *armadillo* is a little armored animal. A *peccadillo* is a little sin. (Do you speak Spanish? *Pecar* is to sin.)

Flash your friends: How to use flashcards

Go out and buy three packages of the largest index cards you can find: white and two other colors. Put all the roots, prefixes, and suffixes you learn that have negative connotations on cards of one color. For example, *ne-* means bad or not; put it on a brown card. *Ben-* means good; put it on a pink card. *-ous* means full of. It doesn't "feel" good or bad; it's neutral. Put it on a white card.

When you get to the exam, you may encounter the word *nefarious.* You know you've seen it before, but you can't for the life of you remember what it means. Then a little picture unfolds in front of your eyes: You see *ne-* on a brown card. Aha! If it's on a brown card, it must be something negative. Just knowing that much often helps you to get the right answer.

Say the analogy is NEFARIOUS : SAINT. Normally, you assume that the words are synonyms and say, "A saint *is* nefarious." However, remembering that *ne-* is on a brown card, which means that it is negative, makes you change the sentence to "A saint is *not* nefarious,"

because saints are generally considered pretty good. (I make no comments about the New Orleans Saints football team, strong though the temptation is.)

There is no right or wrong way to classify the roots. If you think that a root is positive, fine, it's positive. If you think that a root is negative, fine, it's negative. The whole purpose of flashcards is to help you associate the words. Go with whatever works for *you.*

Bonus! When you come across a word that incorporates the root, put that word on the card as an example. That way, you learn both the root and the vocabulary word: two for the price of one. If you're reading a newspaper article about a program that will have a *salubrious* effect on the economy, note that *sal-* means health (I cover that root later) and *-ous* means full of. You know immediately that the word means healthful. Put it on both the *sal-* card and the *-ous* card. You'll learn the vocabulary without realizing it.

3. *-ous* = **full of (very):** Someone *joyous* is full of joy. Someone *amorous* is full of *amour,* or love. Someone *pulchritudinous* is full of beauty, and therefore beautiful.

4. *-ist* = **a person:** A *typist* is a person who types. A *pugilist* is a person who fights (*pug-* means war or fight), a boxer. A *pacifist* is a person who believes in peace, a noncombatant (*pac-* means peace or calm).

5. *-ify (-efy)* = **to make:** To *beautify* is to make beautiful. To *ossify* is to make bone. (If you break your wrist, it takes weeks to ossify again, or for the bone to regenerate.) To *deify* is to make into a deity, a god.

6. *-ize* = **to make:** To *alphabetize* is to make alphabetical. To *immunize* is to make immune. To *ostracize* is to make separate from the group, to shun.

7. *-ate* = **to make:** To *duplicate* is to make double. To *renovate* is to make new again (*nov-* means new). To *placate* is to make peaceful or calm (*plac-* means peace or calm).

8. *-ity* = **noun suffix that doesn't actually mean anything; it just turns a word into a noun:** *Jollity* is the noun form of jolly. *Serenity* is the noun form of serene. *Timidity* is the noun form of timid.

The Terminator: Eliminating Dumb Answers

The first answer to eliminate is the backward one. Putting answers in reverse order is a common trap. If the question goes from greater to lesser (OVERJOYED : CONTENT), there is almost certainly a trap answer that goes from lesser to greater (displeased : furious). Look for it.

Another good answer to eliminate is one that duplicates the *meaning* rather than the relationship between the words. The question may be PROFESSOR : EDUCATED. The words are synonyms. A good answer to eliminate is teacher : moronic. Even though a professor is a teacher and those words have the same meaning, the *relationship* between the trap answer words is antonymous, not synonymous.

Finally, forget about humor. Anything funny or trying to be funny is outta there. Correct answers are almost always dull and boring.

Déjà Vu Review

Before going on to the practice questions, review what you've discovered about analogy questions. Don't forget to use the simple two-step approach to answering an analogy question:

1. **Use both words in a *descriptive* sentence.**

2. **Use the exact same sentence on each answer choice.**

Even if you don't have a clue what the words in an analogy mean, you can often get the correct answer by using the following five tips. These tips help you to identify the relationship between the words well enough to make a reasonable guess.

↳ Turn a verb into an infinitive.

↳ Identify which part of speech — noun, verb, or adjective — the question words are.

↳ Use roots, prefixes, and suffixes.

↳ Look for the *salient features* of a word.

↳ Identify common relationships.

Ten words that Cindy Crawford never hears

obese	rotund
corpulent	fleshy
flaccid	homely
drab	frowzy
unkempt	slovenly

Chapter 3

The Dirty Dozen:
Analogy Practice Questions

• •

*R*eady to practice what I've been preaching? Here are The Dirty Dozen Analogy practice questions to get you into the swing of things. This chapter is loaded with good vocabulary words. Don't forget to pay extra-careful attention to the words in this font: *vocabulary word*. Just consider this entire chapter stamped with a big ol' vocabulary icon!

Q 1. PEANUT : SHELL ::

   (A) atom : proton

   (B) clock : dial

   (C) corn : husk

   (D) emollient : solid

   (E) enamel : tooth

Make a simple sentence defining the relationship between the words : "A peanut is surrounded by a shell." Corn is surrounded by a husk.

Choice E is backward. The enamel is not surrounded by the tooth but vice versa. Keep your eyes open for a backward answer among the answer choices; one is frequently put there to getcha.

Q 2. HYMN : SONG ::

   (A) screech : whisper

   (B) waltz : dance

   (C) misnomer : correction

   (D) discussion : altercation

   (E) smile : reproof

A simple sentence is "A hymn is a type of song." A waltz is a type of dance. A *screech* is a loud noise, just the opposite of a whisper. Your tires screech when you take the corner wide in your rush to get to the GRE, having overslept that morning. (I know — I shouldn't even joke about such a thing!) In choice C, a *misnomer* is the wrong name, calling someone Tracy instead of Stacy, for example. It therefore is not a correction but a mistake. An *altercation* is a disagreement. While it may be a discussion, the answer is not as close to being synonymous as is choice B. In choice E, a *reproof* is a condemnation, a criticism.

3. CHUCKLE : MERRIMENT ::

   (A) goose bumps : denial

   (B) blush : glee

   (C) scowl : perfidy

   (D) wince : discomfort

   (E) shout : fury

Make your sentence: "A chuckle indicates merriment" or "A chuckle is the result of merriment." *Merriment* is just what it looks like, happiness. The suffix *-ment* doesn't mean anything; it just turns a word into a noun, such as content and contentment, or argue and argument. A wince (an involuntary shrinking back or flinching) indicates discomfort. You wince when your Dearly Beloved says to you, "We *have* to talk." In choice A, *goose bumps* indicate cold or fright, not denial. Choice B could trap a careless reader who thinks that because *glee* means happiness or merriment, this answer fits. In choice C, perfidy means disloyalty. Choice E is a "mebbe so, mebbe not" answer. A shout may indicate fury (you shout at the ATM when it gobbles up your bankcard and shreds it), but the connection is not absolute. Always look for the salient or outstanding feature of the word. *Correct Answer:* D.

Remember: Choose an answer based on the *relationship* between the words, not on the meanings of the words. The question can be about houses and the answer about cantaloupes; they don't have to have any connection whatsoever.

4. COW : TERRIFY ::

   (A) praise : denounce

   (B) interest : fascinate

   (C) invigorate : exhaust

   (D) soothe : agitate

   (E) diminish : lessen

Okay, suppose that you have no idea what the word *cow* as a verb means. You can still get this question right by the process of elimination. Choices A, C, and D all have the relationship of antonyms. Because they can't all be correct, they must all be wrong. You now know that *cow* and *intimidate* are not antonyms. As quickly as that, you've narrowed the answers down to two, but can you narrow the answers down even further? The relationship between the words in choice B is lesser to greater; that is, interesting someone is less intense than fascinating that person. Because *terrify*, in the question, is such a strong word, it's unlikely that the first word, *cow*, is something even stronger. Just so you know, *to cow* means to intimidate, to browbeat. *Correct Answer:* B.

Words have more than one meaning. A test question may key into this fact. If your first response seems to make no sense in the context of the question ("Why would a cow terrify anyone?"), think of alternate meanings of the word or words.

5. XENOPHOBIC : STRANGERS ::

   (A) claustrophobic : Christmas

   (B) hydrophobic : fires

   (C) agoraphobic : open spaces

   (D) pyromaniac : animals

   (E) romantic : love

You may not know the word xenophobic, but you can deduce that *phobic* means fearful of because you know such relatively easy words as *hydrophobia* (fear of water) and *claustrophobia* (fear of closed spaces). Therefore, make the sentence: "Xenophobic is fearful of strangers." *Agoraphobic* means fearful of open spaces. An agoraphobe is often afraid to leave the house at all. When it's your turn to shovel the snow off the front walk, you may suddenly turn into an agoraphobe.

Choice A is a lame attempt at humor (and won't be found on the actual GRE, which has no humor at all, lame or otherwise). Claustrophobic does not mean fearing Santa Claus and Christmas. Hydrophobic means fearing water, not fires. Someone who is a *pyromaniac* has a love of fire. Someone romantic has a love of love, not a fear of love. *Correct Answer:* C.

6. ELEGIAC : JOY ::

   (A) innocuous : harmful

   (B) phlegmatic : peace

   (C) implacable : tranquility

   (D) dynamic : energy

   (E) disparaging : insults

Something elegiac is not full of joy. An *elegy* is a sad or mournful poem. Something *innocuous* is not full of harm. (Figure this out using the roots: *In-* usually means not; *noc* means harm; *-ous* means full of: not full of harm.)

Often, if you don't know a word, you make the "is" sentence: Elegiac is joy. But in this case, to make you miss the question and, therefore, help you to remember the word *elegiac* (sad or mournful), I made it the opposite. But you can still get this question correct because choice D, *dynamic*, does mean full of energy, and choice E, *disparaging*, does mean full of insults. Because two answers can't both be correct, they must both be wrong. Knowing that should send you back to the drawing board to change from an "is" to an "is not" sentence.

Choice B, *phlegmatic*, means calm, composed. Now that you know this word, you can remain phlegmatic when you encounter it on the GRE and not panic. Choice C, *implacable*, means unchangeable, stubborn. An implacable toddler yells "NO!" no matter what the harassed parents suggest. (Do you see the roots? im- means not; *plac* means peace or calm; *-able* is able to be. Someone implacable is "unable to be calmed down," or just plain stubborn.) *Correct Answer:* A.

7. PECCADILLO : TRANSGRESSION ::

   (A) felony : crime

   (B) nibble : bite

   (C) alias : name

   (D) cacophony : noise

   (E) eructation : volcano

You know the suffix *-illo* means small or little. Make the sentence : "A peccadillo is a small transgression." You don't even have to know what the words mean to get a good sentence. (A *peccadillo* is a small wrong or fault. A *transgression* is a trespass or sin, a wrong.) A *nibble* is a small bite. In choice C, *alias* is a different name, not a small name. In D, *cacophony* is a bad or harsh sound, such as my singing voice or the sounds of an orchestra warming up. The roots help you to define this word; *caco* means bad, *phon* means sound: bad sound. Choice E is my gift to you, a little comic relief. An *eructation* is a belch. Although a volcano may eructate, an eructation itself is not a volcano. *Correct Answer:* B.

8. PROGNOSTICATION : SOOTHSAYER ::

   (A) tumult : arbitrator

   (B) duplicity : idiot

   (C) fanaticism : zealot

   (D) adulation : adult

   (E) retrospection : prophet

Whoa! Suddenly these words have gotten terribly hard. Try saying: "Prognostication *is* sooth-sayer." Therefore, you are looking for two answer words that are synonyms or at least mean *nearly* the same thing.

Fanaticism is the state of being a fanatic (did you know that the word *fan,* like a rock star's groupie, comes from the word *fanatic?*), being really into something. **Zealous** also means very into something, enthusiastic, involved. The words are synonyms. A zealot is one who is zealous.

You may have known the words for choice C but not for the other answers. Let's review them quickly. You may be familiar with tumult in another form, **tumultuous,** which means wild, chaotic, disorganized. An **arbitrator** is a mediator, a go-between in a fight or controversy. An arbitrator's job would be to stop the tumult, to calm things down and bring about a rational discussion. The words are closer to antonyms than synonyms.

By the way, a favorite ETS trick is to give you a common word in an uncommon form, just to confuse you and make your life miserable. For example, do you know this word?

   RUTH

Seeing it all by itself like that, you may swear that you'd never seen the word before. But you probably know it in another form:

   RUTHLESS

Ah, you know that **ruthless** means cruel, without pity or compassion. Work backwards. If ruth-less means *without* pity, ruth must mean *with* pity. **Ruth** is pity or compassion, kindness, mercy. Ruth used to be a very popular girl's name.

The moral of the story is, when you see a word that looks slightly familiar, knock it around a little bit. Change its form to see whether you can discover its meaning more easily. Tumult is just the noun form of the more common word, tumultuous.

In B, **duplicity** is the quality of being *dup,* or double, as in double-dealing, double-crossing, double-talking. Benedict Arnold was noted for his duplicity. It has nothing to do with being an idiot. However, there is a trick here. A **dupe,** or a person who has been double-crossed or swindled, is in fact rather idiotic. This would be an easy trap to fall for.

Choice D is silly. Adulation has nothing to do with being an adult. **Adulation** is hero worship, extreme admiration. You may have adulation for a war hero, or for the person who discovers the cure for cancer.

The words in choice E are also closer to antonyms than to synonyms. **Retrospection** is a look back, a review. At my 16th birthday party, my parents showed home movies of me naked in the bathtub at 6 months, me crawling around on a rug at 7 months, and so on. They called it the Suzee Retrospective. I called it Death By Embarrassment. A **prophet** is supposed to prophesy or predict the future, not look back at the past. *Correct Answer:* C.

9. EXCULPATE : BLAME ::

(A) demean : average

(B) compromise : peril

(C) proliferate : abundance

(D) perturb : exasperation

(E) exonerate : guilt

Just to keep you on your toes, I put in a question in which the right answer actually did have the same meaning as the question words. This situation is rare, but I always want to emphasize to you that my suggestions are tips, not rules. Never shut off your own brain in favor of mine. To *exculpate* is to remove the blame. Think of the roots: *ex-* means out of or away from; *culp* means guilt or blame; *-ate* means to make: To make away from the guilt or blame. When your roommate comes in breathing fire because someone has borrowed his car and put a big dent in it, you thank your lucky stars that you went to class with friends in their car that day and have witnesses to exculpate you. To *exonerate* is the same thing, to remove the guilt or blame. A defense attorney sends his or her investigators out looking for evidence to exonerate the client.

To *compromise* means to imperil, to put into danger. For example, a young girl who stays out all night long with her date — even though they are just talking — compromises her reputation. A government official seen fraternizing with lobbyists may be compromising her integrity, putting it into some question or doubt. As you learned with *cow* in question 4, words may have more than one meaning. The first definition most people provide for *compromise* is to come to terms by mutual concession, to meet in the middle and agree. As that meaning has no connection with peril, you need to wrack your brains for another, less-common meaning.

In choice C, to *proliferate* is to grow in number or size, to become more abundant. The most common meaning of *pro-* on the GRE is big or much; a proliferation is an abundance, very much. In choice D, *to perturb* is to exasperate, to annoy or harass. If you missed this question, you are probably perturbed and exasperated with yourself. *Correct Answer:* E.

10. DESICCATE : MOISTURE ::

(A) sanction : restrictions

(B) enervate : energy

(C) swindle : chicanery

(D) attenuate : attention

(E) derogate : epithets

To *desiccate* is to dry out, to remove moisture. (Ever hear of desiccated liver tablets? Some health food stores sell them for people who don't want to eat liver and would prefer to ingest it in dehydrated or pill form.) You can figure out this relationship by knowing that *de-* means out of or away from: A desiccant moves moisture out of or away from something. To enervate is to devitalize, to remove the energy from, to weaken.

Choice A, to *sanction* is to restrict. You probably know about economic sanctions, in which a government prohibits businesses from working with companies in other countries. To sanction, therefore, is to add restrictions rather than to take them away. In choice C, to *swindle* is to cheat or trick, as in swindling someone out of his money. *Chicanery* is trickery in matters of law. To swindle is not to take away chicanery but to add to it. In choice D, to *attenuate* is not to take away attention (you didn't fall for such a cheesy trick, did you?) but to make slender, thin, or diluted. An *emaciated* person looks attenuated. In choice E, to *derogate* is to denounce or be critical of. An *epithet* is a descriptive term, often one used derogatorily or critically. *Correct Answer:* B.

11. TOADY : SYCOPHANT ::

    (A) recluse : pedant

    (B) heretic : leader

    (C) malingerer : prodigy

    (D) bluestocking : gymnast

    (E) miser : penny-pincher

If you don't know the words in the question, you're not alone. They are very difficult words, put there in the hopes that you remember what to do when you don't have a clue: First, try making the words synonyms. Make the simple sentence: A toady is a sycophant. As it turns out, that's correct. Both a *toady* and a *sycophant* are over-flatterers, kiss-ups, yes-men. A groupie to a rock star is a toady and a sycophant. A student trying to get the professor to turn a borderline A-/B+ into the A is a toady and a sycophant. In the correct answer, E, a *miser* (a cheapskate, someone stingy) is in fact a penny-pincher. A penny-pincher is a cheap person, one who "pinches" pennies, holding them securely, not letting them go or spending them.

Here are the definitions for the other words. A *recluse* is a hermit, a solitary person. You may have heard this word in another form, reclusive. A *pedant* is a teacher, especially one who is overly precise and didactic. A *heretic* is a rebel, particularly one who doesn't agree with the orthodox religion. Joan of Arc was burned at the stake as a heretic. A *malingerer* is one who pretends to be sick in order to get out of work. All of us have been malingerers on the morning of a big exam at school, swearing to a variety of symptoms that would kill an ox. A *prodigy* is a highly talented person (Mozart was a child prodigy). A *bluestocking* is a learned woman, especially one in literary circles. She has nothing to do with gymnastics. *Correct Answer:* E.

12. PUGILIST : BELLICOSE ::

    (A) benefactor : beguiling

    (B) chatterbox : taciturn

    (C) narcissist : charismatic

    (D) scholar : erudite

    (E) imbecile : obsequious

A *pugilist* is a boxer, one who fights (the root *pug* means war or fight and *-ist* is a person). *Bellicose* is like belligerent: hostile, argumentative, fighting. The test sentence is: "A pugilist is bellicose." If you don't know the words and assume they are synonyms, you are right. A scholar is in fact *erudite*, which means well-educated or scholarly. In choice A, a *benefactor* is a person who does good, one who brings *benefits* (to use a more common form of the word). He or she probably would not be *beguiling*, which means tricking or confusing. In choice B, a *chatterbox* is just what it looks like, one who chatters or talks a lot. *Taciturn* means not talkative, of few words. A chatterbox is not taciturn.

Have you heard of a tacit agreement? It's an unspoken agreement. Try to think of more common or familiar forms of the word. If you can remember how you use those in context, you can often get a "good enough" definition for a difficult word.

In choice C, a *narcissist* is a person overflowing with self-love, someone who thinks he or she is just the most wonderful thing around. While the narcissist may think he or she is *charismatic* (inspiring loyalty), 'tain't necessarily so. In choice E, an *imbecile* is a feebleminded person, a fool (what most of us feel like when we don't know all these words). An imbecile may or may not be *obsequious*, which means excessively flattering. Remember the toady and sycophant from a previous question? Now *they* would be obsequious. *Correct Answer:* D.

Chapter 4

If Opposites Attract, Why Are Antonyms So Repulsive?

In This Chapter

▶ Is that all there is? The format of an antonym question

▶ Let's get this over with fast: The approach

▶ What to do when you ain't got a clue

▶ Bad things come in small packages: Tricks, traps, and tips

Think of the antonyms as the terrible twos of the vocabulary world. Just like a *cantankerous* (grumpy) kid who answers your "Good morning!" with "No, it's not; it's a bad morning!" the GRE's Antonym questions are looking to contradict everything.

Is That All There Is? The Format

Antonyms are a fish out of water, a word out of context (a cliché out of a *For Dummies* book). Questions in the Antonym section feature one word in capital letters followed by five lower-case answer choices. The prima donna antonym stands alone. You have no context to help you to define the vocabulary. It's you against the word. For example:

LOQUACIOUS:

  (A) quotidian

  (B) taciturn

  (C) contentious

  (D) guileless

  (E) perfunctory

I'm looking *forward* to this	
harbinger	auguries
prescient	portent
presage	prognosticate
prognosis	bode

You have to keep your sense of *humor*

levity	ribald
jocose	puckish
wag	jocular
risible	badinage
japing	jollity
twit	mirth

Your task is to define the question word and then choose the answer with the most nearly opposite meaning. The good news is that doing so takes almost no time. These questions are over with faster than your last relationship. The bad news is that some of this vocabulary is so difficult you may think you've wandered into the Greek GRE by mistake.

Let's Get This Over with Fast: The Approach

The antonyms are the least complicated portion of the GRE. Take a simple two-step approach:

1. **Define the question word.**
2. **Choose the opposite.**

Sounds simple, right? It is . . . *if* you know what the question word means. If the question word is *happy,* choose *sad.* If the question word is *tall,* choose *short.* So far, so good. But what happens when you *don't* know what the question word means?

It's a *sad* day when you don't know your vocabulary

Weltschmerz	lachrymose
jeremiad	dour
doleful	lugubrious
maudlin	saturnine
contrite	bereft

What to Do When You Ain't Got a Clue

Suppose that you look at a word and think it looks more like an inkblot test than like any vocabulary word you've ever seen. The word may be *cadging*. Not a clue, right? (And no, it's not a typo or a misspelling of "cage.") What do you do next? You have three options:

1. **Dissect and define the term using roots, prefixes, and suffixes.**

   As I point out in Chapter 3, roots, prefixes, and suffixes are the real key to vocabulary on the GRE. Unfortunately, you haven't learned a root, prefix, or suffix for *cadging*. Proceed to step 2.

2. **Eliminate answer choices that are synonyms of each other.**

   Suppose that choice A is *bubbly* and choice D is *effervescent*. Both words mean exuberant, joyful. Because two answer choices cannot both be correct, they must both be wrong.

3. **Bail out! Choose an answer and leave the scene as quickly as possible.**

   Suppose that you have no idea what the word means. It has no identifiable root, prefix, or suffix. No two of the answer choices mean the same thing. There's no way to narrow the answers down. What happens now? Guess and go. Choose something, anything, and go on to the next question.

The biggest mistake that you can make on an antonym question is to waste time. The longer you sit there, staring at the word, scratching your head, and waiting for heavenly revelation, the more the test-makers in their dark cubbyholes chortle with glee at your struggling in the *quagmire* (bog) they designed for you. Get through an Antonym question quickly: You either know it, or you don't know it, and then you're outta there. Think of an Antonym question as a blind date. You can tell in the first few minutes whether something's happening or not. (P.S. *Cadging* means begging or scrounging. GRE students often cadge notes from friends for classes.)

That's easy for you to *say*

declaim	exhort
stentorian	philippic
persiflage	pontificate
raconteur	prolix
voluble	tergiversate

Bad Things Come in Small Packages: Tricks, Traps, and Tips

How, you wonder, can there be tricks and traps in a one-word question? Read 'em and weep.

Ignore the synonym

You may be lucky enough to encounter a very difficult word that you just happen to remember. Suppose that the question word is *pulchritudinous*. If you have already gone through the analogies portion of this book, you remember that pulchritudinous means beautiful. Choice A is "beautiful." You are so pleased with yourself for remembering this hard word that you choose A ("Ah, there it is!") and go your merry way. It isn't until you're boasting to your friend later that afternoon about having remembered *pulchritudinous* that your mistake dawns on you: You were supposed to choose the *antonym,* not the synonym. In short: If you see a word in the answer choices whose meaning is the same, or nearly the same as the question, ignore it. It's put there just to ruin your day.

Use roots, prefixes, and suffixes

As I mention throughout this material, roots, prefixes, and suffixes (RPS) can save you when you have to wade through this polysyllabic pit. If you have not yet learned the prefixes and suffixes in the analogies chapter, I strongly suggest you do so now. You can analyze even the most difficult word by using roots. Even if you can't get the exact definition, you can get a general idea of the word well enough to choose it or lose it.

Suppose that the question word is *abjure*. You don't know what it means, but you recall that the prefix *ab-* means away from. A queen abdicates a throne, or goes away from a throne. One of the answer choices is embrace. To embrace something is to take it as your own, to accept it, as in embracing the principles of democracy. If you trust your roots-sense and choose this, you can get a hard question correct in just a few seconds. (To *abjure* is to renounce or reject.)

Memorize connotation cards

I talk in Chapter 2 about creating flashcards for the roots, prefixes, and suffixes. You should have those cards completed by now and should be ready to move on to a more sophisticated type of flashing: *connotation cards*.

Just how *boring* is this vocabulary?

ennui	trite
platitude	hackneyed
prosaic	vapid
listless	soporific
bromide	tedious
somniferous	banal

It takes a lot of *guts* to know these words

audacity	intrepid
doughty	redoubtable
undaunted	effrontery
impudent	uncowed

Notice that I'm not wasting your time or mine by giving you a list of a thousand words. It would be useless for you to sit down and try to memorize so many. You'd get to a point where each new word would **supplant** (displace, push out) a previous word. So how *can* you cram the most vocabulary into the least brain space? Memorize groups of words by their connotation.

A **connotation** is an association or idea, an implication. It is what the word means to you, how you remember it. Use index cards to cluster words by their connotations. For example, on one side of a card, write *fat,* and on the other side, write *thin*. Every time you encounter a word that has one of these meanings, put it on the card. On the fat side, you may have corpulent, fleshy, rotund, and obese. On the thin side, you might have emaciated, attenuated, svelte, and lanky.

Suppose you get to the exam and you see the word *svelte* but can't for the life of you remember what it means. In your mind's eye, you see the word on the *fat/thin* card. Voilà! Or on second thought: Ooops! Wait a minute: Does *svelte* mean fat, or does it mean thin?

Write words with positive meanings in red ink and words with negative meanings in black ink. Maybe you consider being thin better than being fat. Write all the *thin* words in bright red ink to make them stand out. Write all the *fat* words in black ink. During the exam, you can remember that *svelte* is a red word on the *fat/thin* card, so it must mean thin. You'll be surprised how many questions you can get correct without knowing precise definitions, just hazy general concepts.

Hip, hip, hooray! Words of *praise*

laud	extol
paean	accolade
eulogy	plaudits
encomium	sycophant
kudos	toady
panegyric	obsequious

Don't anticipate and misread

The GRE often features some pretty bizarre-looking words. My favorite is *froward* (stubborn). At least once a year, some student calls me, overjoyed at having "conquered" the GRE: "Suzee, you won't believe it. The GRE had a typo. One of the antonyms said *froward* instead of *forward*. However, the answer choice 'backward' was there, so I had no trouble figuring it out." No, no, a thousand times, no! The GRE has no typos. The GRE has no spelling errors. The GRE has no heart. It's very easy to see what you want to see rather than to read what's actually shown on the screen. Double-check that you have read the word correctly, not rewritten the test to match your preconceptions.

Peroration (A Summing Up)

An Antonym question requires a simple, two-step approach:

1. **Define the word.**
2. **Choose the opposite.**

Antonyms are small but deadly. Remembering the following can help you get through these questions efficiently:

✔ Use roots, prefixes, and suffixes.

✔ Eliminate answer choices that are synonyms of each other.

✔ Look for and avoid the answer choice that is a synonym of the question word.

✔ Learn vocabulary words in clusters using connotation cards.

✔ Don't anticipate and misread unusual words (such as *froward*).

Are you sick to *death* of vocabulary?

dirge	morbid
demise	obsequies
valetudinarian	noxious
elegy	insalubrious
cadaver	wan

Chapter 5

Unattractive Opposites: Antonym Practice Questions

You say you've been using a dictionary for a pillow for the last six weeks, believing some of the words and their definitions would penetrate your skull by osmosis? Here's a chance to test your theory. (Consider this chapter to have one big, looming Vocabulary icon attached to it.)

1. CHANGING

   (A) lightweight

   (B) cautious

   (C) immutable

   (D) delicious

   (E) soft

You can get this question correct by the process of elimination. The opposite of changing is not changing, or unchanging. You know that lightweight, cautious, delicious, and soft do not mean "not changing," which narrows the answers down quickly to the correct one. Use your roots to define *immutable*. *Im-* means not; *mut* means change. Im-mut-able literally means not changeable, unchanging. *Correct Answer:* C.

2. RECUPERATE

   (A) sicken

   (B) invent

   (C) operate

   (D) elongate

   (E) balance

To **recuperate** is to regain your health. The opposite is to sicken. Choice C has a small trap in it. A person recuperating may have been operated on, but just because an answer choice seems connected to the question word (both *recuperate* and *operate* have to do with health) does not mean the choice is correct.

Did you use your common sense to eliminate choice B? What word could possibly be the opposite of *invent*? As far as I know, no word means "uninvent." If you can't think of a logical opposite for a word, then it probably is not an antonym of the question. *Correct Answer:* A.

3. OPAQUE

(A) old-fashioned

(B) angry

(C) improper

(D) outdated

(E) transparent

Something *opaque* is not clear, not see-through. It blocks the light (*op* means block or against). Something transparent is clear, does not block the light. Did you notice that you can eliminate choices A and D because they are synonyms of each other? If two words mean the same (or nearly the same), they can't both be correct and therefore must both be wrong. *Correct Answer:* E.

4. LOQUACIOUS

(A) elegant

(B) quiet

(C) overweight

(D) excited

(E) incapable

Loq means speech or talk; *-ous* means full of or very. Someone loquacious is full of talk, very talkative. The opposite is quiet. *Correct Answer:* B.

Most of my students are quite loquacious in telling me that their biggest problem is vocabulary. They just plain can't remember pages and pages and pages of words. My suggestion is always the same: Concentrate on learning roots, prefixes, and suffixes, which can expand your vocabulary exponentially. In this book, you can find lists of roots, prefixes, and suffixes in Chapters 2 and 6.

5. SKEPTICAL

(A) fast-acting

(B) punctual

(C) depressed

(D) credulous

(E) effervescent

If you are *skeptical,* you are dubious or doubtful. You are looking for a word that means not doubtful. Eliminate the words you do know — choices A, B, and C. *Credulous* can be defined using the roots: *cred* means trust or belief; *-ous* means full of or very. Someone credulous is full of trust, naive, gullible — just the opposite of skeptical. Effervescent means bubbly. When an *Effer*dent (a denture-cleaning tablet) is put into a glass of water, it bubbles. *Correct Answer:* D.

6. VIABLE

(A) solid

(B) moribund

(C) vital

(D) integral

(E) irreplaceable

If you chose C, you fell for the trap. *Vital* means essential, critical. Just because it has a *vi* like the question word does not mean vital is the right answer (and anyway, you are looking for antonyms, not synonyms). Choices C, D, and E are similar enough in meaning that selecting one over the others would be hard. You can't have three right answers, so eliminate them all.

Viable means capable of working or developing adequately, livable. A plan for learning several new roots like *vi* (meaning life) daily is viable (it can be done). *Moribund* means near death or extinction. A company that is bankrupt and firing employees may be described as moribund. *Correct Answer:* B.

7. SALUBRIOUS

   (A) unhealthy

   (B) serendipitous

   (C) dour

   (D) rapid

   (E) monumental

Salubrious means healthful, wholesome, salutary (*sal* means health, *-ous* means full of). Unhealthy is as logical an opposite as you're ever going to find. Choice B, *serendipitous,* means fortuitous, a happy, lucky occurrence. It would be serendipitous to walk out your front door and find a hundred dollar bill on your doorstep. Choice C, *dour,* means gloomy. Finding out that the hundred dollar bill you so serendipitously found on the sidewalk features a picture not of Ben Franklin but of Alfred E. Newman will leave you dour. *Correct Answer:* A.

8. IRASCIBLE

   (A) mendacious

   (B) serpentine

   (C) phlegmatic

   (D) fatigued

   (E) tepid

Irascible means hot-tempered, easily angered. Choice C, *phlegmatic,* means slow, having a stolid temperament, not easily excited to action. Choice A, *mendacious,* means lying, dishonest, untruthful. Don't confuse the adjective mendacious, meaning dishonest, with the noun *mendicant,* a beggar. A mendicant may be mendacious when he tells you how he's going to spend the quarter you just gave him. Choice B, *serpentine,* means like a snake, twisting or turning. The road to Pike's Peak is a serpentine road. Choice E, *tepid,* means lukewarm. A tepid response to a marriage proposal should send you to your lawyer's office to get a prenuptial agreement. *Correct Answer:* C.

9. FRANGIBLE

   (A) refulgent

   (B) histrionic

   (C) unbreakable

   (D) unfriendly

   (E) masculine

Frangible means breakable. The opposite, amazingly enough, is unbreakable. Choice A, *refulgent,* means shining, radiant, gleaming. Choice B, *histrionic,* means theatrical, hysterical, dramatic. *Correct Answer:* C.

10. PALLIATE

    (A) laud

    (B) appraise

    (C) exacerbate

    (D) befriend

    (E) mitigate

To *palliate* is to soften, lessen, or assuage. You can palliate an insult by smiling to take the sting out. Choice C, *exacerbate,* is to make more severe, to aggravate. You exacerbate a fight when you slam the door in your opponent's face. Choice A, to *laud,* is to praise. (Think of app<u>laud</u>.) Choice D, to *befriend,* is to make a friend of. (*Be* is a prefix meaning completely; however, you can basically ignore this prefix. To befriend someone is simply to "friend" him.) Choice E, *mitigate,* is the same as palliate. To mitigate is to lessen or decrease, to make less severe. You may have heard of "mitigating circumstances." Hot wiring and stealing a car is a felony that can land you in prison; taking the car because your wife is in labor and you have to get to the hospital pronto is a mitigating circumstance (but if you take *my* car, you have *unmitigated* gall!). *Correct Answer:* C.

11. CONDIGN

    (A) incapable

    (B) inevitable

    (C) inconsistent

    (D) unremitting

    (E) undeserved

Condign means deserved or appropriate. A condign punishment for those of you who do not laugh at my jokes is to spend eternity listening to your parent's old record albums. The opposite (logically enough) is undeserved. *Correct Answer:* E.

12. SALACIOUS

    (A) wholesome

    (B) rustic

    (C) noxious

    (D) merry

    (E) puissant

Salacious means lustful, lecherous, lewd — the opposite of wholesome. Choice B, *rustic,* means rural, appropriate for the country. A rustic outfit would be plus fours and a shooting stick. Choice E, *puissant,* means strong, influential, powerful. *Correct Answer:* A.

Did you fall for the trap answer, C? *Sal-* means health; *-ous* means full of. No one can fault you if you thought salacious meant "full of health." However, the word for that is salubrious. Choice C, *noxious,* means poisonous. It is a good antonym for salubrious but not for salacious.

No, no, don't panic. Of course, this section is hard for you. But I have news for you: It's just as hard for native English speakers. It's true! Your average American has no more idea of the meanings of *prolix* (verbose and long-winded) and *salubrious* than you do. Everyone is equal when it comes to needing to learn roots, prefixes, and suffixes.

Chapter 6

Finish What You Start: Sentence Completions

In This Chapter

▶ Drawing a blank: What Sentence Completion questions look like

▶ Cutting away the deadwood: Dissecting and simplifying the sentences

▶ Sweeping away the trash: Eliminating wrong answers

Sentence Completion questions are the blind dates of the GRE. What you see is not necessarily what you get . . . or what you want. Looks can be deceiving. Don't judge a book by its cover. Beauty is only skin deep. Let's see, have I left out any other trite, banal, hackneyed clichés? The point of all this babbling is that Sentence Completion questions can be sneaky, tricky, duplicitous, and worse than they look. Fortunately, there are ways to beat the questions at their own game.

What Sentence Completion Questions Look Like

A Sentence Completion question consists of one sentence with one or two blanks. Your job, should you choose to accept it, is to fill in those blanks. Usually only one word goes in each blank; occasionally, however, the blank requires a few words or a short phrase instead. Here is an example:

Disgusted at having to spend the entire weekend studying for the GRE instead of going hang gliding, Faye - - - - her book across the room with such - - - - that it soared high into the sky, causing three of her neighbors to call the UFO hot line.

(A) tossed ... gentleness

(B) hurled ... ferocity

(C) pitched ... glee

(D) carried ... gloom

(E) conveyed ... reluctance

The key word in this example is *disgusted*, indicating strong, negative emotions. Only choice B offers two words that match the tone of *disgusted*. *Correct Answer:* B.

Looking at the Sentence and Drawing a Blank

Do you look at Sentence Completion questions and draw a blank? (Sorry, I couldn't resist.) Knowing where to start is a great confidence builder and time-saver. Try the following steps.

1. **Read the entire sentence for its gist.**

2. **If possible, predict words to fit the blanks.**

3. **Insert the answer choices.**

The following sections explain these steps.

Read the entire sentence

Although this may seem obvious, many people read until they get to the first blank and then head for the answers. The problem is that the sentence may change in midstream, messing everything up. Note, for example, the big difference between

Having been coerced by her mother into accepting a blind date, Mitzi was ---- *because* Marty turned out to be ----.

— and —

Having been coerced by her mother into accepting a blind date, Mitzi was ---- *although* Marty turned out to be ----.

In the first example, you may want to say something like this:

Having been coerced by her mother into accepting a blind date, Mitzi was *ecstatic* because Marty turned out to be *gorgeous*.

In the second example, you could say the following:

Having been coerced by her mother into accepting a blind date, Mitzi was *content* although Marty turned out to be *mediocre*.

How you fill in the blanks depends on the middle term — in this case the conjunction *because* or *although*.

Keep in mind that the purpose of Sentence Completion questions is to measure your ability to recognize words and phrases that logically and stylistically complete the meaning of the sentences.

If possible, predict words to fit the blanks

Notice the careful hedge, "if possible." You can't *always* predict words. But it's amazing how often you can get close. Consider the following example:

Hal was ---- when his new computer arrived because he realized he'd have no excuses now for not finishing his homework.

You can predict that the word should be something negative, such as *depressed, sad,* or *unhappy.* (If your vocabulary is up to the task, you can also predict negative words such as *lachrymose, dolorous,* and *lugubrious.*)

Did you predict something positive, such as *happy* or *glad?* If you did, you probably headed for the answers before you read the entire sentence. What did I just tell you in the preceding section? Tsk, tsk.

Insert the answer choices

Don't try to save time by hurrying through Sentence Completion questions. You just need to plug and chug. Plug in every answer choice and chug through the whole darn sentence again. Occasionally, you can eliminate answers because you know the word *must* be positive, but that answer choice is negative. After you eliminate everything you can, you must insert the remaining answers into the blanks and read through the sentences that result. Try the following example:

As a public relations specialist, Susan realizes the importance of ---- and ---- when dealing with even the most exasperating tourists.

(A) dignity ... etiquette

(B) fantasy ... realism

(C) kindness ... patience

(D) courtesy ... compassion

(E) truth ... honesty

Because the two blanks are connected by *and,* the words in those blanks should be synonyms (or almost synonyms). They may not need to mean exactly the same thing, but they certainly should not be opposites. They should be on the same wavelength. That means you can eliminate choice B because *fantasy* and *realism* are opposites. That's the only answer, however, that you can eliminate immediately. The others are all close enough in meaning to fit together.

This leaves you with no choice but to plug and chug. Insert every answer and see which one makes the most sense. The right answer here is choice C. Choice A looks pretty good, but you don't "treat someone with etiquette." *Etiquette* is a system of rules for manners. Choice D also looks pretty good, but treating with compassion someone who is *exasperating* is not as logical as treating the person with patience. Choice E is very tempting until you plug it into the sentence. *Truth* and *honesty* are synonyms, but they don't fit as well in the context of the sentence as do *kindness* and *patience. Correct Answer:* C.

Forget about taking a lot of shortcuts. After you eliminate the obviously incorrect answers, take your sweet time going back and inserting every remaining answer into the sentence. Sentence Completion answers aren't right or wrong so much as good, better, or best. Sometimes all the answers seem to "sorta fit"; your job is to choose the one that fits best.

TNT: Dynamite Traps 'n' Tricks

Let me introduce you to the nasty little gremlins lurking in the Sentence Completion questions and give you some suggestions for dealing with them. The basic steps to take are as follows:

1. **Look for key connecting words that may change the meaning of the sentence.**

2. **Predict positive or negative words to fit in the blanks.**

3. **Don't waste time scratching your head over questions with vocabulary that is totally unfamiliar to you: Make a guess and go on to the next question.**

The following sections explain these steps.

Connections count

Changing *and* to *or* or *because* to *however* can change everything, as this example shows:

> Buzz was content to - - - - *and* - - - - on his weekend, answering to no one but himself, doing exactly as he liked.

Perhaps you would fill the blanks with *rest..relax*. You know that the concepts are synonyms. Now check this out:

> Buzz was content to - - - - *or* - - - - on his weekend, answering to no one but himself, doing exactly as he liked.

The *or* changes everything. You may fill the blanks with *sleep...party* or perhaps *work...play*. You know that the concepts must be opposites here.

Some common connecting words are:

although	and	because
but	but for	despite
either/or	however	in spite of
moreover	nonetheless	or
therefore		

Whenever you see the preceding words, your antennae should go up, putting you on the alert for a plot twist — a trap of some sort.

Use your crystal ball

Sometimes the sentences are so long and *convoluted* (twisting or turning) that you can't make heads or tails of them. In that case, dissect the sentence. (A sentence so confusing probably makes you bloodthirsty or *sanguinary* enough to want to dismember something right about then.) Isolate just a bit of the sentence around the blank and try to predict whether that blank requires a positive or negative word. Consider the following:

> "Blah blah blah blah blah blah blah blah blah blah blah," Frances cursed - - - -.

Because people rarely curse or swear nicely, you can predict that the blank must be filled with a negative word. Maybe Frances curses *harshly, rudely,* or *viciously* (or *stridently, stentorianly,* or *fulminatingly*). You can eliminate answer choices such as *sweetly, kindly,* or *courteously* (as well as *benignly, amiably,* or *decorously*).

Guess and go!

Many times you can get the right answer in Sentence Completion questions by the process of elimination. You may have a hazy idea what type of word (positive or negative) or words (antonyms or synonyms) go into the blank or blanks. But what happens if you can't eliminate any answers because you don't know what any of the words mean? Hit the road, Jack. Get outta there fast. If you are making a wild guess anyway, why spend time deliberating over it? Guess and go!

A vocabulary helper bonus

You are no doubt delighted to know that roots, prefixes, and suffixes help you immensely on the Sentence Completion vocabulary, just as they do on the Analogies and Antonyms sections. If you don't know what the words mean, use your RPS to figure them out (see Chapter 2 for more on RPS). For example, consider the following sentence:

> Jane refused to eulogize Donald, saying that she thought he was a - - - - fellow.

Obviously, the entire sentence depends on the meaning of eulogize. If it means something bad, Jane refused to bad-mouth Donald and thought that he was a swell fellow. If it means something good, Jane refused to say anything good about Donald, thinking he was a bad fellow. Which is it? As you may recall, *eu* (along with *ben* and *bon*) means good. You also learned the

suffix *-ize*, which means to make. And *log* means speech or talk. You can reason that *to eulogize* means to make good speech or talk. If she refused "to make good speech or talk" about Donald, she didn't like him. Fill the blank with a bad word, such as *rotten, terrible,* or *disgusting.*

Try this one:

> Ashamed of his obvious trembling and - - - - when confronted by the farmer's wife, Blind Mickey told his two good friends, "I thought I was a man, but I'm just a mouse."

You need a word here that means fear. The right answer may be trepidation. You can figure out the word if you know that the root *trep* means fear.

Although she usually was of a cheerful nature, Patty was - - - - when she heard the history professor assign a paper that would be due the first day back after Spring Break.

(A) ebullient

(B) indolent

(C) supercilious

(D) enigmatic

(E) lugubrious

Okay. You know that the blank needs to be filled with a word that means sad, gloomy, or glum. So far so good. But then you get to the answer choices, and life as you know it ceases to exist. You don't know *any* of those words. You can't get this one right except by randomly guessing. Fill in something, anything, and zoom on to the next question.

Leaving you hanging on this sentence would be too vicious, even for me. After all, I'm only an *unofficial* test-maker, a tyrant-in-training, as it were. The correct answer is E. Lugubrious means sad. As for the other words, ebullient means happy, overjoyed. Indolent means lazy, laid back. Supercilious means stuck-up, conceited. Enigmatic means mysterious, difficult to figure out. An enigma is a puzzle or a mystery, such as the enigma of how you ever let yourself in for something as soul-leeching as this exam. *Correct Answer:* E.

Getting Back to Your Roots

Chapter 2 presents basic prefixes and suffixes. It's time now to increase your vast storehouse of knowledge by adding some of the important roots. The following is just a short list, but it is representative of what can greatly help you to figure out GRE *sesquipedalian* (foot and a half long!) vocabulary words.

If English is not your first language, vocabulary may be the hardest part of the exam for you. Using roots, prefixes, and suffixes can help you greatly.

- ✔ *som* = **sleep:** Take *Som*inex to get to sleep. If you have in*som*nia, you can't sleep. (The prefix *in-* means not.)

- ✔ *sop* = **sleep:** A glass of warm milk is a *sop*orific. So is a boring professor.

- ✔ *son* = **sound:** A *son*ic boom breaks the sound barrier. Dis*son*ance is clashing sounds. (My singing, quite frankly, is so bad that the governor declared my last opera a disaster aria!) A *son*orous voice has a good sound.

- ✔ *phon* = **sound:** *Phon*ics helps you to sound out words. Caco*phon*y is bad sound; eu*phon*y is good sound. Homo*phon*es are words that sound the same, such as *red* and *read*.

- ✔ *path* = **feeling:** Something *path*etic arouses feeling or pity. To sym*path*ize is to share the feelings (literally, to make the same feeling). Anti*path*y is a dislike — literally, a feeling against, as in: No matter how much the moron apologizes, you still may harbor *antipath*y toward the jerk who parked right behind you and blocked you in, making you late for a date and causing all sorts of unfortunate romantic repercussions.

- ✔ *mut* = **change:** The Teenage *Mut*ant Ninja Turtles *mut*ated, or changed, from mild-mannered turtles to pizza-gobbling crime fighters. Something im*mut*able is not changeable, but remains constant. Don't confuse *mut* (change) with *mute* (silent).

- ✔ *meta* = **beyond, after:** A *meta*morphosis is a change of shape beyond the present shape.

- ✔ *morph* = **shape:** Something a*morph*ous is without shape. *Morph*ology is the study of shape. ("Yes, of course, I take my studies seriously. I spend all weekend on *morph*ology at the beach.")

- ✔ *loq, log, loc, lix* = **speech or talk:** Someone *loq*uacious talks a lot. (That person is literally full of talk.) A dia*log*ue is talk or conversation between two people. E*loc*ution is proper speech. A pro*lix* person is very talkative. (Literally, he or she engages in big, or much, talk.)

- ✔ *cred* = **trust or belief:** Something in*cred*ible is unbelievable, such as the excuse: "I would have picked you up on time, Sweetheart, but there was a 75-car pile-up on the freeway." If you are *cred*ulous, you are trusting and *naive* (literally, full of trust). In fact, if you're credulous, you probably actually feel sorry for me being stuck in traffic.

Be careful not to confuse the words *credible* and *credulous*. Something *credible* is trustable or believable. A credible excuse can get you out of trouble if you turn a paper in late. *Credulous,* on the other hand, means full of trust, naive, or gullible. The more credulous your professor is, the less credible that excuse needs to be.

- ✔ *gyn* = **woman:** A *gyn*ecologist is a physician who treats women. A miso*gyn*ist is a person who hates women.

- ✔ *andro* = **man:** Commander Data on *Star Trek II: The Next Generation* is an *andro*id; he's a robot shaped like a man. Someone *andro*gynous exhibits both male (*andro*) and female (*gyn*) characteristics (literally, he/she is full of man and woman) — for example, the character Pat on the TV show *Saturday Night Live* is androgynous.

- ✔ *anthro* = **human or mankind:** *Anthro*pology is the study of humans (not just men and not just women but humans in general). A mis*anthro*pe hates humans (an equal-opportunity hater: he or she hates both men and women alike).

- ✔ *pac* = **peace, calm:** Why do you give a baby a *pac*ifier? To calm him or her down. To get its name, the *Pac*ific Ocean must have appeared calm at the time it was discovered.

- ✔ *plac* = **peace, calm:** To *plac*ate someone is to calm him or her down or to make peace with that person. You placate your irate sweetheart, for example, by sending a dozen roses (hint, hint). Someone im*plac*able is someone you are not able to calm down — or someone really stubborn. If those roses don't do the trick, for example, your sweetheart is too implacable to placate.

✔ *pug* = **war, fight:** Someone *pug*nacious is ready to fight. A *pug*ilist is a person who likes to fight — such as a professional boxer. (Did you ever see those big sticks that Marines train with in hand-to-hand combat — the ones that look like Q-Tips with a thyroid condition? Those are called *pug*il sticks.)

✔ *bellu, belli* = **war, fight:** If you're *belli*gerent, you're ready to fight — in fact, you're downright hostile. An ante*bellu*m mansion is one that was created before the Civil War. (Remember that *ante-* means *before*. You can find this word in the prefixes section.)

✔ *pro* = **big, much:** *Pro*fuse apologies are big, much — in essence, a *lot* of apologies. A *pro*lific writer produces a great deal of written material.

Note: Pro has two additional meanings less commonly used on the GRE. It can mean *before,* as in "A *pro*logue comes before a play." Similarly, to *pro*gnosticate is to make knowledge before or to predict. A *pro*gnosticator is a fortune-teller. *Pro* can also mean *for.* Someone who is *pro* freedom of speech is in favor of freedom of speech. Someone with a *pro*clivity toward a certain activity is for that activity or has a natural tendency toward it.

✔ *gnos* = **knowledge:** A doctor shows his or her knowledge by making a dia*gnos*is (analysis of the situation) or a pro*gnos*is (prediction about the future of the illness). An a*gnos*tic is a person who doesn't know whether a god exists. Differentiate an *agnostic* from an *atheist:* An atheist is literally without God, a person who believes there is no god. An agnostic is without knowledge, believing a god may or may not exist.

✔ *scien* = **knowledge:** A *scien*tist is a person with knowledge. Someone pre*scien*t has forethought or knowledge ahead of time — for example, a prognosticator (a fortune-teller, remember?). After you learn these roots, you'll be closer to being omni*scien*t — all-knowing.

✔ *de* = **down from, away from (to put down):** To *de*scend or *de*part is to go down from or away from. To *de*nounce is to put down or to speak badly of, as in *de*nouncing those hogs who chow down all the pizza before you get to the party.

Many unknown words on the GRE that start with *de* mean to put down in the sense of to criticize or bad-mouth. Here are just a few: demean, denounce, denigrate, derogate, deprecate, decry.

✔ *ex* = **out of, away from:** An *ex*it is literally out of or away from it — *ex*-it. (This is probably one of the most logical words around.) To *ex*tricate is to get out of something. You can extricate yourself from an argument by pretending to faint, basking in all the sympathy as you're carried away. To *ex*culpate is to get off the hook — literally to make away from guilt. *Culp* means guilt. When the president of the Hellenic Council wants to know who TP'ed the dean's house, you can claim that you and your sorority sisters are not *culp*able.

✔ *greg* = **group, herd:** A con*greg*ation is a group or herd of people. A *greg*arious person likes to be part of a group — is sociable. To se*greg*ate is literally to make away from the group. *Se-* means apart or away from, as in *separate, sever, sequester,* and *seclusion.*

✔ *luc, lum, lus* = **light, clear:** Something *lum*inous is shiny and full of light. Ask the teacher to e*luc*idate something you don't understand (literally, to make clear). *Lus*trous hair reflects the light and is sleek and glossy.

✔ *ambu* = **walk, move:** In a hospital, patients are either bedridden (they can't move) or ambulatory (they can walk and move about). A somn*ambu*list is a sleepwalker. *Som-* means sleep; *-ist* is a person; *ambu* is to walk or move. A *somnambulist,* therefore, is a person who walks or moves in his or her sleep.

Enough for now. You'll find no *paucity* (lack or scarcity) of roots to learn, but these should provide you with a good foundation.

A fun word: Antepenultimate

Most people know that *ultimate* means *the last,* just as Z is the ultimate letter of the alphabet. But which letter is the antepenultimate? Give up? It's *X.* The ultimate is the last; the penultimate is the second to last; the antepenultimate is the third to last (literally, *before the second to last*). Therefore, if you have three younger brothers, you can introduce them as your antepenultimate, penultimate, and ultimate siblings.

A Sense of Completion: Review

Before you go on to the practice questions in the following chapter, take some time to review the following approaches and tricks, as discussed earlier in this chapter.

Approaches

1. **Read the entire sentence for its gist.**

2. **If possible, predict words to fit into the blanks.**

3. **Insert *every* answer choice into the blanks and reread the sentence.**

Tricks

✔ Look for key connecting words that may change the meaning of the sentence.

✔ Predict positive or negative words to fit in the blanks.

✔ Guess quickly on questions with answers that depend entirely on unknown vocabulary.

And, of course, you want to remember that using a few basic RPS (roots, prefixes, and suffixes) can help you to figure out the killer vocabulary.

A whale of an exam

QUESTION: What do the GRE and *Moby Dick* have in common?

ANSWER: They both feature the following vocabulary.*

prodigious	fathom	ruefully
blunder	fastidious	tyro
antediluvian	wretched	omnipotent
voracious	incensed	cadge
heinous	precipice	descry
effulgent	inert	leviathan
floundering	disparaging	sagacious
depict	incredulous	superficial
conflagration	dogged	indiscriminate

* Oh sure, you can probably think of other commonalties, such as (1) no one ever finishes either one; (2) they are leading causes of migraine headaches, and so on, but honestly, this is the real answer. All these GRE words are found in *Moby Dick.*

Chapter 7

Reality Check: Sentence Completion Practice Questions

• •

*I*t's that time again — when you use it or lose it. Answering the following questions should reinforce what you learned in the preceding chapter about Sentence Completion questions. I made these sentences much more amusing than the deadly dull ones on the actual GRE, but the difficulty level and the vocabulary are the same.

1. Although dismayed by the pejorative comments made about her inappropriate dress at the diplomatic function, Judy - - - - her tears and showed only the most calm and - - - - visage to her critics.

   (A) obviated ... agitated

   (B) suppressed ... placid

   (C) exacerbated ... unfazed

   (D) monitored ... incensed

   (E) curtailed ... articulate

Look at the second blank first. Often the second blank is easier to predict than the first.

If Judy had a calm *and* (something) *visage* (a visage is a countenance, a facial expression), the (something) must go hand in hand with calm. Although it doesn't have to be an exact synonym, the second word can't be an antonym, either. Look for a word that means calm. *Placid* means calm, tranquil, as you know from the root *plac*, meaning peace. Check the rest of the second words. *Agitated* means upset or worried, just the opposite of what you're looking for. *Unfazed* may be good, as it means not bothered by. (Erudite types are unfazed by seeing how that word is spelled, knowing that *unphased* is a trap often found on grammar exams.) *Incensed* means upset, burning mad (think of burning incense). *Articulate* means well-spoken. Her visage, or facial expression, would not be well-spoken, although Judy herself may be. So, you've narrowed the answers down to B and C, based on the second words alone. Now check out the first words.

To *exacerbate* is to make worse. Words as hard as this one can exacerbate your headache. But if you choose this answer, you let your insecurity complex get the better of you. It's normal to think, "Oooh, big hard word; it must be the right answer." That's not to say the question doesn't feature hard words, but they may be the trap answers, not the correct answers. *Suppress* means to hold back and fits the sentence perfectly. *Correct Answer:* B.

Take a quick look at some of the other vocabulary. To *obviate* is to prevent, as in your learning these words now obviates your falling for traps by choosing them later. To *curtail* is to shorten (think of cutting off the tail of a word when you cur*tail* it).

Did you take note of the word *although?* A key word like that can change the meaning of the entire sentence. If it weren't there, you may think that Judy in fact burst out crying from the criticism rather than holding back.

2. Although there are those writers who carp and - - - - about the current depressed state of our economy, many people insist that such writers don't speak for the common man (or woman) who believes in the - - - - of the nation and the security of its future.

    (A) lampoon ... uniformity

    (B) grouse ... resilience

    (C) complain ... morbidity

    (D) laud ... strength

    (E) ridicule ... chaos

As I advise in Chapter 6, try to predict the words to fit into the blank or, failing that, predict the sense (positive or negative) of the words. You can predict here that the first word must be something bad (because the writers are carping, or griping, about a depressed economy) and that the second word must be something good (because the average man or woman believes in the future of the country). Eliminate all second words that are not good: *morbidity* (meaning gruesomeness) and *chaos* (meaning confusion and disorganization). Eliminate all first words that are not negative: *laud*, meaning to praise, as in to app*laud*. Now you've narrowed the choices down to just two.

To *lampoon* is to ridicule (think of the satirical magazine, the *National Lampoon*). That may fit, but the second blank doesn't make much sense. Sure, it's good to believe in the uniformity, or unity, of a country, but that's not related to worrying about the depressed state of its economy. Choice B, *grouse,* is to complain or grumble. (The poet Dorothy Parker wrote a great stanza that says, "Cavil, quarrel, grumble, grouse/I ponder on the narrow house/I shudder at the thought of men/I'm due to fall in love again!") And *resilience* is elasticity, the state of springing back. The average person thinks the economy will stage a comeback. *Correct Answer:* B.

3. The speaker, ironically, - - - - the very point he had stood up to make, and hurriedly sat down, hoping no one had caught his - - - -.

    (A) prognosticated ... summation

    (B) divulged ... information

    (C) refuted ... solecism

    (D) duplicated ... duplicity

    (E) ferreted out ... mistake

Predict that the second blank must be something negative, as the speaker hoped no one had noticed it. That eliminates answers A (a *summation* is just what it looks like, a summary, and is not necessarily bad) and B (information is also neutral). Now try the sentence with the remaining answer choices inserted.

To *refute* is to disprove or show to be false. It would be *ironic* (the opposite of what is expected) if the speaker were to disprove the very point he stood up to make. A *solecism* is an inconsistency, a mistake. *Correct Answer:* C.

Take a moment to go through the other words to increase your vocabulary. (As you realize by now, you can narrow down many of the Sentence Completion questions to just two or three answers through the process of elimination. But to get the one, right answer you have to know the words.) To *prognosticate* is to predict. *Pro* means before; *gnos* means knowledge; *ate* means to make. To prognosticate is to "make knowledge before," to predict.

If you chose A, you probably fell for the trap of looking only at the answer choices and not reinserting them into the sentence. Yes, something ironic is the opposite of what is expected, and a prognostication is the opposite of a summation, but that answer doesn't fit when reinserted into the sentence. Be sure to take your time and go back to the sentence with each answer choice. The Sentence Completion section is not a place to try to save seconds.

In choice B, to *divulge* is to reveal. That first word works, but the second does not. It's not ironic to divulge the very information you stand up to say; it's normal.

In choice D, duplicity is an interesting word. The root *dup* means double, but duplicity is not "doubleness" in the sense of two of something. *Duplicity* is deception, being two-faced. A traitor is noted for his or her duplicity. And in choice E, to *ferret out* is to search diligently, as a detective ferrets out clues to help his client. You ferret out the tips and traps scattered throughout these explanations to help you to remember them.

4. Although often writing of - - - - activities, Emily Dickinson possessed the faculty of creating an eclectic group of characters ranging from the reticent to the epitome of - - - -.

   (A) questionable ... taciturnity

   (B) mundane ... effrontery

   (C) egregious ... discretion

   (D) horrific ... stoicism

   (E) commensurate ... composure

This is the first question in the batch that you may have wanted to make a wild guess at. The entire question depends on vocabulary, and all the vocabulary is very difficult. If you encounter a question of this sort on the exam, don't waste too much time on it. Make a quick guess and go on to the next question.

If you know that *reticent* means shy and holding back, you can predict that the second blank must be the opposite of that, something bold and forward. *Effrontery* is shameless boldness and audacity. You have effrontery when you ask your boss for a raise right after he or she chews you out for bungling a project and costing the company money. Effrontery is the only second blank that fits. *Taciturnity* is the noun form of the word *taciturn,* meaning quiet, not talkative, not forward. *Stoicism* is not showing feelings or pain. Only a stoic can look at words such as these without shrieking or ripping out her hair.

Turning to the first blanks, *mundane* means common, worldly. Mundane activities are the day-to-day tasks, nothing exciting like winning a lottery or visiting Antarctica. *Egregious* means terrible or flagrant. An egregious mistake is right out there for the world to see. *Commensurate* means equivalent to or proportionate. Your score on this section will be commensurate with your vocabulary. *Correct Answer:* B.

5. Dismayed by the - - - - evidence available to her, the defense attorney spent her own money (even though that would leave her nearly - - - -) to hire a private investigator to acquire additional evidence.

   (A) dearth of ... affluent

   (B) scanty ... insolvent

   (C) vestigial ... pecuniary

   (D) immense ... bankrupt

   (E) impartial ... penurious

Predict words to fit into the blanks. If the attorney is dismayed by evidence and hires an investigator to get *more* evidence, there must not have been much evidence to begin with. Predict the first word means not very much. *Scanty* means barely sufficient. A *dearth of* is a lack of. Those are the only two that fit for the first blank. *Vestigial* means not fully developed; for example, the tailbone of humans is a vestigial tail. *Immense* means large, just the opposite of what you want.

The words "even though" tell you that spending her own money to gather the extra evidence would have a negative effect on the attorney. She was nearly *insolvent,* or bankrupt. Choice A, *affluent,* means rich, wealthy, or — as a smart-aleck friend of mine says — financially over-supplied. That doesn't work, eliminate that choice.

In choice C, *pecuniary* means consisting of or pertaining to money matters. This could be a trick answer, as you know that the costs have to do with money as well. However, the first word definitely doesn't fit in this sentence. In choice E, *penurious* means poor, needy, destitute. It fits the second blank, but the first blank doesn't work with this answer. *Impartial* evidence is neutral, neither good nor bad. *Correct Answer:* B.

6. Unwilling to be labeled - - - -, Gwenette slowly and - - - - double-checked each fact before expounding upon her theory to her colleagues at the convention.

(A) precipitate ... meticulously

(B) hasty ... swiftly

(C) rash ... desultorily

(D) efficacious ... haphazardly

(E) painstaking ... heedlessly

The key here is pure vocabulary. You can probably predict the types of words you need, knowing that the first word must mean too fast and careless and the second word slow and careful. But if you don't have a clue what any of the words mean, don't waste time scratching your head over this one. Just guess and go.

Precipitate, hasty, and *rash* all mean overly quick, leaping before looking. Those fit the first blank. *Efficacious* means efficient and effective, something Gwenette wants to be labeled. *Painstaking* means meticulous, careful, and attentive to detail, another good thing to be. Dump choices D and E.

You know the second blank must be something good. *Meticulous* means careful with detail, paying careful attention. It is pretty much the opposite of *swiftly* (quickly), *desultorily* (aimlessly, not methodically), *haphazardly* (unsystematically, not methodically), and *heedlessly* (not paying attention). *Correct Answer:* A.

Even if you don't know the exact meanings of the words, you often have an idea whether they are positive or negative — whether they have good or bad connotations. If you sense that a word is bad when you need a good word, eliminate that answer choice. You'll be pleasantly surprised at how often your subconscious leads you to the correct answer.

If you didn't grow up in the United States, you may not be able to "sense" the meanings (good or bad) of words. In that case, it's even more important for you to make a *quick* guess and go on.

Chapter 8

Readings That Can Affect Your Future: Blood Pressure, Astrology, and the GRE

• •

In This Chapter

▶ Three commonly tested reading passages
▶ Questions worth your time/questions not worth your time
▶ Tricks to make life easier

• •

Feared by more students than Monday's mystery meat in the college cafeteria, Reading Comprehension questions on the computer-based test (CBT) comprise 8 out of 30 verbal questions. The number can vary slightly, but in general, approximately 27 percent of your verbal score is determined by the Reading Comprehension questions.

For those of you used to taking pencil and paper tests, the reading passages on the computer can be quite a challenge. On a paper test, you have the option of skipping around and finding a passage you like (maybe you prefer a science passage to a humanities passage). You also have the option of skipping a question and coming back to it later. Those options are gone with the CBT. You get only one reading passage at a time; you can't preview several and choose your favorite. Also, you must choose and confirm an answer before the computer will go on to the next question.

On the computer, you'll probably have to scroll up and down to read and reread the passage. (For those of you not familiar with computers, *scrolling* means you use the mouse to push a bar on the right side of the screen up or down to move the text up or down on the screen.) Most likely, the entire passage cannot fit on the screen at once.

Why Do They Call It Reading Comprehension If I Don't Understand a Thing I've Read?

The origin of the *misnomer* (wrong name) "Reading Comprehension" is a great topic for a *deipnosophist*. (A deipnosophist is one who converses eruditely at the dinner table. Don't worry; you don't have to know the word for the GRE. I just threw it in so you could sound smart to your friends.) For now, you don't care so much what the section is called; you just want to get through it. The following information presents an overview of the types of passages you may encounter, the best approach to each distinct type of passage, and tips and traps for answering the questions based on those passages. Start by seeing what a Reading Comp question looks like.

Which of the following best describes the tone of the passage?

(A) sarcastic

(B) ebullient

(C) objective

(D) saddened

(E) mendacious

All questions can be answered from information stated or implied in the passage. You aren't expected to answer questions based on your own knowledge, and you don't need to know anything special about science or humanities to answer these questions.

The Three Commonly Tested Reading Passages

In their torture chambers over the years (would someone please call Amnesty International?), the test-makers have decided to write passages based on biological or physical sciences, social sciences, and humanities. The following sections offer a preview of the passages to help you separate the devastating from the merely intolerable.

Beam me up, Scotty! Biological and physical science passages

A science passage is straightforward, giving you information on how laser beams work, how to build a suspension bridge, how molecular theory applies, and so on. Although the passage itself may be very booooooooring to read (because it is full of just facts, facts, and more facts), this type of passage is often the easiest passage for people because it has so few tricks and traps.

Reading tip

Time to talk reality here: You're not going to remember — and maybe not even understand — what you read in a science passage. It's all just statistics and dry details. No matter how carefully and slowly you read through it the first time, you're almost certain to need to go back through the passage a second time to find specific facts. You end up reading the passage twice. Why waste time? Zip through the passage, just to get a general idea of what it's about and where the information is. (Paragraph one tells how molecules combine; paragraph two tells how scientists are working to split the atom; paragraph three tells. . . .) You may want to jot down a one-or-two-word note on your scratch paper to summarize each paragraph: Molecules. Atoms. Research. No need to waste time understanding every nuance if you can get the answer right by going back and finding the specific fact quickly. Because science passages can be done so quickly, work on them first.

Bonus: What happens if you swallow a molecule of uranium? You get atomic ache!

Science passages are best for slow readers because you're not really *reading* the passages; you're skimming them. You don't have to understand what you read; just identify some key words.

Question tip

You can often answer science questions directly from the facts provided in the passage itself. They are rarely the inference type that requires you to read between the lines and really think about what the author is saying, what point he or she is trying to make, how she feels about the subject, and so on. Here's an example:

The author states that spices were used

   I. to improve the taste of food.

   II. for medicinal purposes.

   III. to preserve food before refrigeration.

   IV. as a substitute for cash.

(A) I and III only

(B) I, II, and IV only

(C) I, II, and III only

(D) II and III only

(E) I, II, III, and IV

To answer the question, return to the passage and look for the specific answers — which should be easy to locate if you made those handy little notes during your first run-through (in this case, the notation may be *Purposes*).

It's not a disease: The social sciences passage

The GRE usually includes one social sciences passage. It may be about history, psychology, business, or a variety of other topics. The term *social sciences* is broad enough, in other words, to include whatever the test-makers want it to include. The social sciences passage is often the most interesting of the passages you encounter. It may give you a perspective on history that you didn't know or tell you insights into psychology or sociology that you can use to manipulate your friends. (Who says the GRE is useless?)

Reading tip

In many ways, social sciences passages are nearly the opposite of science passages. The questions here deal more with inferences and less with explicitly stated facts. You must read the passages slowly and carefully, therefore, trying to understand not only what is said, but also what is implied. Think about what you are reading.

Question tip

The questions that follow social sciences passages may not be as straightforward as those for a biological or physical science passage. You may not be able to go back to a specific line and pick out a specific fact. Instead, you are asked to understand the big picture, to comprehend what the author meant but didn't come right out and say. You may be asked why an author included a particular example or explanation. In other words, you're expected to be a mind reader. Here's an example:

The author's primary motive in discussing Dr. Buttinski's theory was to

(A) impress the reader with Dr. Buttinski's importance.

(B) show that Dr. Buttinski overcame great odds to become a psychologist.

(C) ridicule Dr. Buttinski's adversaries, who disagreed with the theory.

(D) predict great things for Dr. Buttinski's future.

(E) evaluate the effect Dr. Buttinski's theory has had on our everyday lives.

Determining the author's motive involves as much reasoning as reading. No sentence specifically says: "Okay, listen up, troops. I'm going to tell you something, and my motive for doing so is blah, blah, blah." You need to read the passage slowly enough to develop an idea of why the author is telling you something and what exactly he or she wants you to take from this passage. Going back and rereading the passage doesn't do you much good; thinking about what you read does.

In the sample question provided here, every answer given probably would be true in the context of the passage itself. That is, the author probably thought Dr. Buttinski was important, probably believed that Dr. Buttinski had to overcome great odds to be a psychologist, and so on. Keep in mind, however, what the question is asking: *Why* did the author mention this specific thing? You must probe the author's mind.

Gimme a break, I'm only human: The humanities passages

Humanities passages may be about humans (well, duh!) or about art, music, philosophy, drama, or literature. The passages are usually positive, especially if they are talking about a person who was a pioneer in his or her field, such as the first African-American astronaut or the first female doctor. Think about this logically: If the GRE bothers with writing about someone, that someone must have been pretty darn great or done something noteworthy. Keep this sense of admiration, even awe, in mind as you answer the questions related to the passage.

Reading tip

Have fun with the passage. This is the only passage you may actually enjoy reading. You don't need to zoom through it to finish before you fall asleep as you must with the science passages. You don't need to read it carefully for between-the-lines understanding as you must read the social sciences passages. You can read this passage normally. Pretend that you are reading an article in *People* magazine, for example.

Question tip

While the humanities passages don't require meticulous between-the-lines reading, the questions are another matter. The questions following a humanities passage often require you to get into the mind of the author, to read between the lines and make inferences. While reading a passage about a particular person, for example, you are supposed to ascertain not just what the person accomplished but why he worked towards his goals and what mark he hoped to leave on the world. Here's an example:

It can be inferred from the passage that Ms. Whitecloud would be most likely to agree with which of the following statements?

(A) A good divorce attorney must take the broader view and in effect represent the marriage itself rather than either of the spouses.

(B) The job of a divorce attorney is similar to that of a psychologist, attempting to ascertain why the marriage failed and address that issue rather than just the legal issues.

(C) The most important function of a divorce attorney is to protect the interests of the children of the marriage.

(D) A divorce attorney's job is merely to represent the legal interests of his or her client and does not include becoming a "friend" to the spouses.

(E) A divorce attorney represents his or her success by how quickly the divorce is accomplished.

All or Nothing: Questions to Take Seriously; Questions to Laugh Off

Knowing how to approach the GRE Reading Comprehension passages is extremely important. Even more important than the passages themselves, however, are the questions following each passage. After all, the admissions officer at Harvard is not going to say to you, "Hey, tell me about that GRE passage you read about the curative properties of heavy metal music." The admissions officer is far more likely to ask, "How many questions did you answer correctly on the Reading Comprehension portion?" No matter how carefully you read the passage, no matter how well you understand it, you must be able to put that knowledge to work to answer the questions that follow those passages.

So just what kind of questions are you most likely to encounter in the Reading Comprehension portions of the test? The following sections describe the several basic question types you may face in the dark alleys of the GRE.

It's the attitude, dude: The attitude or tone question

The author's attitude may be described as . . .

The tone of the passage is . . .

These two questions are variations on a single theme. What is the tone of the passage or the attitude of the author? Nothing in the passage answers this type of question directly. You can't find any one line reading: "In my opinion, which, by the way, is sardonic, the importance of. . . ." You simply must reason this one out.

Table 8-1 lists the tone or attitude likely found in each type of reading passage.

Table 8-1	Predominant Tones or Attitudes Found in GRE Reading Passages	
Passage Type	**Tone or Attitude**	**Explanation**
Physical or biological sciences	Neutral or positive	A physical or biological science passage gives you just the facts. The author rarely evaluates the facts one way or the other and rarely expresses an opinion. After all, how opinionated can someone be about a color spectrum?
Social sciences	Positive or neutral	A social sciences passage may be about how some event unfolded or some theory was developed. For example, a passage may talk about history, presenting the good events and downplaying the bad ones. Think positive, or at the very worst, neutral.
Humanities	Positive or neutral	If the passage is about an individual, it is probably positive, saying good and respectful things about that person and his or her accomplishments. If it is about the other topics of humanities, such as art, music, philosophy, drama, and literature, it may be either positive or neutral. Only very rarely does a humanities passage have a negative tone.

Do you notice a pattern here? Everything is either neutral or positive, positive or neutral. Because so many of the tones or attitudes of the Reading Comprehension passages are positive or neutral, certain words are often good to choose as answers to attitude or tone questions. With neutral passages, the term *objective* (which means neutral, not taking one side or the other, not subjective or opinionated) is often a correct answer. Don't simply turn off your own brain and choose *objective* automatically, of course, but it's a good guess if you're stumped for an answer. Think of a passage as neutral until proven otherwise.

The following list offers several common positive words. Each word is followed by a more unfamiliar term that has the same meaning:

Common Positive-Attitude Word	More Difficult Word with the Same Meaning
Optimistic	Sanguine
Praising	Laudatory
Admiring	Reverential

You get the idea. Wrong answers — that is, negative answers — may include the words in the following list. Remember: These are words that you usually don't want to choose.

Common Negative-Attitude Word	More Difficult Word with the Same Meaning
Ridiculing	Lampooning
Sarcastic	Sardonic
Belittling	Denigrating

The answer choices to an attitude or tone question often use quite difficult vocabulary. If you know from reading the passage that the author is delighted with something, which of the following would you choose to describe his attitude: *phlegmatic, dogmatic, ebullient, cantankerous, lethargic*? The right answer is *ebullient*, which means bubbling over with enthusiasm or excitement — but how many people know that word? I mean, it's not as if your best friend asks you, "So, how are you today?" and your immediate response is, "Well, I'm ebullient, thanks; and you?" If you don't know the vocabulary in the answer choices, *quickly* make a wild guess and go on. It can be very frustrating to do so, because you know what kind of word you are looking for, but when you can't define the answer choices, all you're doing is wasting time. Guess and go.

What's the big idea: Main idea or best title

You can bet the farm (but, of course, only in states with legalized gambling) that you'll see a few main idea or best title questions; each Reading Comprehension passage usually has one. This type of question can assume any of the following forms:

> The main idea of the passage is . . .
>
> The primary purpose of the author is . . .
>
> The best title for the passage is . . .

The best place to find the main idea of the passage is in its topic sentence, which is usually the first or second sentence of the first paragraph. The topic sentence *may* be the last sentence of the passage, but such a structure is rare. Your game plan upon encountering one of these questions should be to head right back to the first sentence to locate a main idea.

Suppose that the passage begins as follows:

> The uses to which latex has been applied have exceeded the wildest fantasies of its creators.

What is the main idea of the passage: The uses of latex? The applications of latex? The many products made of latex?

After you've read the entire passage, all the darn answers in the main idea question may look pretty good. That's because they usually consist of facts stated in the passage. Just because something is true and just because it is discussed in the passage doesn't mean it's necessarily the main idea.

Really try or fly right by: How much time is it worth?

The main idea or best title question is worth a few minutes of your time. Go back and reread the first few sentences. Even if you don't have time to read the entire passage — or even get started on it — you can often hustle up an answer to this question by glancing at one sentence.

Because Reading Comprehension passages are almost always positive or neutral, the main idea/best title is almost always positive or neutral, too. Eliminate any negative answer choices right away.

The main idea of this passage is

(A) the submission and shame of the Native Americans.

(B) the unfair treatment of Native Americans.

(C) how Native Americans are taking charge of their own destinies.

(D) why Native Americans fail.

(E) the causes behind Native American problems.

Because all the answers but C are negative, choose C. Humanities passages are often about people who have beaten the odds: inspirational pioneers and leaders. The passage is certain to be very admiring of those people. *Correct Answer:* C.

Don't pester me with details: The detail or fact question

One type of question very straightforwardly asks you about information explicitly stated in the passage. If a question begins with the phrase "According to the passage . . ." you've hit a detail or fact question — which is usually a very easy question to answer correctly. All you need to do is identify the key words in the question, return to the reading passage, and skim for those words. The answer is usually within a few sentences of those key words.

According to the passage, what two elements make up Drake's Elixir?

The key words are *Drake's Elixir*. Go back to the passage and find the exact answer.

According to the passage, why did Mr. Sanchez win a medal during the war?

The key words in this question are *Mr. Sanchez, medal,* and *war.* Go back to the passage and find the exact answer.

"According to the author" is not the same thing as "According to the passage." The two phrases may look the same, but author questions are often more difficult than passage questions and are not as straightforward. A question that asks you about the author may be more of a read-between-the-lines question than one about the passage — something you can answer only if you truly understand what you read. An "according to the passage" question, on the other hand, can often be answered even without reading the whole passage by skimming for the key words.

The power of positive thinking: Negative or exception questions

One type of GRE question is a trained killer: the negative or exception question. Here are a few ways this question may be worded:

Which of the following is *not* true?

Which of the following is *least* likely?

With which of the following would the author *disagree?*

All of the following are true *except* . . .

The questions are phrased in the negative, which makes them very tricky. You are actually looking for four correct answers and then by the process of elimination choosing the one that is not correct. It's easy to get confused and even easier to waste a lot of time. This is a good question to laugh off, to guess at randomly.

Toga! Toga! Toga! The Roman numeral question

A Roman numeral question looks like this:

The author mentions which of the following as support for her argument against unilateral intervention?

   I. economic considerations

  II. moral obligations

 III. popular opinion

(A) I only

(B) II only

(C) III only

(D) I and II only

(E) I, II, and III

Roman numeral questions are usually time-wasters. In effect, you have to go back and reread almost the whole passage to find whether I, II, or III was mentioned anywhere. A common trap is to have I and II mentioned close together . . . and then have III mentioned far down the passage. Most people find I and II and then when III doesn't appear to be hanging around, choose I and II only, going down the tubes. (Hey, maybe the test-makers get bonus points for every student they snare with a trick, rather like a cop writing speeding tickets to meet his quota in a speed trap. Just a thought.) With a Roman numeral question, you have to make a commitment (did I just lose half my male readers?). You have to commit to rereading most of the passage just in case one of the concepts is floating around where you least expect it. If you are not willing (or able) to commit the time, forget about the question. Just make a random guess and go on.

Bonus: What do you call a pig who won't make a commitment? A hedge hog!

The Swing Vote: Extending the Author's Reasoning

You've learned which questions you should always do carefully and which questions you should usually guess at. The GRE has one more type of question that, although it has become increasingly rare, you need to be prepared to meet. This type of question asks you to extend the author's reasoning to another situation. The GRE may give a situation that is analogous, or similar to, the one described in the Reading Comprehension passage and then ask you to determine how the author's reasoning would or would not work in the new situation. The tone or attitude of this type of passage may be positive, neutral, or negative. Here's an example:

Which of the following would the author most likely feel would be a valid issue to appear on a referendum, based on his argument in the preceding passage?

 (A) the right to die

 (B) term limits for members of Congress

 (C) expansion of the powers of the judiciary

 (D) increased student involvement in college application processes

 (E) tax rate increases

This type of question may be ridiculously easy or annoyingly difficult. If you understand the passage well and understand the author's reasoning, this question is simple. Sometimes you can answer this question without understanding the entire passage, as long as you have some general idea of the author's purpose in writing the passage.

Don't immediately choose an answer just because it refers to the topic discussed in the passage. For example, the passage may be about education. The trap answer to the previous question would be choice D. However, you are asked to extend the author's reasoning to an *analogous* situation. The situation can be about the right to die or about congressional term limits or about anything else.

Something up My Sleeve: Tricks for Making Life a Little Easier

Now that you know about the types of passages and primary types of questions, it's time for the fun stuff: the tricks.

Reading passages you'll never see on the GRE

✔ **Biological Science:** Cannibalism and You: The Science of Pigging Out at a Barbecue

✔ **Social Science (Psychology):** The End of Political Correctness: An Analysis of Howard Stern and Rush Limbaugh

✔ **Social Science (Behaviorism):** An excerpt from *Confessions from the Funny Farm*, Chapter Two: How the GRE Pushed Me over the Edge

✔ **Humanities:** The Developer of the Prefrontal Lobotomy: "Inspiration struck while I was studying for the GRE," says Famous Surgeon

---

Be positive or neutral, not negative

I will say this over and over until you are exasperated enough to cut off my air supply. Because most of the passages are positive or neutral, most of the correct answers are positive or neutral. Because the test-makers don't want to get sued for saying mean and vicious things about anyone, they are generally sweet and charming (and probably go home, kick the dog, and evict a few widows and orphans just to get pent-up frustrations out of their systems after having to be so nice at work all day long). Be sweet and charming right back at 'em; choose positive, goody-goody answer choices.

Choose answers containing key words

The key words, often found in the topic sentence, are what the whole passage is about. The right answers usually feature those words. If the passage is about Chicano history, the right answer often has the words *Chicano history* in it. Don't immediately choose an answer *only* because it has the key words in it, but if you can narrow the answers down to two, choose the one with the key words.

Be wishy-washy, not dramatic

The test-makers realize that people have different points of view. They don't want to be *dogmatic* (narrow-minded), saying, "This is the right way, the only way. Zip your lip and don't argue." They want to hedge their bets, leave some space for personal interpretation. And, of course, they don't want to get sued. If you have two answers, choose the more moderate or wishy-washy of the two. Wimp out big time.

Suppose that you have narrowed the answer choices to two:

(A) The author hates discrimination.

(B) The author is saddened by the discrimination and tries to understand its causes.

Choice B is the kinder, gentler, wimpier answer and would probably be correct.

Eponymous words

An **eponym** is a word derived from the name of a person. For example, the cardigan sweater got its name from the Earl of Cardigan (who would probably much rather be remembered for the garment than for his other claim to fame: He was the leader of the Light Brigade). Here are a few eponyms to add to your GRE vocabulary.

bowdlerize: to omit indecent words or phrases in a book or piece of writing (you bowdlerize a love letter before you let your roommate read it). Dr. Thomas Bowdler, an English physician, published in 1818 a ten-volume edition of Shakespeare's plays called *The Family Shakespeare.* He left out all the dirty parts. For example, instead of "Out, damn'd spot!" the line reads, "Out, crimson spot!"

boycott: You would think that Mr. Boycott started the practice of boycotting, wouldn't you? Just the opposite: He was the victim of the first boycott. Charles Boycott was a retired English Army captain who refused to lower rents to his farmer tenants after a few bad harvests and was accused of exploiting the poor. The locals harassed him, stealing his crops, refusing to sell his products in their stores, until he was hounded out of the county. Today, when you refuse to have anything to do with someone, you are said to boycott him.

Draconian: extremely harsh and severe. When you tell your professor that dropping your grade one whole letter just because you turned in a report one day late is truly Draconian, you are harking all the way back to about 620 B.C. Draco was an Athenian who wrote a code of laws that made nearly every crime punishable by death, even laziness and, uh, urinating in public. The word Draconian came to apply to any laws that were just too darn cruel or strict.

maverick: an individualist, an unconventional person. Samuel Maverick, who lived during the 1800s, was a Texas rancher whose unbranded cattle roamed free.

Maverick's neighbors refused to hand back his strays, claiming that because they were unbranded, there was no proof they were his. The word eventually evolved into meaning anything "without a brand," or unusual, unique.

Quisling: a traitor. Vidkun Quisling was a Norwegian politician who turned traitor in World War II, siding with Hitler. He was shot by a firing squad at the end of the war, but his name lives on to torment GRE-takers.

simony: the buying or selling of religious or sacred objects or privileges. Simon Magus (who is often described as a "reformed wizard"— great job description!) offered St. Peter and St. John money to give him their religious abilities. The word simony was especially popular in the Middle Ages, when people would sell pardons, indulgences, and the like.

Bonus! You probably already know these words, but did you know they are eponyms, too?

diesel: a type of fuel, named for Rudolf Diesel, a German engineer.

mausoleum: a large tomb or memorial, named for King Mausolus, King of Calia in ancient Greece about 370 B.C.

nicotine: the (possibly) addictive stuff in tobacco, named for French diplomat Jean Nicot.

saxophone: a musical instrument, invented by and named after Adolphe Sax, a Belgian musician of the early to mid 1800s.

shrapnel: fragments thrown out by a shell or a bomb, invented in 1802 by Lieutenant General Henry Shrapnel, an English army officer.

silhouette: profile or shadow of a face, named after Etienne de Silhouette (1709-1767), a French finance minister.

The Final Paragraph: Review

You've learned a lot in this chapter. Take a moment to review the key points before you jump into the practice exam in Chapter 9.

Approaches

- ✔ Identify the type of reading passage: biological and physical science, social sciences, humanities
- ✔ Identify the type of question (for example, main idea or best title, detail or fact, negative or exception, Roman numeral, extending the author's reasoning) and decide how much time to invest in it

Tricks

- ✔ Be positive or neutral, not negative
- ✔ Choose answers containing key works
- ✔ Be wishy-washy, not dramatic

Chapter 9

Practice What I Preach: Reading Comprehension Practice Questions

●●

This section features two reading passages and nine questions. For now, don't worry about timing yourself. Try to identify each selection as one of the types of reading passages described in Chapter 8 (science, humanities, and so on) and use the tips I gave you for reading that type of passage. As you answer the questions, try to identify whether each question is attitude/tone, main idea/best title, Roman numeral, and so on and then try to recall any traps inherent to that type of question.

Passage 1

Line Microbiological activity clearly affects the mechanical strength of leaves. Although it cannot be denied that with most species the loss of mechanical strength is the result of both invertebrate feeding and microbiological breakdown, the example of *Fagus sylvatica* illustrates loss without any sign of invertebrate attack being evident. *Fagus* shows little sign of
(05) invertebrate attack even after being exposed for eight months in either lake or stream environment, but results of the rolling fragmentation experiment show that loss of mechanical strength, even in this apparently resistant species, is considerable.

Most species appear to exhibit a higher rate of degradation in the stream environment than in the lake. This is perhaps most clearly shown in the case of *Alnus*. Examination of the
(10) type of destruction suggests that the cause for the greater loss of material in the stream-processed leaves is a combination of both biological and mechanical degradation. The leaves exhibit an angular fragmentation, which is characteristic of mechanical damage, rather than the rounded holes typical of the attack by large particle feeders or the skeletal vein pattern produced by microbial degradation and small particle feeders. As the leaves become less
(15) strong, the fluid forces acting on the stream nylon cages caused successively greater fragmentation.

Mechanical fragmentation, like biological breakdown, is to some extent influenced by leaf structure and form. In some leaves with a strong midrib, the lamina break up, but the pieces remain attached by means of the midrib. One type of leaf may break clean while
(20) another tears off and is easily destroyed once the tissues are weakened by microbial attack.

In most species, the mechanical breakdown will take the form of gradual attrition at the margins. If the energy of the environment is sufficiently high, brittle species may be broken across the midrib, something that rarely happens with more pliable leaves. The result of attrition is that where the areas of the whole leaves follow a normal distribution, a bimodal
(25) distribution is produced; one peak composed mainly of the fragmented pieces, the other of the larger remains.

To test the theory that a thin leaf has only half the chance of a thick one for entering the fossil record, all other things being equal, Ferguson (1971) cut discs of fresh leaves from 11 species of leaves, each with a different thickness, and rotated them with sand and water in a (30) revolving drum. Each run lasted 100 hours and was repeated three times, but even after this treatment, all species showed little sign of wear. It therefore seems unlikely that leaf thickness alone, without substantial microbial preconditioning, contributes much to the probability that a leaf will enter a depositional environment in a recognizable form. The results of experiments with whole fresh leaves show that they are more resistant to fragmentation than (35) leaves exposed to microbiological attack. Unless the leaf is exceptionally large or small, leaf size and thickness are not likely to be as critical in determining the preservation potential of a leaf type as the rate of microbiological degradation.

1. Which of the following would be the best title for the passage?

(A) Why Leaves Disintegrate

(B) An Analysis of Leaf Structure and Composition

(C) Comparing Lakes and Streams

(D) The Purpose of Particle Feeders

(E) How Leaves' Mechanical Strength Is Affected by Microbiological Activity

The main idea, main purpose, or best title is found in the topic sentence, which is usually the first sentence of the passage. The correct answer here is taken nearly word-for-word from the first sentence. Note that because the passage is talking primarily about leaves, that word needs to be in the title, which eliminates choices C and D right off. Choice A is too broad; there may be other causes of disintegration that the passage doesn't mention. Choice B is too specific. The passage mentions leaf structure but doesn't make that topic its primary focus. *Correct Answer:* E.

2. Which of the following is mentioned as a reason for leaf degradation in streams?

I. mechanical damage

II. biological degradation

III. large particle feeders

(A) II only

(B) I and II only

(C) I and III only

(D) II and III only

(E) I, II, and III

Paragraph two of the passage tells you that ". . . loss of material in stream-processed leaves is a combination of biological and mechanical degradation." Statement III is incorrect, because lines 12 and 13 specifically state that the pattern of holes is contrary to that of large particle feeders. *Correct Answer:* B.

3. The conclusion the author reached from Ferguson's revolving drum experiment was that

(A) leaf thickness is only a contributing factor to leaf fragmentation.

(B) leaves submersed in water degrade more rapidly than leaves deposited in mud or silt.

(C) leaves with a strong midrib deteriorate less than leaves without such a midrib.

(D) microbial attack is exacerbated by high temperatures.

(E) bimodal distribution reduces leaf attrition.

Lines 31–33 tell you that it's unlikely that leaf thickness *alone* affects the final form of the leaf. You probably need to reread that sentence a few times to understand it, but this is the type of question you should take the time to be sure you answer correctly — a detail or fact question. Choice B introduces facts not discussed in the passage; there was no talk of leaves in mud or silt. Choice C is mentioned in the passage but not in Ferguson's experiments. Be careful to answer *only* what the question is asking; the mere fact that a statement is true or is mentioned in the passage means nothing if the question isn't asking about that point. Nothing appears in the passage about high temperatures, which eliminates choice D. (Did you know the word *exacerbated?* It means made worse — like this reading passage probably exacerbated your headache.) Choice E sounds pretentious and pompous — and nice and scientific — but again has nothing to do with Ferguson. To answer this question correctly, you need to return to the passage to look up Ferguson specifically, not merely rely on your memory of the passage as a whole. *Correct Answer:* A.

4. The tone of the passage is

   (A) mesmerizing.

   (B) biased.

   (C) objective.

   (D) argumentative.

   (E) disparaging.

You *had* to get this question correct. If you missed this question, please consider yourself totally humiliated. *Correct Answer:* C.

Most of the time, a science passage has a neutral, objective, unbiased tone. The author neither praises nor criticizes anything; he or she just gives the facts. *Biased* means prejudiced, having an opinion one way or the other, and is just the opposite of the correct answer. GRE passages are rarely argumentative, especially science passages. If you chose A or E, you let your insecurities get the better of you: "Oooh, big hard word. I don't know it. It must be the right answer!" *Mesmerizing* means hypnotic or captivating. You probably weren't held spellbound by this passage (if you were, hey, get a life!). By the way, do you know who Franz Mesmer was? He was called "the father of hypnotism." What we now know as hypnotism used to be called Mesmerism after Franz. (No extra charge for the fascinating facts.) In choice E, *disparaging* means in a degrading manner, speaking slightingly of. Disparaging is a negative answer, and as Chapter 8 says, GRE passages are rarely negative in tone.

5. The author most likely is addressing this passage to

   (A) gardeners.

   (B) botanists.

   (C) hikers.

   (D) mechanical engineers.

   (E) Adam and Eve.

The passage is talking about the microbiological activity affecting the strength of leaves. (You know this because you already answered a best title question on the topic — question number 1.) Although choosing D is tempting, given the topic of the passage, mechanical engineers are usually interested more in machines than in leaves. Botanists are the ones who would most likely read this passage. The advice is probably too technical for gardeners, choice A, and is waaaay too specific for hikers, choice C. Choice E was added for comic relief. (If anyone needed to know how and why leaves disintegrate, especially fig leaves, it would be Adam and Eve. . . .) *Correct Answer:* B.

Passage II

Line   Multinational corporations frequently encounter impediments in their attempts to
explain to politicians, human rights groups, and (perhaps most importantly) their consumer
base why they do business with, even seek closer business ties to, countries whose human
rights records are considered heinous by United States standards. The CEOs propound that
(05) in the business trenches, the issue of human rights must effectively be detached from the
wider spectrum of free trade. Discussion of the uneasy alliance between trade and human
rights has trickled down from the boardrooms of large multinational corporations to the
consumer on the street who, given the wide variety of products available to him, is eager to
show support for human rights by boycotting the products of a company he feels does not
(10) do enough to help its overseas workers. International human rights organizations also are
pressuring the multinationals to push for more humane working conditions in other countries and to in effect develop a code of business conduct that must be adhered to if the
American company is to continue working with the overseas partner.

    The president, in drawing up a plan for what he calls the "economic architecture of our
(15) times," wants economists, business leaders, and human rights groups to work together to
develop a set of principles that the foreign partners of United States corporations will volun-
tarily embrace. Humans rights activists, incensed at the nebulous plans for implementing
such rules, charge that their agenda is being given low priority by the State Department. The
president vociferously denies their charges, arguing that each situation is approached on its
(20) merits without prejudice, and hopes that all the groups can work together to develop principles based on empirical research rather than political fiat, emphasizing that the businesses
with experience in the field must initiate the process of developing such guidelines. Business
leaders, while paying lip service to the concept of these principles, fight stealthily against
their formal endorsement as they fear such "voluntary" concepts may someday be given the
(25) force of law. Few business leaders have forgotten the Sullivan Principles, in which a set of
voluntary rules regarding business conduct with South Africa (giving benefits to workers and
banning apartheid in the companies that worked with U.S. partners) became legislation.

6. Which of the following best states the central idea of the passage?

    (A) Politicians are quixotic in their assessment of the priorities of the State Department.

    (B) Multinational corporations have little if any influence on the domestic policies of their
    overseas partners.

    (C) Voluntary principles that are turned into law are unconstitutional.

    (D) Disagreement exists between the desires of human rights activists to improve the
    working conditions of overseas workers and the pragmatic approach taken by the
    corporations.

    (E) It is inappropriate to expect foreign corporations to adhere to American standards.

The main idea of the passage is usually stated in the first sentence or two. The first sentence
of this passage discusses the difficulties that corporations have explaining their business ties
to certain countries to politicians, human rights groups, and consumers. From this statement,
you may infer that those groups disagree with the policies of the corporations. *Correct
Answer:* D.

In choice A, do you know the word *quixotic?* It means idealistic, impractical (think of the fic-
tional character Don Quixote tilting at windmills). Although the president in this passage
may not be realistic in his assessment of State Department policies, his belief is not the main
idea of the passage.

Just because a statement is (or may be) true does not necessarily mean it's the correct
answer to a question. The answer choices to a main idea question in particular often are
correct or at least look plausible.

To answer a main idea question, I like to pretend that a friend of mine just came up behind me and said, "Hey, what 'cha reading there?" My first response is the main idea: "Oh, I read this passage about how corporations are getting grief from politicians and other groups because they do business with certain countries." *Before* you look at the answer choices, predict in your own words what the main idea is. You'll be pleasantly surprised at how close your prediction is to the correct answer (and you won't be confused by all the other plausible-looking answer choices).

Choice E is a moral value, a judgment call. An answer that passes judgment, one that says something is morally right or morally wrong, is almost never the correct answer.

7. According to the passage, the president wants the voluntary principles to be initiated by businesses rather than by politicians or human rights activists because

    (A) businesses have empirical experience in the field and thus know what the conditions are and how they may/should be remedied.

    (B) businesses make profits from the labor of the workers and thus have a moral obligation to improve their employees' working conditions.

    (C) workers will not accept principles drawn up by politicians whom they distrust but may agree to principles created by the corporations that pay them.

    (D) foreign nations are distrustful of U.S. political intervention and are more likely to accept suggestions from multinational corporations.

    (E) political activist groups have concerns that are too dramatically different from those of the corporations for the groups to be able to work together.

When a question begins with the words "according to the passage," you need to go back to the passage and find the exact answer. In lines 21–22, you are told that ". . . businesses with experience in the field must initiate the process of developing such guidelines." Great — but what if you don't know the word *empirical*, which means based on experiment or experience rather than on theory? Keep reading. The rest of the sentence divulges the right answer. Don't tune out as soon as you encounter a difficult word.

Choices B, C, D, and E are all judgment calls. You are assuming facts not in evidence, as the lawyers say. Although you personally may believe the statements in these answer choices to be true, they don't answer the specific question. *Correct Answer:* A.

8. Which of the following best describes the reason the author mentions the boycott of a corporation's products by its customers?

    (A) to show the difficulties that arise when corporations attempt to become involved in politics.

    (B) to predict the inevitability of failure of any plan that does not involve customer input.

    (C) to disagree with the president's contention that big business is the best qualified to draw up the voluntary principles of workplace conduct.

    (D) to indicate the pressures that are on the multinational corporations.

    (E) to ridicule the consumers for believing that their small boycott would significantly affect the sales of a multinational corporation.

This question is one of those mind-reading questions that I warned you about. You are expected to get into the author's mind and understand why he or she said what he or she did. The concept of the consumer boycott follows closely the main idea of the passage, which is that the corporations have difficulty trying to explain themselves and their actions to all sorts of groups, including their customers. From this, you may infer that the point of the statement is to indicate the pressures placed on the corporations.

The next line in the passage states that human rights organizations *also* are pressuring multinational corporations, leading you to infer that the consumers are applying pressure. Remember that one of your tips is to expand your horizons. Read until you find what you think is the right answer . . . and then read a little further.

Choices C and E begin with negative words, *disagree* and *ridicule*. Negative answer choices are rarely correct. Be careful, however, not to take this tip as a hard and fast rule. If you go back to the correct answer to Question 6, you can see that you may interpret that answer as negative.

Choice B seems logical; common sense tells you that a company that ignores its customers will probably fail. However, a strong, dramatic word like *inevitably* is rarely correct. Few things in life are inevitable, as I've said before: just death, taxes, and the GRE. *Correct Answer:* D.

9. Which of the following statements about the Sullivan Principles can best be inferred from the passage?

   (A) They had a detrimental effect on the profits of those corporations doing business with South Africa.

   (B) They represented an improper alliance between political and business groups.

   (C) They placed the needs of the foreign workers over those of the domestic workers whose jobs would therefore be in jeopardy.

   (D) They will be used as a model to create future voluntary business guidelines.

   (E) They will have a chilling effect on future adoption of voluntary guidelines.

Choice A is the major trap here. Perhaps you assumed that because the companies seem to dislike the Sullivan Principles, they hurt company profits. However, nothing was said in the passage about profits. Maybe the companies still made good profits but objected to the Sullivan Principles, well, on principle. The companies just may not have wanted such governmental intervention even if profits weren't decreased. If you chose A, you read too much into the question and probably didn't read the rest of the answer choices.

In choice E, the words *chilling effect* mean negative effect, discouraging effect. Think of something with a chilling effect as leaving you cold. If your friend asks you to taste some soup because the dog loved it when he lapped up a few swallows, the statement about canine cuisine can have a chilling effect on your desire to taste the soup. Because few corporations have forgotten the Sullivan Principles, you may infer that these principles may discourage the companies from agreeing to voluntary principles in the future. *Correct Answer:* E.

In order to get this question correct, you really need to understand the whole passage. If you didn't know what was going on here, you would be better off to just guess and go. An inference question usually means you have to read between the lines; you can't just go back to one specific portion of the passage and get the answer quickly.

Part III
Two Years of Math in 58 Pages: The Dreaded Math Review

In this part . . .

No, no, please don't go get your pillow and PJs. I promise that this math review won't put you to sleep. I'm not going to start at $1 + 1 = 2$ and take you through every math concept you've learned since kindergarten; I have more respect for you than that. This math review neither insults you nor wastes your time. Here, I keep the instruction down to what you really need for the GRE.

If you've been out of school for a while, don't despair. After you go through the math review, do as many of the math problems as you can. The answer explanations review the formulas and concepts again and again and again; some of them are bound to come back to you.

Chapter 10
More Figures Than a Beauty Pageant: Geometry Review

• •

In This Chapter

▶ Angles

▶ Triangles

▶ Similar figures

▶ Area problems

▶ Quadrilaterals and other polygons

▶ Shaded area problems

▶ Circles

• •

*Q*uestion: How can you learn geometry?

Answer: Do it by degrees!

You Gotta Have an Angle: Angles

Angles are a big part of the GRE geometry problems. Fortunately, understanding angles is easy after you memorize a few basic concepts. And keep in mind the best news: You don't have to do proofs. Finding an angle is usually a matter of simple addition or subtraction. These three rules generally apply to the GRE:

> ✔ There are *no negative angles.*
>
> ✔ There are *no zero angles.*
>
> ✔ It is extremely unlikely that you'll see any fractional angles. (For example, an angle won't measure 45 ½ degrees or 32 ¾ degrees.)

Angles are whole numbers. If you're plugging in a number for an angle, plug in a whole number, such as 30, 45, or 90.

1. **Angles greater than zero but less than 90 degrees are called** *acute.* Think of an acute angle as being *a cute* little angle.

Acute

2. **Angles equal to 90 degrees are called *right angles*.** They are formed by perpendicular lines and are indicated by a box in the corner of the two intersecting lines.

Right

A GRE trap is to have two lines appear to be perpendicular and look as if they form a right angle. Do not assume this to be true. An angle is a right angle *only* if (A) you're expressly told, "This is a right angle"; (B) you see the perpendicular symbol ($\perp$) indicating that the lines form a 90-degree angle; or (C) you see the box in the angle. Otherwise, you may be headed for a trap!

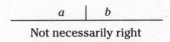

Not necessarily right

3. **Angles that sum up to 90 degrees are called *complementary angles*.**

Complementary

Think of *C* for corner (the lines form a 90-degree corner angle) and *C* for complementary.

4. **An angle that is greater than 90 degrees but less than 180 degrees is called *obtuse*.** Think of obtuse as *obese*; an obese (or fat) angle is an obtuse angle.

Obtuse

5. **An angle that measures exactly 180 degrees is called a *straight angle*.**

Straight

6. **Angles that sum up to 180 degrees are called *supplementary angles*.**

Supplementary

Think of *S* for straight angles and *S* for supplementary angles. Be careful not to confuse complementary angles (*C* for complementary; *C* for corner) with supplementary angles (*S* for supplementary; *S* for straight). If you're likely to get these confused, just think alphabetically. *C* comes before *S* in the alphabet; 90 comes before 180 when you count.

7. **An angle that is greater than 180 degrees but less than 360 degrees is called a *reflex angle*.**

Reflex angle

Think of a reflex angle as a reflection or mirror image of an acute angle. It makes up the rest of the angle when there's an acute angle.

Reflex angles are rarely tested on the GRE.

8. Angles around a point total 360 degrees.

360 degrees

9. Angles that are opposite each other have equal measures and are called *vertical angles.* Note that vertical angles may actually be horizontal. Just remember that vertical angles are across from each other, whether they are up and down (vertical) or side by side (horizontal).

10. Angles in the same position (corresponding angles) around two parallel lines and a transversal have the same measures.

When you see two parallel lines and a transversal, number the angles. Start in the upper-right corner with 1 and go clockwise. For the second batch of angles, start in the upper-right corner with 5 and go clockwise:

$1=3=5=7$ $2=4=6=8$

Note that all the odd-numbered angles are equal and all the even-numbered angles are equal.

Be careful not to zigzag back and forth when numbering, like this:

$l_1 \parallel l_2$

If you zig when you should have zagged, you can no longer use the tip that all even-numbered angles are equal to one another and all odd-numbered angles are equal to one another.

11. The exterior angles of any figure are supplementary to the interior angles and total 360 degrees.

Exterior

Triangle Trauma: Triangles

1. A triangle with three equal sides and three equal angles is called *equilateral*.

Equilateral

2. A triangle with two equal sides and two equal angles is called *isosceles*.

Isosceles

3. Angles opposite equal sides in an isosceles triangle are also equal.

Isosceles

4. A triangle with no equal sides and no equal angles is called *scalene*.

Scalene

5. In any triangle, the largest angle is opposite the longest side.

6. In any triangle, the sum of the lengths of two sides must be greater than the length of the third side. This is often written as $a+b>c$, where a, b, and c are the sides of the triangle.

7. In any type of plane triangle, the sum of the interior angles is 180 degrees.

Often a trap question wants you to assume that different-sized triangles have different angle measures. Wrong! A triangle can be seven stories high and have 180 degrees or be microscopic and have 180 degrees. The size of the triangle is irrelevant; every triangle's internal angles sum up to 180 degrees.

8. The measure of an exterior angle of a triangle is equal to the sum of the two remote interior angles.

When you think about this rule logically, it makes sense. The sum of supplementary angles is 180. The sum of the angles in a triangle is 180. Therefore, angle $x=180-(y+z)$ or angle $x=180-a$. That must mean that $a=y+z$

Similar figures

1. The sides of similar figures are in proportion. For example, if the heights of two similar triangles are in a ratio of 2:3, then the bases of those triangles are in a ratio of 2:3 as well.

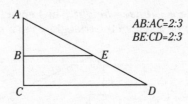

2. **The ratio of the areas of similar figures is equal to the square of the ratio of their sides.**
   For example, if each side of figure A is $\frac{1}{3}$ the length of each side of similar figure B, then the area of figure A is $\frac{1}{9}\left[\left(\frac{1}{3}\right)^2\right]$ the area of figure B.

Two similar triangles have bases 5 and 25. Which of the following expresses the ratio of the areas of the two triangles?

(A) 1:5

(B) 1:15

(C) 1:25

(D) 2:15

(E) 3:5

The ratio of the sides is $\frac{1}{5}$. The ratio of the areas is the *square* of the ratio of the sides: $\frac{1}{5} \times \frac{1}{5} = \frac{1}{25}$. Note that answer E is a trap for the unwary. You can't figure out the exact area of either figure because you don't know the height. (The area of a triangle is $\frac{1}{2} base \times height$.) However, you aren't asked for an area, only for the ratio of the areas, which you can deduce from the formula discussed. *Correct Answer:* C.

Bonus: What do you suppose the ratio of the *volumes* of two similar figures is? Because volume is found in cubic units, **the ratio of the volumes of two similar figures is the *cube* of the ratio of their sides.** If figure A has a base of 5 and similar figure B has a base of 10, then the ratio of their volumes is 1:8 ($\left[1{:}2\right]^2$ which is $\frac{1}{2} \times \frac{1}{2} \times \frac{1}{2} = \frac{1}{8}$).

Don't assume that figures are similar; you must be told that they are.

Area

1. **The area of a triangle is $\frac{1}{2} base \times height$.** The height is always a line perpendicular to the base. The height may be a side of the triangle, as in a right triangle.

The height may be inside the triangle. It is often represented by a dashed line and a small 90-degree box.

The height may be outside the triangle. This is very confusing and can be found in trick questions. ***Remember:*** You can always drop an altitude. That is, put your pencil on the tallest point of the triangle and draw a line straight from that point to the base. The line can be outside the triangle.

2. The perimeter of a triangle is the sum of the lengths of the sides.

Pythagorean theorem

You have probably studied the Pythagorean theorem (known colloquially as PT). Keep in mind that it works only on *right* triangles. If a triangle doesn't have a right or 90-degree angle, you can't use any of the following information.

In any right triangle, you can find the lengths of the sides with the formula:

$$a^2 + b^2 = c^2$$

where *a* and *b* are the sides of the triangle and *c* is the hypotenuse. The hypotenuse is always opposite the 90-degree angle and is always the longest side of the triangle. Why? Because if one angle in a triangle is 90 degrees, no other angle can be more than 90 degrees. All the angles must total 180 degrees, and there are no negative or 0 angles. Because the longest side is opposite the largest angle, the hypotenuse is the longest side.

Pythagorean triples

It's a pain in the posterior to have to do the whole PT formula every time you want to find the length of a side. You'll find four very common PT ratios in triangles.

1. **Ratio 3:4:5:** In this ratio, if one side of the triangle is 3, the other side is 4, and the hypotenuse is 5.

Because this is a ratio, the sides can be in any multiple of these numbers, such as 6:8:10 (twice 3:4:5), 9:12:15 (three times 3:4:5), or 27:36:45 (nine times 3:4:5).

2. **Ratio 5:12:13:** In this ratio, if one side of the triangle is 5, the other side is 12, and the hypotenuse is 13.

Because this is a ratio, the sides can be in any multiple of these numbers, such as 10:24:26 (twice 5:12:13), 15:36:39 (three times 5:12:13), or 50:120:130 (ten times 5:12:13).

3. **Ratio** $s:s:s\sqrt{2}$ where s stands for the side of the figure. Because two sides are the same, this formula applies to an isosceles right triangle, also known as a 45:45:90 triangle. If one side is 2, then the other side is also 2, and the hypotenuse is $2\sqrt{2}$.

 This formula is great to know for squares. If a question tells you that the side of a square is 5 and wants to know the diagonal of the square, you know immediately that it is $5\sqrt{2}$. Why? A square's diagonal cuts the square into two isosceles right triangles (*isosceles* because all sides of the square are equal; *right* because all angles in a square are right angles). What is the diagonal of a square of side 64? $64\sqrt{2}$. What is the diagonal of a square of side 12,984? $12,984\sqrt{2}$.

There's another way to write this ratio. Instead of $s:s:s\sqrt{2}$, you can write it as $\left(\frac{s}{\sqrt{2}}\right):\left(\frac{s}{\sqrt{2}}\right):s$. Of course, the s still stands for the side of the triangle, but now you've divided everything through by $\sqrt{2}$. Why do you need this complicated formula? Suppose that you're told that the diagonal of a square is 5. What is the area of the square? What is the perimeter of the square? Chances are good that one of the trap answers is "It cannot be determined from the information given." Chances are even better that you may fall for that trap answer.

However, if you know this formula, $\left(\frac{s}{\sqrt{2}}\right):\left(\frac{s}{\sqrt{2}}\right):s$, you know that s stands for the hypotenuse of the triangle, which is the same as the diagonal of the square. If $s = 5$, then the side of the square is $5/\sqrt{2}$, and you can figure out the area or the perimeter. Once you know the side of a square, you can figure out just about anything.

4. **Ratio** $s:s\sqrt{3}:2s$: This is a special formula for the sides of a 30:60:90 triangle.

This type of triangle is a favorite of the test-makers. The important thing to keep in mind here is that the hypotenuse is twice the length of the side opposite the 30-degree angle. If you get a word problem saying, "Given a 30:60:90 triangle of hypotenuse 20, find the area" or "Given a 30:60:90 triangle of hypotenuse 100, find the perimeter," you can do so because you can find the lengths of the other sides.

Thanks 4 Nothing: Quadrilaterals

1. Any four-sided figure is called a *quadrilateral*.

Quadrilateral

The interior angles of any quadrilateral total 360 degrees. Any quadrilateral can be cut into two 180-degree triangles.

2. A *square* is a quadrilateral with four equal sides and four right angles.

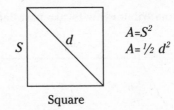

Square

The area of a square is *side*² (also called *base × height*), or ½ (*diagonal*)².

3. A *rhombus* is a quadrilateral with four equal sides and four angles that are not necessarily right angles.

Rhombus

A rhombus often looks like a drunken square, tipsy on its side and wobbly. The area of a rhombus is ½ $d_1 d_2$ (½ *diagonal 1 × diagonal 2*).

Any square is a rhombus, but not all rhombuses are squares.

4. A *rectangle* is a quadrilateral with two opposite and equal pairs of sides. That is, the top and bottom sides are equal, and the right and left sides are equal. All angles in a rectangle are right angles (*rectangle* means right angle).

Rectangle

The area of a rectangle is *length × width* (which is the same as *base × height*).

5. A *parallelogram* is a quadrilateral with two opposite and equal pairs of sides. The top and bottom sides are equal, and the right and left sides are equal. Opposite angles are equal but not necessarily right (or 90 degrees).

Parallelogram

The area of a parallelogram is *base × height*. Remember that the height always is a perpendicular line from the tallest point of the figure down to the base. Diagonals of a parallelogram bisect each other.

All rectangles are parallelograms, but not all parallelograms are rectangles.

6. A *trapezoid* is a quadrilateral with two parallel sides and two nonparallel sides.

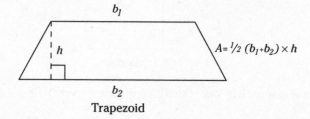

Trapezoid

The area of a trapezoid is $\frac{1}{2}(base\ 1 + base\ 2) \times height$. It makes no difference which base you label *base 1* and which you label *base 2* because you're adding them together anyway. Just be sure to add them *before* you multiply by ½.

Quaint quads: Bizarre quadrilaterals

Some quadrilaterals don't have nice, neat shapes or special names.

Don't immediately see a strange shape and say that you have no way to find the area of it. You may be able to divide the quadrilateral into two triangles and find the area of each triangle. You may also see a strange quadrilateral in a shaded-area problem; I tell you more about those in the next section.

Leftovers again: Shaded-area problems

Think of a shaded area as a *leftover*. It is "left over" after you subtract the unshaded area from the total area.

Shaded areas are often very unusual shapes. Your first reaction may be that you can't possibly find the area of that shape. Generally, you're right, but you don't have to find the area directly. Instead, be sly, devious, and sneaky; in other words, think the GRE way! Find the area of the total figure, find the area of the unshaded portion, and subtract.

1. $s = 8$

    Area of square $= 64$

2. $r = 4$

    Area of circle $= 16\pi$

3. Shaded area $= 64 - 16\pi$

Missing Parrots and Other Polly-Gones: More Polygons

Triangles and quadrilaterals are probably the most common polygons tested on this exam. Here are a few other polygons you may see:

Number of Sides	Name
5	pentagon
6	hexagon (think of *x* in six and *x* in hex)
7	heptagon
8	octagon
9	nonagon
10	decagon

1. **A polygon with all equal sides and all equal angles is called *regular*.** For example, an equilateral triangle is a regular triangle, and a square is a regular quadrilateral.

   You usually will not be asked to find the areas of any polygons with more than four sides. You may be asked to find the *perimeter,* which is just the sum of the lengths of all the sides. You also may be asked to find the exterior angle measure, which is always 360.

2. **The exterior angle measure of *any* polygon is 360.**

Total interior angle measure

You may also have to find the interior angle measure. Use this formula:

$(n-2)180°$, where n stands for the number of sides

For example, the interior angles of the following polygons are

- ✔ **Triangle:** $(3-2)180 = 1 \times 180 = 180°$
- ✔ **Quadrilateral:** $(4-2)180 = 2 \times 180 = 360°$
- ✔ **Pentagon:** $(5-2)180 = 3 \times 180 = 540°$
- ✔ **Hexagon:** $(6-2)180 = 4 \times 180 = 720°$
- ✔ **Heptagon:** $(7-2)180 = 5 \times 180 = 900°$
- ✔ **Octagon:** $(8-2)180 = 6 \times 180 = 1,080°$
- ✔ **Nonagon:** $(9-2)180 = 7 \times 180 = 1,260°$
- ✔ **Decagon:** $(10-2)180 = 8 \times 180 = 1,440°$

Have you learned that proportional multiplication is a great timesaving trick? Numbers are in proportion, and you can fiddle with them to make multiplication easier. Suppose that you're going to multiply 5×180. Most people have to write down the problem and then work through it. But because the numbers are in proportion, you can double one and halve the other: Double 5 to make it 10. Halve 180 to make it 90. Now your problem is 10×90, which you can multiply to 900 in your head.

Try another one: $3 \times 180 = ?$ Double the first number: $3 \times 2 = 6$. Halve the second number: $^{180}/_2 = 90$. $6 \times 90 = 540$. You can do this shortcut multiplication in your head very quickly and impress your friends.

One interior angle

If you are asked to find the average measure of one angle in a figure, the formula is

$$\frac{(n-2)180°}{n}$$

where n stands for the number of sides (which is the same as the number of angles).

Pentagon: $\dfrac{(5-2) \times 180}{5} = \dfrac{(3 \times 180)}{5} = \dfrac{540}{5} = 108$

Because all angles are equal in a regular polygon, the same formula applies to one angle in a regular polygon.

If you are given a polygon and are *not* told that it's regular, you can't solve for just one angle.

What's the measure of angle *x*? It cannot be determined. You can't assume that it is

$$\frac{(7-2)180}{7} = \frac{900}{7} = 128.57$$

Be sure to divide through by *n*, the number of sides (angles), not by $(n-2)$. If you divide through by $(n-2)$, you always get 180 ($\frac{900}{5} = 180$). Knowing this, triple-check your work if you come up with 180 for an answer to this type of problem; you may have made this very typical but careless error.

Volume

1. **The volume of any polygon is $(\textbf{\textit{area of base}}) \times \textbf{\textit{height}}$.** If you remember this formula, you don't have to memorize any of the following more specific formulas.

2. **Volume of a cube:** e^3

Cube

A cube is a three-dimensional square. Think of a die (one of a pair of dice). All of a cube's dimensions are the same; that is, *length = width = height*. In a cube, these dimensions are called *edges*. The volume of a cube is $edge \times edge \times edge = edge^3 = e^3$.

3. **Volume of a rectangular solid:** $l \times w \times h$

Rectangular solid

A rectangular solid is a box. The base of a box is a rectangle, which has an area of *length × width*. Multiply that by height to fit the original formula: $Volume = (area\ of\ base) \times height$, or $V = l \times w \times h$.

4. **Volume of a cylinder:** $(\pi r^2)\ height$

Cylinder

Think of a cylinder as a can of soup. The base of a cylinder is a circle. The area of a circle is πr^2. Multiply that by the height of the cylinder to get $(area\ of\ base) \times height = (\pi r^2) \times height$. Note that the top and bottom of a cylinder are identical circles. If you know the radius of either the top base or the bottom base, you can find the area of the circle.

Total surface area (TSA)

1. **The total surface area, logically enough, is the sum of the areas of all the surfaces of the figure.**

2. **TSA of a cube:** $6e^2$

Cube

A cube has six identical faces, and each face is a square. The area of a square is $side^2$. Here, that is called $edge^2$. If one face is $edge^2$, then the total surface area is $6 \times edge^2$, or $6e^2$.

3. **TSA of a rectangular solid:** $2(lw) + 2(hw) + 2(lh)$

Rectangular solid

A rectangular solid is a box. You need to find the area of each of the six surfaces. The bottom and top have the area of $length \times width$. The area of the left side and right side is $width \times height$. The front side and the backside have the area of $height \times length$. Together, they total $2(lw) + 2(wh) + 2(hl)$ or $2(lw + wh + hl)$.

4. **TSA of a cylinder:** $(circumference \times height) + 2(\pi r^2)$

Cylinder

This is definitely the most difficult TSA to figure out. Think of it as pulling the label off the can, flattening it out, finding its area, and then adding that to the area of the top and bottom lids.

The label is a rectangle. Its length is the length of the circumference of the circle.

Its height is the height of the cylinder. Multiply *length × height* to find the area of the label.

You also need to find the area of the top and bottom of the cylinder. Because each is a circle, the TSA of the top and bottom is $2(\pi r^2)$. Add everything together.

I'm Too Much of a Klutz for Coordinate Geometry

The horizontal axis is the *x*-axis. The vertical axis is the *y*-axis. Points are labeled (*x,y*) with the first number in the parentheses indicating how far to the right or left of the vertical line the point is and the second number indicating how far above or below the horizontal line the point is.

The intersection of the *x*- and *y*-axes is called the *point of origin,* and its coordinates are (0,0). A line connecting points whose *x*- and *y*-coordinates are the same forms a 45-degree angle.

If you're asked to find the distance between two points, you can use the distance formula (which is based on the Pythagorean theorem):

$$\sqrt{(x_2 - x_1)^2 + (y_2 - y_1)^2}$$

Find the distance from (9,4) to (8,6).

$9 = x_1$

$8 = x_2$

$4 = y_1$

$6 = y_2$

$(8-9)^2 = -1^2 = 1$

$(6-4)^2 = 2^2 = 4$

$1 + 4 = 5$

$\sqrt{5}$ is the distance between the two points.

Running Around in Circles

Did you hear about the rube who pulled his son out of college, claiming that the school was filling his head with nonsense? As the rube said, "Joe Bob told me that he learned πr^2. But any fool knows that pie are round; *cornbread* are square!"

Circles are among the less-complicated geometry concepts. The most important things are to remember the vocabulary and to be able to distinguish an arc from a sector and an inscribed angle from an intercepted arc. Here's a quick review of the basics.

1. A radius goes from the center of a circle to its circumference (perimeter).

Radius

2. A circle is named by its center.

circle M

Center

3. A diameter connects two points on the circumference of the circle, going through the center, and *is equal to two radii*.

Diameter

4. A chord connects any two points on a circle. The longest chord in a circle is the diameter.

Chords

Here's a lovely question you may see on the test. Choose

A if the quantity in Column A is greater.

B if the quantity in Column B is greater.

C if the two quantities are equal.

D if the relationship cannot be determined from the information given.

Column A	*Column B*
Area of a circle of radius 6	Area of a circle of longest chord 12

Many people choose D for this question. Although it's usually true that in QCs a geometry question with no figure is D because it *de*pends on how you draw the picture, a circle is frequently an exception to this tip. A circle is a circle is a circle; it rarely depends on how you draw it. The key here is knowing that the *longest chord* is a fancy-schmancy way of saying the *diameter*. Because the diameter is twice the radius, a circle of diameter (or longest chord) 12 has a radius of 6. Two circles with radii of 6 have the same area. (Don't waste even a nanosecond figuring out what that area actually is; it's irrelevant to comparing the quantities in the two columns.) *Correct Answer:* C.

<table>
<tr><td>*Column A*</td><td>*Column B*</td></tr>
<tr><td>Area of a circle of radius 10</td><td>Area of a circle of chord 20</td></tr>
</table>

If you chose C, you fell for the trap. A chord connects any two points on a circle. The *longest* chord is the diameter, but a chord can be any ol' thing. *Correct Answer:* D.

5. **The perimeter of a circle is called the *circumference*. The formula for the length of a circumference is $2\pi r$ or πd** (logical, because $2\ radii = 1\ diameter$ diameter).

circumference

Bonus: You may encounter a wheel question in which you're asked how much distance a wheel covers or how many times a wheel revolves. The key to solving this type of question is knowing that one rotation of a wheel equals one circumference of that wheel.

A child's wagon has a wheel of radius 6 inches. If the wagon wheel travels 100 revolutions, approximately how many feet has the wagon rolled?

(A) 325

(B) 314

(C) 255

(D) 201

(E) It cannot be determined from the information given.

One revolution is equal to one circumference: $C = 2\pi = 2\pi 6 = 12\pi = approximately\ 37.68$ inches. Multiply that by $100 = 3,768\ inches = 314\ feet$. Choice E is definitely the worst guess that you can make. If you have a radius, you can solve for nearly anything having to do with circles. Remember that there's a difference between "it cannot be determined" and "*I* cannot determine it." Just because you personally may not know what to do doesn't mean the problem is not "doable." If you're guessing, guess something else. *Correct Answer:* B.

6. **The area of a circle is $\pi\ radius^2$.**

$A=16\pi$

7. A central angle has its endpoints on the circumference of the circle and its center at the center of the circle. The degree measure of a central angle is the same as the degree measure of its intercepted arc.

$\overset{\frown}{AC}=90°$

8. An inscribed angle has both its endpoints and its center on the circumference of the circle. The degree measure of an inscribed angle is half the degree measure of its intercepted arc.

You may see a figure that looks like a string picture you made at summer camp, with all sorts of lines running every which way. Take the time to identify the endpoints of the angles and the center point. You may be surprised at how easy the question suddenly becomes.

In this figure, find the sum of the degree measures of angles $a+b+c+d+e$.

$\overset{\frown}{XY}=20°$

Note: Figure not drawn to scale.

(A) 65

(B) 60

(C) 55

(D) 50

(E) 45

Each angle is an inscribed angle. That means it has half the degree measure of the central angle, or half the degree measure of its intercepted arc. If you look carefully at the endpoints of these angles, they're all the same: *XY*. Arc *XY* has a measure of 20°. Therefore, each angle is 10°, for a total of 50. *Correct Answer:* D.

9. When a central angle and an inscribed angle have the same endpoints, the degree measure of the central angle is twice that of the inscribed angle.

10. The degree measure of a circle is 360.

11. An *arc* is a portion of the circumference of a circle. The degree measure of an arc is the same as its central angle and twice its inscribed angle.

To find the length of an arc, follow these steps:

1. **Find the circumference of the entire circle.**

2. **Put the degree measure of the arc over 360 and then reduce the fraction.**

3. **Multiply the circumference by the fraction.**

Find the length of arc *AC*.

(A) 36π

(B) 27π

(C) 18π

(D) 12π

(E) 6π

Take the steps one at a time. First, find the circumference of the entire circle. $C = 2\pi r = 36\pi$. Don't multiply π out; problems usually leave it in that form. Next, put the degree measure of the arc over 360. The degree measure of the arc is the same as its central angle, 60°. $\frac{60}{360} = \frac{1}{6}$. The arc is ⅙ of the circumference of the circle. Multiply the circumference by the fraction: $36\pi \times \frac{1}{6} = 6\pi$. *Correct Answer:* E.

Try another one. After you get the hang of these, they're kinda fun.

Angle *ROS* = 6°

Find the length of arc *RS* in this figure.

(A) ⅓π

(B) π

(C) 3π

(D) 4π

(E) 12

First, find the circumference of the entire circle. $C = 2\pi r = 10\pi$. Second, put the degree measure of the arc over 360. Here, the inscribed angle is 6°. Because an inscribed angle is ½ of the central angle and ½ of its intercepted arc, the arc is 12°. $\frac{12}{360} = \frac{1}{30}$. The arc is 1/30 of the circle. Finally, multiply the circumference by the fraction: $10\pi \times \frac{1}{30} = \frac{10}{30}\pi = \frac{1}{3}\pi$. The length of the arc is ⅓π. *Correct Answer:* A.

20

Be very careful not to confuse the *degree measure* of the arc with the *length* of the arc. The length is always a portion of the circumference, always has a π in it, and always is in linear units. If you chose E in this example, you found the degree measure of the arc rather than its length.

12. **A *sector* is a portion of the area of a circle. The degree measure of a sector is the same as its central angle and twice its inscribed angle.**

To find the area of a sector, do the following:

1. **Find the area of the entire circle.**

2. **Put the degree measure of the sector over 360 and then reduce the fraction.**

3. **Multiply the area by the fraction.**

Finding the area of a sector is very similar to finding the length of an arc. The only difference is in the first step. Whereas an arc is a part of the *circumference* of a circle, a sector is a part of the *area* of a circle. Try a few examples for sectors.

Find the area of sector *ABC*.

(A) 64π

(B) 36π

(C) 16π

(D) 12π

(E) 6π

First, find the area of the entire circle. $A = \pi r^2 = 64\pi$. Second, put the degree measure of the sector over 360. The sector is 90°, the same as its central angle: $^{90}/_{360} = ^{1}/_{4}$. Third, multiply the area by the fraction: $64\pi \times ^{1}/_{4} = 16\pi$. *Correct Answer:* C.

Find the area of sector *XYZ* in this figure.

(A) 9.7π

(B) 8.1π

(C) 7.2π

(D) 6.3π

(E) 6π

First, find the area of the entire circle. $A = \pi r^2 = 81\pi$. Second, put the degree measure of the sector over 360. A sector has the same degree measure as its intercepted arc, here 36°: $^{36}/_{360} = ^{1}/_{10}$. Third, multiply the area by the fraction: $81\pi \times ^{1}/_{10} = 8.1\pi$. *Correct Answer:* B.

Chapter 11

Gotta Catch Some (Xs, Ys, and) Zs: Algebra and Other Sleeping Aids

- -

In This Chapter

▶ Bases and exponents

▶ Ratios

▶ Symbolism

▶ Algebra basics and the FOIL method

▶ Roots and radicals

▶ Probability

- -

*T*rivia Question: Where was algebra supposedly invented?

Answer: Algebra was invented in Zabid, Yemen, by Muslim scholars. See — you can't blame the Greeks for everything!

The Powers That Be: Bases and Exponents

Many GRE questions require you to know how to work with bases and exponents. The following sections explain some of the most important concepts.

1. **The *base* is the big number (or letter) on the bottom. The *exponent* is the little number (or letter) in the upper-right corner.**

    In x^5, x is the base; 5 is the exponent.

    In 3^y, 3 is the base; y is the exponent.

2. **A base to the zero power equals one.**

    $x^0 = 1$

    $5^0 = 1$

    $129^0 = 1$

There is a long, *soporific* (sleep-causing) explanation as to why a number to the zero power equals one, but you don't really care, do you? For now, just memorize the rule.

3. A base to the second power is *base*×*base*.

This is pretty familiar stuff, right?

$$x^2 = x \times x$$

$$5^2 = 5 \times 5$$

$$129^2 = 129 \times 129$$

The same is true for bigger exponents. The exponent tells you how many times the number is repeated. For example, 5^6 means that you write down six 5s and then multiply them all together.

$$3^9 = 3 \times 3 \times 3 \times 3 \times 3 \times 3 \times 3 \times 3 \times 3$$

4. A base to a negative exponent is the reciprocal of something.

This one is a little more confusing. A *reciprocal* is the upside-down version of something. (Here's a **conundrum** [or riddle]: Is the North Pole the reciprocal of the South Pole?) When you have a negative exponent, just put the base and exponent under a 1 and make the exponent positive again.

$$x^{-4} = \frac{1}{(x^4)}$$

$$5^{-3} = \frac{1}{(5^3)}$$

$$129^{-1} = \frac{1}{(129^1)}$$

The *number* is *not* negative. When you flip it, you get the reciprocal, and the negative just sort of fades away. *Don't* fall for the trap of saying that $5^{-3} = -\left(\frac{1}{5}\right)^3$ or $-\frac{1}{125}$.

When you take a base of 10 to some power, the number of the power equals the number of zeros in the number.

$$10^1 = 10 \text{ (one zero)}$$

$$10^4 = 10,000 \text{ (four zeros)}$$

$$10^0 = 1 \text{ (zero zeros)}$$

5. To multiply like bases, add the exponents.

You can multiply two bases that are the same; just add the exponents.

$$x^3 \times x^2 = x^{(3+2)} = x^5$$

$$5^4 \times 5^9 = 5^{(4+9)} = 5^{13}$$

$$129^3 \times 129^0 = 129^{(3+0)} = 129^3$$

You cannot multiply *unlike* bases. Think of it as trying to make dogs multiply with cats — it doesn't work. All you end up with is a miffed meower and a damaged dog.

$$x^2 \times y^3 = x^2 \times y^3 \text{ (no shortcuts)}$$

$$5^2 \times 129^3 = 5^2 \times 129^3 \text{ (you actually have to work it out)}$$

6. To divide like bases, subtract the exponents.

You can divide two bases that are the same by subtracting the exponents.

$$x^5 \div x^2 = x^{(5-2)} = x^3$$

$$5^9 \div 5^3 = 5^{(9-3)} = 5^6$$

$$129^4 \div 129^0 = 129^{(4-0)} = 129^4$$

(Did I getcha on that last one? It should make sense. Any base to the zero power is 1. Any number divided by 1 is itself.)

Did you look at the second example, $5^9 \div 5^3$, and think that it was 5^3? It's easy to fall into the trap of dividing instead of subtracting, especially when you see numbers that just beg to be divided, like 9 and 3. Keep your guard up.

7. Multiply the exponents of a base inside and outside the parentheses.

That's quite a mouthful. Here's what it means:

$$\left(x^2\right)^3 = x^{(2\times3)} = x^6$$

$$\left(5^3\right)^3 = 5^{(3\times3)} = 5^9$$

$$\left(129^0\right)^3 = 129^{(0\times3)} = 129^0$$

Try a few QC questions testing this concept.

The answer choices are

A if the quantity in Column A is greater.

B if the quantity in Column B is greater.

C if the two quantities are equal.

D if the relationship cannot be determined from the information given.

Column A	_Column B_
x^3	$\dfrac{x^7}{x^4}$

$x^{(7-4)} = x^3$, no matter what the value of x is. *Correct Answer:* C.

Column A	_Column B_
$\left(x^3\right)^4$	x^{12}

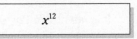

No matter what value x has, the two columns are the same: $x^{12} = x^{12}$. *Correct Answer:* C.

24

Column A	Column B
$\left(x^3\right)^4$	12

Everything *depends on* the value of x. Boy, this trap is really easy to fall for. You are so busy thinking of $3 \times 4 = 12$ that you may be tempted to choose C. But the automatic shut down valve in the back of your brain should alert you to the fact that *when two columns appear to be equal, it is usually a trap.* (See Chapter 13 for more information on this QC trick.) *Correct Answer:* D.

8. To add or subtract like bases to like powers, add or subtract the numerical coefficient of the bases.

The *numerical coefficient* (a great name for a rock band, don't you think?) is simply the number *in front of* the base. Notice that it is not the little exponent in the right-hand corner but the full-sized number to the left of the base.

In $31x^3$, 31 is the numerical coefficient.

In $-8y^2$, -8 is the numerical coefficient.

In x^3, the numerical coefficient is 1, because any number is itself times 1; the 1 is not always written out. Good trap.

In $37x^3 + 10x^3 = 47x^3$, just add the numerical coefficients: $37 + 10 = 47$.

In $15y^2 - 10y^2 = 5y^2$, just subtract the numerical coefficients: $15 - 10 = 5$.

You cannot add or subtract like bases with *different exponents.*

$13x^3 - 9x^2$ is *not* equal to $4x^3$ or $4x^2$ or $4x$. All it is equal to is $13x^3 - 9x^2$. The bases *and* exponents must be the same for you to add or subtract the terms.

Column A	Column B
$16x^4 - 4x^3$	$12x$

The answer depends on the value of x. If you chose C, you fell for the trap I just discussed. *Correct Answer:* D.

9. You cannot simply add or subtract the numerical coefficients of unlike bases.

Again, this is like working with cats and dogs. They don't mingle.

$16x^2 - 4y^2 = 16x^2 - 4y^2$

It is *not* $12x^2$ or $12y^2$ or $12xy^2$.

Column A	Column B
$10x^3 - 2y^3$	$8xy$

It depends on the values of x and y. C is the trap answer. *Correct Answer:* D.

Keep It in Proportion: Ratios

After you know the tricks, ratios are some of the easiest problems to answer quickly. I call them "heartbeat" problems because you can solve them in a heartbeat. Of course, if someone drop-dead gorgeous sits next to you and makes your heart beat faster, it may take you two heartbeats to solve a ratio problem. So sue me.

1. **A ratio is written as $\frac{of}{to}$ or of:to.**

   The ratio *of* sunflowers *to* roses roses = sunflowers:roses.

   The ratio *of* umbrellas *to* heads = $\frac{umbrellas}{heads}$.

2. **A possible total is a multiple of the sum of the numbers in the ratio.**

   You may be given a problem like this: At a party, the ratio of blondes to redheads is ⅘. Which of the following can be the total number of blondes and redheads at the party?

   Mega-easy. Add the numbers in the ratio: 4 + 5 = 9. The total must be a multiple of 9: 9, 18, 27, 36, and so on. If this "multiple of" stuff is confusing, think of it another way: The sum must divide evenly into the total. That is, the total must be divisible by 9. Can the total, for example, be 54? Yes, 9 goes evenly into 54. Can it be 64? No, 9 does not go evenly into 64.

After a rough hockey game, Bernie checks his body and finds that he has three bruises for every five cuts. Which of the following can be the total number of bruises and cuts on poor ol' Bernie's body?

(A) 53

(B) 45

(C) 35

(D) 33

(E) 32

Add the numbers in the ratio: 3 + 5 = 8. The total must be a multiple of 8 (or, looking at it another way, the total must be evenly divisible by 8). Only E is a multiple of 8: 8 × 4 = 32. *Correct Answer: E.*

Did you notice the trap answers? 53 is a good trap because it features both 5 and 3, the numbers in the ratio. 45 is a trap. If you multiply 3 × 5 = 15, you may think that the total has to be a multiple of 15. No, the total is a multiple of the *sum,* not of the product. *Add* the numbers in the ratio; don't multiply them. 35 again has both terms of the ratio. 33 is a multiple of 3. Only 32 is a multiple of the *sum* of the terms in the ratio.

One more, because you should always get this type of problem correct.

Trying to get Willie to turn down his stereo, his downstairs neighbor pounds on the ceiling and shouts up to his bedroom. If she pounds 7 times for every 5 times she shouts, which of the following can be the total number of poundings and shouts?

(A) 75

(B) 57

(C) 48

(D) 35

(E) 30

Add the numbers in the ratio: $7 + 5 = 12$. The total must be a multiple of 12 (it must be evenly divisible by 12). Here, only 48 is evenly divisible by 12. Of course, 75 and 57 try to trick you by using the numbers 7 and 5 from the ratio. Choice D is the product of 7×5. *Correct Answer:* C.

Notice how carefully I have been asking which *can be* the *possible* total. The total can be *any* multiple of the sum. If a question asks you which of the following *is* the total, you have to answer, "It cannot be determined." You know only which *can be* true.

<u>Column A</u>	<u>Column B</u>

Ratio of CDs to tapes = 2:9

Total of CDs and tapes	11

You know the total must be a multiple of 11, but it can be an infinite number of terms: 11, 22, 33, 44, 55, and so on. This trap has destroyed a lot of overly confident students over the years. *Correct Answer:* D.

When given a ratio and a total and asked to find a specific term, do the following in order:

1. **Add the numbers in the ratio.**

2. **Divide that sum into the total.**

3. **Multiply that quotient by each term in the ratio.**

4. **Add the answers to double-check that they sum up to the total.**

Pretty confusing stuff. Take it one step at a time.

Yelling at the members of his team, which had just lost 21–0, the irate coach pointed his finger at each member of the squad, calling everyone either a wimp or a slacker. If there were 3 wimps for every 4 slackers and every member of the 28-man squad was either a wimp or a slacker, how many wimps were there?

1. **Add the numbers in the ratio:** $3 + 4 = 7$.

2. **Divide that sum into the total:** $28/7 = 4$.

3. **Multiply that quotient by each term in the ratio:** $4 \times 3 = 12$; $4 \times 4 = 16$.

4. **Add to double-check that the numbers sum up to the total:** $12 + 16 = 28$.

Now you have all the information you need to answer a variety of questions: How many wimps were there? Twelve. How many slackers were there? Sixteen. How many more slackers than wimps were there? Four. How many slackers would have to be kicked off the team for the number of wimps and slackers to be equal? Four. The GRE's Math Moguls can ask all sorts of things, but if you've got this information, you're ready for anything they throw at you.

Be sure that you actually do step 4, adding the terms to double-check that they sum up to the total again. Doing so will catch any careless mistakes you may have made. For example, suppose you divided 7 into 28 and got 3 instead of 4. Then you said that there were 3×3, wimps, and 3×4, or 12, slackers. That means that the total was $9 + 12 = 21$ — *ooooops!* You know the total has to be 28, so you can go back and try again. You'll also catch a careless mistake in your multiplication. Suppose that you correctly divide 7 into 28 and get 4. But when you multiply 4×3, you get 43 instead of 12. (Hey, when the adrenaline's flowing during the exam, you'd be surprised at the kinds of mistakes you can make.) When you add the numbers, you get $43 + 16 = 59$ instead of the 28 that you know is the total.

It takes longer to talk through these steps than it does to do them. After you learn this technique, it makes a lot of sense. Think of ratios as cliques. If there are 3 boys for every 5 girls, there are 8 kids in one clique. If there are 48 kids at a party, there must be 6 cliques (8 divided into 48 = 6). If there are 6 cliques at 3 girls per clique, there are $6 \times 3 = 18$ girls. If there are 6 cliques at 5 boys each, there are $6 \times 5 = 30$ boys.

Things Aren't What They Seem: Symbolism

You may encounter two basic types of symbolism problems. If so, do one of the following:

✔ Substitute the number given for the variable in the explanation.

✔ Talk through the explanation to see which constraint fits and then do the indicated operations.

1. Substitute for the variable in the explanation.

You see a problem with a strange symbol. It may be a variable inside a circle, a triangle, a star, or a tic-tac-toe sign. That symbol has no connection to the real world at all. Don't panic, thinking that your teachers forgot to teach you something. Symbols are made up for each problem.

The symbol is included in a short explanation. It may look like this:

$$a \# b \# c = \frac{(a+b)^c}{(b+c)}$$

$$x * y * z = \frac{z}{x} + \left(\frac{y}{z}\right)^x$$

$$m @ n @ o = mm + no - om$$

Again, the symbols don't have any meaning in the outside world; they mean only what the problem tells you they mean, and that meaning holds true only for this problem.

Below the explanation is the question itself:

$3 \# 2 \# 1 =$

$4 * 6 * 8 =$

$2 @ 5 @ 10 =$

Your job is one of substitution. Plug in a number for the variable in the equation. Which number do you plug in? The one that's in the same position as that variable. For example:

$$a \# b \# c = \frac{(a+b)^c}{(b+c)}$$

$$3 \# 2 \# 1 = \frac{(3+2)^1}{(2+1)} = \frac{5}{3}$$

Because a was in the first position and 3 was in the first position, substitute a 3 for an a throughout the equation. Because b was in the second position and 2 was in the second position, substitute a 2 for a b throughout the equation. Because c was in the third position and 1 was in the third position, substitute a 1 for a c throughout the equation.

Do the same for the other problems.

$$x * y * z = \frac{2}{x} + \left(\frac{y}{z}\right)^x$$

$$4 * 6 * 8 = \left(\frac{2}{4}\right) + \left(\frac{6}{8}\right)^4 = 2 + \left(\frac{6}{8}\right)^4 = 2 + .316 = 2.316$$

$$m @ n @ o = mn + no - om$$

$$2 @ 5 @ 10 = (2 \times 5) + (5 \times 10) - (10 \times 2) = 10 + 50 - 20 = 40$$

This is the simpler of the two types of symbolism problems. Just substitute the number for the variable and work through the equation.

2. **Talk through the explanation and do the operations.**

This type of symbolism problem may seem more confusing until you've done a few. Then it becomes so easy that you wonder why you didn't see it before. Here are two possibilities.

$$\boxed{\begin{array}{l} \textcircled{x} = 3x \text{ if } x \text{ is odd.} \\ \textcircled{x} = \dfrac{x}{2} \text{ if } x \text{ is even.} \end{array}}$$

Solve for $\textcircled{5} + \textcircled{8}$.

First, talk through the explanation. You have something in a circle. If that something in the circle is odd, you multiply it by 3. If that something in the circle is even, you divide it by 2.

In the question, there's a 5 in the circle. Because 5 is odd, you multiply it by 3 to get $5 \times 3 = 15$. In the second half of the question, there's an 8 in a circle. Because 8 is even, you divide it by 2. $\frac{8}{2} = 4$ Now add $15 + 4 = 19$.

Don't keep going. Do *not* say, "Well, 19 is odd, so I have to multiply it by 3, getting 57." You can bet that 57 is one of the trap multiple-choice answers.

You may still think of this second type of problem as a plug-in or substitution problem because you are plugging the number into the equation for *x* and working it through. However, you first have to figure out which equation to plug it into. That requires talking things through. You have to understand what you're doing in this type of problem. Try another:

$$\boxed{\begin{array}{l} \triangle{x} = 3x + \frac{1}{3}x \text{ if } x \text{ is prime} \\ \triangle{x} = x^2 + \sqrt{x} \text{ if } x \text{ is composite} \end{array}}$$

$$\triangle{16} + \triangle{3} =$$

Aha! Now you have to know some math vocabulary. *Prime numbers* are numbers greater than 1, and cannot be divided other than by 1 and themselves. Examples are 2, 3, 5, 7, 11, and 13. *Composite numbers* are numbers that *can* be divided other than by just 1 and themselves, like 4, 6, 8, 9, 10, and 12. The first thing you do is decide whether the term in the triangle is a composite number or a prime number.

In $\triangle{16}$ because 16 is a composite number, use the second equation. Square 16: $16 \times 16 = 256$. Take the square root of 16: $\sqrt{16} = 4$. Add them together: $256 + 4 = 260$.

In $\triangle{3}$, because 3 is a prime number, use the first equation. $3^2 + \frac{1}{3}(3) = 9 + 1 = 10$. Add the two solutions: $260 + 10 = 270$.

Sometimes, the solutions have symbols in them as well. Here's an example:

$$\boxed{\begin{array}{l}\text{ⓧ} = \tfrac{1}{2}\, x \text{ if } x \text{ is composite.} \\[4pt] \text{ⓧ} = 2x \text{ if } x \text{ is prime.}\end{array}}$$

Solve for ⑤ × ⑩.

(A) ⑮

(B) ㉕

(C) ㊿

(D) ⑩⓪

(E) It cannot be determined from the information given.

First, you know to eliminate answer E. This is the sucker's answer, the one for people who have no idea what the cute little circle means and are clueless as to where to begin. You know by now that you *can* solve a symbolism problem — and pretty quickly, too.

Because 5 is prime, you multiply it by 2: $5 \times 2 = 10$.

Because 10 is composite, you multiply it by $\frac{1}{2}$: $10 \times \frac{1}{2} = 5$

Multiply: $10 \times 5 = 50$.

Noooo! Don't choose answer C; that's the trap answer. Choice C doesn't say 50; it says ㊿. That means that you have to solve the answer choice to see what it really is. Think of it as a choice in disguise with a false beard and glasses. Because 50 is even, you take half of it: $50 \div 2 = 25$. That's not the answer you want. Now go through the rest of the choices:

⑮: Because 15 is composite, multiply it by $\frac{1}{2}$: $15 \times \frac{1}{2} = 7.5$.

㉕: Because 25 is composite, multiply it by $\frac{1}{2}$: $25 \times \frac{1}{2} = 12.5$.

⑩⓪: Because 100 is composite, multiply it by $\frac{1}{2}$: $100 \times \frac{1}{2} = 50$. You have a winner!

Whenever you see a symbol, get to work. That symbol may be in the question or in the answer choices. You still follow the explanation. But remember the trap I already discussed: Be super careful not to keep on going. That is, when you come up with 50 as your answer, don't say, "Well, 50 is composite, so I have to multiply it by ½, getting 25." Stop when there are no more symbols. *Correct Answer:* D.

Have you studied functions? Maybe not in school, but if you've read the preceding material on symbolism, you have just studied functions. A function is very much like the symbolism you've just read about. You may see a problem like this:

$f(x) = (2x)^3$. Solve for $f(2)$.

The *f* stands for function. You do the same thing you did before: Talk through the problem. You say, "I have something in parentheses. My job is to multiply that something by two and then cube the whole disgusting mess." In other words, just plug in the 2 where you see an *x* in the explanation.

$$f(2) = (2 \times 2)^3 = 4^3 = 64$$

Try another one.

$f(x) = x + x^2 + x^3$, Solve for $f(10)$.

Just plug the 10 in for the x: $f(10) = 10 + 10^2 + 10^3 = 10 + 100 + 1,000 = 1,110$.

Now that you've acquired this skill, you can call yourself "fully functional."

Abracadabra: Algebra

You must be able to do three basic algebra concepts for the GRE.

- ✔ Solve for x in an equation.
- ✔ Use the FOIL method.
- ✔ Factor down a quadratic equation and take an algebraic expression from its final form back to its original form of two sets of parentheses.

To solve for x, follow these steps:

1. **Isolate the variable which means getting all the x's on one side and all the non-x's on the other side.**

2. **Add all the x's on one side; add all the non-x's on the other side.**

3. **Divide both sides of the equation by the number in front of the x.**

Now you try it: $3x + 7 = 9x - 5$

1. **Isolate the variable. Move the $3x$ to the right, *changing the sign* to make it $-3x$.**

   Forgetting to change the sign is one of the most common careless mistakes students make. The test makers realize that and often include trap answer choices to catch this mistake.

2. **Move the -5 to the left, *changing the sign* to make it $+5$. You now have $7 + 5 = 9x - 3x$.**

3. **Add the x's on one side; add the non-x's on the other side.**

   $12 = 6x$

4. **Divide both sides through by what is next to the x.**

   $\dfrac{12}{6} = \dfrac{6x}{6}$

   $2 = x$

If you're weak on algebra or know that you often make careless mistakes, plug the 2 back into the equation to make sure that it works.

$3(2) + 7 = 9(2) - 5$

$6 + 7 = 18 - 5$

$13 = 13$

If you absolutely hate algebra, see whether you can simply plug in the answer choices. If this were a Problem-Solving question with multiple-choice answers, you could plug 'n chug.

$3x + 7 = 9x - 5$. Solve for x.

(A) 5

(B) 3½

(C) 2

(D) 0

(E) −2

Don't ask for trouble. Keep life simple by starting with the simple answers first. That is, try plugging in 5. When it doesn't work, don't bother plugging in 3½. That's too much work. Go right down to 2. If all the easy answers don't work, then you can go back to the hard answer of 3½, but why fuss with it unless you absolutely have to? *Correct Answer:* C.

Curses! FOILed again

The second thing you need to know to do algebra is how to use the FOIL method. FOIL stands for *First, Outer, Inner, Last* and refers to the order in which you multiply the variables in parentheses. With the equation $(a+b)(a-b) =$

1. Multiply the *First* variables: $a \times a = a^2$.

2. Multiply the *Outer* variables: $a \times -b = -ab$.

3. Multiply the *Inner* variables: $b \times a = ba$ (which is the same as ab).

4. Multiply the *Last* variables: $b \times -b = -b^2$.

Add like terms: $-ab + ab = 0ab$. (Remember that you can multiply numbers forward or backward, such that $ab = ba$.) The positive and negative ab cancel each other out. You're left with only $a^2 - b^2$.

Try another one $(3a+b)(a-2b)$

1. Multiply the *First* terms: $3a \times a = 3a^2$.

2. Multiply the *Outer* terms: $3a \times -2b = 6 - ab$.

3. Multiply the *Inner* terms: $b \times a = ba$ (which is the same as ab).

4. Multiply the *Last* terms: $b \times -2b = -2b^2$.

5. Combine like terms $-6ab + ab = -5ab$. The final answer: $3a^2 - 5ab - 2b^2$.

You should memorize the following three FOIL problems. Don't bother to work them out every time; know them by heart.

1. $(a+b)^2 = a^2 + 2ab + b^2$

    You can prove this equation by using FOIL: $(a+b)(a+b)$

    a. Multiply the *First* terms: $a \times a = a^2$.

    b. Multiply the *Outer* terms: $a \times b = ab$.

    c. Multiply the *Inner* terms: $b \times a = ba$ (which is the same as ab).

    d. Multiply the *Last* terms: $b \times b = b^2$.

    e. Combine like terms: $ab + ab = 2ab$.

    Final solution: $a^2 + 2ab + b^2$.

2. $(a-b)^2 = a^2 - 2ab + b^2$

   You can prove this equation by using FOIL: $(a-b)(a-b)$.

   a. Multiply the *First* terms: $a \times a = a^2$.

   b. Multiply the *Outer* terms: $a \times -b = -ab$.

   c. Multiply the *Inner* terms: $-b \times a = -ba$ (which is the same as $-ab$).

   d. Multiply the *Last* terms $-b \times -b = +b^2$.

   e. Combine like terms: $-ab + -ab = -2ab$.

   f. Final solution: $a^2 - 2ab + b^2$.

   Be careful to note that the b^2 at the end is *positive,* not negative, because multiplying a negative times a negative gives a positive.

3. $(a-b)(a+b) = a^2 - b^2$

   You can prove this equation by using FOIL: $(a-b)(a+b)$.

   a. Multiply the *First* terms: $a \times a = a^2$.

   b. Multiply the *Outer* terms: $a \times b = ab$.

   c. Multiply the *Inner* terms: $-b \times a = -ba$ (which is the same as $-ab$).

   d. Multiply the *Last* terms: $-b \times b = -b^2$.

   e. Combine like terms: $ab + -ab = 0ab$.

   Final solution: $a^2 - b^2$. Note that the middle term drops out because $+ab$ cancels out $-ab$.

Memorize these three equations. Doing so saves you time, careless mistakes, and acute misery on the actual exam.

Fact or fiction: Factoring

Now you know how to do algebra forward; are you ready to do it backward? The third thing you need to know is how to factor down a quadratic equation and take an algebraic expression from its final form back to its original form of two sets of parentheses.

Given $x^2 + 13x + 42 = 0$, solve for x. Take this problem one step at a time.

1. **Draw two sets of parentheses.**

   $(\ )(\ ) = 0$.

2. **To get x^2, the *First* terms have to be x and x. Fill those in.**

   $(x)(x) = 0$.

3. **Look now at the *Outer* terms.**

   You need two numbers that multiply together to be $+42$. Well, there are several possibilities: $42 \times 1, 21 \times 2,$ or 6×7. You can even have two negative numbers: $-42 \times -1, -21 \times -2,$ or -6×-7. You aren't sure which one to choose yet. Go on to the next step.

4. **Look at the *Inner* terms.**

   You have to add two values to get $+13$. Now you know that you need *two positive* values to get the $+13$. What's the first thing that springs to mind? $6 + 7$, probably. Hey, that's one of the possibilities in the preceding step! Plug it in and try it.

   $(x+6)(x+7) = x^2 + 7x + 6x + 42 = x^2 + 13x + 42$.

Great, but you're not finished yet. If the whole equation equals zero, then either $(x+6)=0$ or $(x+7)=0$. That's because the only way to make a product zero is to make one of the factors zero. Therefore, x can equal -6 or -7.

Again, if you have a multiple-choice problem, you can simply try the answer choices. Never start doing a lot of work until you absolutely have to.

Too Hip to Be Square: Roots and Radicals

To simplify working with square roots (or cube roots or any radicals), think of them as variables. You work the same way with $\sqrt{7}$ as you do with x, y, or z.

Addition and subtraction

1. **To add or subtract *like* radicals, add or subtract the number in front of the radical (your old friend, the numerical coefficient).**

   $2\sqrt{7}+5\sqrt{7}=7\sqrt{7}$ $\qquad$ $2x+5x=7x$

   $9\sqrt{13}-4\sqrt{13}=5\sqrt{13}$ $\qquad$ $9x-4x=5x$

2. **You *cannot* add or subtract unlike radicals (just as you cannot add or subtract unlike variables).**

   $6\sqrt{5}+4\sqrt{3}=6\sqrt{5}+4\sqrt{3}$ (You cannot add the two and get $10\sqrt{8}$.)

   $6x+4y=6x+4y$ (You cannot add the two and get $10xy$.)

Don't glance at a problem, see that the radicals are not the same, and immediately assume that you cannot add the two terms. You may be able to simplify one radical to make it match the radical in the other term.

$\sqrt{52}+\sqrt{13}=2\sqrt{13}+\sqrt{13}=3\sqrt{13}$

To simplify: Take out a perfect square from the term. $\sqrt{52}=\sqrt{4}\times\sqrt{13}$. Because $\sqrt{4}=2$, $\sqrt{52}=2\sqrt{13}$.

$\sqrt{20}+\sqrt{45}=\left(\sqrt{4}\times\sqrt{5}\right)+\left(\sqrt{9}\times\sqrt{5}\right)=2\sqrt{5}+3\sqrt{5}=5\sqrt{5}$.

Beware! You must simplify *first*. You can't say that $\sqrt{20}+\sqrt{45}=\sqrt{65}=8.06$. When you work out the correct answer, $5\sqrt{5}$, you see that it's not 8.06, but 11.18.

Multiplication and division

1. **When you multiply or divide radicals, you just multiply or divide the numbers and then pop the radical sign back onto the finished product.**

   $\sqrt{5}\times\sqrt{6}=\sqrt{30}$

   $\sqrt{15}\div\sqrt{5}=\sqrt{3}$

2. **If you have a number in front of the radical, multiply it as well. Let everyone in on the fun.**

   $6\sqrt{3}\times4\sqrt{2}=$

   $6\times4=24$

   $\sqrt{3}\times\sqrt{2}=\sqrt{6}$

   $24\sqrt{6}$

Try this example:

$37\sqrt{5} \times 3\sqrt{6} =$

(A) $40\sqrt{11}$

(B) $40\sqrt{30}$

(C) $111\sqrt{11}$

(D) $111\sqrt{30}$

(E) $1,221$

$37 \times 3 = 111$ and $\sqrt{5} \times \sqrt{6} = \sqrt{30}$, so $111\sqrt{30}$. Straightforward multiplication. *Correct Answer:* D.

Inside out

When there is an operation under the radical, do it first and then take the square root.

$$\sqrt{\frac{x^2}{40} + \frac{x^2}{9}}$$

First, solve for $\frac{x^2}{40} + \frac{x^2}{9}$. You get the common denominator of 360 (40×9) and then find the numerators: $9x^2 + 40x^2 = \frac{49x^2}{360}$. *Now* take the square roots: $49x^2 = 7x$ (because $7x \times 7x = 49x^2$). $\sqrt{360} = 18.97$. Gotcha, I bet! Did you say that $\sqrt{360} = 6$? Wrong! $\sqrt{36} = 6$, but $\sqrt{360} =$ approximately 18.97. Beware of assuming too much; you can be led down the path to temptation.

Your final answer is $\frac{7x}{18.97}$. Of course, you can bet that the answer choices will include $\frac{7x}{6}$.

Probably Probability

Probability questions are usually word problems. They may look intimidating, with a lot of words that make you lose sight of where to begin. Two simple rules can solve nearly every probability problem tossed at you.

1. Create a fraction.

To find a probability, use this formula:

$$P = \frac{\text{Number of possible desired outcomes}}{\text{Number of total possible outcomes}}$$

Make a probability into a fraction. The denominator is the easier of the two parts to begin with. The denominator is the total possible number of outcomes. For example, when you're flipping a coin, there are two outcomes, giving you a denominator of 2. When you're tossing a die (one of a pair of dice), there are six outcomes, giving you a denominator of 6. When you're pulling a card out of a deck of cards, there are 52 outcomes (52 cards in a deck), giving you a denominator of 52. When 25 marbles are in a jar and you're going to pull out one of them, there are 25 possibilities, giving you a denominator of 25. Very simply, the *denominator* is the whole shebang — everything possible.

The *numerator* is the total possible number of the things you want. If you want to get a head when you toss a coin, there is exactly one head, giving you a numerator of 1. The chances of tossing a head, therefore, are ½, one possible head, two possible outcomes altogether. If you want to get a 5 when you toss a die, there is exactly one 5 on the die, giving you a numerator of 1. Notice that your numerator is *not* 5. The number you want happens to be a 5, but there is only *one* 5 on the die. The probability of tossing a 5 is ⅙: There are one 5 and six possible outcomes altogether.

If you want to draw a jack in a deck of cards, there are four jacks: hearts, diamonds, clubs, and spades. Therefore, the numerator is 4. The probability of drawing a jack out of a deck of cards is ⁴⁄₅₂ (which reduces to ⅟₁₃). If you want to draw a jack of hearts, the probability is ⅟₅₂ because there is only one jack of hearts.

A jar of marbles has 8 yellow marbles, 6 black marbles, and 12 white marbles. What is the probability of drawing out a black marble?

Use the formula. Begin with the denominator, which is all the possible outcomes: $8 + 6 + 12 = 26$. The numerator is how many there are of what you want: 6 black marbles. The probability is ⁶⁄₂₆, which can be reduced or (as is more customary) changed to a percentage. What's the probability of drawing out a yellow marble? ⁸⁄₂₆. A white marble? ¹²⁄₂₆. *Correct Answer:* ⁶⁄₂₆ or ³⁄₁₃ or 23%.

A drawer has 5 pairs of white socks, 8 pairs of black socks, and 12 pairs of brown socks. In a hurry to get to school, Austin pulls out a pair at a time and tosses them on the floor if they are not the color he wants. Looking for a brown pair, Austin pulls out and discards a white pair, a black pair, a black pair, and a white pair. What is the probability that on his next reach into the drawer he will pull out a brown pair of socks?

This problem is slightly more complicated than the preceding one, although it uses the same formula. You began with 25 pairs of socks. However, Austin, that slob, has thrown 4 pairs on the floor. That means that there are only 21 pairs left. The probability of his pulling out a brown pair is ¹²⁄₂₁, or ⁴⁄₇, or about 57%. *Correct Answer:* 57%.

A cookie jar has chocolate, vanilla, and strawberry wafer cookies. There are 30 of each type. Bess reaches in, pulls out a chocolate and eats it, and then in quick succession pulls out and eats a vanilla, chocolate, strawberry, strawberry, chocolate, and vanilla. Assuming that she doesn't get sick or get caught, what is the probability that the next cookie she pulls out will be a chocolate one?

Originally, there were 90 cookies. Bess has scarfed down 7 of them, leaving 83. Careful! If you're about to put ³⁰⁄₈₃, you're headed for a trap. There are no longer 30 chocolate cookies; there are only 27 because Bess has eaten 3. The probability is now ²⁷⁄₈₃, or about 33%. *Correct Answer:* 33%.

Probability must always be between zero and one. You cannot have a negative probability and you cannot have a probability greater than 1, or 100%.

2. Multiply consecutive probabilities.

What is the probability that you'll get two heads when you toss a coin twice? You find each probability separately and then *multiply* the two. The chance of tossing a coin the first time and getting a head is ½. The chance of tossing a coin the second time and getting a head is ½. Multiply those consecutive probabilities: ½ × ½ = ¼. The chances of getting two heads is one out of four.

What is the probability of tossing a die twice and getting a 5 on the first toss and a 6 on the second toss? Treat each toss separately. The probability of getting a 5 is ⅙. The probability of getting a 6 is ⅙. Multiply consecutive probabilities: ⅙ × ⅙ = ⅟₃₆.

Here's a good trick question.

	<u>*Column A*</u>		<u>*Column B*</u>

A fair die is tossed twice.

Chances of getting a 5 on the first toss and a 2 on the second toss	Chances of getting a 6 on both tosses

If you chose A, you fell for the trap. You may think that it's harder to roll the same number twice, but the probability is the same as rolling two different numbers. Treat each roll separately. The probability of rolling a 5 is $\frac{1}{6}$. The probability of rolling a 2 is $\frac{1}{6}$. Multiply consecutive probabilities: $\frac{1}{6} \times \frac{1}{6} = \frac{1}{36}$. For Column B, treat each toss separately. The probability of rolling a 6 is $\frac{1}{6}$. The probability of rolling a second 6 is $\frac{1}{6}$. Multiply consecutive probabilities: $\frac{1}{6} \times \frac{1}{6} = \frac{1}{36}$. *Correct Answer:* C.

If you've had a course in statistics, you may have learned about independent events, mutually exclusive events, and interdependent events. Forget about them; they're not on the GRE. The material you just learned is about as complicated as probability gets.

Chapter 12

Miscellaneous Math You Probably Already Know

• •

In This Chapter

▶ Time, rate, and distance problems

▶ Averages

▶ Percentages

▶ Number sets and prime and composite numbers

▶ Mixture, interest, and work problems

▶ Absolute value

▶ Order of operations

▶ Units of measurement

▶ Decimals and fractions

▶ Statistics

▶ Graphs

• •

*Y*ou probably already know the material in this chapter, but a quick review can't hurt you. (The humor — now that's another story!)

DIRTy Math: Distance, Rate, and Time

D.I.R.T. Distance Is Rate × Time. $D = RT$. When you have a time, rate, and distance problem, use this formula. Make a chart with the formula across the top and fill in the spaces on the chart.

Jennifer drives 40 miles an hour for two and a half hours. Her friend Ashley goes the same distance but drives at one and a half times Jennifer's speed. How many *minutes* longer does Jennifer drive than Ashley?

Do *not* start making big, hairy formulas with x's and y's. Jennifer has no desire to be known as Madame x; Ashley refuses to know y. Make the DIRT chart.

| *Distance* | = | *Rate* | × | *Time* |

When you fill in the 40 mph and 2½ hours for Jennifer, you can calculate that she went 100 miles. Think of it this simple way: If she goes 40 mph for one hour, that's 40 miles. For a second hour, she goes another 40 miles. In a half-hour, she goes ½ of 40, or 20 miles. (See? You don't have to write down $40 \times 2\frac{1}{2}$ and do all that pencil pushing; use your brain, not your yellow #2.) Add them together: $40 + 40 + 20 = 100$. Jennifer has gone 100 miles.

Distance	Rate	×	Time
100 (Jennifer)	40 mph		2½ hours

Because Ashley drives the same distance, fill in 100 under distance for her. She goes one and a half times as fast. Uh-uh, put down that pencil. Use your brain! 1×40 is 40; $\frac{1}{2} \times 40$ is 20. Add $40 + 20 = 60$. Ashley drives 60 mph. Now this gets really easy. If she drives at 60 mph, she drives one mile a minute. (60 minutes in an hour, 60 miles in an hour. You figure it out, Einstein.) Therefore, to go 100 miles takes her 100 minutes. Because your final answer is asked for in minutes, don't bother converting this to hours; leave it the way it is.

Distance	Rate	×	Time
100 (Ashley)	60 mph		100 minutes

Last step. Jennifer drives 2½ hours. How many minutes is that? Do it the easy way, in your brain. One hour is 60 minutes. A second hour is another 60 minutes. A half hour is 30 minutes. Add them together: $60 + 60 + 30 = 150$ minutes. If Jennifer drives for 150 minutes and Ashley drives for 100 minutes, Jennifer drives 50 minutes more than Ashley. However, Ashley gets a speeding ticket, has her driving privileges taken away by an irate father, and doesn't get to go to this weekend's party. Jennifer goes and gets her pick of the hunks, ending up with Tyrone's ring and frat pin. The moral of the story: Slow . . . but steady!

Distance	Rate	×	Time
100 (Jennifer)	40 mph		150 minutes
100 (Ashley)	60 mph		100 minutes

Be careful to note whether the people are traveling in the *same* direction or *opposite* directions. Suppose that you're asked how far apart drivers are at the end of their trip. If you are told that Jordan travels 40 mph east for 2 hours and Connor travels 60 mph west for 3 hours, they are going in opposite directions. If they start from the same point at the same time, Jordan has gone 80 miles one way, and Connor has gone 180 miles the opposite way. They are 260 miles apart. The trap answer is 100, because careless people (not *you!*) simply subtract $180 - 80$.

It All Averages Out: Averages

You can always do averages the way Ms. Jones taught you when you were in third grade: Add all the terms, and then divide by the number of terms.

$5 + 11 + 17 + 23 + 29 = 85$.

$\frac{85}{5} = 17$

Or you can save wear-and-tear on the brain cells and know the following rule:

1. **The average of evenly spaced terms is the middle term.**

   First, check that the terms are evenly spaced. That means that there is an equal number of units between each term. Here, the terms are six apart. Second, circle the middle term, which here is 17. Third, go home, make popcorn, and watch the late-night movie with all the time you've saved.

Try another one. Find the average of these numbers:

32, 41, 50, 59, 68, 77, 86, 95, 104

Don't reach for your pencil. You look and see that the terms are all nine units apart. Because they are evenly spaced, the middle term is the average: 68.

This is an easy trick to love, but don't march down the aisle with it yet. The tip works only for *evenly spaced* terms. If you have just any old batch of numbers, such as 4, 21, 97, 98, 199, you can't look at the middle term for the average. You have to find the average of those numbers the old-fashioned way.

Find the average of these numbers:

3, 10, 17, 24, 31, 38, 45, 52

First, double-check that they are evenly spaced. Here, the numbers are spaced by sevens. Next you look for the middle number . . . and there isn't one. You can, of course, find the two central terms, 24 and 31, and find the middle between them. That works, but what a pain. Not only that, but suppose that you have 38 numbers. It's very easy to make a mistake as to which terms are the central ones. If you're off just a little bit, you miss the question. Instead, use rule number two:

2. **The average of evenly spaced terms is** $\frac{(first + last)}{2}$.

Just add the first and the last terms, which are obvious at a glance, and divide that sum by 2. Here, $3 + 52 = 55$. $\frac{55}{2} = 27.5$

Note: Double-check using your common sense. Suppose that you made a silly mistake and got 45 for your answer. A glance at the numbers tells you that 45 is not in the middle and therefore cannot be the average.

This tip works for *all* evenly spaced terms. It doesn't matter whether there is a middle number, as in the first example, or no middle number, as in the second example. Go back to the first example.

32, 41, 50, 59, 68, 77, 86, 95, 104

Instead of finding the middle term, add the first and last terms and divide by 2, like this: $32 + 104 = 136$. $\frac{136}{2} = 68$. Either way works.

Missing term average problem

You are likely to find a problem like this:

A student takes seven exams. Her scores on the first six are 91, 89, 85, 92, 90, and 88. If her average on all *seven* exams is 90, what did she get on the seventh exam?

This is called a *missing term average problem* because you are given an average and asked to find a missing term. Duh.

1. **You can do this the basic algebraic way.**

$$\text{Average} = \frac{\text{Sum}}{\text{Number of terms}}$$

$$90 = \frac{\text{Sum}}{7}$$

Because you don't know the seventh term, call it x. Add the first six terms (and get 535) and x.

$$90 = \frac{(535 + x)}{7} \quad \text{Cross-multiply:} \quad 90 \times 7 = 535 + x$$

$$630 = 535 + x$$

$$95 = x$$

The seventh exam score was 95.

2. **You can do these problems the commonsense way.**

There is another quick way to do this problem. You've probably done it this way all your life without realizing what a genius you are.

Suppose that your dad tells you that if you average a 90 for the semester in advanced physics, he'll let you take that summer trip through Europe with your buddies that the two of you have been arguing about for months (he figures he's safe because there's no way you're going to get such a high grade in that incredibly difficult class). You take him at his word and begin working hard.

On the first exam, you get 91 and you're +1 point. That is, you're one point above the ultimate score you want, a 90. On the second exam, you get 89 and you're −1. On that test, you're one point below the ultimate score you want, a 90. On the third exam, you get an 85, which is −5. You're five points below the ultimate score you want, a 90.

Are you getting the hang of this? Here's how it looks.

$$91 = +1$$
$$89 = -1$$
$$85 = -5$$
$$92 = +2$$
$$90 = 0$$
$$88 = -2$$

The +1 and −1 cancel each other out, and the +2 and −2 cancel each other out. You're left with −5, meaning you're five points in the hole. You have to make up those five points on the last exam or get five points *above* what you want for your ultimate score. Because you want a 90, you need a 95 on the last test.

Try another, using the no-brainer method. A student takes seven exams. She gets an 88 average on all of them. Her first six scores are 89, 98, 90, 82, 88, and 87. What does she get on the seventh exam?

$$\text{Average} = 88$$

$$89 = +1$$
$$98 = +10$$
$$90 = +2$$
$$82 = -6$$
$$88 = 0$$
$$87 = -1$$

The +1 and −1 cancel. Then you have $(10 + 2) = +12$ and −6, for a total of +6. You are six points *above* what you need for the ultimate outcome. You can afford to lose six points on the final exam or to be six points *below* the average. That gives you an 82.

You may be given only five out of seven scores and asked for *the average of the missing two* terms. Do the same thing and then divide by 2.

Average of seven exams: 85

Scores of the first five exams: 86, 79, 82, 85, 84

Find: The average score of each of the remaining exams

Algebraic way: $85 = \dfrac{(86 + 79 + 82 + 85 + 84) + x + x}{7}$

Cross-multiply: $595 = 416 + 2x$

$595 - 416 = 2x$

$179 = 2x$

$89.5 = x$

Commonsense way:

Average $= 85$

$86 = +1$

$79 = -6$

$82 = -3$

$85 = 0$

$84 = -1$

The +1 and −1 cancel each other out. You are left with −9 for *two* exams or −4.5 per exam. If you are *down* four and a half points, you must *gain* those four and a half points on each of the two exams:

$85 + 4.5 = 89.5$

 The shortcut, commonsense way is quick and easy, but don't forget to make the change at the end. That is, if you decide that you are *minus eight* points going into the final exam, you need to be *plus eight* points on that last exam to come out even. If you subtract eight points from the average rather than add them, you'll probably come up with one of the trap answers.

Weighted averages

In a *weighted average,* some scores count more than others.

Number of Students	Score
12	80
13	75
10	70

If you are asked to find the average score for the students in this class, you know that you can't simply add 80, 75, and 70 and divide by three because the scores weren't evenly distributed among the students. Because 12 students got an 80, multiply $12 \times 80 = 960$. Do the same with the other scores:

$13 \times 75 = 975$

$10 \times 70 = 700$

$960 + 975 + 700 = 2,635$

Divide *not by three* but by the total number of students: $35(12 + 13 + 10)$

$$\frac{2635}{35} = 75.29$$

You can often answer a Quantitative Comparison question on weighted averages without doing all the work, as demonstrated in the following. (See Chapter 13 for more information about QC questions and how to answer them.)

The answer choices are

A if the quantity in Column A is greater.

B if the quantity in Column B is greater.

C if the two quantities are equal.

D if the relationship cannot be determined from the information given.

Column A		_Column B_
Clothing	_Quantity_	_Cost per Item_
Black T-shirts	5	$20
Denim shirts	8	$25
Blue jeans	20	$30

Average cost per item of clothing	$25

You can work this whole problem out, finding the cost of all the T-shirts, denim shirts, and jeans and then dividing that cost by the number of items of clothing. When you do all that work, you get 27.27 (and a headache and a sore pencil-pushing finger). Or you can use your brain and common sense: 13 items are $25 or less, and 20 items are $30. Therefore, there are more items at above $25 than below $25. The average must be more than $25. Remember, because this is a QC problem, you don't need to solve it through for the final, precise solution; you need only enough information to compare the quantities in the two columns. *Correct Answer:* A.

Percentage Panic

The mere mention of the word *percent* may strike terror in your heart. There's no reason to panic over percentages; there are ways of getting around them.

1. **Ignore their very existence. You can express a percentage as a decimal, which is a lot less intimidating. You do so by putting a decimal point two places to the left of the percentage and dropping the % sign.**

   $35\% = .35$ $83\% = .83$ $50\% = .50$ $33.3\% = .333$ $66.6\% = .666$

   If you have a choice of working with decimals or percentages, it's better to choose decimals.

2. **Another way to ignore a percentage is to convert it to a fraction. The word *percent* means *per cent,* or *per hundred.* Every percentage is that number over 100.**

   $50\% = {}^{50}\!/_{100}$ $33\% = {}^{33}\!/_{100}$ $75\% = {}^{75}\!/_{100}$

   If you can't ignore the percentage, remember that a percent is

   $$\frac{\text{Part}}{\text{Whole}} \times 100, \text{ or } \frac{is}{of} \times 100$$

   What percent *is* 45 *of* 90? Put the part, 45, over the whole, 90. Or put the *is,* 45, over the *of,* 90:

   $${}^{45}\!/_{90} = {}^{1}\!/_{2} \times 100 = {}^{100}\!/_{2} = 50\%$$

   42 *is* what percent *of* 126? Put the part, 42, over the whole, 126. Or put the *is,* 42, over the *of,* 126.

   $${}^{42}\!/_{126} = {}^{1}\!/_{3} \times 100 = {}^{100}\!/_{3} = 33\tfrac{1}{3}\%$$

   Here's a little harder one: What is 40% of 80? You may be tempted to put the *is,* 40, over the *of,* 80, and get ${}^{40}\!/_{80} = {}^{1}\!/_{2} \times 100 = {}^{100}\!/_{2} = 50\%$. However, when the problem is worded this way, you don't know the *is.* Your equation must be ${}^{x}\!/_{80} = {}^{40}\!/_{100}$. Cross-multiply: $3200 = 100x$. $x = 32$. There's an easier way to do it: *of* means times, or multiply. Because $40\% = .40$, multiply $.40 \times 80 = 32$.

Life has its ups and downs: Percent increase/decrease

You may see a problem asking you what percent increase or decrease occurred in the number of games a team won or the amount of commission a person earned. To find a percent increase or decrease, use this formula:

$$\text{percent increase or decrease} = \frac{\text{number increase or decrease}}{\text{original whole}}$$

In basic English, to find the percent by which something has increased or decreased, you take two simple steps:

1. **Find the *number* (amount) by which the thing has increased or decreased.** For example, if a team won 25 games last year and 30 games this year, the number increase was 5. If a salesperson earned $10,000 last year and $8,000 this year, the number decrease was 2,000. Make that the numerator of the fraction.

2. **Find the *original whole.*** This figure is what you started out with before you increased or decreased. If a team won 25 games last year and won 30 games this year, the original number was 25. If the salesperson earned $10,000 last year and $8,000 this year, the original number was 10,000. Make that the denominator.

You now have a fraction. Make it a decimal, and multiply by 100 to make it a percentage.

42

In 1992, Coach Jarchow won 30 prizes at the county fair by tossing a basketball into a bushel basket. In 1993, he won 35 prizes. What was his percent increase?

(A) 100

(B) 30

(C) 16⅔

(D) 14.28

(E) .1̄6̄6̄

The number by which his prizes increased, from 30 to 35, is 5. That is the numerator. The original whole, or what he began with, is 30. That is the denominator. *Correct Answer:* C.

$$\tfrac{5}{30} = \tfrac{1}{6} = 16\tfrac{2}{3}\%$$

If you chose E, I fooled you. The question asks what *percent* increase there was. If you say E, you're saying that there was a .1̄6̄6̄ percent increase. Not so. The .1̄6̄6̄ increase *as a percentage* is 16⅔%. If you chose D, you fell for another trap. You put the 5 increase over the 35 instead of over the 30.

Two years ago, Haylie scored 22 goals at soccer. This year, she scored 16 goals. What was her approximate percentage decrease?

(A) 72

(B) 37.5

(C) 27

(D) 16

(E) .2̄7̄

Find the number of the decrease: 22 − 16 = 6. That is the numerator. Find the original whole from which she is decreasing: 22. That is the denominator. $\tfrac{6}{22} \approx .\overline{27}$, or approximately 27 percent. *Correct Answer:* C.

If you chose A, you put 16 over 22 instead of putting the decrease over the original whole. If you chose E, again you forgot the difference between .27 and .27 *percent.* If you chose B, you put the decrease of 6 over the new amount, 16, rather than over the original whole. Note how easy these traps are to fall for. My suggestion: Write down the actual formula and then plug in the numbers. Writing down the formula may be boring, but doing so takes only a few seconds and may save you points.

Here's a tricky question that many people do in their heads (instead of writing down the formula and plugging in numbers) and blow big time.

Carissa has three quarters. Her father gives her three more. Carissa's wealth has increased by what percent?

(A) 50

(B) 100

(C) 200

(D) 300

(E) 500

Did you fall for the trap answer, C? Her wealth has doubled, to be sure, but the percent increase is only 100. You can prove that with the formula: The number increase is 75 (she has three more quarters, or 75 cents). Her original whole was 75. $^{75}/_{75} = 1 = 100\%$. *Correct Answer:* B.

When you double something, you increase by 100 percent because you have to subtract the original "one" you began with. When you triple something, you increase by 200 percent because you have to subtract the original you began with. For example, if you had three dollars and you now have nine dollars, you have tripled your money but increased by only 200 percent. Do the formula: number increase = 6 dollars. Original whole = 3 dollars. $^{6}/_{3} = 2 = 200$ percent. Take a wild guess at what percent you increase when you quadruple your money? That's right, 300 percent. Just subtract the original 100 percent.

Ready, Sets, Go: Number Sets

There's no escaping vocabulary. Even on the math portion of the test, you need to know certain terms. How can you solve a problem that asks you to "state your answer in integral values only" if you don't know what integral values are? Here are the number sets with which you'll be working.

- **Counting numbers:** 1, 2, 3 . . . Note that 0 is *not* a counting number.

- **Whole numbers:** 0, 1, 2, 3 . . . Note that 0 *is* a whole number.

- **Integers:** . . . –3, –2, –1, 0, 1, 2, 3 . . . When a question asks for *integral values,* it wants the answer in integers only. For example, you can't give an answer like 4.3 because that's not an integer. You need to round down to 4.

- **Rational numbers:** Rational numbers can be expressed as $^{a}/_{b}$, where *a* and *b* are integers.

  Examples: 1 (because $1 = \frac{1}{1}$ and 1 is an integer), ½ (because 1 and 2 are integers), $\frac{9}{2}$ (because 9 and 2 are integers), and $-\frac{4}{2}$ (because –4 and 2 are integers).

Notice that every number set so far has included the previous number sets. Whole numbers include counting numbers, integers include counting numbers and whole numbers, and rationals include counting numbers, whole numbers, and integers.

- **Irrational numbers:** The highly technical definition here is *anything not rational.* That is, an irrational number cannot be written as $^{a}/_{b}$, where *a* and *b* are integers. Numbers whose decimals do not terminate and do not repeat can't be written as a fraction and therefore are irrational.

  Examples: π cannot be written *exactly* as 3.14; it is nonterminating and nonrepeating. $\sqrt{2}$ is approximately 1.4142 but is nonterminating and nonrepeating.

  Irrational numbers *do not* include the previous number sets. That is, irrational numbers don't include counting numbers, whole numbers, integers or rational numbers.

✔ **Real numbers:** Briefly put, all of the preceding. Real numbers include counting numbers, whole numbers, integers, rationals, and irrationals. For all practical purposes, real numbers are everything you think of as numbers. When a question tells you to "express your answer in real numbers," don't sweat it. That's almost no constraint at all, because nearly everything you see is a real number.

There are such critters as *imaginary* numbers, which are *not* on the GRE. (Most of you probably stopped reading right there, figuring that you don't even want to hear about them if they're not going to be tested. I don't blame you.) Imaginary numbers are expressed with a lowercase *i* and are studied in upper-division math classes. I won't go into them here because, once again, *they are not tested on the GRE*. All numbers on the GRE are real numbers.

Prime and Composite Numbers

Prime numbers are positive integers that have exactly two positive integer factors; they cannot be divided by numbers other than 1 and themselves. Examples include 2, 3, 5, 7, and 11.

There are a few lovely tricks to prime numbers.

✔ Zero is *not* a prime number (by definition). Why? Because it is divisible by more than two factors. Zero can be divided by 1, 2, 3, and on to infinity. Although division by zero is undefined (and isn't tested on the GRE), you can divide zero by other numbers; the answer of course is always zero. $0 \div 1 = 0$; $0 \div 2 = 0$; $0 \div 412 = 0$.

✔ One is *not* a prime number (by definition). There are not two factors of 1. It cannot be divided only by 1 *and* itself. Confused? Don't worry about it. Just memorize the fact that 1 is not a prime number.

✔ Two is the *only* even prime. People tend to think that all prime numbers are odd. Well, almost. Two is prime because it has only two factors; it can be divided only by 1 and itself.

✔ Not all odd numbers are prime. Think of 9 or 15; those numbers are odd but not prime because they have more than two factors and can be divided by more than just 1 and themselves. $9 = (1 \times 9)$ *and* (3×3). $15 = (1 \times 15)$ *and* (3×5).

Composite numbers have more than two factors and can be divided by more than just 1 and themselves. Examples: 4, 6, 8, 9, 12, 14, and 15.

Note that composite numbers (called that because they are *composed* of more than two factors) can be even or odd.

Don't confuse *prime* and *composite* and *even* and *odd* with *positive* and *negative*. That's an easy mistake to make in the confusion of the exam. If a problem that you know should be easy is flustering you, stop and ask yourself whether you're making this common mistake.

I said that 0 and 1 are not prime. They are also not composite. What are they? Neither. You express this as "0 and 1 are neither prime nor composite." It's rather like wondering whether zero is positive or negative. You say, "Zero is neither positive nor negative." Why should you know this? Here's an example when the information can win you ten points (the approximate value of one correct math question).

The answer choices are

    A if the quantity in Column A is greater.

    B if the quantity in Column B is greater.

    C if the two quantities are equal.

    D if the relationship cannot be determined from the information given.

Column A	_Column B_
The number of prime numbers from 0 to 10 inclusive	The number of prime numbers from 11 to 20 inclusive

The prime numbers from 0 to 10 inclusive are 2, 3, 5, and 7. Note that 0 and 1 are *not* prime. If you count either or both as prime, you miss an otherwise very easy question. In Column B, the prime numbers from 11 to 20 inclusive are 11, 13, 17, and 19. Both columns have four prime numbers. *Correct Answer:* C.

I'm All Mixed Up: Mixture Problems

A mixture problem is a word problem that looks much more confusing than it actually is. There are two types of mixtures: those in which the items remain separate (when you mix peanuts and raisins, you still have peanuts and raisins, not pearains or raispeans) and those in which the two elements blend (these are usually chemicals, like water and alcohol). Check out the separate mixture first.

Marshall wants to mix 40 pounds of beads selling for 30 cents a pound with a quantity of sequins selling for 80 cents a pound. He wants to pay 40 cents per pound for the final mix. How many pounds of sequins should he use?

The hardest part for most students is knowing where to begin. Make a chart.

	Pounds	*Price*	*Total*
Beads	40	$.30	$12.00
Sequins	x	$.80	.80x
Mixture	40 + x	$.40	.40(40 + x)

Reason it out. In pennies, the cost of the beads (1200) plus the cost of the sequins (80x) must equal the cost of the mixture (1600 + 40x). Note that you dump the decimal point (officially, you multiply by 100 to get rid of the decimal point, but really, you dump it). Now you have a workable equation:

$$1200 + 80x = 1600 + 40x$$

$$80x - 40x = 1600 - 1200$$

$$40x = 400$$

$$x = 10$$

Careful! Keep in mind what x stands for. It represents the number of pounds of sequins, what the question asks for.

Go back and double-check by plugging this value into the equation. You already know that Marshall spent $12 on beads. If he buys 10 pounds of sequins for 80 cents, he spends $8, for a total of $20. He spends that $20 on 50 pounds: $2000 \div 50 = 40$. How about that, it works!

Greed Is Great: Interest Problems

This is a pretty problem: PRTI, to be exact. $P =$ Principal, the amount of money you begin with, or the amount you invest. $R =$ Rate, the interest rate you're earning on the money. $T =$ Time, the amount of time you leave the money in the interest-bearing account. $I =$ Interest, the amount of interest you earn on the investment. A problem usually asks you how much interest someone earned on his or her investment.

The formula is $PRT = I$. Principal × Rate × Time = Interest.

Janet invested $1,000 at 5 percent annual interest for one year. How much interest did she earn?

This is the simplest type of problem. Plug the numbers into the formula.

$PRT = I$

$1,000 \times .05 \times 1 = 50$. She earned $50 interest.

The answer choices may try to trap you with variations on a decimal place, making the answers 5, 50, 500, and so on. You know that $5\% = \frac{5}{100} = .05$; be careful how you multiply.

These problems are not intentionally vicious (unlike 99 percent of the rest of the GRE, right?). You won't see something that gets crazy on interest rates, like "5 percent annual interest compounded quarterly for 3 months and 6 percent quarterly interest compounded daily," blah, blah, blah.

(Useless but fascinating trivia: In Bulgarian, the word for *thank you* is pronounced *blah-go-dah-ree-uh*. But a shortened form, like *thanks,* is simply *blah.* If your mother takes you to task for being a smart aleck and going "blah, blah, blah" when she talks, you can innocently claim that you're practicing your Bulgarian and are just thanking her for her wisdom.)

All Work and No Play: Work Problems

The formula most commonly used in a work problem is

$$\text{Work} = \frac{\text{Time put in}}{\text{Capacity (time to do the whole job)}}$$

Find each person's contribution. The denominator is the easy part; it represents how many hours (minutes, days, weeks, and so on) it would take the person to do the whole job, working alone. The numerator is how long the person has already worked. For example, if Janie can paint a house in four days and has been working for one day, she has done ¼ of the work. If Evelyn can paint a house in nine days and has been working for five, she has done ⅝ of the project.

So far, so good. The problem comes when more than one person works at the task. What happens when Janie and Evelyn work together?

Janie working alone can paint a house in six days. Evelyn working alone can paint it in eight days. Working together, how long will it take them to paint the house?

Find Janie's work: $\frac{x}{6}$. Find Evelyn's work: $\frac{x}{8}$. Together, the two fractions must add up to 1, the entire job.

$$\frac{x}{6} + \frac{x}{8} = 1$$

Multiply by the common denominator, 48, to eliminate the fractions.

$$\frac{48x}{6} + \frac{48x}{8} = 48$$

$$8x + 6x = 48$$

$$14x = 48$$

$$x = \text{approximately } 3.43.$$

It would take the two women working together about 3.43 days to paint the house.

Double-check by using your common sense. If you get an answer of 10, for example, you know that you must have made a mistake because the two women working together should be able to do the job *more quickly* than either one working alone.

Reading between the Lines: Absolute Value

The absolute value is the magnitude of a number. So much for the official definition. The *Dummies* definition (that is, the easy way to think about it) of *absolute value* is the positive form of a number. Absolute value is indicated by two vertical parallel lines (like this: $|\ |$).

Any number within those lines is read as "The absolute value of that number." For example, $|3| = 3$ is read as "The absolute value of three equals three." That seems straightforward enough, but what if the number inside the straight lines is negative? Its absolute value is still positive: $|-3| = 3$. Here's a tricky problem you're likely to see on the exam.

$$-|-3| = -3$$

The answer may seem contrary to common sense. Isn't a negative times a negative a positive? True, but you have to work from the inside out. The absolute value of negative three is three. Then you multiple three by the negative to get negative three. *Correct Answer:* -3. Here's another example that's even a little harder.

$$-|-|-5|\ | =$$

Here's the official way to work the problem (**Hint:** The word *official* is a clue that in a minute I'm going to give you an unofficial, much easier way to solve this.) Work from the inside out. Say it to yourself as you go along: "The absolute value of negative five is 5. Then the negative of that is negative 5. But the absolute value of negative 5 is 5. And finally, the negative of that is -5." *Correct Answer:* -5.

Do you see the super-shortcut for the above example? You actually don't have to work the problem out at all! Anything and everything inside the absolute value signs is going to be positive. Then the one negative sign outside changes the whole problem to negative. You don't, in other words, have to go through the intermediate steps. With an absolute value, look to see whether a negative sign is outside the first absolute value symbol. If it is, the number is negative. If it's not, the number is positive. Simple as that.

Smooth Operator: Order of Operations

When you have several operations (addition, subtraction, multiplication, division, squaring, and so on) in one problem, there is a definite order in which you must perform the operations:

1. **Parentheses**. Do what's inside the parentheses first.

2. **Power.** Do the squaring or the cubing, whatever the exponent is.

3. **Multiply or divide.** Do these left to right. If multiplication is to the left of division, multiply first. If division is to the left of multiplication, divide first.

4. **Add or subtract.** Do these left to right. If addition is to the left of subtraction, add first. If subtraction is to the left of addition, subtract first.

An easy *mnemonic* (memory) device for remembering these is *Please Praise My Daughter And Son* (PPMDAS): Parentheses, Power, Multiply, Divide, Add, Subtract.

$$10(3-5)^2 + (30/5)^0 =$$

First, do what's inside the parentheses: $3-5=-2$. $30/5 = 6$. Next, do the power: $-2^2 = 4$. $6^0 = 1$. (Did you remember that any number to the zero power equals one?) Next, multiply: $10 \times 4 = 40$. Finally, add: $40 + 1 = 41$. *Correct Answer:* 41. Try another.

$$3 + (9-6)^2 - 5(8/2)^{-2} =$$

First, do what's inside the parentheses: $9-6=3$. $8/2 = 4$. Second, do the powers: $3^2 = 9$. $4^{-2} = 1/(4^2) = 1/16$. Multiply: $5 \times 1/16 = 5/16$. Finally, add and subtract left to right. $3 + 9 = 12$. Then $12 - 5/16 = 11^{11}/_{16}$. *Correct Answer:* $11^{11}/_{16}$.

Measuring Up: Units of Measurement

Occasionally, you may be expected to know a unit of measurement that the test makers deem obvious but which you have forgotten. Take a few minutes to review this brief list.

International students, in particular, need to memorize these as you may not have grown up using some of the same units of measurement as those used in the United States (and on the GRE).

1. **Quantities**

   16 ounces = 1 pound

   2,000 pounds = 1 ton

   2 cups = 1 pint

   2 pints = 1 quart

   4 quarts = 1 gallon

You can calculate that a gallon has 16 cups, or eight pints. To help you remember, think of borrowing a cup of sugar. Sugar is sweet, and you have a Sweet 16 birthday party: 16 sweet cups of sugar in a gallon. It may be silly, but the best memory aids usually are.

2. **Length**

   12 inches = 1 foot

   3 feet (36 inches) = 1 yard

   5,280 feet (1,760 yards) = 1 mile

Everyone knows that there are 12 inches in a foot. How many square inches are there in a square foot? If you say 12, you've fallen for the trap. $12 \times 12 = 144$ square inches are in a square foot.

Here's how you may fall for that trap in an otherwise easy problem.

The answer choices are

A if the quantity in Column A is greater.

B if the quantity in Column B is greater.

C if the two quantities are equal.

D if the relationship cannot be determined from the information given.

Column A	*Column B*
Number of square inches in 3 square feet	36

Your first reaction is to think that the columns are equal because there are 12 inches to a foot and $12 \times 3 = 36$. However, a square foot is $12 \times 12 = 144$ inches. Because 144×3 is definitely greater than 36 (don't waste any time doing the math), the answer is A. *Correct Answer:* A.

Bonus: How many cubic inches are there in a cubic foot? Not 12, and not even 144. A cubic foot is $12 \times 12 \times 12 = 1,728$ cubic inches.

3. Time

> **60 seconds = 1 minute**
>
> **60 minutes = 1 hour**
>
> **24 hours = 1 day**
>
> **7 days = 1 week**
>
> **52 weeks = 1 year**
>
> **365 days = 1 year**
>
> **366 days = 1 leap year**

Leap year is an interesting concept in terms of math problems. It comes around every four years. The extra day, February 29, makes 366 days in the year. Why do you need to know this? Suppose that you see this problem:

Mr. Pellaton's neon sign flashes four hours a day, every day all year, for four years. If it costs him three cents a day for electricity, how much will he owe for electricity at the end of the fourth year?

You may be tempted to say that this problem is super easy — multiply 365×4 to find the number of days and then multiply that number by .03. Wrong-o! You forgot that extra day for leap year, and your answer is off by three cents. You *know* that the test makers will have that wrong answer lurking among the answer choices just to trap you. Whenever there is a four-year period, look out for the leap year with an extra day.

What's the Point: Decimals

Here's where a calculator would be very helpful. Until the test makers join the twentieth century and let you use a calculator, however, you'll have to rely on brain power, not battery power. (By the way, did you know that students taking the SAT and ACT are now allowed to use a calculator? Things are changing.)

Adding and subtracting decimals

Line up the decimal points vertically and add or subtract the numbers.

$$\begin{array}{r} 3.09 \\ 4.72 \\ 31.9 \\ \underline{121.046} \\ 160.756 \end{array}$$

If you're rushed for time and don't want to do the whole problem, go to extremes. The extremes are the far-left and far-right columns. Often, calculating them alone gives you enough information to choose the right answer to a multiple-choice problem. In this case, you can look at the far right, which is the thousands column, and know that it has to end in a 6. Suppose that the answer choices are

(A) 160.999

(B) 160.852

(C) 160.756

(D) 159.831

(E) 159.444

You know immediately that C has to be the correct choice.

Maybe more than one of the answer choices uses the correct digit for the far-right column. Okay, you're flexible; head for the far-left column, which here is the hundreds place. You know in this problem it has to be a 1. The answer choices are

(A) 160.756

(B) 201.706

(C) 209.045

(D) 210.006

(E) 301.786

Only choice A has the correct far-left number.

Multiplying decimals

The biggest trap is keeping the number of decimal points correct. The number of decimal places in the product (the number you get when you multiply the terms together) must be the same as the sum of the number of decimal places in all the terms.

$$5.06 \times 3.9 =$$

$$\begin{array}{r} 5.06 \\ \times 3.9 \\ \hline 19.734 \end{array}$$

There are two decimal places in the first term and one in the second, for a total of three. Therefore, the final answer must have three decimal places.

The shortcut you learned for addition and subtraction works here as well. Go to extremes. Look at the far-right and far-left terms. You know that $6 \times 9 = 54$, such that the last digit in the answer has to be a 4. You can eliminate wrong answers by using that information. You know that $5 \times 3 = 15$, but you may have to carry over some other numbers to make the far-left value greater than 15 (as it turns out here). At least you know that the far-left digits must be 15 *or more*. An answer choice starting with 14, 13, or anything less than 15 can be eliminated.

Dividing decimals

Turn the decimals into integers by moving the decimal point to the right the appropriate number of places for both terms, the one you are dividing and the one you are dividing by (called the *divisor*, should you happen to care).

$$4.44 \div .06 = {}^{444}\!/_{6} = 74$$

I won't spend much time on decimals because you almost certainly won't spend much time on them yourself. Just remember two things:

- Keep a wary eye on the decimal point; its placement is often a trap for the careless.
- Go to extremes: Determine the far-left or far-right digit and use that information to eliminate incorrect answer choices.

Broken Hearts, Broken Numbers: Fractions

Fractions strike fear into the hearts of most mere mortals. Fortunately, the number of fraction problems on the GRE is small and getting smaller all the time.

Adding or subtracting

1. **You can add or subtract fractions only when they have the same denominator.**

$$\frac{1}{3} + \frac{4}{3} = \frac{5}{3}$$

$$\frac{3}{8} - \frac{2}{8} = \frac{1}{8}$$

2. **When fractions have the same denominator, add or subtract the numerators only.**

3. **When fractions don't have the same denominator, you have to find a common denominator.**

You can, of course, multiply all the denominators, but that often doesn't give you the *lowest* common denominator. You end up with some humongous, overwhelming number that you'd rather not work with. Instead, use this little trick:

4. **To find the lowest common denominator, identify the highest denominator and count by it.**

   Find the lowest common denominator of 15 and 6. Sure, you can multiply $15 \times 6 = 90$, but that's not the *lowest* common denominator. Instead, count by 15's because it's the larger of the two. 15? No, 6 doesn't go into that. 30? Yes, both 15 and 6 go into 30. That's the *lowest* common denominator.

   Try another one: Find the lowest common denominator for 2, 4, and 5. Count by 5s: 5? No, 2 and 4 don't go into it. 10? No, 4 doesn't go into it. 15? No, 2 and 4 don't go into it. 20? Yes, all the numbers divide evenly into 20. That number is much smaller than the one you get when you multiply $2 \times 4 \times 5 = 40$.

5. **In many problems, you don't even have to find the lowest common denominator. You can find any common denominator by multiplying the denominators.**

$$\frac{4}{15} + \frac{1}{6} =$$

   The common denominator is $15 \times 6 = 90$. Cross-multiply: $4 \times 6 = 24$. The first fraction becomes $\frac{24}{90}$. Cross-multiply: $1 \times 15 = 15$. The second fraction becomes $\frac{15}{90}$. Now add the numerators: $24 + 15 = 39$. Put the sum over the common denominator: $\frac{39}{90}$. Can you reduce? Yes, by 3: $\frac{13}{30}$.

   Do the same thing when working with variables instead of numbers.

$$\frac{a}{b} - \frac{c}{d} =$$

   Find the common denominator by multiplying the two denominators: $b \times d = bd$. Cross-multiply: $a \times d = ad$. Cross-multiply: $c \times b = cb$. Put the difference of the results of the cross-multiplication over the common denominator: $\dfrac{(ad - cb)}{bd}$

Multiplying fractions

This is the easy one. Just do it. Multiply horizontally, multiplying the numerators and then multiplying the denominators.

$$\frac{3}{4} \times \frac{2}{5} = \frac{(3 \times 2)}{(4 \times 5)} = \frac{6}{20} = \frac{3}{10}$$

Always check whether you can cancel before you begin working to avoid having to deal with big, awkward numbers and to avoid having to reduce at the end. In the preceding example, you can cancel the 4 and the 2, leaving you with

$$\frac{3}{{}_2\cancel{4}} \times \frac{\cancel{2}^1}{5} = \frac{(3 \times 1)}{(2 \times 5)} = \frac{3}{10}$$

You get to the right solution either way; canceling in advance just makes the numbers smaller and easier to work with.

Dividing fractions

To divide by a fraction, invert it (turn it upside down) and multiply.

$$\frac{1}{3} \div \frac{2}{5} = \frac{1}{3} \times \frac{5}{2} = \frac{5}{6}$$

Mixed numbers

A *mixed number* is a whole number with a fraction tagging along behind it, like $2\frac{1}{3}$, $4\frac{2}{5}$, or $9\frac{1}{2}$. Multiply the whole number by the denominator and add that to the numerator. Put the sum over the denominator.

$$2\tfrac{1}{3} = (2 \times 3) + 1 = 7 \rightarrow \tfrac{7}{3}$$
$$4\tfrac{2}{5} = (4 \times 5) + 2 = 22 \rightarrow \tfrac{22}{5}$$
$$9\tfrac{1}{2} = (9 \times 2) + 1 = 19 \rightarrow \tfrac{19}{2}$$

The Stats Don't Lie: Statistics

Don't panic; statistics are tested on the GRE only in the most rudimentary way. If you can master three basic concepts, you can do any statistics on this exam. Those concepts are median, mode, and range.

Median

Simply put, the *median* is the middle number when all the terms are arranged in order. Think of the median strip, which is the middle of the road. Median = middle. Be sure you arrange the numbers in order (increasing or decreasing, it makes no difference) before you find the median.

Find the median of -3, 18, -4, $\frac{1}{2}$, 11.

(A) -3

(B) 18

(C) -4

(D) $\frac{1}{2}$

(E) 11

Put the numbers in order: -4, -3, $\frac{1}{2}$, 11, 18. The one in the middle, $\frac{1}{2}$, is the median. It's as simple as that. *Correct Answer:* D.

Do not confuse median (middle) with mean. A mean is simply the average.

Mode

The *mode* is the most frequent number. I suggest you put the numbers in order again. Then look for the one that shows up the most often. It's the mode.

Find the mode of 11, 18, 29, 17, 18, –4, 0, 19, 0, 11, 18.

(A) 11

(B) 17

(C) 18

(D) 19

(E) 29

There are three 18s but no more than two of any other number. *Correct Answer:* C.

Range

The *range* is the distance from the greatest to the smallest. In other words, you take the biggest term and subtract the smallest term and that's the range.

Find the range of the numbers 11, 18, 29, 17, 18, –4, 0, 19, 0, 11, 18.

(A) 33

(B) 29

(C) 19

(D) 0

(E) –4

Ah, did this one getcha? True, 33 is not one of the numbers in the set. But to find the range, subtract the smallest from the largest number: $29 - -4 = 29 + 4 = 33$. *Correct Answer:* A.

The only trap you are likely to see in the statistics questions is in the answer choices. The questions themselves are quite straightforward, but the answer choices may assume that some people don't know one term from another. For example, one answer choice to a median question may be the mean (the average). One answer choice to a range question may be the mode. Mentally note the word in the question that tells you what you are looking for to keep from falling for this trap.

A Picture Is Worth a Thousand Words: Graphs

On the computer-based test, you may have one or two graphs. When you have a graph, all the questions following it are kept together. In other words, you won't have a graph with a question, then a question on something else, then a second graph question. Even the GRE isn't that vicious!) Four basic types of graphs show up frequently:

- **Circle or pie graph:** The circle represents 100 percent. The key to this graph is noting of what total the percentages are part. Below the graph you may be told that in 1994, 5,000 students graduated with Ph.D.s. If a 25-percent segment on the circle graph is labeled "Ph.D.s in history," you know to say that the number of history Ph.D.s is 25 percent of 5,000, or 1,250.

✔ **Two axes line graph:** A typical line graph has a bottom and a side axis. You plot a point or read a point from the two axes. This is probably the simplest type of graph you will encounter.

✔ **Three axes line graph:** This type of graph is rare. It has a left side axis, a bottom axis, and a right side axis. The left axis, for example, may represent the number of crates of a product while the right side axis represents the percentage that those crates are of the whole shipment. You read the points on the graph the same way as you read them on a two axes graph, simply paying special attention that you answer what the question is asking you. If the question asks you for the number of crates, read the left side. If the question asks you for the percentage of crates, read the right side.

✔ **Bar graph:** A bar graph has vertical or horizontal bars. The bars may represent actual numbers or percentages. If the bar goes all the way from one side of the graph to the other, it represents 100 percent.

Some questions use two graphs in one problem. The following is such an example.

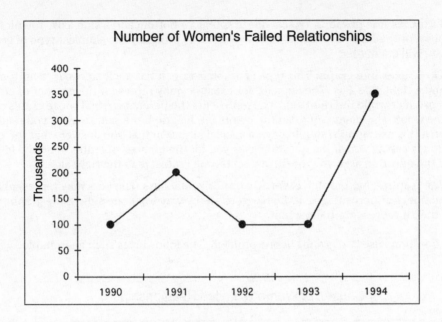

Two graphs here must be read in conjunction. The first graph is a bar graph going from 0 to 100 percent. Read the graph by *subtracting* to find the appropriate percentage. For example, in 1990, job conflict begins at 20 and goes to 50, a difference of 30 percent. You'd be falling for a trap were you to say that job conflicts were 50 percent. In 1993, His Mother (as a cause of failed relationships) goes from 80 to 100, or 20 percent.

The second graph gives you the actual number of failed relationships in thousands. Be sure to look at the labels of the axes. For example, in 1990, there were not 100 failed relationships but 100,000. Use the graphs together to find out the number of relationships caused to fail by a particular event or situation. For example, in 1991, there were 200,000 failed relationships. Also in 1991, age differences (from 70 to 80, or 10 percent) made up 10 percent. Multiply 10 percent or $.10 \times 200,000 = 20,000$ relationships.

Ready to try some practice questions? Usually, there are three to five questions below a graph. Answer the following two questions based on the two practice graphs.

How many relationships did women have from 1990 to 1994 inclusive?

(A) 850

(B) 8,500

(C) 85,000

(D) 850,000

(E) It cannot be determined from the information given.

Did I getcha? The title of the graph says it all: The Causes of Women's *Failed* Relationships. You have no way to determine how many relationships worked. *Correct answer:* E.

The number of women's relationships in 1994 that failed due to job conflicts was what percent greater than the number of women's relationships in 1992 that failed due to age differences?

(A) 700

(B) 600

(C) 500

(D) 120

(E) 7

In 1994, job conflicts accounted for 40 percent of women's failed relationships (from 20 to 60). Because there were 350,000 failed relationships in 1994, multiply $.40 \times 350,000 = 140,000$. In 1992, age differences accounted for 20 percent of women's failed relationships (60 to 80). In 1992, there were 100,000 failed relationships. Multiply $.20 \times 100,000 = 20,000$. *Correct answer:* B.

If you chose answer D, you simply subtracted the two amounts: $140,000 - 20,000 = 120,000$.

If you chose choice E, 7, or choice A, 700, you fell for the trap. Take the job conflicts number, 140,000, and put it over the age differences number — 20,000. $140,000 \div 20,000 = 7$. The 7 translates to 700 percent. If you're confused why 7 is 700 percent, not 7 percent, or why 7 times is 600 percent greater than, go back to the percentages section of the math review.

Part IV
Your Number's Up: Math Questions

The 5th Wave — By Rich Tennant

BASEBALL TRAPEZOID

STEALING 2ND
$A = \frac{1}{2}(b_1 + b_2) \times h$

"For the next month, instead of practicing on a baseball diamond, we'll be practicing on a baseball trapezoid. At least until everyone passes the geometry section of the GRE test."

In this part . . .

There are two types of people in the world: those who never met an equation they didn't like . . . and those who wish they had never met an equation at all. The following math chapters and practice questions can be a lot of fun.

In these chapters, you learn all sorts of good tricks. Sure, I also sneak in some Real Math (stuff such as formulas and rules), but I really focus on the tricks and traps you're likely to see on the GRE, including tips for sidestepping them. But please note: The GRE math has no relation to the Real World. Just review it, ace the math sections, and be done with it.

The math section features two types of problems: Quantitative Comparisons and Problem Solving questions. You get the unexpected pleasure of using your brain, your whole brain, and nothing but your brain to solve these problems. In other words, you can't use a calculator. You may not bring in your own calculator, and the computer you will be using won't have any calculator functions available to you. You will be given some scratch paper (you may not bring in your own; scratch paper will be provided for you) that you can use to jot down calculations . . . or to gnaw on and rip up if you get totally frustrated!

Note: When you take this exam on the computer, you'll see the two types of math questions interspersed. For example, you may see one Quantitative Comparisons question, then two Problem Solving questions, then another Quantitative Comparisons question, and so on. The directions for each type are available on-screen to you at any time. In these printed materials, all the questions of one type are grouped together, so that you don't have to keep flipping back and forth to the directions.

Chapter 13

The Incomparable Quantitative Comparisons

A riddle for you: What do quicksand and quantitative comparisons have in common?

Answer: They both can suck you in and pull you down before you realize what's happening.

Quantitative comparisons (QCs) consist of 14 or so questions, but a zillion or more traps. The QCs rarely require power math; they require paranoia (to recognize the traps) and finesse (to avoid the traps). Hmmm, "Paranoia & Finesse." Sounds like a firm of attorneys, doesn't it?

Where Did All the Answers Go? The QC Format

A QC question lists a quantity in Column A and another quantity in Column B. The quantities can be numbers, variables, equations, words, figures, compromising photos of you at the last fraternity party — anything. Your job is to compare the quantity in Column A to the quantity in Column B. (Hence the title, "Quantitative Comparisons." I bet some rocket scientist got big bucks for thinking this one up!)

No answer choices are given below the quantities in QC questions. You are to compare the quantities and

▸ Choose A if the quantity in Column A is greater than the quantity in Column B.

▸ Choose B if the quantity in Column B is greater than the quantity in Column A.

▸ Choose C if the quantity in Column A is equal to the quantity in Column B.

▸ Choose D if not enough information is provided for you to determine the relationship between the quantities.

Got all that? Just choose A if A is bigger, B if B is bigger, C if they're the same (with C standing for *Same,* if you spell as badly as I do), and D if you can't tell (as in D for *duuuuuh!*).

As Easy as π: Approaching QC Questions

The hardest part of a QC question is knowing where to begin. You can save considerable time — and frustration — if you develop good habits now that carry over to the exam later. Follow this simple three-step approach:

1. **Solve for the quantity in Column A.** You may solve an equation, talk through a word problem, or do nothing but look at what's given. Here are some examples of what you may see in Column A.

   Column A

   $$x^2$$

   40% of 340

   The number of miles hiked by Ken, who kikes at 3mph for $6\frac{1}{2}$ hours

2. **Solve for the quantity in Column B.** Again, this can mean solving an equation, talking through a word problem, or just looking at the column. Here are some examples:

   Column B

   $$x^3$$

   40% of 340

   18

3. **Compare the two columns.**

   Sounds simple enough, right? Wait until you see some of the traps that they can build into the QCs.

Gotchas and Other Groaners: Tips, Traps, and Tricks

QCs have so many tricks and traps that I give you a separate section for each one, with a few examples to illustrate how easily you can fall for the traps.

As unbalanced as the rest of us

If the columns look equal, it's a trap. If two columns appear at first glance to be equal, a trap is almost always involved. Suppose that you see this question:

Column A	_Column B_
π	3.14

Your gut reaction may be to choose C because they are equal. At school, you've had 3.14 drilled into your head as π. (If you've been out of school for quite a while, you may be very pleased with yourself for remembering that. Put the self-congratulations on hold; you've just fallen for a trap.) But π is only *approximately* 3.14; it is actually larger. The correct answer to this problem is A. For convenience, π is rounded to two decimal places: 3.14. Actually, however, π continues as a nonrepeating, nonterminating decimal: 3.141592. . . . *Correct Answer:* A.

Column A	_Column B_
$.0062 \times 3600$	$6200 \times .3600$

Again, you probably checked that the number of digits and decimal places is the same and chose C. But the answer is B. When you multiply them out, Column A equals 22.32 and Column B equals 2,232. *Big* difference. The moral of the story: If your first reaction is that the problem is a no-brainer — that the answer is obviously, clearly, undoubtedly C — slap yourself upside the head and work through the problem. *Correct Answer:* B.

No scale, no sale

If a figure is not drawn to scale, the answer is often choice D. A problem may show a figure. Underneath the picture may appear the words: "***Note:*** Figure not drawn to scale." This message should be a warning buzzer, alerting you to the presence of a built-in trap. If a figure is not drawn to scale, you can't rely on it. Because you can't just eyeball it to figure things out, you need solid information such as the lengths of lines or the measures of angles. If that information is not provided, you often can't determine the relationship between the columns and must choose D.

Column A   _Column B_

Note: Figure not drawn to scale.

Column A	_Column B_
x	y

Sure, x and y each appear to be 45 degrees. Go ahead and choose C. You'll blow the GRE, never get into grad school, and end up walking some rich woman's poodles for a living, lamenting, "If only I had noticed that the figure was not drawn to scale!"

Because the figure is not drawn to scale, you can't use it to estimate. You can't look at the figure and deduce that x and y are equal. Yes, x and y add up to 90 degrees. That's because angles along a straight line add up to 180 degrees, and you already have a right angle: $180 - 90 = 90$. But you *don't* know how much of the 90 is x and how much is y. Are they 45 and 45? 60 and 30? 89 and 1? The figure is not to scale, so any of those values may be correct. Because you don't have enough information to compare the quantities, choice D is the right answer. *Correct Answer:* D.

<u>*Column A*</u>   <u>*Column B*</u>

Note: Figure not drawn to scale.

2x	y

If you fell for this one, you can kiss your 800 good-bye. This is a classic D. Yes, yes, the figure appears to be an isosceles right triangle. You know that the two x's are equal and that the angles in a triangle add up to 180 degrees. But no one said that angle y is 90 degrees. What's that you say? It *looks* like 90 degrees? Tooooo bad. You can't look at the figure if it's not drawn to scale. As far as you know, angle y may be 89 degrees or 91 degrees or all sorts of other possibilities. Maybe $x = 40$, so $2x = 80$ and $y = 100$. Maybe $x = 60$, so $2x = 120$ and $y = 60$. What? That can't be, because it's obvious that this is not an equilateral triangle with all angles equal? Nothing is obvious; you can't use the figure if it's not drawn to scale. Because anything is possible, choose D. *Correct Answer:* D.

"Not drawn to scale" problems have fallen out of favor with the GRE lately. In my opinion, these problems were just too easy for students to get right, so the GRE naturally took them off the test. Don't be surprised if you don't see a "not drawn to scale" problem — but be prepared just in case you do. (You will definitely see some on the practice exams. I want you to be prepared for every possibility.)

Win, lose, or draw

If the answer *depends on* how you draw the figure, choose D. Approximately one third of GRE math is geometry. Many of the QC geometry problems are word problems that give no figures or diagrams. These questions often demand that you draw the figure yourself. In that case, the answer may depend on how you draw the figure.

<u>*Column A*</u>   <u>*Column B*</u>

Area of a decagon	Area of a pentagon

The trap answer is A. True, a decagon has ten sides and a pentagon has five sides, and true, $10 > 5$, even in new math. The correct answer, however, depends on how you draw the figures: and how long each side is. For example, I can draw the shapes three different ways:

If everything *deeeeee*-pends on the *deeeeee*-rawing, choose D. *Correct Answer:* D.

<u>**Column A**</u>   <u>**Column B**</u>

A skating rink is 5 miles from a yogurt shop
and 6 miles from a restaurant.

| Distance from the yogurt shop to the restaurant | 1 mile |

Did you fall for the trap answer, C? Two tips come into play here:

- ✔ **If the columns look equal, it's a trap.**
- ✔ **If the answer depends on how you draw the figure, choose D.**

Here are a couple ways of drawing the figure:

Picture perfect

If a picture is drawn, the answer is rarely D. This is the flip side of the preceding tip. The GRE is rather wishy-washy about figures. The directions say something like this: "Questions have figures that are drawn as accurately as possible, but you should use mathematics, not estimation or measurement based on the figure, to answer the questions." Huh? What does all that mean? It means that the figures really are pretty much drawn to scale, but that the GRE doesn't want you just looking at a figure to get the answer; the GRE wants you to calculate and do things the hard, "official" way. My advice is this: Don't worry about scale. As far as you're concerned, the figures are to scale unless a note specifically says otherwise. Your measurements would have to be incredibly precise for the lack of exact scale to mess you up. The answer, therefore, is rarely D when a figure is given.

Keep in mind that these are just tips, not rules. That means that they work most of the time, but not always. (I have seen, for example, some questions with figures that were unsolvable, requiring a D answer.) Never shut off your own brain in favor of a tip. The purpose of a tip is just to make you think twice before falling for a trap.

<u>Column A</u>   <u>Column B</u>

$a+b$	$d+e$

Angle a is a vertical angle to angle d, meaning that they are opposite and of equal measure. Angle b is a vertical angle to angle e, meaning that they are opposite and of equal measure. Because each part of Column A is equal to its counterpart in Column B, both columns are equal. *Correct Answer:* C.

At first glance, you may be tempted to choose D for this problem because no numbers are given. It's true that you cannot solve for the exact measure of $a+b$ or the exact measure of $d+e$, but the question doesn't expect you to do so. This section is not about problem solving; it's quantitative comparisons — all you need to do is compare the quantities. You can compare them here (and see that they are equal), so D is wrong.

<u>Column A</u>   <u>Column B</u>

Number of square units in area of the triangle	100

Fight the temptation to choose D automatically just because you don't have numbers for the lengths of the sides of the triangle. You know that the figure is drawn to scale; you can probably compare the quantities.

The formula for the area of a triangle is $\frac{1}{2}\,base \times height$. What is the base? You don't know, but you *do* know that it is less than the base of the rectangle because the sides of the triangle don't extend all the way to the sides of the rectangle. Just call it *less than 20*. How much is the height? You don't know, but you *do* know that it is less than 10 because the top and bottom of the triangle don't touch the top and bottom of the rectangle. Call it *less than 10*. Multiply *less than* 10 × *less than* 20 = *less than 200*. Half of *less than 200* is *less than 100*. Because *less than 100* is smaller than 100, choose B. *Correct Answer:* B.

Been there, done that

Cancel quantities that are identical in both columns. Think of it as clearing the decks or simplifying the picture. A QC problem is like a scale — a balance. If something is the same on one side as on the other, it doesn't affect the balance — you can ignore it. Be careful that you cancel only *identical* things; -5 does not cancel 5, for example.

Column A	*Column B*
$x^2 - 21$	$x^2 - 35$

Cancel the x^2 in both columns. Copy the problem on your scratch paper, just so you can have the joy of scratching out the identical quantities. That leaves you with -21 and -35. Caution! Remember that a *negative* 21 is greater than a *negative* 35. *Correct Answer:* A.

Column A	*Column B*
$a > b > c > 2$	
$(a+b)^2$	$(a-b)^2$

You can't cancel out the a and b on both sides and say that the columns are equal. $(a+b)^2$ is *not* the same as $(a-b)^2$. You should memorize these two expressions (they are discussed in detail in Chapters 10–12):

$$(a+b)^2 = a^2 + 2ab + b^2 \qquad\qquad (a-b)^2 = a^2 - 2ab + b^2$$

Now you can cancel identical terms: slash off the a^2 and the b^2 from both columns. You are left with $+2ab$ in Column A and $-2ab$ in Column B. Because both a and b are greater than 2, you don't need to worry about negatives or fractions. *Correct Answer:* A.

In the preceding problem, you don't need to do any pencil-pushing if you reason the answer out. Because a is greater than b and both a and b are positive numbers (greater than 2), you know that the sum $(a+b)$ must be greater than the sum $(a-b)$. Squaring a larger (positive) number gives you more than squaring a smaller number. You can deduce that Column A is bigger without doing any paperwork.

Six of one, a half dozen of the other

Compare each part of Column A to its counterpart in Column B. Again, think of QCs as a scale. If both parts of Column A are greater, or "heavier," than both parts of Column B, A is greater.

Column A	*Column B*
$\dfrac{17}{21} + \dfrac{47}{80}$	$\dfrac{19}{81} + \dfrac{23}{97}$

Don't even *think* about reaching for your pencil to work this problem through. Compare each part of Column A to its counterpart in Column B. Which is greater: $^{17}/_{21}$ or $^{19}/_{81}$? Reason that 17 is more than half of 21, whereas 19 is much less than half of 81. The same is true for the second pair of numbers. You know that 47 is more than half of 80; 23 is less than half of 97. Because both parts of Column A are greater than both parts of Column B, A is the answer. No muss, no fuss. *Correct Answer:* A.

Of course, some spoilsport always wants to know what happens if one part of Column A is greater than its counterpart in Column B, but the other part of Column A is less than its counterpart in Column B. Doesn't happen. Why? It ruins the trick that the test makers want you to recognize and use — you'd miss the entire point of the question. The question would reach back to a basic arithmetic, pull-out-your-pencil problem. If lightning strikes and that problem does arise, well, you have no choice but to lift a finger. *Which* finger you lift is up to you.

Keep plugging away

When plugging in numbers, use 1, 2, 0, –1, –2, ½ — in that order. This is the best tip you're likely to get outside a racetrack. Whenever you have variables, *plug in numbers*. Instead of randomly choosing any old numbers, plug in these Sacred Six: 1, 2, 0, –1, –2, ½. You should memorize these numbers and throw them into a problem whenever possible. These numbers cover most of the contingencies: positive, negative, zero, odd, even, fraction, and 1, which has special properties.

Column A	Column B
x^2	x^4

The *trap* answer is B. Everyone says that, *of course,* something to the fourth power is greater than the same number squared. (A variable must have the same value in Column A as in Column B *within any one problem.* That is, if x is 5 in Column A, it is also 5 in Column B. Always. No exceptions. A rose is a rose is a rose.)

Ah, but whenever you hear yourself saying *"of course,"* you know that you're headed for a trap. Play the *what if* game: What if $x = 1$? Then the two columns are alike, and answer C prevails. What $x = 2$? Then Column $A = 4$ and Column $B = 16$, and the answer is B. Therefore, the answer can be A or it can be B, depending on what you plug in. If an answer *depends* on what you plug in, choose D. *Correct Answer:* D.

Notice that you didn't have to go through all the Sacred Six numbers. As soon as you find that you get two different answers, you can stop. If plugging in 1 and 2 gives you the same answer, you should go on to 0, –1, –2, and ½, plugging in as many as necessary. You'll be pleasantly surprised, however, to find out how often 1 and 2 alone get the job done.

Column A	Column B
$^1/_x$	$^x/_1$

The *trap* answer is B. Most people think that Column A comes out to be a fraction of less than 1. It may . . . or it may not. And who's to say that x is more than 1 in the first place? Play the *what if* game again.

What if $x = 1$? Then the columns are equal, and choice C is correct. What if $x = 2$? Then Column B is greater. It depends on what you plug in, so choose D. *Correct Answer:* D.

On the real exam, you would stop here, but for now, plug in a few more numbers to see what else can happen. You can't plug in 0 because the problem tells you that x is not equal to 0 (division by 0 is undefined). What if $x = -1$? Then Column A is -1 and Column B is -1; they're equal. What if $x = -2$? Then Column A $= -\frac{1}{2}$, Column B $= -2$; now A is bigger. You've seen all the possibilities at this point: A can be bigger, B can be bigger, or the two columns can be the same. I haven't even gotten into fractions yet. And if it's all the same to you, I won't.

Looking like a hundred bucks

Plug in 100 for dollars and percentages. This is an exception to plugging in the Sacred Six $(1, 2, 0, -1, -2\frac{1}{2})$. If a question deals with dollars or percentages, plug in 100 to make it a nice round number. I'm all for an easy life here.

Column A	Column B

A book bag costs x dollars.

Cost of the book bag on sale at 60% off	$.6x$

If you make the book bag cost $100, you can easily determine that 60 percent of 100 is 60; subtract $100 - 60$ and you get 40. In Column B, $.6(100) = 60$. The answer is B. This type of problem is easy to miss because of carelessness. Many people choose C automatically. Of course, you know by now that *if the columns look equal, it's probably a trap.* You should slow down, plug in 100, and work out the problem. *Correct Answer:* B.

Column A	Column B

One year's interest on x dollars at 6% annual interest	$12

Gotcha! I threw this one in to remind you once again that these are *tips,* not rules, and that you should never sacrifice common sense in favor of tips. Sure, if you plug in 100 for x dollars, you know that the interest is $6 and B is the answer. But what if $x = \$1,000,000$? Then Column A is significantly larger. Here, the correct answer *de*pends on which value you plug in for x. Although 100 often works, it is not infallible. Think! *Correct Answer:* D.

Get outta that rut

Plug in consecutive terms first and then nonconsecutive terms. If you need to plug in numbers for two or three variables, first plug in the numbers all in a row: 1, 2, and 3. Then try it again, plugging in numbers that are not in a row: 1, 5, and 7. Sometimes the spacing between the numbers makes a difference.

When pigs fly . . .

Question: Can you ever plug in all the Sacred Six and still fall for the trap?

Answer: Yeah, you can (although it's unlikely). Here's an example:

Column A	Column B
$\frac{1}{x}$	3

Now you play the *what if* game. What if $x = 1$? Then Column B is larger. What if $x = 2$? Then Column B is larger. Because x is not equal to 0 (division by 0 is undefined), you skip to the next number in the Sacred Six. What if $x = -1$? Column B is still larger. What if $x = -2$? Yes, yes, Column B is still larger. Finally, what if $x = \frac{1}{2}$

$x = \frac{1}{2}$? Then Column $A = 2$ (to divide by a fraction, invert and multiply) and Column B is still larger. Now, 99 percent of the Thinking World would choose B at this point and feel very confident. And 99 percent of the Thinking World would go straight down the tubes. The answer, in fact, is **D**. What if $x = \frac{1}{3}$? Then Column $A = 3$, and the two columns are equal — choice C. If the answer could be B and could also be C, the answer *de*pends and therefore is choice D.

A problem in which the Sacred Six don't do the job for you is incredibly rare, but it could happen. Sorry about that. This is a *tip*, not a rule. It's not perfect. Close, though. . . .

<u>**Column A**</u>	<u>**Column B**</u>
$a < b < c$	
$\dfrac{a+c}{2}$	b

The normal response is to plug in consecutive numbers: 1, 2, and 3. If you do that, Column A is $1 + 3$, or 4, divided by $2 = 2$. In Column B, b is 2. The columns are equal. *Uh-oh!* You know by now that *if the columns look equal, it's often a trap* and you should double-check your work.

Plug in some nonconsecutive numbers: 1, 5, and 7. Now Column A is $1 + 7 = 8$, divided by $2 = 4$. In Column B, b is 5. Now the answer is B. If the answer *de*pends on which values you plug in for the variables, choose D. *Correct Answer:* D.

<u>**Column A**</u>	<u>**Column B**</u>
$y + z$	x

The *trap* answer is C. The right answer is D because the answer *de*pends on which numbers you plug in. If you plug in 3, 2, and 1, $y + z = 2 + 1 = 3$. Because $x = 3$, the columns are equal. But plug in nonconsecutive numbers: 100, 2, and 1. Now $y + z = 2 + 1 = 3$. But $x = 100$; Column B is larger. The answer can be C or B — it *de*pends on what you plug in. Choose D. *Correct Answer:* D.

Familiarity Breeds Content (ment): A Review

Before going on to the sample questions in the following chapter, review the approach and the tricks described here.

Approach

1. Solve for the quantity in Column A.

2. Solve for the quantity in Column B.

3. Compare the two quantities.

4. Choose A if the quantity in Column A is greater than the quantity in Column B.

   Choose B if the quantity in Column B is greater than the quantity in Column A.

   Choose C if the quantity in Column A is equal to the quantity in Column B.

   Choose D if you don't have enough information to determine the relationship between the quantities.

Tricks

✔ If the columns look equal, the question is usually a trap.

✔ If a figure is not drawn to scale, the answer is often choice D.

✔ If the answer *de*pends on how you draw the figure, choose D.

✔ If a picture is drawn to scale, the answer rarely is D.

✔ Cancel quantities that are identical in both columns.

✔ Compare each part of Column A to its counterpart in Column B.

✔ When plugging in numbers, use 1, 2, 0, −1, −2, and ½ in that order.

✔ Plug in 100 for dollars and percentages.

✔ Plug in consecutive terms first and then nonconsecutive terms.

Chapter 14

Putting It All Together: QC Practice Questions

• •

*I*f you're waiting until someone makes a movie of this stuff, forget it. You're outta luck. The information on quantitative comparisons in the preceding chapter is all she wrote (so to speak). If you didn't read it carefully, please go back and do so now — before you humiliate yourself on this practice exam.

All done? Good. Now, check your ego at the door or it may get trashed on this exam. I've written a dozen problems that incorporate the meanest, the cruelest, the stupidest traps you're likely to see on the real GRE. How many are *you* going to fall for?

The answer choices are

A if the quantity in Column A is greater.

B if the quantity in Column B is greater.

C if the two quantities are equal.

D if the relationship cannot be determined from the information given.

<u>Column A</u>	<u>Column B</u>

1.

$$10\left[(4\times 3)^2 + 5^0\right]$$

1,440

This question tests two concepts: order of operations and the zero exponent. Always do what is inside of the parentheses first: $4 \times 3 = 12$. $12^2 = 144$. Then do what's inside the brackets. $5^0 = 1$. Any number to the zero power equals one. Add: $144 + 1 = 145$. Then multiply by what's outside the brackets: $10 \times 145 = 1,450$. *Correct Answer:* A.

If you chose C, you thought that 5^0 was zero, giving you $144 + 0 = 144$; $144 \times 10 = 1,440$. Look out for the zero exponent; it is often in tricky questions. Also, double-check all your C answers. I've found more traps in which people choose C than all the other traps combined.

<u>Column A</u>	<u>Column B</u>

A cubic box has a total surface area of 600 square units.

2.

Number of cubic units in the volume of the box	1,000

The total surface area of a cube is the sum of the areas of all surfaces. A cube has six surfaces: $600 \div 6 = 100$. Each surface of the cube, which is a square, has an area of 100. That means each edge is 10, because the area of a square is *side* $\times$ *side*. The volume of a cube is *edge*^{3}. $10 \times 10 \times 10 = 1,000$. *Correct Answer:* C.

Many of the geometry problems ask you to go forwards and backwards. You're given a volume and asked to find a total surface area, or vice versa. You may be given a circumference and asked to find a sector, or vice versa. Be comfortable enough with the geometry formulas to work problems inside out, upside down, and any which way. If you don't know how to find a volume and a total surface area, return to the thrilling pages of Chapter 10.

Column A	_Column B_
3. $\sqrt{66+85}$	12

First add the numbers under the square root sign. $66 + 85 = 151$. Then take the square root of that. Stop! Don't have a panic attack right here. No, you are not allowed to use a calculator. That's the bad news. The good news is that you don't have to. You don't have to get an exact answer for a QC problem; you just have to compare the quantities in the columns. Look for a perfect square close to 151. How about 144, which is 12^2, or 169, which is 13^2. Because 151 is between 144 and 169, the square of it must be between 12 and 13. You couldn't care less exactly how much it is. (Do not bother finding the exact square root!) As long as it's more than 12, Column A is larger. _Correct Answer:_ A.

Column A	_Column B_
4. $.10 \times 10 \times 100$	1

You needn't have withdrawal pains from your calculator. This problem is much easier than it looks. Multiply $.10 \times 10$ to get 1. You know that $1 \times 100 = 100$, which is certainly greater than 1. That's all you have to do. If you chose C, you got careless and were swayed by the hypnotic power of the columns. Don't let the C's mesmerize (hypnotize) you; double-check them any time you encounter them. _Correct Answer:_ A.

Column A	_Column B_

On a road trip, Kimberly drove 600 miles and used 45 gallons of gas.
Her friend Whitney drove half as far and used 30 gallons of gas.

Column A	_Column B_
5. Miles per gallon of Kimberly's car	Miles per gallon of Whitney's car

This is a basic arithmetic problem. To find the mileage, divide the number of miles driven by the gallons used. $600 \div 45$ compared to $300 \div 30$. _Correct Answer:_ A.

Before you begin making the pencil scratches, look at both columns. You'll be surprised how often you don't have to work through the actual arithmetic. You know that $300 \div 30$ is 10; you can do that in your head. Is $600 \div 45$ more than 10, equal to 10, or less than 10? It's more than 10, because $600 \div 60$ would be 10. Stop right there. You don't have to work the problem through to the bitter end; just compare the quantities. I want you to be able not only to get all the QC questions correct but also to get them correct quickly.

Column A	_Column B_
6. $18y + 18x$	$18y - 18x$

You didn't fall for the cheesy and *egregious* (heinous, truly terrible) trap built into this very simple question, did you? If so, please consider yourself totally humiliated. One tip you learned in the lecture was to cross off quantities that are identical in both columns. Cancel the $18y$. You are now left with $18x$ compared to $-18x$. Common sense tells you that $18x$ is greater. Common sense should take a flying leap. There's nothing common about the QC questions. Play the *what-if* game: What if $x = 1$? Then A is greater. What if $x = 2$? Then A is still greater. Ah, but what if $x = 0$? Then the columns are equal. If the answer *de*pends on what you plug in, choose D. *Correct Answer:* D.

The more variables you have, the greater the likelihood that the answer is D, because those variables could, well, vary. Whenever you plug in, use the Sacred Six you learned in Chapter 13. (If you skipped Chapter 13 and went right to the practice problems, you missed some good stuff. Here's your second chance.) Plug in 1, 2, 0, −1, −2, and ½, in that order. You won't usually have to plug them *all* in. As soon as you get two different possibilities, you know the answer *de*pends on what you plug in, and you choose D.

Column A	*Column B*
$ab = -40$	

7.

$(a+b)^2$	$(a-b)^2$

Did you memorize the expanded form of these two expressions $(a+b)^2 = a^2 + 2ab + b^2$? (If you don't know how I got that, go back to the discussion of FOIL methods in Chapter 11.) $(a-b)^2 = a^2 - 2ab + b^2$. Now use the trick also taught in Chapter 11: Cancel quantities that are identical in both columns. Slash off a^2 and b^2. You're left with $+2ab$, which would be -80, compared to $-2ab$, which would be $+80$ (because a negative times a negative is a positive). Correct Answer: B.

If you chose A, you got careless with your negative. Keeping the signs straight is one of the most important things you can do in any algebra problem. During the computer-based exam, write the problem on your scratch paper just to be sure of avoiding this type of careless mistake (easy to make when you're working a problem through in your mind).

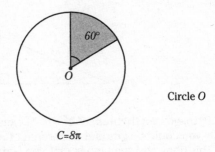

Circle O

$C = 8\pi$

Column A	*Column B*

8.

Area of the shaded region	3π

A shaded portion of a circle is called a sector. Its area is a fraction of the area of the circle. To find the area of a sector, first find the area of the circle. The formula for the area of a circle is $\pi \times radius^2$. You have to work backwards from the circumference to find the radius. The circumference of a circle is $2\pi \times radius$ $C = 8\pi$, so $2\pi r = 8\pi$, or $r = 4$. Area $= \pi r^2$ or 16π.

Next, you know that the degrees in a circle total 360. The shaded portion has a 60-degree angle, making it ⅙ (⁶⁰⁄₃₆₀) of the circle. Multiply the fraction by the area: ⅙ × 16π = ¹⁶⁄₆π or ⅝π, which is less than 3π. *Correct Answer:* B.

The geometry review section has a good discussion of everything to do with circles, including sectors. Circles, in my not-so-humble opinion, are among the easiest of the geometry problems to get correct. Consider these "gimmes."

Column A	*Column B*
9. $\frac{47}{299} + \frac{18}{101}$	$\frac{17}{31} + \frac{7}{13}$

Did you see the shortcut? Surely you know by now that you are not expected to do common denominators and go through all the garbage math. If it's a QC problem, there's usually a trick. Use my tip: *Compare each element of Column A to its counterpart in Column B.* That is, compare $\frac{47}{299}$ to $\frac{17}{31}$. Because 47 out of 299 is less than half, and 17 out of 31 is more than half, Column B is larger. Next, compare the remaining two quantities. Because 18 out of 101 is less than half and 7 out of 13 is more than half, Column B is larger here as well. Both parts of Column B are greater than both parts of Column A; B is greater. *Correct Answer:* B.

And for you people who insist on creating drama: No, the test makers will not, repeat, will *not* give you a problem of this sort in which one quantity is larger in Column A but the other quantity is larger in Column B. Doing so would defeat the point that this question is asking. Believe it or not, the test makers don't get a fiendish glee out of watching you do a lot of pencil pushing. They're trying to see whether you're smart enough to *avoid* doing the work.

Column A	*Column B*

Michelle and Mike begin walking and go 5 miles due north.
Their friend Devrae begins at the same point and goes 12 miles due west.

10. Shortest distance from Michelle to Devrae	13 miles

Did I trick you? True, usually when a geometry problem has no picture drawn, the answer is D. However, if you draw this picture, you see that you get a right triangle of sides 5 and 12.

You can use the Pythagorean theorem of $a^2 + b^2 = c^2$ and find that $5^2 + 12^2 = (25 + 144) = 169$; $169 = c^2$; $c = 13$. Or you could be grateful you weren't too *parsimonious* (cheap) to plunk the dough down for this book and remember that you learned in the math review one of the Pythagorean Triples, which is 5:12:13. That is, in a right triangle (which is true if one person goes due north and the other person goes due west) if one side is 5, and the other side is 12, the hypotenuse must be 13. You don't have to do the work at all. *Correct Answer:* C.

Did you have trouble figuring out the square root of 169? You should have memorized certain square roots and perfect squares, as given in the math review. If you didn't do so, you could, of course, always work backwards from the Column B quantity: $13 \times 13 = $ (son of a gun!) 169. Once again I say unto you: Don't panic, especially over square roots. In my experience, I've never seen a GRE question that depended on your being able to find an exact square root. I have seen a *plethora* (an abundance), indeed a *superfluity* (an excessive number) of problems that can be answered by knowing the basic Pythagorean Triples, which just happen to be given and explained in the math review.

Column A   **_Column B_**

11.

| The greatest prime factor of 1,210 | The greatest prime factor of 12,100 |

A prime factor is a prime number, a number that can be divided only by itself and 1. The prime numbers are 2, 3, 5, 7, 11, and so on. (Notice that 0 and 1 are not prime numbers.) To factor down a number ending in 0, divide by 10. For Column A, that gives you 121×10. You should have memorized your perfect squares and know that $121 = 11 \times 11$. For Column B, dividing by 10 gives you $1,210 \times 10$. Divide by 10 again to get $121 \times 10 \times 10$. Because 10 factors down into 2 and 5, the greatest prime factor of both columns is 11. *Correct Answer:* C.

Column A   **_Column B_**

$9x^2 - 4x = 69; \ 3x^2 - 10x = -3.$

12.

| $x^2 + x$ | 15 |

This is a straightforward algebra problem. Traps are rarely found in algebra problems; they usually are pretty basic. Here, write the two expressions vertically and either add or subtract to make the numerical coefficients (the numbers before the x^2 and the x) the same.

$$9x^2 - 4x = 69$$
$$3x^2 - 10x = -3$$

If you add, you get $12x^2 - 14x = 66$, not the same numerical coefficient. Because the numerical coefficients are not the same, no variable "drops out" or can be canceled. On to plan B. If adding the equations doesn't work, subtract the second equation, which means changing the signs on all the numbers.

$$9x^2 - 4x = 69$$
$$-3x^2 + 10x = 3$$

You get $6x^2 + 6x = 72$. Divide both sides through by 6 to get $x^2 + x = 12$. *Correct Answer:* B.

Chapter 15

Real Math at Last: Problem Solving

Problem Solving is a rather ritzy name for "regular" math problems. A Problem-Solving question, amazingly enough, actually expects you to solve a problem. This is different from the Quantitative Comparison questions (covered in Chapter 13), in which you often don't need to solve the problem through to the bitter end — you just compare the quantities. (Who thinks of these catchy names anyway? How much do they get paid, and where can I apply for the job?)

Strategic Planning: The Attack Strategy

Are you an Algebra Ace? Mathematics Master? Geometry Guru? Me neither. Isn't it lucky that you don't have to be any of those things to do well on the Problem-Solving questions? To improve your chances of acing the material, try to understand and apply the few strategies discussed here.

I realize that some of you who are reading this book haven't taken math classes in a long, long time. Maybe you are a senior in college and, because you tested out of your math while you were still in high school, never took any math at all in college. Maybe you're returning to school after spending several years off working or having a family or traveling or pursuing the idle and decadent lifestyle of the independently wealthy. Whatever the cause, you may be so rusty in math that your pencil creaks when you pick it up. I realize that you are not going to get every single math question correct; you should realize that you don't have to. The following suggestions help you to maximize your points with a minimum of time and bother.

1. **Read the problem through carefully and jot down on your scratch paper what the question is asking for.**

   People who are especially math-phobic miss this crucial point very often. It's easy to "predict" or "anticipate" what the question is asking for and not take note of what it really wants. Your goal is to give 'em what they want. If the question asks for a circumference, circle or jot down the word *circumference* and don't solve for an area. If the question wants you to find the number of hours already worked rather than the total number of hours a job would take, be sure that you supply that figure.

   Of course, of course, *of course,* the answer choices feature trap answers; this goes without saying on the GRE. If you find the area of a figure, it will be a trap answer to a question that wants the perimeter. Just because the answer you got is staring you in the face does not mean that it is the correct answer. It might be . . . or it might be a trap. Before you press the CONFIRM button on your computer, go back and look at the information: Are you answering the right question?

2. **Preview the answer choices; look to see how precise your answer has to be and how careful you have to be on the decimal points.**

   If the answer choices are 4, 5, 6, 7, and 8, you probably have to solve the problem to the bitter end, calculating rather than estimating. This type of problem may take a long time. However, if the answer choices are .05, .5, 5, 50, and 500, you know that the digit is definitely going to be a 5 and that you have to keep your decimal point straight. You may be able to use common sense on that problem and estimate the answer without working it out.

3. **Solve the problem forwards and backwards.**

   Work out the problem and get an answer; then plug that answer back into the problem to make sure that it makes sense. If you found the average of 4, 6, 7, 9, and 10 to be 36, you can look at the answer and reason that you made a mistake somewhere because the average can't be bigger than the biggest number. (Did you see the mistake? If you got 36, you found the sum of the terms but forgot to divide by the number of terms. "Interim" answers of this sort are common trap answer choices on the GRE.)

Four Commonsense Suggestions

 The Problem-Solving questions are much more straightforward than the Quantitative Comparison (QC) problems presented in Chapter 13. There aren't as many tricks or traps, but you can learn a few good, fairly commonsense techniques that can speed up your work or help you avoid careless mistakes.

Eliminate illogical (dumb) answer choices

You know how some teachers always reassure students by saying, "Oh, there's no such thing as a dumb question or answer; just try!" Wrong. There *are* such things as dumb answers. If you're asked for the temperature of a liquid and one of the answer choices is –200° Fahrenheit, it's unlikely that a liquid would be that cold; it would freeze and no longer be a liquid! If you're asked for the age of a person and one answer is 217, I'd like to know what kind of vitamins that person has been taking! When you preview the answers, dump the ones that seem to make no sense.

Don't choose a "close enough" answer

Suppose that you do a ton of calculations and get the answer 36. One of the answer choices is 38. Don't shrug and say, "Ahh, close enough; I must have made a mistake somewhere." You sure did, and you're about to make a second mistake by being lazy and choosing an answer that's close. *Remember:* Close counts only in horseshoes (which you may want to bring to the exam for luck, come to think of it) and hand grenades (which may be what you feel has hit you when you see some of these math questions!).

Don't let me scare you *too* much about the math. The GRE does not, repeat does *not,* test trigonometry or calculus. It tests basic arithmetic, algebra, and geometry. Even if you haven't had those subjects in years, you can cover enough in a quick math review to do well. As a private tutor, I recently worked with a student in her 60s who wanted to go back to graduate school after her husband passed away. She had never taken geometry in her life because the subject wasn't required when she applied to college 40 years ago. She memorized formulas, went through some sample problems, kept an eye open for tricks, and did just as well as anyone else.

Give your pencil a workout

During the computer-based test, you are given scratch paper — you can't use your own; the proctor supplies it and will give you as much as you want, a few sheets at a time — and you can scribble to your heart's content. As you'll see when you go through the sample questions and practice exam, writing down formulas and plugging numbers into them or drawing pictures and putting numbers on the pictures is an excellent means of avoiding careless errors and clarifying and organizing thoughts. Don't think you're wasting time by using your pencil; you may actually be saving time by avoiding confusion.

I'm Sure I Know You from Somewhere: A Quick Review

Before going on to the sample questions, let's review the approach and the tricks.

Approach

Although a Problem-Solving question is a basic multiple-choice math question similar to what you've done on exams all your life, using these commonsense suggestions can help you to answer the questions more quickly and with fewer errors.

1. **Read the problem through carefully and circle or jot down what the question is asking for.**
2. **Preview the answer choices.**
3. **Solve the problem forwards and backwards (plugging in the multiple-choice answers).**

Tricks

The test-makers know all the traps students can fall for and delight in building those traps into the questions. Just because the answer you got is one of the answer choices in front of you does not mean that your answer is correct. Keep the following tricks in mind as you go through the Problem-Solving questions:

- Eliminate illogical (dumb) answer choices.
- Don't choose a "close enough" answer.
- Plug in numbers, write down formulas, and draw pictures. Give your pencil a workout.

Chapter 16

A Chance to Show Off: Problem-Solving Practice Questions

● ●

*S*o you think that you understand everything from the lecture? Prove it! I'm calling your bluff. Let's see you ace these practice questions.

1. At a park, the ratio of softball players to volleyball players is 3:4. If the total number of softball and volleyball players is 63, how many more volleyball players than softball players are in the park?

   (A) 3

   (B) 4

   (C) 6

   (D) 9

   (E) 12

The total of a ratio is a multiple of the sum of the numbers in that ratio. In simple English that means you add the numbers in the ratio: $3 + 4 = 7$. Think of 7 as the number of athletes in one clique or one batch. In 63, there are 9 cliques or batches, because $^{63}/_7 = 9$. If there are 9 batches of 3 softball players, that's 27. If there are 9 batches of 4 volleyball players, that's 36. $36 - 27 = 9$. *Correct Answer:* D.

Ratios should be among the easiest of questions to answer correctly. The math review has a very easy explanation of how to get through these problems without even lifting your pencil.

2. What is the length of side *x* in the figure above?

   (A) 48

   (B) 40

   (C) 35

   (D) 32

   (E) 30

Because the longest side of any right triangle is always the hypotenuse (the side opposite the right or 90-degree angle), you know that answers less than or equal to 32 are wrong. Eliminate choices D and E.

You could of course do this problem the long and boring way, using the Pythagorean theorem to find that $a^2 + b^2 = c^2$. That means you have to square 24, square 32, and then find the square root of whatever humongous number results. (Don't ask me what it is; I'm not about to do all that hard work.) At this stage, you should be reminding yourself that there should be an easier way. And there is.

Right triangles have their sides in specific proportions or ratios, called the Triples. If you haven't learned these yet, go back to Chapter 10 and do so right now. You'll save yourself a lot of work (and points) if you memorize some special triples. The one that works here is the most common on the test: 3:4:5. Each side is a multiple of those terms. The first side is 3×8, or 24. The next side is 4×8, or 32. That means the last side must be 5×8, or 40. Brain overload avoided. *Correct Answer:* B.

3. Given a regular hexagon of side 5, what is the sum of the interior angles?

   (A) 900

   (B) 720

   (C) 540

   (D) 360

   (E) 180

The term *regular* just means that all sides and all angles are equal. For example, an equilateral triangle and a square are regular figures. The interior angles of a figure are found with the formula $(n-2)$ 180 degrees, where n stands for the number of sides of the figure. Because a hexagon has six sides (think of the x in *six* and the x in *hex* to help you to remember this), your formula is $(6-2)180 = (4 \times 180) = 720$. *Correct Answer:* B.

If you chose C, you fell for the trap. You let the 5, which is the *length* of the side, be the number of sides. The two numbers are totally different: six sides, each measuring 5 units. Only the number of sides is important here.

Chapter 10 provides a very good analysis of how to find the interior (and exterior) angles of any figure. Because geometry problems are the easiest to get right once you've learned formulas, I suggest that you spend the majority of your study time working on geometry if you have only a limited time to work on this material.

4.

> $\textcircled{x} = x^2$ if x is prime.
> $\textcircled{x} = (x+1)^2$ if x is composite.

Solve for $\textcircled{3} + \textcircled{4}$.

   (A) 41

   (B) 34

   (C) 25

   (D) 23

   (E) 7

This is a symbolism problem. Talk your way through it, substituting the number in the circle for the x in the directions. First, you have $\textcircled{3}$. Because 3 is a prime number (a prime number has no positive integer factors other than one and itself), you use the first line of the directions. Square 3 to get 9. Next you have a $\textcircled{4}$. Because 4 is composite (it has factors other than just one and itself), you use the second line of directions. Add 1 to the 4 first and then square the sum. $1+4=5$; $5^2 = 25$. Now add the two answers: $9+25=34$. *Correct Answer:* B.

Did you fall for one of the trap answers? If you added 1 to both terms and squared them, you got choice A. If you didn't add 1 to either term but squared them alone, you got choice C. I want you to avoid a false sense of security. The mere fact that the answer you got is among the answer choices doesn't mean it's the correct answer (although if it's not there, it's definitely the wrong answer).

5. Given that $a \neq 0$, solve for $\dfrac{a^2 a a^3}{a^4}$.

   (A) $a^{3/2}$

   (B) a^1

   (C) a^2

   (D) a^3

   (E) a^9

This is a relatively simple problem, once you know how to work with bases and exponents. When you multiply like bases, you add the exponents. Keeping in mind that a by itself is a^1, you get $a^{(2+1+3)} = a^6$. When dividing like bases, subtract the exponents like this $a^{(6-4)} = a^2$. The answer is not $a^{3/2}$; even the GRE wouldn't put an answer that nasty on the exam. Well, let me **renege** (take back) that statement. It would put an answer that nasty on the test; the answer just wouldn't be correct. *Correct Answer:* C.

If you chose B, you forgot that a is the same as a^1. You thought it was a^0 and added $a^{(2+0+3)} = a^5$. But any number to the zero power is 1, not that number itself.

Yes, you guessed it: There's an explanation in the math review of working with bases and exponents. It's to your advantage to go back and study it now.

6. $a - 3b + c = 15$; $6a - 2b + 6c = 23$. $b =$

   (A) $^{11}/_{5}$

   (B) 1

   (C) $^{15}/_{11}$

   (D) $^{-60}/_{11}$

   (E) $^{-67}/_{16}$

To find b, you have to make the a and c variables "drop out." That means you need to subtract one equation from the other until you are left only with b. Multiply the first equation by 6 so that you have $6a - 18b + 6c = 90$. Then subtract the second equation from that. It looks like this:

$$\begin{array}{r} 6a - 18b + 6c = 90 \\ -\quad 6a - 2b + 6c = 23 \\ \hline \end{array}$$

When you subtract, you change the signs on the second term. That means you have $6a - 6a$; the a's drop out. You have $-18b + 2b = -16b$. You have $6c - 6c$; the c's drop out. All you have now is $-16b = 67$. Divide both sides through by the -16: $b = ^{-67}/_{16}$. *Correct Answer:* E.

Part V
Getting into Analysis: Analytical Ability

The 5th Wave   By Rich Tennant

THOUGH HIS "CALL" TO THE SCHOOL NEVER WENT THROUGH, GARY WAS PLEASED TO LATER FIND THAT AN ANALYTICAL ABILITY SCORE WASN'T REQUIRED AS PART OF THEIR ADMISSION REQUIREMENTS.

©RICHTENNANT

Hmm—still no dial tone.

In this part . . .

The Analytical Ability section torments you with two types of questions: Analytical Reasoning (sometimes called logic games) and Logical Reasoning. In these chapters, you get to play mind games, using logic to make diagrams, identify assumptions, and analyze evidence — fun stuff.

Before you go through these sections, check that the schools you're applying to use the Analytical Ability score — many don't. Sweating through stuff that may not even count would be the biggest mind game of all!

Chapter 17

A Section Only Mr. Spock Could Love: Analytical Ability

. . . .

▶ Distinguishing Analytical Reasoning (logic games) from Logical Reasoning (critical thinking) questions

▶ Recognizing and diagramming the four main types of logic games

▶ Finding shortcuts for long and confusing logic passages

. . . .

No, Analytical Ability is not what a potential proctologist must display. Analytical Ability is the reasoning and logic portion of the GRE. Your Analytical Ability score is the third score you'll see on your score report: Verbal, Math, Analytical. Like the Verbal and Math scores, it ranges from 200 to 800.

Many schools do *not* look at the Analytical Ability scores. Let me repeat that statement, as this information may be critical to your study program: *Many schools do not care about your Analytical Ability scores.* Before you go through this section, before you read any further, read the university bulletins or call the admissions offices of the graduate schools to which you're applying and find out whether the Analytical Ability scores are important to your admission chances. If they are not, congratulations! You don't have to suffer through the rest of this chapter (but I do recommend making some effort on test day. The graduate programs to which you are applying may wonder what kind of person you are if you have good Verbal and Math scores and only a 200 Analytical score.) However, one warning: Don't simply talk to the receptionist in the admissions office and take his or her word for it that the Analytical Ability scores do not count. Get that policy in writing.

For those of you who are still tuned in, welcome to the most bizarre section of the GRE. Analytical Ability is not something tested in everyday life. French doesn't require you to make diagrams or charts of the relationships between things; World History 101 rarely has small passages of which you must find the underlying assumption. In other words, you have not taken a lot of exams with this style of question on it.

Fun and Games: The Format

The GRE features about 10 logical reasoning questions and 25 questions based on about 6 logic games (called Analytical Reasoning). As with the other sections of the GRE, the two types of questions will be mixed throughout the test section. For example, you may start out with two logical reasoning questions, then get a game with three questions, another game with four questions, a third game with five questions, three logical reasoning questions, some more logic games, and so on.

Logic Games: Analytical Reasoning

I'll start with the games; the fun comes next. A logic game has two basic parts. First is the set of statements or conditions, sometimes called the facts. These statements describe the relationship between or among people, items, or events. You may, for example, be given statements about colleagues and asked which professors can work together on a committee. You may be told facts about events that can happen on certain days of the week. Perhaps a game will tell you about possible combinations of items. Here are examples of statements you may see in different games:

Amelia cannot sit at the same table as Britta.

Flu shots are given on Mondays, Tuesdays, and Wednesdays except when measles shots are given on the same day.

Justine is taller than Cristina and weighs less than Marco.

Following the statements is a set of three or more questions, presented one at a time, that tests your understanding of how the statements work together. Each question in a group is independent of the others. That is, you do not have to answer the first question correctly to answer the second question. Following are a few sample questions:

How many different groups of at least three people can Amelia be part of?

On which day of the week are no shots given at all?

Which of the following represents the order of the students from tallest to shortest?

Take your time going through a logic game. You can answer the questions in less time if you get a good handle on the game, carefully consider the meaning of each statement, and make deductions. Remember that the first games are worth more than the later ones, so don't rush through the earlier games unless you are completely stuck. If you don't have time to attack the last game with all of your reasoning powers, just make wild guesses until you finish. These last questions don't have much of an effect on your score, and you want to be sure you finish (one or two of those guesses could very well be correct).

Here's a basic approach that works for any of the several types of logic games.

You Can't Tell the Players without a Program

Make a "program" of the players by writing down the pool of people or events. For example, if the question talks about five professors, Mahaffey, Negy, O'Leary, Plotnitz, and Quivera, you jot down M, N, O, P, and Q on your scratch paper.

My telling you to write down this pool of people may seem simplistic, but your not doing so can cost you points during the heat of the battle. It's very easy to have five people, four of whom are asked about frequently. The fifth poor forgotten soul often is ignored . . . until a trap question near the end. Write the pool down and refer to it often.

Picture This: The Diagram

Usually, you can make a diagram to show the relationship between the people or events. Here are a few of the most common diagrams:

✔ **Calendar:** A calendar game is very straightforward; draw a calendar and fill in the events that happen on particular days.

✔ **Ordering or sequencing:** You may have an ordering or sequencing relationship game in which some people are taller or heavier than others. You would write a line of people, with A above B if A is taller than B, C at the bottom if she is the shortest, and so on.

✔ **Grouping or membership:** This game asks you which items or people could belong to which group. For example, membership in a club may require four out of five characteristics. Often this type of question doesn't require a graph per se but a lot of "if . . . then" statements such as "If A is in the group, then B is not." You can also think of these as mathematical statements: $A \neq B$. I've put a few games of this type in the short quiz that follows in the next chapter; the serious diagramming I'm saving for the Practice Exams 1 and 2 found at the end of the book.

✔ **Personal characteristics:** In this game, you are given information about people and asked what those people can or cannot do based on their characteristics. For example, you may be told that Trent has a fear of heights and Lucilla has a fear of horses. If the question asks, "Which of the following could go on a horseback ride along a mountain crest?" you know to eliminate Trent and Lucilla from the group.

The preceding examples are by no means the only types of games you could get; they are simply the most common. Most games you see will be a variation on one of these. As you go through the practice exam, you'll see several different types of games. After you finish both practice exams, take a few minutes to go back through the analytical games. Label each one by type and decide which types you're great at, which ones you could happily live without, and which you may choose to make wild guesses on if they are near the end of the section.

Artifices, Ruses, and Wiles: A Trap by Any Other Name Still Stinks

Logic games are full of traps; be on the lookout for them. The following suggestions may help you to recognize and overpower the worst of them.

Read the entire game first. Do not start making a diagram as soon as you get to the first statement. You can make several different styles of diagrams; don't decide which type is for you until after you read all the statements.

You cannot and should not make a diagram for every single type of game. Sometimes you will simply write statements such as $A \neq B$ or *If B, then not C*. Occasionally, a game may have more than one diagram. Be flexible and realize that you may have to create two or even three diagrams, any of which could be true under a particular set of conditions.

Focus on an *always/never* statement. Some statements are 100 percent absolute. They give info such as, "Darnay never goes to the clinic on Tuesdays" or "Puff is the smallest cat." You love those types of statements, as there are no ifs, ands, or buts about them. Look for them first and circle them. You want to keep them in the front of your mind as those statements often let you eliminate answer choices immediately. For example, if a question asks you which is the order of cats from largest to smallest, eliminate any answer that doesn't have Puff at the very end. Usually, you can narrow your answers down to two or three immediately.

Be alert to multiple contingencies. A game may ask you which clubs a person can join. If you find by going through the statements that Rod could belong to either the swim team or the chess team, be sure to note both possibilities. Maybe the question asks which space Charlene can take at the conference table, and you find she can sit in either seat four or seat five. Make diagrams illustrating both possibilities.

Don't carry over info given by a preceding question. So there you are. You've created a beautiful diagram, all parts in place, everything perfect. Then you get to question 18 and it adds something new, such as, "Boomer decides he doesn't want to sit next to Twyla but must sit next to a blonde. Which of the following could be the seating order?" That piece of new info means you have to go back and redo your entire diagram. Usually doing so chews up a lot of time. If you are behind in your desired pace at this point, I suggest you make a random guess and move on to the next question. If you decide to tackle the question rather than guess, be sure not to transfer info to the next question. That is, when you're ready to answer question 19, go back to your original diagram that has Boomer sitting next to Twyla. The test makers know that students have a tendency to carry over info and design answers to trap those who make that mistake.

Don't confuse forward and backward. You may have one game that requires you to make "if . . . then" statements: "If it rains, then I'll go to the library." Don't turn that statement around and say, "If I go to the library, it will be raining." Not necessarily. I may be forced to go to the library on a gorgeous, sunny day because my term paper is due and I can't *procrastinate* (delay) any longer.

It Makes Sense to Me: Logical Reasoning

Logical Reasoning questions consist of short paragraphs, sometimes just a sentence or two. You read the passage and then answer questions such as these:

Which of the following is the author's underlying assumption?

Which of the following statements would most *weaken* the author's conclusion?

The author's conclusion would be most *strengthened* by which of the following?

Which of the following arguments is most likely to explain the seeming contradiction between the author's statement and his actions?

The author quotes the doctor to make the point that . . .

Which of the following is the best conclusion to the paragraph above?

The statement above follows most logically from which of these statements?

When Nothing Is Reason-able: Tricks and Traps

Here are a few suggestions to help you to maximize your points in this section.

Identify exactly what the question is asking. The most important step in Logical Reasoning is identifying what the question wants. Are you to identify an assumption? Find a strengthening argument? Predict what would weaken the argument?

Predict an answer and quickly eliminate those choices that do not come close. Scratch paper is not just for logic games. Use the vertical columns numbered 1–5 that you drew during the general instructions to the test to cross off choices that you know are incorrect.

Dedicate more time to your strongest questions. You certainly want to do everything you can to get any type of Logical Reasoning question right during the first part of the test, but later on, spend more time working on your strengths. I've written these practice exams to give you a smattering of all sorts of Logical Reasoning questions. After you finish with the tests, go back and identify which types of questions you always get right and which ones you usually miss. Maybe you're better at questions that require very little reading but a lot of analysis, like the short variety of parallel-reasoning questions. Maybe you're better at questions that test less formal logic and more reading, such as "conclusion to the paragraph" questions. Because most people don't get every analytical ability question right, it only makes sense to concentrate on those that you do best. You may just want to guess quickly at the questions you know are in your weakest area and hope you get to some your strong suit questions shortly.

All Good Things Must End: Review

The Analytical Ability portion of the GRE has two types of questions: Analytical Reasoning (also called logic games) and Logical Reasoning (also called Critical Reasoning or Critical Thinking).

Analytical Reasoning

When you encounter an Analytical Reasoning question, remember the following:

Approach

- ✔ Three or more questions are based on a set of statements.
- ✔ Make a pool of the people or events in the game.
- ✔ Read the *entire* game first and then make a diagram showing the relationship between the set of statements.

Tricks

- ✔ Focus on an *always/never* statement.
- ✔ Be alert to different contingencies.
- ✔ Don't confuse forward and backward.

Logical Reasoning

These tips can help you to survive (triumph over!) the Logical Reasoning questions.

- ✔ Carefully — and suspiciously — read short (two-to-five sentence), but often confusing paragraphs.
- ✔ Identify what the question is asking for: an assumption, a strengthening/weakening statement, and so on.

Chapter 18

Just How Logical Are You? Analytical Ability Practice Questions

● ●

Now you have your chance to see whether your parents were right when they yelled at you all those years, "Sometimes you make no sense at all!" Use your logic and reasoning skills to answer the following questions.

 The good news here (besides the fact that a lot of schools don't even count this analytical section) is that Analytical Ability questions have fewer traps than the rest of the GRE. For a change, you can actually use your common sense and answer these questions directly without having to be paranoid and insecure.

Questions 1–3 are based on the following information.

An independent television station shows movies every day of the week between 8 and 10 p.m. One week, the station must decide on which days it will show movies of the following genres: one western, one romance, two dramas, and three comedies. The selections must conform to the following conditions:

> The western must be shown later in the week than the romance.
>
> A comedy is shown on Wednesday.
>
> The romance may not be shown the night before or night after a drama is shown.
>
> Comedies may not be shown three nights in a row.

ANALYSIS. This game involves arranging a sequence for a given week. A good way to keep track of the information is to draw a calendar for the week.

Su	M	Tu	W	Th	F	Sa
—	—	—	—	—	—	—

You don't really need to label the blanks, given your familiarity with calendars, but doing so may help you to place the movies faster.

Next, go to the rule(s) that can easily be incorporated into the diagram. You don't have to follow the rules in order; start with the one that is the simplest to diagram.

The second rule may be represented as follows:

Su	M	Tu	W	Th	F	Sa
—	—	—	C	—	—	—

Summarize the rule about westerns and romances (westerns must be shown later in the week than romances) by writing something on the order of "R, then W. Not W, then R." This information allows you to deduce, for example, that westerns (W) may not be shown on Sunday and romances (R) on Saturday or else the rule would be violated. Show this on your diagram as follows:

Su	M	Tu	W	Th	F	Sa
__	__	__	C	__	__	__

R, then W. Not W, then R.

Summarize the other two rules by jotting a quick note, such as "no D, then R and no R, then D" and "no C, then C, then C." Now you've put all the info from words into diagrams or quick notes, and you are ready to tackle the questions.

1. Which of the following is an acceptable lineup for the week's movies?

   (A) drama, western, drama, comedy, romance, comedy, comedy

   (B) comedy, comedy, romance, western, drama, drama, comedy

   (C) comedy, comedy, drama, comedy, romance, drama, western

   (D) drama, drama, comedy, comedy, comedy, romance, western

   (E) drama, comedy, drama, comedy, comedy, romance, western

On the GRE, often the first question after a game simply asks you for the order of an arrangement. Usually, the best way to answer this question is by the process of elimination. The test maker has done all the work for you. You know that one of the sequences must be correct while all the others have at least one thing wrong with them. The best way to approach such a question is to take one rule at a time and eliminate the choice(s) that violate it.

Because W must be after R, choice A is out. No D, then R and no R, then D? Get rid of choice C. No C, then C, then C? Eliminate choice D. Finally, knock out choice B because a C is not shown on Wednesday. Only the correct answer, choice E, is left. *Correct Answer:* E.

2. If the romance is shown on Friday, which of the following is *not* necessarily true?

   (A) The romance is shown after all the comedies have been shown.

   (B) A comedy is shown on Sunday.

   (C) The western is shown on Saturday.

   (D) Comedies are shown on consecutive nights.

   (E) Both dramas are shown in the first half of the week.

Take the information in the question and add it to your diagram: *Correct Answer:* B.

Su	M	Tu	W	Th	F	Sa
__	__	__	C	__	R	__

R, then W. Not W, then R.

With the R on Friday, the W must shown on Saturday:

Su	M	Tu	W	Th	F	Sa
__	__	__	C	__	R	W

The only movies left are D and D and C and C. Given that D may not go next to R, C must be on Thursday:

Su	M	Tu	W	Th	F	Sa
__	__	__	C	C	R	W

You can't use C, then C, then C, so put a D in Tuesday:

Su	M	Tu	W	Th	F	Sa
__	__	D	C	C	R	W

This is as far as you can go. C can go in Sunday, and D is shown on Monday or vice versa.

When you have two options, be sure to keep track of both of them. You frequently encounter questions in which you can have two possibilities; don't arbitrarily choose one. In this case, B may be true, but it is not *necessarily* true. If you are unsure, check the remaining choices. A quick check reveals that the other choices are *definitely* true.

3. If the western is shown the night immediately before the first comedy of the week, how many different sequences of movie genres are possible?

   (A) two

   (B) three

   (C) four

   (D) five

   (E) six

You know that W cannot be shown on Sunday. Because it has to be shown the night before the first comedy, this leaves two possibilities for the western: Monday or Tuesday. See what happens with W on Monday:

Su	M	Tu	W	Th	F	Sa
__	W	C	C	__	__	__

(C is on Tuesday because the W is shown the immediately preceding night.)

Because of "R, then W," R must be shown on Sunday:

Su	M	Tu	W	Th	F	Sa
R	W	C	C	__	__	__

Because of "no C, then C, then C," a D must be shown on Thursday:

Su	M	Tu	W	Th	F	Sa
R	W	C	C	D	__	__

You have two possibilities: D on Friday, and C on Saturday **or vice versa.** This does not make the answer choice A, however. You still have to see what happens with W on Tuesday:

Su	M	Tu	W	Th	F	Sa
__	__	W	C	__	__	__

With this setup, R could go on Sunday:

Su	M	Tu	W	Th	F	Sa
R	_	W	C	_	_	_

Because W must be shown the night before the first C, the only movie you can go on Monday is D:

Su	M	Tu	W	Th	F	Sa
R	D	W	C	_	_	_

But wait, R and D may not go together, therefore this is not a possibility. What if R is shown on Monday?

Su	M	Tu	W	Th	F	Sa
_	R	W	C	_	_	_

Put a D in Sunday because W must be shown before the first C.

Su	M	Tu	W	Th	F	Sa
D	R	W	C	_	_	_

But wait, once again we have R and D together — which is not allowed. Therefore, there are only two possibilities and the correct answer is A. *Correct Answer:* A.

4. *Ricardo:* My wife and I tried to get marital counseling. The counselors who could see us were too expensive, and the counselors whose fees were reasonable were too busy to fit us into their schedules. My wife and I have decided that counseling cannot help us.

Which of the following statements, if true, would most weaken Ricardo's conclusion?

(A) Marital counseling succeeds only with motivated people who are willing to do the exercises and role-playing suggested by the counselors.

(B) People who go to expensive counselors have better results than those who go to more moderately priced counselors.

(C) Ricardo and his wife will eventually find an affordable counselor who has time for them.

(D) Husbands are often more critical of marital counseling than are wives, who are willing to continue even when frustrated.

(E) Counselors are only human and cannot be as unbiased as they would like to be as they have feelings of their own.

First, identify the conclusion. It is that counseling can't help Ricardo and his wife. Ricardo uses his current inability to find a counselor to leap to this conclusion. He assumes that his wife and he will never see a counselor. The best way to weaken an argument is to contradict the assumption. Choice C does just this. This choice points out that Ricardo can't use the current unavailability of counselors to make a conclusion about future effectiveness.

Eliminate choices D and E right away because they do nothing to indicate that counseling might succeed, which is necessary to contradict Ricardo's conclusion. If you're in a rush and don't have time to figure out the answer, you can guess among choices A, B, and C. *Correct Answer:* C.

5. *Mr. Janowski:* Adolescents should be steered away from a career in dentistry. There are so many breakthroughs in cavity prevention today that the need for a dentist will soon be minimal.

   Mrs. Hogan: That's true. The last time I went to a dentist it wasn't for a cavity at all but to get an implant when I knocked my tooth out playing street hockey with my son.

   Which of the following may be said of Mrs. Hogan's comment?

   (A) It contradicts the point made by Mr. Janowski.

   (B) It gives an example that supports the assumption made by Mr. Janowski.

   (C) It assumes facts not in evidence.

   (D) It redefines terms.

   (E) It uses an invalid definition to buttress a weak assumption.

   Mrs. Hogan appears to agree with what Mr. Janowski says, but her words in fact contradict his conclusion. He is saying that dentists are not necessary because children no longer get cavities. She shows that a dentist has functions other than to fill a cavity, thus disproving his statement that dentists are no longer necessary.

   If you chose B, you fell for the trap. You probably read the "That's true" uttered by Mrs. Hogan and got no further. Reading the whole statement would tell you that while she thought she was agreeing with Mr. Janowski, she was proving his premise wrong.

   Choice C means nothing. What facts? What evidence? If you chose this answer, you went for the "best-sounding" choice, the one that sounded the most pretentious and analytical. Choices D and E are wrong because there are no definitions given in the passage, let alone redefined or defined incorrectly. *Correct Answer:* A.

6. Fraud is the intentional misrepresentation upon which a person is intended to rely and upon which he does rely to his detriment. If a person is accidentally misled and suffers an injury (for example, if he is given erroneous financial advice), he may not sue for fraud. If a person relies on something that he was never supposed to find out, the person making the false statement that was not meant to be overheard is not liable for fraud because there was no intentional misrepresentation. Similarly, if the person were intended to rely on the information, and did, but actually benefited from the information, there is no fraud because there was no detrimental effect of the reliance.

   Which of the following is best supported by the information above?

   (A) If even one element of those required for fraud is absent, there is no fraud.

   (B) If an investor loses money after being advised to invest in a restaurant by its new owner, the restaurant owner is not guilty of fraud.

   (C) An assembly-line worker warns a machinist that the machinist is about to be fired. If the machinist quits and finds a new job that pays less than half of what he made before, the machinist can rightfully sue the assembly-line worker for fraud.

   (D) If there is harm from relying on the information, but the harm eventually turns to gain, there is no fraud.

   (E) A physician tells a patient to take some medication and exercise regularly to improve her physical condition. If the patient takes the medication but the condition worsens, the patient has a legitimate case of fraud against the physician.

The passage gives the elements that make up fraud and then provides examples of how not having those elements negates the fraud. Choice B does not necessarily follow from the stimulus because the restaurant owner may have intentionally misled the investor by providing bogus reports of the restaurant's financial health, status, and so on. Choice C is out because the assembly-line worker's information was probably accurate. In addition, the machinist is likely better-off with his new job than he would have been had he stayed and been fired (although unemployment benefits may have been substantial). Choice D is a little tougher to eliminate. The passage does say that there is no fraud if there is no harm. However, it does not say that there is no fraud if the harm eventually turns to gain. Be very careful not to take the information and make more of it than is there. Choice E is no good because the physician may have given very sound advice. The most obvious potential problem is that the patient did not follow the physician's advice regarding exercise. *Correct Answer:* A.

Part VI

It All Comes Down to This: Full-Length Practice GREs

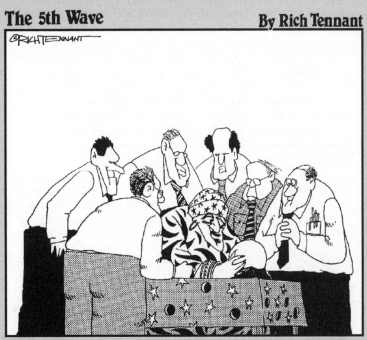

The 5th Wave   By Rich Tennant

"THE IMAGE IS GETTING CLEARER NOW... I CAN ALMOST SEE IT... YES! THERE IT IS — THE ANSWER IS $3ab^2 \times 7d^3 - \sqrt{19L} + U\frac{3}{4}m \div \pm 100 . (15) 7\frac{2}{3} \phi Q69$."

In this part . . .

*J*ust when you think your brain can't be stuffed with one more factoid, relief is at hand. You finally get to download some of the information you've been inputting for the past 18 chapters. Trust me; you'll feel better when you let it all out.

This unit has two full-length exams that are as close to the actual GRE as I can get without having briefcase-bearing barristers pounding on my door. I take these tests seriously, and you should, too — do them under actual test conditions, sitting in a quiet room and timing yourself. Open books are definitely out (sorry!). I have spies everywhere; I'll know if you cheat on these tests. There will be a knocking at your door one foggy night . . . .

After you've done your duty on these two practice exams, you'll have a good time going through the answer explanations, which are nowhere near as dry and stuffy as the exam itself.

Chapter 19

How to Ruin a Perfectly Good Day, Part I: Practice Exam 1

● ●

You are now ready to take a sample GRE. Like the actual GRE, the following exam consists of one 30-minute verbal section, one 45-minute quantitative section, and one 60-minute analytical section. The actual GRE may also include one additional verbal, quantitative, or analytical section, which does not count toward your GRE score. Because this section will not be identified as one that will not be scored, you must give every verbal, quantitative, and analytical section your best effort. You may also get an extra section that will be identified as experimental, meaning that it won't affect your score. Here, I don't include the experimental sections because I don't want to put you through any more anguish and agony than absolutely necessary. You're welcome.

You are familiar with the question formats by now, so you should not have to read the instructions for each specific question type. Nevertheless, take as much time as you need to go through the tutorial, which precedes the timed part of the exam. Do not start the test until you are comfortable with how to scroll down passages, graphs, and figures, mark an answer, and turn the clock off and on. The tutorial covers these topics, along with some other basic information. Even if you are extremely comfortable with using the computer to take the GRE, use the tutorial time to block the outside world from your mind and focus on the task ahead of you.

Please take the test under normal exam conditions and approach it as if it were the real test. This is serious stuff here!

1. **Work when you won't be interrupted (even though you'd probably welcome any distractions).**

2. **Use scratch paper that is free of any prepared notes. (On the actual GRE, you will get blank scratch paper before your test begins. You will have a little time before the clock starts to jot down a few notes and formulas and a series of columns of numbers or letters that you may want to use to help you eliminate answer choices, but you may not whip out a ready-made version of such test-taking aids.)**

3. **Turn off the clock at the beginning of each test section and be very careful on the first five questions. Remember that these earlier questions contribute more to your score than do the later questions.**

4. **If a question is truly impossible for you, guess and move on. You do not have the option of skipping the question and coming back to it. The computer will not let you move on until you mark and confirm an answer.**

5. **Make sure that you get to the end of the test section (30th question for verbal, 28th question for quantitative, and 35th question for analytical). If you have to, make wild guesses to reach the end before time expires. Unanswered questions will hurt your score more than incorrect ones will.**

6. If you get to the last question before time expires, you have the option of answering it right away and finishing your test early (you can't use the time to go back and check your work) or relaxing for a while and marking your answer shortly before time expires. If you feel pumped up and you're on a roll, do the former. Give yourself the breather if you feel bombarded by the test.

7. Do not leave your desk while the clock is running on any one section.

8. You will get a one-minute break after the first section and the option to take a ten-minute break after the second section.

After you complete the entire test, check your answers with the answer key at the end of this chapter. You can find a section at the end of Chapter 21 that explains your score. Go through the answer explanations to ALL the questions, not just the ones you miss. There is a plethora of worthwhile information there, material that provides a good review of everything you went over in the lectures. I even tossed in a few good jokes to keep you somewhat sane.

Answer Sheet

Begin with Number 1 for each new section. If any sections have fewer than 50 questions, leave the extra spaces blank.

Verbal Section

1. Ⓐ Ⓑ Ⓒ Ⓓ Ⓔ	26. Ⓐ Ⓑ Ⓒ Ⓓ Ⓔ
2. Ⓐ Ⓑ Ⓒ Ⓓ Ⓔ	27. Ⓐ Ⓑ Ⓒ Ⓓ Ⓔ
3. Ⓐ Ⓑ Ⓒ Ⓓ Ⓔ	28. Ⓐ Ⓑ Ⓒ Ⓓ Ⓔ
4. Ⓐ Ⓑ Ⓒ Ⓓ Ⓔ	29. Ⓐ Ⓑ Ⓒ Ⓓ Ⓔ
5. Ⓐ Ⓑ Ⓒ Ⓓ Ⓔ	30. Ⓐ Ⓑ Ⓒ Ⓓ Ⓔ
6. Ⓐ Ⓑ Ⓒ Ⓓ Ⓔ	31. Ⓐ Ⓑ Ⓒ Ⓓ Ⓔ
7. Ⓐ Ⓑ Ⓒ Ⓓ Ⓔ	32. Ⓐ Ⓑ Ⓒ Ⓓ Ⓔ
8. Ⓐ Ⓑ Ⓒ Ⓓ Ⓔ	33. Ⓐ Ⓑ Ⓒ Ⓓ Ⓔ
9. Ⓐ Ⓑ Ⓒ Ⓓ Ⓔ	34. Ⓐ Ⓑ Ⓒ Ⓓ Ⓔ
10. Ⓐ Ⓑ Ⓒ Ⓓ Ⓔ	35. Ⓐ Ⓑ Ⓒ Ⓓ Ⓔ
11. Ⓐ Ⓑ Ⓒ Ⓓ Ⓔ	36. Ⓐ Ⓑ Ⓒ Ⓓ Ⓔ
12. Ⓐ Ⓑ Ⓒ Ⓓ Ⓔ	37. Ⓐ Ⓑ Ⓒ Ⓓ Ⓔ
13. Ⓐ Ⓑ Ⓒ Ⓓ Ⓔ	38. Ⓐ Ⓑ Ⓒ Ⓓ Ⓔ
14. Ⓐ Ⓑ Ⓒ Ⓓ Ⓔ	39. Ⓐ Ⓑ Ⓒ Ⓓ Ⓔ
15. Ⓐ Ⓑ Ⓒ Ⓓ Ⓔ	40. Ⓐ Ⓑ Ⓒ Ⓓ Ⓔ
16. Ⓐ Ⓑ Ⓒ Ⓓ Ⓔ	41. Ⓐ Ⓑ Ⓒ Ⓓ Ⓔ
17. Ⓐ Ⓑ Ⓒ Ⓓ Ⓔ	42. Ⓐ Ⓑ Ⓒ Ⓓ Ⓔ
18. Ⓐ Ⓑ Ⓒ Ⓓ Ⓔ	43. Ⓐ Ⓑ Ⓒ Ⓓ Ⓔ
19. Ⓐ Ⓑ Ⓒ Ⓓ Ⓔ	44. Ⓐ Ⓑ Ⓒ Ⓓ Ⓔ
20. Ⓐ Ⓑ Ⓒ Ⓓ Ⓔ	45. Ⓐ Ⓑ Ⓒ Ⓓ Ⓔ
21. Ⓐ Ⓑ Ⓒ Ⓓ Ⓔ	46. Ⓐ Ⓑ Ⓒ Ⓓ Ⓔ
22. Ⓐ Ⓑ Ⓒ Ⓓ Ⓔ	47. Ⓐ Ⓑ Ⓒ Ⓓ Ⓔ
23. Ⓐ Ⓑ Ⓒ Ⓓ Ⓔ	48. Ⓐ Ⓑ Ⓒ Ⓓ Ⓔ
24. Ⓐ Ⓑ Ⓒ Ⓓ Ⓔ	49. Ⓐ Ⓑ Ⓒ Ⓓ Ⓔ
25. Ⓐ Ⓑ Ⓒ Ⓓ Ⓔ	50. Ⓐ Ⓑ Ⓒ Ⓓ Ⓔ

Quantitative Section

1. Ⓐ Ⓑ Ⓒ Ⓓ Ⓔ   26. Ⓐ Ⓑ Ⓒ Ⓓ Ⓔ
2. Ⓐ Ⓑ Ⓒ Ⓓ Ⓔ   27. Ⓐ Ⓑ Ⓒ Ⓓ Ⓔ
3. Ⓐ Ⓑ Ⓒ Ⓓ Ⓔ   28. Ⓐ Ⓑ Ⓒ Ⓓ Ⓔ
4. Ⓐ Ⓑ Ⓒ Ⓓ Ⓔ   29. Ⓐ Ⓑ Ⓒ Ⓓ Ⓔ
5. Ⓐ Ⓑ Ⓒ Ⓓ Ⓔ   30. Ⓐ Ⓑ Ⓒ Ⓓ Ⓔ
6. Ⓐ Ⓑ Ⓒ Ⓓ Ⓔ   31. Ⓐ Ⓑ Ⓒ Ⓓ Ⓔ
7. Ⓐ Ⓑ Ⓒ Ⓓ Ⓔ   32. Ⓐ Ⓑ Ⓒ Ⓓ Ⓔ
8. Ⓐ Ⓑ Ⓒ Ⓓ Ⓔ   33. Ⓐ Ⓑ Ⓒ Ⓓ Ⓔ
9. Ⓐ Ⓑ Ⓒ Ⓓ Ⓔ   34. Ⓐ Ⓑ Ⓒ Ⓓ Ⓔ
10. Ⓐ Ⓑ Ⓒ Ⓓ Ⓔ   35. Ⓐ Ⓑ Ⓒ Ⓓ Ⓔ
11. Ⓐ Ⓑ Ⓒ Ⓓ Ⓔ   36. Ⓐ Ⓑ Ⓒ Ⓓ Ⓔ
12. Ⓐ Ⓑ Ⓒ Ⓓ Ⓔ   37. Ⓐ Ⓑ Ⓒ Ⓓ Ⓔ
13. Ⓐ Ⓑ Ⓒ Ⓓ Ⓔ   38. Ⓐ Ⓑ Ⓒ Ⓓ Ⓔ
14. Ⓐ Ⓑ Ⓒ Ⓓ Ⓔ   39. Ⓐ Ⓑ Ⓒ Ⓓ Ⓔ
15. Ⓐ Ⓑ Ⓒ Ⓓ Ⓔ   40. Ⓐ Ⓑ Ⓒ Ⓓ Ⓔ
16. Ⓐ Ⓑ Ⓒ Ⓓ Ⓔ   41. Ⓐ Ⓑ Ⓒ Ⓓ Ⓔ
17. Ⓐ Ⓑ Ⓒ Ⓓ Ⓔ   42. Ⓐ Ⓑ Ⓒ Ⓓ Ⓔ
18. Ⓐ Ⓑ Ⓒ Ⓓ Ⓔ   43. Ⓐ Ⓑ Ⓒ Ⓓ Ⓔ
19. Ⓐ Ⓑ Ⓒ Ⓓ Ⓔ   44. Ⓐ Ⓑ Ⓒ Ⓓ Ⓔ
20. Ⓐ Ⓑ Ⓒ Ⓓ Ⓔ   45. Ⓐ Ⓑ Ⓒ Ⓓ Ⓔ
21. Ⓐ Ⓑ Ⓒ Ⓓ Ⓔ   46. Ⓐ Ⓑ Ⓒ Ⓓ Ⓔ
22. Ⓐ Ⓑ Ⓒ Ⓓ Ⓔ   47. Ⓐ Ⓑ Ⓒ Ⓓ Ⓔ
23. Ⓐ Ⓑ Ⓒ Ⓓ Ⓔ   48. Ⓐ Ⓑ Ⓒ Ⓓ Ⓔ
24. Ⓐ Ⓑ Ⓒ Ⓓ Ⓔ   49. Ⓐ Ⓑ Ⓒ Ⓓ Ⓔ
25. Ⓐ Ⓑ Ⓒ Ⓓ Ⓔ   50. Ⓐ Ⓑ Ⓒ Ⓓ Ⓔ

Analytical Section

1. Ⓐ Ⓑ Ⓒ Ⓓ Ⓔ   26. Ⓐ Ⓑ Ⓒ Ⓓ Ⓔ
2. Ⓐ Ⓑ Ⓒ Ⓓ Ⓔ   27. Ⓐ Ⓑ Ⓒ Ⓓ Ⓔ
3. Ⓐ Ⓑ Ⓒ Ⓓ Ⓔ   28. Ⓐ Ⓑ Ⓒ Ⓓ Ⓔ
4. Ⓐ Ⓑ Ⓒ Ⓓ Ⓔ   29. Ⓐ Ⓑ Ⓒ Ⓓ Ⓔ
5. Ⓐ Ⓑ Ⓒ Ⓓ Ⓔ   30. Ⓐ Ⓑ Ⓒ Ⓓ Ⓔ
6. Ⓐ Ⓑ Ⓒ Ⓓ Ⓔ   31. Ⓐ Ⓑ Ⓒ Ⓓ Ⓔ
7. Ⓐ Ⓑ Ⓒ Ⓓ Ⓔ   32. Ⓐ Ⓑ Ⓒ Ⓓ Ⓔ
8. Ⓐ Ⓑ Ⓒ Ⓓ Ⓔ   33. Ⓐ Ⓑ Ⓒ Ⓓ Ⓔ
9. Ⓐ Ⓑ Ⓒ Ⓓ Ⓔ   34. Ⓐ Ⓑ Ⓒ Ⓓ Ⓔ
10. Ⓐ Ⓑ Ⓒ Ⓓ Ⓔ   35. Ⓐ Ⓑ Ⓒ Ⓓ Ⓔ
11. Ⓐ Ⓑ Ⓒ Ⓓ Ⓔ   36. Ⓐ Ⓑ Ⓒ Ⓓ Ⓔ
12. Ⓐ Ⓑ Ⓒ Ⓓ Ⓔ   37. Ⓐ Ⓑ Ⓒ Ⓓ Ⓔ
13. Ⓐ Ⓑ Ⓒ Ⓓ Ⓔ   38. Ⓐ Ⓑ Ⓒ Ⓓ Ⓔ
14. Ⓐ Ⓑ Ⓒ Ⓓ Ⓔ   39. Ⓐ Ⓑ Ⓒ Ⓓ Ⓔ
15. Ⓐ Ⓑ Ⓒ Ⓓ Ⓔ   40. Ⓐ Ⓑ Ⓒ Ⓓ Ⓔ
16. Ⓐ Ⓑ Ⓒ Ⓓ Ⓔ   41. Ⓐ Ⓑ Ⓒ Ⓓ Ⓔ
17. Ⓐ Ⓑ Ⓒ Ⓓ Ⓔ   42. Ⓐ Ⓑ Ⓒ Ⓓ Ⓔ
18. Ⓐ Ⓑ Ⓒ Ⓓ Ⓔ   43. Ⓐ Ⓑ Ⓒ Ⓓ Ⓔ
19. Ⓐ Ⓑ Ⓒ Ⓓ Ⓔ   44. Ⓐ Ⓑ Ⓒ Ⓓ Ⓔ
20. Ⓐ Ⓑ Ⓒ Ⓓ Ⓔ   45. Ⓐ Ⓑ Ⓒ Ⓓ Ⓔ
21. Ⓐ Ⓑ Ⓒ Ⓓ Ⓔ   46. Ⓐ Ⓑ Ⓒ Ⓓ Ⓔ
22. Ⓐ Ⓑ Ⓒ Ⓓ Ⓔ   47. Ⓐ Ⓑ Ⓒ Ⓓ Ⓔ
23. Ⓐ Ⓑ Ⓒ Ⓓ Ⓔ   48. Ⓐ Ⓑ Ⓒ Ⓓ Ⓔ
24. Ⓐ Ⓑ Ⓒ Ⓓ Ⓔ   49. Ⓐ Ⓑ Ⓒ Ⓓ Ⓔ
25. Ⓐ Ⓑ Ⓒ Ⓓ Ⓔ   50. Ⓐ Ⓑ Ⓒ Ⓓ Ⓔ

Verbal Section

Time: 30 minutes

30 questions

Choose the best answer to each question. Blacken the corresponding oval on the answer grid.

Directions: Choose the answer choice most nearly opposite in meaning to the question word.

1. NADIR – "lowest point"

    (A) segment

    (B) indigenous "native to"

    → (C) zenith 'highest point"

    (D) sagacious – wise

    (E) connection

2. INEPT – bungling or foolish

    (A) profane

    → (B) skilled

    (C) prolific abundant or producing much

    (D) thrifty

    (E) indigenous "native to "

Directions: Each of the following questions features a pair of words or phrases in capital letters, followed by five pairs of words or phrases in lowercase letters. Choose the lowercase pair that most closely expresses the same relationship as that of the uppercase pair.

3. SWAGGER : ARROGANCE ::

    (A) swindle : veracity   cheat é truthfulness

    (B) renege : consistency

    (C) orchestrate : harmony

    (D) wheedle : certitude

    → (E) stagger : imbalance

4. LIONS : PRIDE ::

    → (A) birds : flock

    (B) coyotes : kit

    (C) kangaroos : joey

    (D) swans : cygnet

    (E) wolves : pelt

Go on to next page

Directions: Each of the following sentences has one or two blanks indicating that words or phrases are omitted. Choose the answer that best completes the sentence.

5. Despite his ---- the ---- of the program, the government official was forced to sign the paperwork that continued funding of what everyone knew was a failed experiment that was costing the taxpayers millions of dollars annually.

    (A) demanding . . enhancement

    (B) suggesting . . implementation

    (C) rejecting . . termination

    (D) advocating . . demise

    (E) predicting . . continuation

6. Reluctant to ---- the man as the complete fraud she suspected him to be, Jill chose to attack the weaker points of his theory, ---- them one by one.

    (A) denounce . . debunking

    (B) ridicule . . proving

    (C) castigate . . applauding

    (D) expose . . strengthening

    (E) recommend . . disseminating

Directions: Each passage is followed by questions pertaining to that passage. Read the passage and answer the questions based on information stated or implied in that passage.

Line   The Canyon Pintado Historic District in
         northwest Colorado has been occupied by pre-
         historic people for as long as 11,000 years, includ-
         ing the Fremont culture that left behind rock art
(05)   sites. Fremont rock art has recurring motifs that
         link it both in time and culture. Strange human-
         like figures with broad shoulders, no legs, and
         horned headdresses are similar to the Barrier
         Canyon style of southwestern Utah. Figures with
(10)   shields or shield-like bodies are like Fremont fig-
         ures from the San Rafael region of Southern Utah.
             Some figures have large, trapezoidal shaped
         bodies, stick-like legs, trapezoidal heads, and in
         many cases, are adorned with necklaces. Another
(15)   motif of the Fremont culture is the mountain
         sheep, with graceful curvilinear horns. Designs

such as concentric circles, snake-like lines, hands, corn plants, and rows of dots are also often found in Fremont art. A unique figure in Douglas Creek is Kokopelli, the humpbacked flute (20) player of Anasazi mythology. His presence indicates some kind of tie with the more advanced culture of the Four Corners area.

7. The author mentions the connection to the culture of the Four Corners area to

    (A) challenge the claim that the Fremont culture was the most advanced of its time.

    (B) refute the assertion that Fremont rock art merely copied art from other cultures.

    (C) suggest that the mimicking of art from other cultures may indicate contact between the cultures.

    (D) prove the relationship between art and the level of civilization.

    (E) ridicule the suggestion that there is a connection between artistic images and warfare success.

8. The passage supplies information for answering which of the following questions?

    (A) What significance is there to the lack of legs on the human-like figures?

    (B) What was the purpose of the rock art?

    (C) Were curved lines absent in Fremont rock art?

    (D) How much of the artwork was sacred and how much secular?

    (E) What other cultures besides those in the Four Corners influenced Fremont rock art?

Line   Chile's human history apparently began
(10)   about 10,000 years ago when migrating Indians
         followed the line of the Andes and settled in fer-
         tile valleys and along the coast. The Incas briefly
         extended their empire into the north, but the
         area's remoteness prevented any significant
         effect. In 1541, the Spanish, under Pedro de
(15)   Valdivia, encountered about one million Indians
         from various cultures who supported themselves
         primarily through slash-and-burn agriculture and
         hunting. Although the Spaniards did not find the
         gold and silver they had sought there, they recog-
(20)   nized the agricultural potential of Chile's central
         valley, and Chile became part of the Viceroyalty
         of Peru.

Go on to next page

Chilean colonial society was heavily influenced by the *latifundio* system of large landhold-
(25) ings, kinship politics, the Roman Catholic
Church, and an aggressive frontier attitude stem-
ming from Indian wars. The drive for independence from Spain was precipitated by usurpation
of the Spanish throne by Napoleon's brother
(30) Joseph. A national junta in the name of
Ferdinand — heir to the deposed king — was
formed on September 18, 1810. Spanish attempts
to reimpose arbitrary rule during the
Reconquista led to a prolonged struggle under
(35) Bernardo O'Higgins, Chile's most renowned
patriot. Chilean independence was formally pro-
claimed on February 12, 1818.

The political revolution brought little social
change, however, and 19th century Chilean soci-
(40) ety preserved the essence of the stratified colonial social structure. The system of presidential
absolutism eventually predominated, but the
wealthy landowners continued to control Chile.

Although Chile established a representative
(45) democracy in the early 20th century, it soon
became unstable and degenerated into a system
protecting the interests of the ruling oligarchy. By
the 1920s, the newly emergent middle and working classes were powerful enough to elect a
(50) reformist president, but his program was frustrated by a conservative congress. Continuing
political and economic instability resulted in the
quasidictatorial rule of General Carlos Ibanez
(1924–1932).
(55) After constitutional rule was restored in
1932, a strong middle-class party, the Radicals,
formed. The Radical Party became the key force
in coalition governments for the next 20 years.
The 1920s saw the emergence of Marxist groups
(60) with strong popular support. During the period of
Radical Party dominance (1932–1952), the state
increased its role in the economy. However, presi-
dents generally were more conservative than the
parties supporting them, and conservative political elements continued to exert considerable
power through their influence over the economy
and control of rural voters.

9. Which of the following best describes the
relationship between congress and the
workers in the 1920s?

(A) They were in opposition.

(B) They worked together toward the same
goals.

(C) They took turns governing the country.

(D) They united only once to overthrow
the government.

(E) Congress was composed of workers;
they were one and the same.

10. From lines 32–34, you may infer that the
Chilean government in the 19th century

(A) included a president who was a figurehead without significant power.

(B) was ruled by a dictator who had
absolute power.

(C) was secretly ruled by Spain.

(D) was reigned over by a king.

(E) was an anarchy, without any formal
governmental structure.

11. The primary purpose of this passage is to

(A) argue that Chile advanced when it
became independent of Spanish rule.

(B) contrast Indian culture with that of the
European settlers.

(C) discuss some key factors in the development of Chilean social structures.

(D) advocate that Chile adopt a government
less dominated by the wealthy class.

(E) explain how coalition governments
resolve some inherent tensions.

12. The tone of the passage is

(A) opinionated.

(B) heretical.

(C) objective.

(D) hidebound.

(E) dolorous.

Directions: Choose the answer choice most
nearly opposite in meaning to the question
word.

13. DOCILE

(A) rebellious

(B) tactless

(C) tawdry

(D) vulnerable

(E) inexplicable

Go on to next page

14. EXTROVERTED

(A) bombastic

(B) unnecessary

(C) shy

(D) stationary

(E) ubiquitous

Directions: Each of the following questions features a pair of words or phrases in capital letters, followed by five pairs of words or phrases in lowercase letters. Choose the lowercase pair that most closely expresses the same relationship as that of the uppercase pair.

15. HARDY : STRONG ::

(A) puny : grandiose

(B) unruly : disorganized

(C) stubborn : flexible

(D) dubious : ineligible

(E) lucid : clouded

16. IRON : BLACKSMITH ::

(A) fabric : mason

(B) wood : carpenter

(C) pork : butcher

(D) brides : matchmaker

(E) pranks : jester

Directions: Each of the following sentences has one or two blanks indicating that words or phrases are omitted. Choose the answer that best completes the sentence.

17. To criticize a new employee for working slowly may actually be ----, as the employee becomes so flustered that he slows down even further in an attempt to concentrate on his task.

(A) counterproductive

(B) praiseworthy

(C) worthwhile

(D) essential

(E) reasonable

18. Shocked to hear the students jeering at his proposal that they work on the school grounds to help the school save on grounds-keeping fees, the principal ---- said that the commitment was completely ---- and no one would be penalized for not showing up.

(A) swiftly . . mandatory

(B) hastily . . voluntary

(C) loudly . . irregular

(D) scornfully . . illegal

(E) predictably . . necessary

Directions: Choose the answer choice most nearly opposite in meaning to the question word.

19. AMUSING

(A) humorous

(B) stalwart

(C) temporary

(D) exasperating

(E) unbelievable

20. TEDIOUS

(A) harmonious

(B) craven

(C) picayune

(D) interesting

(E) dull

21. ABSTAIN

(A) sneer

(B) participate

(C) approximate

(D) meander

(E) infuriate

22. STAPLE : ATTACH ::

(A) button : sew

(B) carpet : impede

(C) water : dehydrate

(D) incision : open

(E) petition : review

Go on to next page

23. PRACTICE : IMPROVE ::

    (A) gather : decrease

    (B) praise : ridicule

    (C) research : discuss

    (D) abbreviate : shorten

    (E) coddle : harm

Directions: Each of the following sentences has one or two blanks indicating that words or phrases are omitted. Choose the answer that best completes the sentence.

24. It is unfortunate that Heather's first day on the job was filled with so many mistakes that her supervisor felt - - - - his original recommendation not to hire her.

    (A) justified in

    (B) discontented with

    (C) objective about

    (D) vituperative regarding

    (E) innovative in

25. Unable to complete the project yet - - - - to admit defeat, Liz worked at the task until she was lucky enough to find a solution that nearly - - - - the difficulty.

    (A) proposing . . destroyed

    (B) unwilling . . resolved

    (C) reluctant . . worsened

    (D) eager . . doubled

    (E) determined . . reduced

Directions: Each passage is followed by questions pertaining to that passage. Read the passage and answer the questions based on information stated or implied in that passage.

Studies have shown that certain components of the immune system behave abnormally in people with chronic fatigue syndrome. Chemicals called interleukin-2 and gamma interferon, which the body produces during its battle against cancer and infectious agents, may not be made in normal amounts. There is evidence that a low-grade battle is being waged by the immune system of CFS patients, given the slight increase in the number of white cells that usually accumulate in the blood when people are fighting off an infection. Natural killer cells, though, that also help the body in this battle are found in slightly reduced numbers. It's important to note that clinical depression has the identical small reduction in natural killer-cell activity. In addition, some depressed patients produce higher amounts of antibodies to certain viruses. There may be more of a connection between depression, the immune system, and chronic fatigue syndrome than is realized even now, which introduces the somewhat controversial aspect of the syndrome, its neuropsychological features.

26. Which of the following does the author mention to support his theory that the immune system may be affected by chronic fatigue syndrome?

    (A) Clinical depression may be more physical than psychological.

    (B) Interleukin-2 and gamma interferon are not produced in normal amounts.

    (C) Antibody levels are higher in depressed people than in nondepressed people.

    (D) White-cell levels in people with neuropsychological problems tend to decrease.

    (E) Natural killer cells reduce the number of white blood cells.

27. When the body battles cancer,

    (A) it produces chemicals like gamma interferon.

    (B) it turns against its own immune system.

    (C) it stimulates the condition known as clinical depression.

    (D) it reduces the number of antibodies available to battle viruses.

    (E) it develops abnormal lesions around the area of the cancer.

Go on to next page

Directions: Choose the answer choice most nearly opposite in meaning to the question word.

28. ILLICIT
    (A) expedient
    (B) insufficient
    (C) legal
    (D) affable
    (E) coarse

29. IRRITATE
    (A) badger
    (B) soothe
    (C) pressure
    (D) scratch
    (E) dry

Directions: Each of the following questions features a pair of words or phrases in capital letters, followed by five pairs of words or phrases in lowercase letters. Choose the lowercase pair that most closely expresses the same relationship as that of the uppercase pair.

30. TRUANT : SCHOOL ::
    (A) scholar : library
    (B) worker : office
    (C) deserter : army
    (D) ogre : home
    (E) politician : Congress

STOP   You may check your work on this section only.
Do not go on to the next section until you are told to do so.

Quantitative Section

Time: 45 Minutes

28 questions

Notes:

All numbers used in this exam are real numbers.

All figures lie in a plane.

Angle measures are positive; points and angles are in the position shown.

The answer choices are

- **A** if the quantity in Column A is greater.
- **B** if the quantity in Column B is greater.
- **C** if the two quantities are equal.
- **D** if the relationship cannot be determined from the information given.

Column A	**Column B**

1. a is an integer greater than zero

$\left(\frac{1}{2a}\right)^2$	$\frac{1}{2}a^2$

2. $= (3x)^2 - \frac{1}{3}x$

3. $0 > a > b > c$

$a - c$	$a + b$

4.

Area of the triangle	$25\sqrt{3}$

Column A	**Column B**

5. $16a + 5b = 37;\ 3b - 8a = -21$

$a + b$	2

6.

Area of a rectangle of perimeter 20	Area of a triangle of perimeter 20

7. $a \neq 0, 1$

a^2	1

8. $3a + 5b = 12;\ >3b + 5a = 28$

$3(a + b)$	15

9. A right cylinder of volume 200π cubic units has a height of 8.

Circumference of the base	10

$V = \pi r h$

8

Go on to next page

Column A	_Column B_

10. $2^{25} - 2^{24}$ | 2^{23}

11. A sequence repeats as shown:
$-5, 0, 5, -5, 0, 5, -5, 0, 5.$

Sum of 250th and 251st terms	5

12. Sales = Cost + Profit

The percent by which sales would increase if profits increased by 20 percent	20 percent

Area = 80

13.

Perimeter of the parallelogram	36

14. Bob traveled 40 percent of the distance of his trip alone, went another 20 miles with Anthony, and then finished the last half of the trip alone. How many miles long was the trip?

(A) 240

(B) 200

(C) 160

(D) 100

(E) 50

15. How many sides are in a polygon with interior angles that average 140 degrees each?

(A) 9

(B) 8

(C) 7

(D) 4

(E) 3

16. Gigi and Neville, working together at the same rate, can mow the estate's lawn in 12 hours. Working alone, what fraction of the lawn can Gigi mow in three hours?

(A) ¹⁄₂₄

(B) ¹⁄₁₂

(C) ⅛

(D) ¼

(E) ⅓

8

17.

Number of square units in the shaded portion of the square	20

Go on to next page ⟶

Use the following graphs to answer questions 18–20.

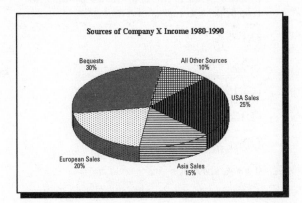

Sources of Company X Income 1980-1990

Bequests 30%
All Other Sources 10%
USA Sales 25%
European Sales 20%
Asia Sales 15%

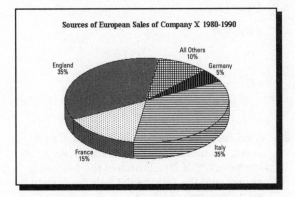

Sources of European Sales of Company X 1980-1990

All Others 10%
England 35%
Germany 5%
France 15%
Italy 35%

18. If Company X received $50,000 in bequests from 1980 through 1990, how much money did it receive from sales to France?

(A) $16,666

(B) $3,333

(C) $5,000

(D) $333

(E) $250

19. From the information given, the 1980 sales to England were what percent of the sales to Italy?

(A) 100

(B) 50

(C) 35

(D) 25

(E) It cannot be determined.

20. From the information given, if sales to Italy accounted for $1 million more than sales to France, how much income came from U.S. sales?

(A) $200,000

(B) $6,250,000

(C) $5 million

(D) $25 million

(E) It cannot be determined.

21. In Li's store, his profit is 320 percent of his cost. If his costs increase by 25 percent but his selling price remains constant, approximately what percent of the selling price is the profit?

(A) 30

(B) 70

(C) 100

(D) 250

(E) 270

22. The remainder when n is divided by 5 is 4. What is the remainder when $3n$ is divided by 5?

(A) 0

(B) 1

(C) 2

(D) 3

(E) 5

Go on to next page

Questions 23 and 24 refer to the following graphs.

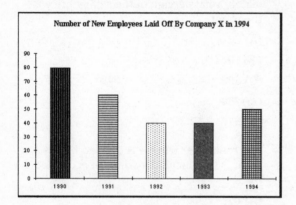

23. If new employees hired in May 1994 were ⅙ of the total employees, new employees laid off in 1994 would be what percent of the total employees in the company?

    (A) 60

    (B) 50

    (C) 33⅓

    (D) 24

    (E) 20

24. In 1995, the increase in the percentage of new employees laid off over that of the previous year was the same as the increase in the percentage of new employees hired between January and February of 1994. How many new employees were laid off in 1995?

    (A) 10

    (B) 20

    (C) 50

    (D) 60

    (E) 75

25. If ten plums cost *a* cents and six apples cost *b* cents, what is the cost of two plums and two apples in terms of *a* and *b*?

    (A) $\dfrac{3a+5b}{15}$

    (B) $3a+5b$

    (C) $15ab$

    (D) $5a+\dfrac{3b}{15}$

    (E) $\dfrac{1}{15ab}$

26. If $x \neq 4$, solve for

    $$\frac{\sqrt{x}+2}{\sqrt{x}-2}$$

    (A) -1

    (B) $\dfrac{x+4}{x-4}$

    (C) $-\sqrt{x}-1$

    (D) $\sqrt{x}+4$

    (E) $\dfrac{x+4\sqrt{x+4}}{x-4}$

27. Two cans each have a height of 10. Can A has a circumference of 10π. Can B has a circumference of 20π. Which of the following represents the ratio of the volume of Can A to the volume of Can B?

    (A) 1:10

    (B) 1:8

    (C) 1:4

    (D) 1:2

    (E) 1:1

28. A plane flies from Los Angeles to New York at 600 miles per hour and returns along the same route at 400 miles per hour. What is the average (arithmetic mean) flying speed for the entire route?

    (A) 460 mph

    (B) 480 mph

    (C) 500 mph

    (D) 540 mph

    (E) It cannot be determined from the information given.

STOP You may check your work on this section only. Do not go on to the next section until you are told to do so.

Analytical Section

Time: 60 minutes

35 questions

Directions: Each question or set of questions is based upon a specific passage or upon a set of conditions. To answer the questions, you may find it useful to draw a diagram or a chart. Select the best answer to each question.

1. Newspaper advertisement: Enroll in Apogee Test Prep! Apogee GRE students average 570 in the verbal, 640 on the quantitative, and 660 on the analytical. Raise your scores to the Apogee!

   Which of the following information would be most useful in evaluating the ad's claim?

   (A) the number of years Apogee Test Prep has been working with GRE students

   (B) the national averages for GRE scores

   (C) the number of hours of instruction offered by Apogee Test Prep

   (D) the GRE scores for Apogee students before they took the course

   (E) whether Apogee's students' scores were high enough to get the students admitted to the graduate schools of their choice

2. Last year, there was only one fatality among circus performers who did acts without a net on the trapeze or the high wire. There were more than five hundred deaths from skateboarding accidents. Therefore, it is more dangerous to skateboard than to perform without a net on the trapeze or high wire in a circus.

   The absurdity of the conclusion in the preceding material would be best illustrated by which of the following?

   (A) comparing the death rates as percentages of all skateboarders versus all circus performers on the trapeze or high-wire who work without a net

   (B) graphing the history of the number of deaths from circus acts versus the number of deaths from skateboarding over a longer period, such as 10 years

   (C) identifying more specifically the causes of the deaths: lack of qualification for the task, equipment failure, outside forces, and so on

   (D) counting severe injuries as well as deaths from the two activities

   (E) comparing the age groups of the average trapeze or high-wire artist to the age group of the average skateboarder and finding the number of deaths as a percentage of that age group

Go on to next page

3. Eating foods prepared with butter or fried in butter is detrimental to your health. Research has proven that the oils in butter clog arteries and cause heart problems. Therefore, it follows that if you want to lead a long and healthy life, you should eliminate butter from your diet.

Which of the following, if true, would most weaken the above conclusion?

(A) No one knows the effects of a completely butter-free diet on the body.

(B) Butter provides nutrients that are essential for good health and cannot be obtained from other sources.

(C) Eating a variety of foods in moderation is the key to a long and healthy life.

(D) Butter substitutes such as margarine also clog arteries and cause heart problems.

(E) Most people do not believe that butter is detrimental to their health and fail to take precautions to eliminate it from their lives.

4. My dentist said that she would use the drill when I visit her today. She used the drill when she filled my bicuspid, put a crown on my molar, and gave me a root canal. I felt a lot of pain on each occasion. I know that I will feel pain today.

The argument above depends on which of the following assumptions?

(A) The drill emits a high-frequency sound that can hurt ears.

(B) The drill will be used for a routine teeth cleaning.

(C) The patient will get a filling, crown, or root canal today.

(D) The drill was the only source of pain for the patient during past visits to the dentist.

(E) Use of the drill always leads to pain for the patient.

Questions 5–8 are based on the following information:

Alphabet Communications is linked by computer terminals *A, B, C, D, E,* and *F.* Messages are sent from one terminal to another by way of systems *X* and *Y.*

I.   System *X* allows only the following messages to be sent:

   A to *B*

   B to *C*

   C to *B*

   C to *E*

   D to *C*

   E to *A*

   A to *E*

II. System *Y* allows the following messages to be sent:

   A to *D*

   D to *A*

   D to *F*

   E to *B*

   F to *A*

III. Messages from one terminal to another may be relayed through one or more other terminals. Messages may switch from *X* to *Y.*

5. If terminal *E* breaks so that it cannot send or receive messages, which message is impossible?

(A) *D* to *B* along system *X*

(B) *D* to *A* along system *X*

(C) *C* to *B*

(D) *F* to *B*

(E) *A* to *B* when system *Y* is used part of the way

6. Which of the following routes does not require a relay through terminal *A*?

(A) *E* to *B* along system *X*

(B) *F* to *C*

(C) *F* to *B*

(D) *D* to *E* when both systems are used

(E) *B* to *E*

Go on to next page

7. One leg of a message along system X takes one second, while a similar connection along system Y takes three seconds. Which of the following takes the least time?

    (A) B to E
    (B) C to D
    (C) A to F
    (D) B to F
    (E) F to B

8. Which of the following messages requires use of both systems?

    (A) A to E
    (B) A to F
    (C) C to B
    (D) C to F
    (E) D to B

Questions 9–13 are based on the following information:

Larissa wants to plant flowers. She has seven flowers and eight spaces in which she may plant them. She has pink petunias, purple zinnias, white daisies, pink carnations, red roses, purple pansies, and purple lilies.

   I. No flowers of the same color can be planted next to each other.

   II. Pansies must be either in the first space or in the seventh space.

   III. Roses must be right before the zinnias and right after the pansies.

   IV. The lilies must be planted in the last space.

   V. A pink flower must be in spaces four and six.

   VI. A white flower must have exactly one space between it and a purple flower.

9. How many spaces are between the daisies and the closest purple flower?

    (A) one
    (B) two
    (C) three
    (D) four
    (E) five

10. Which of the following statements is not necessarily true?

    (A) There are two spaces between the pansies and a pink flower.
    (B) There are three spaces between an empty space and the zinnias.
    (C) The roses are in space two.
    (D) One space is between the carnations and the roses.
    (E) The zinnias are before the carnations.

11. How many flowers will be between the zinnias and the lilies?

    (A) one
    (B) two
    (C) three
    (D) four
    (E) five

12. Which of the following spaces will have no flower planted in it?

    (A) third
    (B) fourth
    (C) fifth
    (D) sixth
    (E) seventh

13. In which space will the carnations be planted?

    (A) two or three
    (B) four or six
    (C) six or seven
    (D) three or five
    (E) one or seven

Go on to next page

Questions 14–16 are based on the following information:

I. Seven batters are ready to play at the league's softball game. Four veterans (John, Karl, Larry, and Moe) played last year. The other three are rookies (Frank, Gary, and Harold).

II. For a rookie to bat, he must be preceded by and followed by a veteran.

III. Gary bats second while his good friend Larry is the last veteran at bat.

IV. The last batter is a veteran.

V. Karl must bat before Moe but after John.

14. Which of the following is not necessarily a true statement?

(A) Harold bats after Gary.

(B) Frank bats before Moe.

(C) Larry bats after all the rookies.

(D) Gary is the first rookie at bat.

(E) Moe bats between Karl and Larry.

15. If Karl and Frank have a fight and Frank refuses to bat next to Karl, which of the following would be the correct batting order?

(A) Larry, Harold, Moe, Frank, Gary, Karl, John

(B) Larry, Harold, Frank, Moe, Karl, Gary, John

(C) Larry, Frank, Moe, Harold, Karl, Gary, John

(D) John, Gary, Karl, Harold, Moe, Frank, Larry

(E) John, Gary, Moe, Karl, Harold, Frank, Larry

16. Which of the following could be the correct order of batters from first to last?

(A) John, Gary, Karl, Frank, Moe, Harold, Larry

(B) John, Gary, Frank, Moe, Karl, Harold, Larry

(C) Karl, Frank, Larry, Gary, Moe, Harold, John

(D) Karl, Harold, Moe, Frank, Larry, John, Gary

(E) Moe, Harold, Larry, John, Gary, Karl, Frank

17. Children today are learning less than children did ten years ago. Teachers spend too much time on administrative matters, such as report cards, PTA meetings, and field trips, and too little time on teaching the basics.

Which of the following, if true, would most strengthen the author's argument?

(A) Teachers spend over 100 school hours on field trips each year.

(B) The amount children learn is directly related to the amount of time teachers teach the basics.

(C) Teachers are spending less time in the classroom today than they did ten years ago.

(D) One out of every twelve students is flunking at least one class in high school.

(E) Parents are less involved in PTA and similar groups today than they were ten years ago.

18. Physicians correctly warn that for a rash to improve, one must stop scratching it no matter how badly it itches. Unfortunately, the lotions and salves physicians prescribe do almost no good. Recent research has shown that keeping ice packs on the rash helps because the skin becomes so numb that the itching ceases.

If all the above statements are true, which of the following is most likely true?

(A) Physicians are incapable of estimating the severity of a skin rash on another person.

(B) No prescription medication is effective in treating skin rash.

(C) Some readily obtainable treatments work better than physician-prescribed medications.

(D) Patients have a greater awareness of what feels good to them than their physicians do.

(E) One suffering from a rash should try over-the-counter lotions and salves before consulting a physician.

Go on to next page

19. All of the finalists in the Miss Universe contest last year were blondes. Therefore, in order to get more dates this year, I am going to dye my hair blond.

    The author of the above passage fails to recognize which of the following?

    (A) This year all the contestants may be redheads, and blondes will be out of fashion.

    (B) What appeals to Miss Universe judges may not be what attracts her potential dates.

    (C) The Miss Universe contestants were not chosen solely because they were blondes.

    (D) There are too many blondes already; redheads are less common and thus get more attention.

    (E) Men do not like to date Miss Universe finalists.

Questions 20–24 are based on the following information:

I. A doctor will give shots only on the day that a patient checks into the hospital for an overnight stay.

II. The check-in day for any particular disease is the same day every week.

III. Emphysema patients can check in on Wednesday and every second day thereafter except Tuesday.

IV. Cancer patients can check in only on those days when both emphysema and pneumonia patients check in.

V. Eczema patients can check in only on Tuesday and Thursday.

VI. Pneumonia patients can check in any day when eczema patients are not checking in, except Sunday.

VII. Colitis patients can check in only on the two consecutive days on which no cancer patients check in.

VIII. The hospital will check in patients on Tuesday through Sunday only.

20. On which day(s) can colitis patients be admitted?

    (A) Saturday and Sunday

    (B) Sunday and Thursday

    (C) Thursday only

    (D) Tuesday and Wednesday

    (E) Wednesday and Friday

21. On which days could the greatest number of patients with different diseases be admitted?

    (A) Monday and Friday

    (B) Wednesday and Thursday

    (C) Wednesday and Friday

    (D) Sunday and Friday

    (E) Monday and Thursday

22. On which day will pneumonia patients but not cancer patients be admitted?

    (A) Sunday

    (B) Monday

    (C) Wednesday

    (D) Friday

    (E) Saturday

23. On which days could both cancer and emphysema patients be admitted?

    (A) Monday and Tuesday

    (B) Tuesday and Wednesday

    (C) Wednesday and Thursday

    (D) Wednesday and Friday

    (E) Thursday and Friday

24. If the schedule were amended and phlebitis patients would also be admitted on every day that neither emphysema patients nor eczema patients were admitted, what days would phlebitis patients be admitted?

    (A) Tuesday

    (B) Wednesday

    (C) Thursday

    (D) Friday

    (E) Saturday

Go on to next page

Questions 25–29 are based on the following information:

Five vacancies have just opened up on the Board of Directors. These vacancies must be filled by three newcomers and two veterans. The newcomers interested in the job are Rusty, Susan, Tawny, Virginia, and Yolanda. The veterans interested in the job are Hank, Ingrid, and Jack.

I.   Hank will not serve with Ingrid.

II.   Neither Tawny nor Virginia will serve with Jack.

III. Yolanda will not serve with Hank.

25. If Hank may serve with Ingrid but all other rules remain in force, which of the following groupings is *not* possible?

    I.   Hank, Rusty, Susan, Tawny, Virginia

    II.   Ingrid, Jack, Rusty, Susan, Yolanda

    III. Hank, Ingrid, Susan, Tawny, Virginia

    IV. Ingrid, Jack, Rusty, Susan, Virginia

    (A) I only

    (B) III only

    (C) I and IV only

    (D) I, III, and IV only

    (E) I, II, III, and IV

26. If Yolanda were replaced by Zane, who has no restrictions on the people with whom he will serve, how many different groups are possible?

    (A) one

    (B) two

    (C) three

    (D) four

    (E) five

27. How many possible groups of persons can serve on the board?

    (A) one

    (B) two

    (C) three

    (D) four

    (E) five

28. Which of the following cannot serve on the board if Ingrid serves?

    (A) Tawny

    (B) Rusty

    (C) Jack

    (D) Yolanda

    (E) Susan

29. If the Board agrees to have six members, three veterans and three novices, how many groupings are possible?

    (A) 0

    (B) 1

    (C) 2

    (D) 3

    (E) 4

30. Angelica has great grades and high SAT scores and is her high school's student body president. She has been accepted to Harvard. Angelica will certainly attend Harvard next year.

The author's conclusion that Angelica will attend Harvard would be most strengthened if it were true that

    (A) Angelica was accepted under the early decision program, which binds accepted applicants to the school and prohibits them from attending any other college.

    (B) grades are the most important factor for admission to Harvard.

    (C) students who are accepted to Harvard attend Harvard.

    (D) Harvard is the most prestigious college in the world.

    (E) Harvard has tougher admission standards than does any other college in the United States.

Go on to next page

31. The opinion polls taken before the 1948 presidential election predicted that the Republican candidate, Thomas Dewey, would defeat the Democratic candidate, Harry Truman, in a landslide. In the actual election, however, Truman was the victor.

    All the following, if true, help to explain the discrepancy between the polls and the actual election EXCEPT

    (A) the last opinion poll was taken more than two weeks before the election.

    (B) the polls were conducted by telephone, and far more Republicans than Democrats owned telephones in 1948.

    (C) Dewey supporters were so confident of victory that they did not bother to vote on Election Day.

    (D) Truman was one of the most effective presidents in history.

    (E) the number of voters polled was far smaller than what mathematicians now consider acceptable to predict a presidential election.

32. Few children don't love ice cream. Athalie is a child.

    Which of the following would best complete the above statement?

    (A) Therefore, Athalie is a typical child.

    (B) Therefore, Athalie probably loves ice cream.

    (C) Therefore, Athalie eats too much ice cream.

    (D) Therefore, Athalie doesn't like ice cream.

    (E) Therefore, Athalie is an atypical child because she is allergic to ice cream.

Questions 33–35 are based on the following information:

I. A survey is made of six dogs, Rover, King, Spot, Lassie, Fido, and Prince. They are ranked in terms of their intelligence and the number of movie contracts they have received.

II. Spot is less intelligent than all the other dogs with the exception of Lassie (who gets the fewest movie contracts of all the dogs).

III. King gets more movie contracts than any other dog even though he is not the most intelligent.

IV. Prince is the fourth most intelligent dog but gets the third highest number of movie contracts because he is so friendly.

V. Rover is the most intelligent dog but gets fewer movie contracts than any other dog except Fido and Lassie.

33. Which of the following could be the order of dogs ranging from the most intelligent to the least intelligent?

    (A) Prince, Fido, King, Rover, Spot, Lassie

    (B) Prince, Rover, Fido, King, Spot, Lassie

    (C) Rover, Fido, King, Prince, Spot, Lassie

    (D) Rover, Spot, Prince, Fido, King, Lassie

    (E) Lassie, Spot, Prince, Fido, King, Rover

34. Which of the following dogs is less intelligent than Prince but gets more contracts?

    (A) Fido

    (B) Rover

    (C) Spot

    (D) Lassie

    (E) King

35. If a seventh dog, Rex, were added to the group and he had half the movie contracts of Prince, which of the following must be true?

    (A) He has more intelligence than Spot.

    (B) He has less intelligence than Prince.

    (C) He gets fewer movie contracts than Spot.

    (D) He gets more movie contracts than King.

    (E) He is friendlier than Prince.

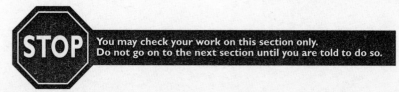

STOP — You may check your work on this section only. Do not go on to the next section until you are told to do so.

Answers to Practice Exam 1

Verbal section	Quantitative section	Analytical section
1. C	1. B	1. D
2. B	2. A	2. A
3. E	3. A	3. B
4. A	4. B	4. E
5. D	5. C	5. B
6. A	6. D	6. E
7. C	7. D	7. A
8. C	8. C	8. D
9. A	9. A	9. A
10. A	10. A	10. D
11. C	11. B	11. C
12. C	12. D	12. E
13. A	13. A	13. B
14. C	14. B	14. B
15. B	15. A	15. D
16. B	16. C	16. A
17. A	17. B	17. B
18. B	18. C	18. C
19. D	19. E	19. B
20. D	20. B	20. A
21. B	21. B	21. C
22. D	22. C	22. E
23. D	23. E	23. D
24. A	24. E	24. E
25. B	25. A	25. C
26. B	26. E	26. B
27. A	27. C	27. A
28. C	28. B	28. A
29. B		29. A
30. C		30. C
		31. D
		32. B
		33. C
		34. C
		35. C

Chapter 20

Practice Exam 1:
Answers and Explanations

Verbal Section

1. **C.** A *nadir* is the lowest point. You may jokingly say that the nadir of your life is having to study for the GRE when all your friends are out partying. The *zenith* is the highest point. The zenith of your life may come when you receive your excellent GRE scores and find that all your studying paid off (especially because you can now gloat about it to your friends)!

   Choice B, *indigenous,* means native to. Cacti are indigenous to the Southwest. Choice D, *sagacious,* means wise. If you have more degrees than a thermostat, you're sagacious.

2. **B.** *Inept* means bungling or foolish. An inept person makes a mess of anything he attempts. The prefix *in-* means not; someone inept is not adept, not skillful. Choice C, *prolific,* means abundant or producing much. An inept person is prolific at creating chaos. Choice E, *indigenous,* means native to. Long-legged blondes are indigenous to California beaches.

3. **E.** To *swagger* is to walk with arrogance, or to strut your stuff. Remember all those bad war movies you watched on Saturday afternoons back in the good old days when all your time wasn't spent studying for this exam? The evil commandant often had a short stick tucked under his arm. That was called a swagger stick, because it was a symbol of his authority and *arrogance* (conceit). To *stagger* is to teeter, to walk with difficulty, or to have trouble maintaining your balance. (Don't confuse *swagger* with *stagger*. You swagger off the football field when you score the winning touchdown. You stagger out of the locker room after drinking too much champagne to celebrate your winning touchdown.)

   To *swindle* is to cheat; *veracity* is truthfulness (*ver* means truth; *-ity* makes the word a noun). You don't cheat someone with truthfulness — you cheat someone with dishonesty.

    If a word in English is difficult, try pronouncing it with the accent of your native language. You may find that the word pronounced in your native accent will sound like a word in your own language that is similar in meaning. For example, *verdad* in Spanish means truth. Knowing that would help you make a connection with *veracity*.

   To *renege* is to go back on your word, or to not be consistent at all. (If you tell your friends that you'll split your lottery winnings with them and then a miracle happens and you actually do win ten gazillion dollars, would you *renege* on your promise? That all depends on your *veracity* in making the statement in the first place.)

   To *orchestrate* is to arrange to achieve a maximum effect. For example, a good hostess orchestrates a dinner party, arranging the seating and the entertainment to give the maximum pleasure to the guests. If you fell for this answer, hang your head in shame. The connection between orchestra and harmony is just a little too hokey, don't you think? One of my goals is to get you thinking the GRE way (don't worry, the condition is not permanent) so that you can recognize cheap tricks like this one.

And finally, to *wheedle* is to beg or flatter. It has nothing to do with *certitude,* which is just what it looks like (certainty, confidence, or assurance). Someone sure of himself or herself probably wouldn't have to beg or wheedle.

4. **A.** A group of lions is a *pride.* A group of birds is a *flock.* Some of these other words are hard, especially if English is not your first language. A *kit* is a baby coyote; a *joey* is a baby kangaroo; a *cygnet* is a baby swan. A *pelt* is the fur of a wolf.

If you think the GRE is a beastly exam, you're right. There are often questions in the analogies requiring you to know the terms for the young of animals, groups of animals, or where animals live; therefore, I'd advise you to learn the terms. Use flash cards. Label one *young animals,* and write on it such terms as kit, joey, and cygnet. Label a second card *habitats* and write things such as den, corral, and sty. Label a third card *groups of animals* and write down pride, pod, and flock. A few minutes of memorization can pay off here, as there are no roots, prefixes, or suffixes to help you define these types of words.

5. **D.** The second blank is the key to this question. If the official were *forced* to sign paperwork, you infer that he didn't want to do so and therefore was against the continuation of the program. He would want the program stopped. The second word must be something like stopped, narrowing the choices down to C and D. The *demise* is the death or conclusion of something. As soon as you have the answers narrowed down to two, if you're in a rush, this is a good time to guess and go.

To *advocate* is to defend or support a cause. The official would support the end or death of the program.

Note any key words or connectors/changers that you encounter. These are words that can change the whole sentence, such as *despite, but, even though, although, nevertheless,* and *nonetheless.* Had the word *despite* not been here, you could have read the sentence to mean that the official wanted the program to continue and therefore signed the paperwork. Choices A, B, and E would work in that case.

6. **A.** You can predict the types of words you need to fill in the blanks. Jill was reluctant to show the man to be a fraud, so she attacked or put down or criticized the weaker points of his theory. To *denounce* is to criticize, to speak harshly of. To *debunk* is to disprove. (*de* = down from, away from, to put down). The first words in choices B, C, and D fit well; the second do not. To *castigate* is to criticize or punish. (For you men who are crossing your legs, relax. *Castigate* does not mean castrate, although both are certainly punishing!) In choice E, to *disseminate* is to spread, to disburse.

7. **C.** First, use the verbs to help to eliminate wrong answers. Passages are rarely negative and don't ridicule anything (choice E). This very factual passage does not *refute* (deny, disprove) anything, eliminating choice B. A strong word like "prove" (choice D) is rarely correct (and how much can be proven in one paragraph, anyway?). Just by examining the verbs, you have narrowed your answers down to a 50-50 guess. (*Remember:* On the CBT, you must guess before the computer goes to the next question. But in any case, a 50-50 shot is a real gift.) Choice A would be tempting except that nowhere does the author make the claim that the Fremont culture was the most advanced, so how can that claim be challenged? Choice C fits with the same motif as that discussed in the previous two questions: Recurring motifs between cultures may indicate connections between those cultures.

8. **C.** Choice A sounds like something that would be interesting to know (Hmmm . . . just why *didn't* the figures have a leg to stand on?), but the passage doesn't supply the answer. Choice B is the trap. Logically, you'd think that a passage about rock art would discuss the purpose of the art, but this very short passage doesn't provide that information. You may be tempted to throw out choice C after you read that sheep were depicted with curvilinear lines and that circles were a frequent motif. However, this

information serves to answer the question in choice C with a definitive "no." The question simply asks which question can be answered. It makes no difference whether the answer is "yes" or "no." Choice D is completely irrelevant; nothing was said about religion. Choice E may have tempted you. The author did mention a possible connection between the Fremont artists and people of the Four Corners area, but you should not take the information further. Nothing was said about people from other cultures beyond those of the Four Corners area.

9. **A.** In lines 38–45, you are told that the conservative congress frustrated the program of a reformist president who had been elected by the workers. From this, you may infer that the congress and the workers were in opposition.

10. **A.** Lines 35–37 say that although presidential absolutism prevailed, "the wealthy landowners continued to control Chile." From this, you may infer that, although there was a president, he was merely a figurehead without any real power.

11. **C.** The "primary purpose" question demands that you walk a fine line: Find an answer that is broad enough to cover the entire passage but not so broad that it brings up issues that are beyond the scope of the passage.

Pay special attention to the first word (typically a verb) in the answers to a primary purpose question. The first word should match the passion or style shown by the author in the passage. The tone of this passage is neutral, which knocks out choices A and D. The author is simply laying out some information for us. She does not take a stand. In addition, these choices contain ideas that the author mentions as parts of an overall development. They are too detailed to be the answer to a primary purpose question. Choice B also contains a verb that doesn't quite match the passage. In the beginning of the passage, the author discusses Indian agriculture and empire and then mentions that the Spanish picked up on these Indian developments. Although there were undoubtedly many differences between the Indians and the Spanish, the author does not describe any in this passage. The verb in choice C, *discuss,* clearly matches the author's tone.

Three verbs are often correct answers to primary purpose questions: *discuss, describe,* and *explain.* The purpose of many passages is to *discuss* an idea, *describe* an event, or *explain* a philosophy. This choice includes social structures, which are mentioned in every paragraph in the passage. Development matches the historical aspects of the passage. Choice E contains a verb that is tempting but doesn't fit as well as *discuss.* The author is not lecturing to you. More importantly, the substance of choice E is too broad for this passage: The author does not discuss coalition governments in general. Even worse, the author does not provide you with any resolutions.

12. **C.** No way did you miss this one. What's my favorite word? Objective! This answer is often (but not always) correct for a tone or attitude question. Here, the passage is narrative, neutral. It simply states the facts. Opinionated means unreasonably stubborn, holding to your own opinion. It's just the opposite of objective, which means open-minded, not prejudging a situation. Heretical means opposed to customary doctrine, especially of a church. (You may be more familiar with another form of the word: *heretic.* A *heretic,* or disbeliever, is often martyred, like Joan of Arc, whose principles were, uh, at stake.) *Hidebound* means stubborn, inflexible. *Dolorous* means sad, mournful . . . what you are if you chose this answer.

13. **A.** *Docile* means easily trained. The opposite is *rebellious* (*belli* means fight or war). *Tactless* means imprudent, indiscriminate. *Tawdry* means tacky, gaudy, or cheap. A tactless person may call her friend's new sweater tawdry. *Vulnerable* means open to attack or damage.

14. **C.** *Extroverted* means outgoing. The opposite is shy. *Bombastic* means big-talking or grandiloquent. *Ubiquitous* means everywhere at once. After you learn these words, you'll be surprised how ubiquitous they are. You will start to see these words in advertisements, editorials, even love letters — well, maybe not every love letter (only those from your more bombastic types!).

Fun Fact: You won't see the word on the GRE, but *ubiety* is a great word to use on your friends, especially the bombastic ones who think their vocabularies are superior to yours. While ubiquitous means everywhere at once, **ubiety** means having the property of being in one particular place at one particular time. For example, the planets have ubiety. If you're so wedded to routine your friends can set their clocks by you, you have ubiety.

15. **B.** *Hardy* means strong. You'd get this question right even if you didn't know the words and assumed that they are synonyms and made the *is* sentence: "Hardy is strong." (When you were young, did you ever read the adventure series of books about the Hardy boys? That name expressed the type of young men the main characters were.) **Unruly** means unable to be ruled, uncontrollable. A group of elementary school kids is unruly when a substitute teacher tries to take over the class. Roots could help you to define choices D and E. *Dubious* means doubtful: *dub-* means doubt; *-ous* means full of. *Lucid* means clear: *luc-* means light or clear. Unless someone has a lucid explanation of why he wants to borrow your car, it's dubious you'll let him take it.

16. **B.** Iron is the raw material with which a blacksmith works. Wood is the raw material with which a carpenter works. Choice D is a pathetic attempt at humor; brides are really not the "raw material" with which a matchmaker works. Answers that are funny — or that are supposed to be funny — are never right. The GRE is about as funny as a zit on your butt.

17. **A.** The gist of the sentence is that criticizing the employee for working slowly makes him work even more slowly. The action, therefore, hurts rather than helps the situation and is counterproductive, meaning having a different result or consequence than what was intended. For example, staying up late studying the Friday night before the GRE may actually be counterproductive; you will be so tired that you may do worse on the exam than you would have had you studied less and slept more.

Try to predict whether the word to fit in the blank should be a "good" or positive word, or a "bad" or negative word. You know that if the employee gets flustered and slows down, something bad has happened. Looking for a negative word allows you to eliminate choices B, C, D, and E.

18. **B.** The key to a Sentence Completion question is usually the second blank; focus on it first. Predict that if no one would be penalized for not showing up, the students didn't have to show up, meaning that their commitment was voluntary. You probably predicted the exact word. Put the rest of choice B into the sentence to make sure it fits: yes, if the principal got jeered at, he probably hastened or rushed to make the rest of his statement.

The second words in answers A and E are exactly the opposite of what you want to say; eliminate them quickly. If something is illegal, the principal wouldn't suggest it, so eliminate choice D. Choice C is possible but doesn't make as much sense in the sentence as choice B.

Sometimes more than one answer "sorta" fits. Your job is to find the answer that fits the best, the one that seems to flow in the sentence. If this seems too subjective (and I've had students get truly upset, sincerely believing their answer just "sounded better" than the correct answer), make a quick guess and go.

19. **D.** The opposite of amusing is *exasperating,* which means annoying. Choice B, *stalwart,* means strong, sturdy, resolute.

20. **D.** *Tedious* means boring or tiresome. The opposite is interesting. Choice C, *picayune,* means minor, or unimportant. In your graduate school essay, see whether you can get away with belittling the GRE as a picayune aspect of your overall application. No one will buy it, but at least you'll impress others with your vocabulary. If you're too *craven* (afraid) to be so witty, you're sentencing the readers to yet another tedious essay.

21. **B.** To *abstain* is to refrain, to hold back (*ab-* means away from). You may abstain from voting in the student elections if you don't like any of the candidates. The opposite is to participate. In choice D, to *meander* is to wander aimlessly, to ramble. To *infuriate* is to annoy greatly, to make furious. A good public speaker will abstain from meandering too much because rambling can infuriate the audience.

22. **D.** The purpose of a staple is to attach something; the purpose of an incision (a cut) is to open something. A surgeon makes an incision to get into your chest, for example.

If you chose A, you fell for a trap. Although a button is sewn on, the purpose of a button is not to sew. Don't fall for a trap answer by looking at the meanings of the words. The fact that buttons and staples both attach items doesn't have any relevance here. You are to look at the relationships between the words, not at their meanings.

The purpose of a carpet is not to *impede,* which is to hold back, to hinder. If you want to go roller skating, then roller skating across a carpet would impede your progress; but impeding progress is not a carpet's primary function. The purpose of water is to *hydrate,* or moisten something, not to *dehydrate,* or dry something out. The purpose of a petition is to suggest or demand that something happen, not to review what happened. If you get up a petition about the GRE, your purpose is to suggest that the exam be abolished from polite society, not to review the status of the exam.

23. **D.** *Practice* and *improve* have a purpose or function relationship: You *practice* in order to *improve;* you *abbreviate* in order to *shorten.* (Did you notice the root *brev,* which means short? A harder word with this root is *brevity,* which means briefness. You may have heard the *cliche,* the overused saying, that brevity is the soul of wit. That means that if you keep it short, they'll think you're smart.) *Coddle,* choice E, means to pamper or treat carefully. Coddled eggs are cooked without having their yolks broken. *Coddle* would be a great name for a dog or cat you spoil rotten.

24. **A.** If the supervisor was afraid to hire a worker who *bungled* (messed up) so badly on her first day, it appears the supervisor's fears were well-founded or justified.

In choice C, *objective* means neutral, unbiased . . . just the opposite of what the supervisor was. Choice D, *vituperative,* means violently abusive. And *innovative* means new, original. A vituperative person may come up with some innovative *epithets* (names, titles) to call the object of his *wrath* (anger).

25. **B.** The only excuse for missing a question such as this one is laziness or carelessness. So many of the Sentence Completion questions test very hard vocabulary that when you get to one like this with very easy vocabulary you should take your time and go through each answer choice carefully to ensure that you find the correct one.

To resolve a difficulty is to solve the problem. If Liz kept working, she was unwilling to abandon the project. Only choices B and C work for the first blank; the second blank in C is just the opposite of what the sentence intends to say.

26. **B.** The first two sentences of the passage tell you that " . . . certain components of the immune system behave abnormally in people with chronic fatigue syndrome" and ". . . interleukin-2 and gamma interferon . . . may not be made in normal amounts." This is a simple detail or fact question.

Choice C is a trap answer. The author does in fact say that antibody levels are higher in depressed people; however, he does not make that statement to support the theory that the immune system may be affected by chronic fatigue syndrome. Just because a statement is true does not mean that it is the correct answer; be sure to address what the question is asking.

Remember, questions usually go in order through the passage, especially through science passages (which require you to find specific facts rather than make inferences). Because this is the first question, go back to the first sentence or two.

For those of you taking the computer-based test, don't worry: The passage will always be available on the screen for you to scroll through and reread as often as you want.

27. **A.** This is a very simple detail or fact question. Lines 3–5 tell you that the body produces chemicals such as interleukin-2 and gamma interferon during its battle against cancer.

    As you have probably noticed by now, the questions on science passages are often easier than questions on other types of passages. Even if the science passages themselves are boring or difficult to understand, the questions relating to them are usually quite straightforward; frequently, you just have to skim for a specific fact or detail.

28. **C.** *Illicit* means illegal. The opposite is legal. *Affable* means friendly (I like to think of *affable* as "af-friend-able").

29. **B.** To *irritate* is to annoy. The opposite is to soothe. Choice A, *badger,* is to harass, bother, annoy. Occasionally, the answer choices feature a word that is a synonym to the question word. It's easy to choose this one, because uppermost in your mind is the definition. "Badger, hmmm. That means to annoy, to irritate. Oh, there it is!" Keep in mind that the name of the game is *antonyms.*

30. **C.** Well, here's a word that every student knows. A *truant* is absent from school. A *deserter* is absent from the army (*de* = down or away from). In choice E, an *ogre* is a monster. (Notice how *ogre* is really o-GRE? Coincidence or cosmic reality? You be the judge.)

Quantitative Section

1. **B.** Plug in numbers. Suppose that $a = 1$. Then Column A is $\frac{1}{2} \times 1$, which is $\frac{1}{2}$, and then $\frac{1}{2}^2$ which is $\frac{1}{4}$. Column B requires you to square the 1 first, which is simply 1, and then multiply by $\frac{1}{2}$ to get $\frac{1}{2}$. So far, Column B is bigger. Try a different number. Suppose that $a = 2$. Then Column A is $\frac{1}{2}$ of 2, which is 1. You know that $1^2 = 1$. Column B is $\frac{1}{2}$ of 4 (because $2^2 = 4$) and Column B is still greater. No matter what you plug in (and you should always plug in more than once, or you'll never know whether the answer depends on what you plug in), Column B is larger.

    Do you remember the Sacred Six you are to plug in for variables? They are 1, 2, 0, –1, –2, and $\frac{1}{2}$. Usually, just plugging in 1 and 2 will do the job for you.

2. **A.** Ah, if you chose C, you got careless.

    Whenever you see a choice C, double- and triple-check it. More traps lie in the C answers than in most of the rest of the answers. If your first instinct is to choose C, you're probably just making some nasty test maker's day by falling for his trap.

    First, you have to say to yourself in English what the symbols means. Say, "I have something in a triangle. First, I multiply that something by 3. Then I square that answer. Then I take a third of that something. Then I subtract the second from the first." In other words, substitute the number in the triangle for the *x* in the equation. For Column A, you have 3×-3, which is –9. Then $-9^2 = 81$. Next, $\frac{1}{3}$ of $-3 = -1$. Finally, $81 - (-1)$ means $81 + 1 = 82$. For Column B, you have $3 \times 3 = 9$. Then $9^2 = 81$. Next, $\frac{1}{3}$ of $3 = 1$. Finally, $81 - 1 = 80$. You had to keep your negatives and positives straight.

    Whenever a problem has a negative variable, double-check your signs. You can easily make a careless mistake with them.

3. **A.** You have absolutely no excuse for missing this problem, even if you did get a brain cramp when you first looked at it. Remember my tip from Chapter 13: Cancel quantities that are identical in both columns. Slash off the *a* in both columns. That leaves you with –*c* and +*b*. Because *c* is negative, a negative *c* is a double negative, which is actually positive. In Column B, *b* remains negative (because a positive times a negative is negative). Because any positive is greater than any negative, Column A is larger.

Did you look at all the variables and choose D, thinking the answer depended on what you plugged in? That's a very good first reaction, but then be sure to do the actual plugging. Say that the numbers are $-1, -2,$ and -3. (Be careful not to get messed up and put $-3, -2, -1$. With negatives, everything is backwards: -1 is greater than -2.)

Column A is $-1-(-3) = -1+3 = 2$. Column B is $-1+(-2) = -3$. Please, please be careful not to overuse and abuse my tips. They are glorious tips and will help you if you treat them with respect. That means when you use a tip, make a commitment to it: Work it through to the end. If you decide that the answer is going to depend on what you plug in, *actually plug in numbers* and work the problem through.

Usually, there are three times when a choice D is valid. You think D when you have a geometry problem with no picture. You think D when a picture specifically says it is not drawn to scale (something that is very rare on the GRE). And you choose D when you have *actually* plugged in different values for variables, *actually* done the work, and *actually* gotten different answers.

4. **B.** If you chose D, you fell for the trap. You probably looked at the question, saw that only one side was given, and figured you didn't have enough info to answer the question. Wrong. You should have reminded yourself of the tip that when a figure is given, the answer is rarely D. (This is the flip of the tip that when a geometry problem gives words but no pictures, it is usually D.)

Do you remember your Pythagorean Triples? They were discussed in Chapter 10. For many right triangles, the sides have a special ratio. For a 30:60:90 triangle, that ratio is $side : side\sqrt{3} : 2\,side$. The side opposite the 30 is the shortest side. Here, that's the 5. The side opposite the 60 is the next shortest side, the "$side\sqrt{3}$" side. Here that would be $5\sqrt{3}$. Although you don't need to know this to find the area of the triangle, the hypotenuse (the side opposite the 90-degree angle) is the longest side, the "2-side" side. Here, it is 10.

The area of a triangle is $\frac{1}{2}\,base \times height$. The base is $5\sqrt{3}$; the height is 5. Therefore, the area is $\frac{1}{2}25\sqrt{3}$. Don't bother finding it exactly; it certainly is less than $25\sqrt{3}$. If you chose C, you did *allllllll* that work, and because you forgot the very last step, missed the stupid question anyway.

How can you prevent making a careless mistake like forgetting to multiply by ½ in this problem? Simple. Write down the formula for the problem immediately on the scratch paper. It may seem childish and extra work, but it takes only a gigasecond and can prevent careless errors. When you see the formula, you plug the numbers into it and work it through.

5. **C.** It's amazing how many questions that require you actually to do the work and solve the problem turn out to be choice C. I'm not saying that you should choose C as soon as you start shoving the pencil around, but the more calculations you do, the more often the answer seems to be C. (That's the flip of the tip in the lecture that if the quantities appear to be equal at first glance, without doing any work, there's probably a trap.) Here, set the equations up vertically:

$16a + 5b = 37$

$-8a + 3b = -21$

You want to either add or subtract to get the same numerical coefficient (the number that goes in front of the variable) for the a and the b. When you add the equations here (and notice how I've moved the a to the front of the second equation, to make the variables add up neatly), you get $8a + 8b = 16$. Divide both sides by 8 to get $a + b = 2$.

You didn't have to go through the whole mess of substitution. That is, you didn't have to say for the first equation that $16a = 37 - 5b$, and then say that $a = {}^{37}\!/_{16} - {}^{5b}\!/_{16}$, and then substitute that for the value of a in the second equation. I'd call that *gratuitous* (uncalled for, unearned, unnecessary) violence. When you have two equations, line them up vertically and work so that either one of the variables drops out (for example, you may have $3b - 3b$) or so that the variables have the same numerical coefficients.

6. **D.** When a geometry problem has no figure drawn, the answer is often choice D because it *de*pends on how the figure is drawn. A rectangle of perimeter 20 can have, for example, sides of 1 and 9 and 1 and 9, making the area 9. Or it can have sides of 6 and 4 and 6 and 4, making the area 24. (The area of a rectangle is *length times width*. If you forgot this, return to the geometry portion of the math review.) A triangle of perimeter 20 can have sides of 4, 7, and 9, or a *plethora* (abundance) of other combinations. And because you don't know whether the triangle is a right triangle, you have no idea what the height is. That height could be a leg of the triangle, be inside the triangle, or be outside the triangle. There is not enough information to compare the quantities.

7. **D.** If you chose A, you fell right for my cunningly devised trap (okay, so it was a cheap trick). Don't forget that a negative squared is a positive. If a were -2, for example, then $-2^2 = 4$, and Column A is larger. And what if a is a fraction? If $a = \frac{1}{2}$, then $\frac{1}{2}^2 = \frac{1}{4}$, and B is bigger. If the answer could be A or could be B, it depends on what you plug in, choice D.

Remember the Sacred Six I asked you to get into the habit of plugging in? They are 1, 2, 0, -1, -2, $\frac{1}{2}$. You don't need to plug in 0 or 1 this time, but you do need to plug in the fraction. You should chant to yourself as if it were a mantra: "positive, negative, zero, fraction."

8. **C.** Line the equations up vertically and either add or subtract them to get the same numerical coefficients (the numbers before the variables). In this case, you add:

$$3a + 5b = 12$$
$$5a + 3b = 28$$
$$\overline{8a + 8b = 40}$$

Now divide both sides of the equation by 8, to get $a + b = 5$. Finally, $3 \times 5 = 15$.

9. **A.** The volume of any figure is (*area of the base $\times$ height*). Because the base of a cylinder is a circle, the volume of a cylinder is π radius^2 $\times$ height. Divide the volume, 200π, by the height, 8, to find that the area of the base is 25π. Because the base is a circle of area $= \pi$ radius^2, the radius is 5. But don't choose B; you're not finished yet.

The circumference of a circle is 2π radius, which here is 10π. If you chose C, you fell for the trap. You forgot your π! The circumference of 10π is actually $10 \times$ approximately 3.14, which is more than 10 (don't bother to figure it out exactly). The moral of the story: Keep your eye on the π.

If your first thought when you look at a problem is that the columns are equal, think again. Usually — not always — you have to do actual calculations to get a C.

Usually when a geometry problem is all words and no pictures, it's choice D, because the comparison will depend on what the picture looks like. This is an exception to the tip, put in just to keep you from using the tips automatically rather than actually thinking the problem through.

10. **A.** What do I mean by giving you a problem like this without allowing you access to your calculator? Well, you have two choices (murder and mayhem are not among them). You can make a quick guess on this problem and pretty much blow it off entirely. Or you can be very smart and realize that if a principle is valid with a large number, it is usually valid with a small number. In other words, instead of 2^{25} or 2^{24}, makt it 2^5 or 2^4. You can quickly figure 2^5 as $2 \times 2 \times 2 \times 2 \times 2 = 32$. Then 2^4 is 16, and $32 - 16 = 16$. Therefore, $2^5 - 2^4$ is 2^4, just as $2^{25} - 2^{24}$ is 2^{24}, not 2^{23}.

11. **B.** There are three terms in the sequence. That means that every third term is 5. Divide 250 by 3 to get 83 with a remainder of 1. That means that the 249th number is 5 (because 249 divides evenly by 3), the 250th number is –5, and the 251st number is 0. Add $-5 + 0 = -5$.

This question was put in to get people to waste their time. Oh sure, you could have counted on your fingers up to the 250th term, but who has that sort of time? Find the closest number that divides by 3 and then work from there.

Did you choose D for this problem? If so, you probably confused "It depends" with "Don't have a clue — duuuh!" Choice D does not mean *you* don't know how to do the problem but rather that no one could do the problem with the *paucity* (lack) of information presented in the problem. Don't take it personally, in other words. Just because you can't do a problem yourself does not indicate it is undoable, or a choice D.

12. **D.** If you chose C, didn't you feel guilty thinking this was just a little bit too easy? Besides, if the columns look equal, there's usually a trap. A percentage means that you must know a part and a whole. For example, if the sales were $100 and the profits went up from 25 to 30, then the sales went up from 100 to 105 (assuming the costs remained the same) and the percent increase was 5 percent. But say that the original sales were $150 and the profits were $10. Then if the profits go up 20 percent to $12, the sales go up only two dollars as well, to $152, and $^2/_{152} = .013$, or roughly 1⅓ percent. The answer *depends* on the original values for both the sales and the profit.

I am less concerned, as a teacher, with your getting the question right than I am with your not missing the question. That may sound *circumlocutional* (arguing in a circle), but it's not really. You have to be sure that you don't miss the question by falling for a trap before your brain has time to process the information and solve the problem. Think of this rather like the physician's creed: First, do no harm.

13. **A.** The area of a parallelogram is *base × height*. You know the base is 10. The height is a straight line from the tallest point of the figure to the base.

Because the area is 80, the height must be 8 (because $10 \times 8 = 80$). That means that the slanted line which is the side of the parallelogram must be more than 8, because a slanted line is longer than a straight line (the shortest distance between two points is a straight line, to indulge in a *hackneyed,* or overused, expression). You don't know what the length of the side actually is, but you know it's more than 8. Ten plus "more than 8" is "more than 18." Two times "more than 18" is "more than 36." Who cares how much more than 36 it is? Not I. You don't have to find the exact perimeter (the sum of the lengths of all the sides); you only have to compare the quantities.

When a figure is given in a QC problem, the answer is rarely D. Usually — but not always, she says, *equivocating* (hedging) madly — the figure provides enough information to compare the quantities, even if there is not enough to come up with a precise answer.

14. **B.** If the last half of the trip were alone, then the 40 percent and the 20 miles are the first half, or 50 percent. Because 50 percent - 40 percent = 10 percent, 20 miles = 10 percent. It may be easier to think in terms of fractions: 10 percent = $^1/_{10}$. One-tenth of *something* is 20; that *something* is 200. (Arithmetically: $^1/_{10}x = 20$. Divide both sides through by 1/10, which means inverting and multiplying by $^{10}/_1$, and $20 \times 10 = 200$.) This was a good problem to talk through; you needed reasoning, not arithmetic.

15. **A.** The formula for the average measure of an interior angle of a polygon is

$$\frac{(n-2)180}{n}$$

where n stands for the number of sides. Solve for n. Here, set up the equation:

$$\frac{(n-2)180}{n} = 140$$

Cross multiply: $(n-2)180 = 140n$.

$180n - 360 = 140n$

$40n = 360$

$n = 9$

If you chose C, you found $(n-2)$. That represents the number of triangles, not the number of sides.

16. **C.** The key to this problem is knowing that Gigi and Neville work at the same rate. If they finish the lawn in 12 hours, each did ½ of the job in 12 hours, meaning it would have taken Gigi working alone 24 hours to finish the lawn. Because 3 hours is ⅛ of 24 hours, she could have done ⅛ of the job in that time.

17. **B.** Think of a shaded area as a leftover. It's what's left over after you have subtracted the unshaded area from the figure as a whole. Because Column A tells you that the figure is a square, you find its area by multiplying side times side: $8 \times 8 = 64$. The diameter of the circle is the same as the length of the square, 8. The radius of a circle is half the diameter, or 4. The area of a circle is $\pi \, radius^2$, or 16π. Find the shaded area by subtracting $64 - 16\pi$.

Do not, I repeat, do not bother actually figuring out how much 16π is. You know that π is slightly larger than 3.14, but I wouldn't even make things that complicated. Just say that π is bigger than 3. Multiply $16 \times 3 = 48$. Subtract $64 - 48 = 16$. The actual area will be even smaller than that because you'll be subtracting some number larger than 48 (whatever you get when you multiply 3.14×16, which I am not about to do, and neither should you). Because 16 is smaller than 20, and the "real" answer will be even smaller than 16, Column B is bigger.

If you've forgotten how to do shaded areas, return to Chapter 10, where I discuss a simple three-step approach.

18. **C.** Bequests account for 30 percent of total income. *Hint:* Ignore the zeros; just let the equation be $50 = .3x$. Divide both sides through by .3 to get x (total income) = 166.67. Then European sales were 20 percent of that, or $166.67 \times .20 = 33.3$. Sales to France were 15 percent of that: $.15 \times 33.3 = 5$.

Estimate wildly. The answer choices are so far apart that you can get away with murder here. Say that Bequests are about a third of the total, making the total 15. Then European sales are 20 percent or a fifth of that, for 3. Then French sales are 15 percent of that, or .45. The only answer even remotely close to that is choice C. If this question really slows you down, just guess.

19. **E.** Read the title on the graphs: They show income and sales from 1980 through 1990. You cannot figure out sales in one particular year. If you chose A, you fell for the trap. And shame on you for being so *credulous* (gullible). You should have been more paranoid than that. If something looks too good to be true, it probably is.

20. **B.** Good problem. If you got this question right, *kudos* and *accolades* and *encomium* (praises) to you. This question takes a lot of backtracking.

Sales to Italy are 20 percent more than sales to France (35 percent - 15 percent), meaning that 20 percent = 1 million, or $\frac{1}{5}$ = 1 million, thus 100 percent = 5 million. But this is 100 percent of the second graph, which is still only 20 percent of the first graph. In other words, the total 5 million in the second graph is 20 percent or $\frac{1}{5}$ of the first graph, such that the total of the first graph is 25 million. (Are you totally confused yet? Just keep reading and no one will get hurt.) USA sales are 25 percent or $\frac{1}{4}$ of that: .25 × $25 million is — hey, stop right there; don't actually do the work out. Estimate. A fourth of 25 is just over 6; the only possible correct answer is B. Don't do all the work until you've checked out the answer choices; often, you can do just a rough estimate and get the correct answer.

21. **B.** Plug in numbers. Because you're dealing with dollars (and with percentages), make the cost be $100. Then the profit is $320 (320% of 100 = 320). The selling price, which is *cost + profit*, equals $420. If the cost, $100, goes up 25%, it is now $125. The selling price remains constant at $420. That means the new profit is (420 – 125 =) 295. The percent that profit is of selling price is $\frac{is}{of} = \frac{295}{420}$ = about 70%.

You could have eliminated answers D and E immediately by using common sense. The profit can never be more than the selling price because the selling price is a combination of cost plus profit.

If you chose A, you found the percentage that the cost was of the selling price ($\frac{125}{420}$). It's a good idea to circle what the question is asking for so that you keep it in mind. The mere fact that the answer you got is one of the multiple choices does not in the least indicate that you got the right answer — only that you may have given the test makers the satisfaction of seeing another fish go for the bait.

22. **C.** You know the remainder cannot be 5; you cannot have 5 left over when you divide by 5. (Think of $\frac{19}{5}$: It's not "1 remainder 5," but 2.) Eliminate choice E.

A great way to simplify a remainder problem is to *plug in numbers*. Choose a number that fits the criterion of the problem: a number divided by 5 has a remainder of 4. How about 9 (because $\frac{9}{5}$ = 1 with 4 left over)? Make n = 9. Then $3n$ = 27. When 27 is divided by 5, the remainder is 2 ($\frac{27}{5}$ = 5 with 2 left over). Still skeptical? Try another number. Say that n = 14 (because $\frac{14}{5}$ = 2 remainder 4). Then $3n$ = 14 × 3 = 42. Finally, $\frac{42}{5}$ = 8 remainder 2.

23. **E.** This relatively simple problem takes two steps. In May there were 50 new employees hired. 50 = 20 percent or $\frac{1}{5}$ of the total (250) employees. If there were 250 employees and 50 of them were laid off, then $\frac{1}{5}$ (back to that same number!) were laid off.

Did you see the shortcut in this problem? The 50 in the top graph is the same as the 50 in the bottom graph. Therefore, whatever percent you have for the top graph is the same as the percent for the bottom graph. You did not need to go through all of that work.

24. **E.** First, figure out the percent increase in new hires between January and February. Twenty new employees were hired in January and 30 were hired in February. To find a percent increase or decrease, you use the formula: *Number increase or decrease divided by original whole* (the number you began with). Here, that's $\frac{10}{20} = \frac{1}{2}$ = 50 percent.

The number of employees laid off in 1994, according to the bottom graph, was 50. The number laid off in 1995 was 50 percent greater than this. Fifty percent of 50 is $\frac{1}{2}$ of 50, or 25. Add 50 + 25 = 75.

Did you fall for choice D? The increase in new hires between January and February was 10, but this does not mean that the number of layoffs in 1995 was 10 higher than the number in 1994. You must figure the *percentage*.

25. **A.** If 10 plums cost a cents, then each plum costs $\frac{1}{10}a$ and 2 plums cost $\frac{2}{10}$ or $\frac{1}{5}a$. If 6 apples cost b cents, then each apple costs $\frac{1}{6}b$ cents, and 2 apples cost $\frac{2}{6}b$ or $\frac{1}{3}b$ cents. Now use 15 as a common denominator for 5 and 3. Convert: $\frac{1}{5}a = \frac{3}{15}a$, and $\frac{1}{3}b = \frac{5}{15}b$.

This pretty confusing problem assumes you have some sort of sick fetish for fractions. You can work out the problem without stooping so low as to deal with those nasty little things at all. The easy way to do this problem is to substitute numbers for the variables. Let $a = 10$, such that each plum costs 1 cent and two plums cost 2 cents. Let $b = 6$ such that each apple costs 1 cent and 2 apples cost 2 cents. Then the total is 4 cents. Plug the same values into the answer choices to see which one comes out to be 4. In a, you have $3(10) + 5(6) = 60$ divided by $15 = 4$.

You must check all the answer choices when you plug in your own numbers. Did you get as far as choice E? If you did, you got 4 there as well $\left(\frac{1}{15} \times 10 \times 6 = \frac{1}{15} \times 60 = 4\right)$. What now? If you get more than one correct answer based on the terms you plug in, plug in different terms and try again.

Suppose that this time $a = 20$ and $b = 6$. Now the cost of each plum is 2 cents, making the cost of two of them 4 cents. The cost of the apples remains the same. Two plums (4 cents) plus 2 apples (2 cents) $(2\text{ cents}) = 6$ cents cents. The new answer you're looking for is 6.

Don't bother going through all of the answer choices again. You've already narrowed the field down to A or E; try just those two.

Now choice A is $(60 + 30) \div 15 = 90 \div 15 = 6$. It works. Choice E is $\frac{1}{15} \times 20 \times 6 = \frac{1}{5} \times 120$, which does not equal 6. Throw away E; A is correct.

I was incredibly kind on this problem in making A the correct answer. A less magnificent human being would have switched answers A and E. Then, if you didn't bother plugging in the answers for every single answer choice and stopped at A, you would fall for the trap.

26. **E.** Does this problem make you think of Egyptian hieroglyphics? Join the crowd. Instead of just saying, "That's History, babe!" and guessing at this problem, make it easy to work through by *plugging in numbers*. Choose a number that has an easy square root. Make $x = 9$ (because $\sqrt{9} = 3$). Now solve the question:

$$\left(\sqrt{9} + 2\right) \div \left(\sqrt{9} - 2\right) = (3 + 2) \div (3 - 2) = \frac{5}{1} = 5$$

Keep in mind that 5 is the answer to the problem. It is not the value of x. Jot the 5 down to the side, draw a circle around it, put arrows pointing to it, do whatever it takes to remind yourself that the answer you want is 5. Now go through each answer choice, seeing which one comes out to be 5. Only choice E works:

$$\left(9 + 4\sqrt{9} + 4\right) \div 9 - 4 = (9 + 4 \times 3 + 4) \div 5 = (9 + 12 + 4) \div 5 = \frac{25}{5} = 5.$$

Be very, very careful not to put 3 in for x in the problem. The $x = 9$; the square root of $x = 3$. I suggest you make a chart to the side, simply writing down $x = 9$ and ANSWER $= 5$.

When you plug in numbers, go through every single answer choice, *soporific* (sleep-inducing) though that may be. If you started with choice E, for example, and made a careless mistake, you would find that choices D, C, and B didn't work either . . . and probably choose A by process of elimination. If you take just a second to work out A, you'll see that it too is wrong, alerting you to the fact that you made a careless mistake somewhere.

For you algebra addicts who can't live without your fix: Simplify the denominator by multiplying each side through by $\left(\sqrt{x} + 2\right)$.

$$\left[\left(\sqrt{x} + 2\right) \div \left(\sqrt{x} - 2\right)\right] \times \left[\left(\sqrt{x} + 2\right)\left(\sqrt{x} + 2\right)\right].$$

The numerator is $\left(\sqrt{x} + 2\right)\left(\sqrt{x} + 2\right)$. Use FOIL (First, Outer, Inner, Last) to multiply these: $\sqrt{x} \times \sqrt{x} = x$. Then $\sqrt{x} \times 2 = 2\sqrt{x}$. Next, $2 \times \sqrt{x} = 2\sqrt{x}$. Finally, $2 \times 2 = 4$. Add: $x + 4\sqrt{x} + 4$.

The denominator is $\left(\sqrt{x}-2\right)\times\left(\sqrt{x}+2\right)$. Use FOIL again to multiply these: $\sqrt{x}\times\sqrt{x}=x$.
Then $x\times2=2x$. Next, $\sqrt{x}\times2=2\sqrt{x}$. Next, $\sqrt{x}\times-2=-2\sqrt{x}$.

The $2\sqrt{x}$ and $-2\sqrt{x}$ cancel each other out, leaving you with $x-4$.

If you took my advice in Chapter 11 and memorized some basic FOIL problems, you knew immediately that $(a+b)(a+b)=a^2+2ab+b^2$ (just substitute x for the a, and 2 for the b). You knew that $(a+b)(a-b)=a^2-b^2$ (substitute the x for the a and the 2 for the b). If you haven't memorized these, go back to Chapter 11 and do so now.

27. **C.** The volume of any figure is $(area\ of\ base)\times height$. The base of a cylinder is a circle. Because the area of a circle is πr^2, the volume of a cylinder is $\pi r^2 h$.

    The circumference of a circle is $2\pi r$. Therefore, the radius of Can A = 5; the radius of Can B = 10. Volume Can A $= 5^2\pi\times10=250\pi$. Volume Can B $=10^2\pi\times10=1000\pi$. Finally, $250\pi:1000\pi=1:4$.

    You may — or may not — be given the necessary formulas to solve this type of question. Don't take any chances: Have the geometry formulas memorized. They're all given in the math review.

28. **B.** If you chose C, my work here has been in vain. To find an average, you add up the terms and then divide by the number of terms. But this is a Time-Rate-Distance problem and the terms here aren't simply 600 and 400. You have to find the length of time spent flying at 600 mph and the length of time spent flying at 400 mph, and then add *those* and divide.

    If you think logically about this problem, know the answer can't be C, but don't want to spend time working it out, you can eliminate a few more answers. You know that the plane must go more time at the slower rate and less time at the faster rate. That means the average is going to be less than half of the "average" 500 mph. Immediately narrow your answers down to A and B. If you're in a hurry, guess and go.

    You probably wanted to make a simple Time-Rate-Distance chart for this problem, right? Good thinking . . . but it won't work here. To make a chart of that sort, you have to have at least two of the three variables. For example, if you know rate and distance, you can find time. But here, you have only one variable, rate. You cannot solve for time and distance. What do you do now? Find a ratio.

    Use a common multiple of 12 (actually, 1,200) miles. In 2 hours, the plane traveling at 600 mph will go 1,200 miles. In 3 hours, the plane traveling at 400 miles will go 1,200 miles. To find the average, add 600 twice and 400 three times . . . and then divide by 5, not by 2. $600+600+400+400+400=2400$. $\frac{2400}{5}=480$.

    Did the words "arithmetic mean" confuse you? They're put there to prevent any lawsuits over confusion of terms. The "average" can mean different things to different people; the "arithmetic mean" is the precise term. Don't worry about it. The info in parentheses is usually there to cover fundamental anatomical regions in case of litigation. You can ignore it.

Analytical Section

1. **D.** The ad claims that Apogee test prep is effective in raising scores. To determine whether this is true, you need to see some data regarding score increases. The problem is that the data indicate scores after the students took the course but do not say by how many points (if any) these scores are higher than what the students were scoring before they took the course. Choice D would allow you to subtract pre-scores from post-scores and see whether the scores went up.

Choice A is very close in that the before-or-after issue does address the heart of the matter about whether scores went up. The problem with choice A is that it isn't of much use when it comes to evaluating the ad's claim. If these scores were achieved before Apogee students took the course, what were they after? Maybe these scores are very impressive, but perhaps the scores were even higher after. (It does seem incongruous that the company would not list the higher, after-course course scores, but the possibility mentioned does exist.) If these scores were achieved after the course, what were they before? Simply knowing whether the scores were from before or after is not enough information.

From one perspective, choice B is useful in that the numbers cited in the ad wouldn't be impressive if the national averages were much higher. However, even if the scores are low, it's still possible that Apogee raised scores. It could be that Apogee students had very low pre-scores.

The argument to rule out choice C is similar to that used to rule out choice A. Consumers may not enroll in the course if they find out that the course doesn't last long; but even if this were the case, the course could still raise scores.

Choice E is out. A GRE student would certainly like to earn scores that will get him or her into graduate school, but the ad makes no claim about this. Even scores that are not good enough for graduate school may still be substantially higher than they were earlier.

2. **A.** The inane conclusion is that skateboarding is more dangerous than performing without a net on a trapeze or high-wire in the circus. This conclusion is based on the fact that, in one year, more skateboarders died than trapeze and high-wire performers died. You could show this conclusion to be flawed by showing the number of deaths among those performers as a percentage of all performers versus the number of deaths of skateboarders as a percentage of all skateboarders. If there are, for example, 100 trapeze artists and 3 died, that's a much larger percentage than if there are 10 million skateboarders and 3,000 died.

Choice B addresses the problem of a longer time span, but it still does not deal with the deaths as a percentage of all involved in the activity. That would be like saying that because more people have died in traffic accidents in the past decade than from jumping out of planes without a parachute, riding in a car is more dangerous than jumping out of a plane without wearing a parachute. Choice C does not change the conclusion. The causes for the death rate do not show that it is illogical to conclude that skateboarding is more dangerous than working the trapeze. Choice D is tempting; however, unless it compares the injuries as a percent of those people involved in the activity, you're right back to the original problem. Choice E talks about a percentage but then goes overboard and brings in the age group question. The original conclusion dealt with everyone in the activity as a whole, not people in various age groups.

3. **B.** The conclusion that you should eliminate butter is predicated on butter's clogging arteries and causing heart problems. This argument assumes that arteries and heart problems are the only factors that matter in regard to the consumption of butter. Perhaps there is a positive factor associated with butter that outweighs the artery and heart problems. Such a factor would argue for the use of butter and thus weaken the conclusion. Choice B does just this. In fact, it argues that one *must* consume butter.

Most of the answer choices seem reasonable, but they don't address the question, which is what weakens the conclusion. Just because most people don't believe butter is detrimental to their health (choice E), for example, does not weaken the conclusion that butter in fact is detrimental. Choice C is probably the second best answer. If eating a variety of foods is the key to a healthy life, butter may be part of that variety; however, choice B discusses butter specifically and thus is a slightly better answer.

Choice A is similar to choice C in that it is too indirect to be a good answer. Choice D would fit in to some extent if the conclusion said that butter is the only thing to eliminate, but this choice is out primarily because one could shoot back with, "Then eliminate butter and all substitutes."

4. **E.** The author's conclusion about feeling pain follows from evidence about the use of a drill. This logically follows only if there is a connection between the drill and pain, which is what choice E provides. If choice E isn't true, you cannot be certain that pain will result.

Choice A is too specific. Earache does not have to be assumed because the drill can produce pain in a variety of ways. Choice B is way off because it provides a reason to think that pain *won't* result from the drill. Choice C assumes more than what needs to be assumed. The patient may be getting an inlay today and may assume that the experience will be similar to her past experiences because the drill will be used. In this argument, she is using the evidence of the drill to conclude that she will feel pain. The author does not need to assume choice D. She may actually *know* (not just assume) that other factors caused her pain, but she is focusing on the drill here.

Questions 5–8

In most mapping games, the actual locations are not important. The games typically reward your ability to keep track of the connections. Put the terminals in a circle (as in Figure 1):

Indicate the connections with arrows. The simplest way to do this is to point the arrows towards the ending point of a connection (see Figure 2). Double-headed arrows indicate that the connections go both ways (for example, *B* to *C* and *C* to *B*).

Figure 1   Figure 2

5. **B.** Draw a diagram for this problem (see Figure 1). Be sure to disconnect terminal *E*. A quick inspection of the connections reveals that choices A, C, and D are all possible, so eliminate those choices. Choice E is possible (see Figure 2):

Figure 1   Figure 2

This leaves choice B as the answer. D can go to C which can go to B, but the message stops there.

6. **E.** If E must transmit on system X, it must go to A, so choice A is out. Choices B and C are similar. F must go to A, so both choices are out. To use both systems from D to E, the connection is D - F - A - E, so choice D is out.

7. **A.** Here are the fastest paths for each choice.

   (A) $B (X) C (X) E$ 2 seconds

   (B) $C (X) E (X) A (Y) D$ 5 seconds

   (C) $A (Y) D (Y) F$ 6 seconds

   (D) $B (X) C (X) E (X) A (Y) D (Y) F$ 9 seconds

   (E) $F (Y) A (X) B$ 4 seconds

8. **D.** Choice A can readily be eliminated as A and E are connected by X. A to D to F can be done with Y, so choice B is out. C to B goes along X, so choice C is out. As for choice D, C could go to B, which won't get anywhere, or E. To move toward F, E must go to A and switch from system X to system Y to move to D. Finally, the message will go from D to F. Note that choice E is out because a D - C - B relay along X will do the job.

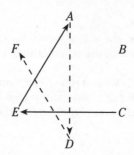

Questions 9–13

Because there are so many flowers to keep straight, make a list or "pool" of them. To the side or on your scratch paper, jot down the flowers: pink petunias, purple zinnias, white daisies, pink carnations, red roses, purple pansies, purple lilies.

Draw eight spaces. Keep in mind that one space will be empty because there are only seven types of flowers. You can drive yourself crazy trying to figure out what goes in that space if you forget this disparity between flowers and available spaces.

Statement I give information that is written off to the side, not in a chart. Jot down a brief not, such as "same colors not together."

Statement II allows you to write purple pansies above space 1 and again above space 7. Be careful to put the note in *both* spaces; you don't know yet which one will finally get the flower.

Statement III tells you that the order is pansies-roses-zinnias. From this, you know that the pansies cannot be in space 7 because there is no room for two types of flowers after space 7. Scratch off the purple pansies from space 7; you have ascertained they go in space 1.

Statement IV puts the lilies in the last space. I don't know about you, but this is my favorite type of statement. Brief, to the point, and no-nonsense. Let's have more of these.

Statement V puts a pink flower, either petunias or carnations, in spaces 4 and 6. Be sure to write *both* petunias and carnations in the blanks. You cannot arbitrarily decide petunias go in 4 and carnations in 6, or vice versa. Keep your options open.

Statement VI deals with a white flower. The only white flower is the daisy. It must go in space 5, resulting in one space between it and the purple zinnias. The other purple flowers are the pansies and lilies. To be one space away from the pansies, the daisies would have to go in space 3, which is already taken up with the zinnias. To be one space away from the purple lilies, the daisies would have to go in space 6, which is already filled with either the petunias or the carnations. Space 5 it is.

purple pansies	red roses	purple zinnias	pink petunias or carnations	white daisies	pink petunias or carnations		purple lilies
1	2	3	4	5	6	7	8

You can now look at the chart and answer any question with *celerity*. (No, not a dieter's worst nightmare; that's celery. **Celerity** means speed.) Note especially that space 7 is empty.

9. **A.** The closest purple flower is the zinnias, only one space away. Keep in mind that this type of question is not trying to trick or trap you; once you have your chart made, the answers are all straightforward.

10. **D.** The carnations can be in space 4, making them two spaces away from the roses, or the carnations can be in space 6, making them four spaces away from the roses. Note how cunningly the question is phrased: "is not necessarily true." That means the statement could be true, but it doesn't have to be.

When you have an "open option" on a chart, a space that "could be" one thing or "could be" another, you will almost always see a question asking about the options. Watch for it.

11. **C.** If you chose D, you fell for the trap. Sure, there are four SPACES between the zinnias and the lilies, but the question asks how many FLOWERS there are between the zinnias and the lilies. There are three.

12. **E.** You could predict that this would be a question, right? If you forgot to leave an empty space, you would lose a lot of time going back and trying to figure out which space is blank. By drawing in the lines and numbering them right away, you avoid making this mistake.

13. **B.** You determined that carnations can go in either space 4 or space 6.

Questions 14–16

First, jot down the pool of men, broken into two categories.

    Rookies: Frank, Gary, Harold

    Veterans: John, Karl, Larry, Moe

Next draw seven dashes or spaces to represent the order in which the men will bat. Use the information given in the statements to fill in the spaces.

Statement I gives you the pool of players, which you have already jotted down.

Statement II tells you that a rookie cannot be first or last, because he must be preceded by and followed by a veteran.

Because statement III says that Gary bats second; put him in space 2. If Larry is the last veteran at bat, he must be the last batter, period, because you have already ascertained (from statement II) that the last batter cannot be a rookie.

Statement IV tells you that the last batter is a veteran. you already knew this.

When a series of statements repeats information, pay attention. You often will see a question along the lines of "Which statement is unnecessary?" or "Which two statements give the same information?"

Statement V tells you that John-Karl-Moe bat in that order . . . but don't assume that they are consecutive batters. There must be rookies between them, because rookies are preceded by and followed by veterans (per statement II). Since a veteran must be before and after Gary, you know that John must be first, followed by Gary and then by Karl.

Your final chart looks like this:

John   Gary   Karl   Frank or Harold   Moe   Frank or Harold   Larry

Note that spaces 4 and 6 could be filled by either Frank or Harold. When a logic game gives you options, when a space may be filled by more than one person, or when a job may be done in more than one way, you will often see a question about that option.

14. **B.** The question is wonderfully vague and *ambiguous* (uncertain; capable of being understood in more than one way). It doesn't ask which is false, or which must be wrong, but which "is not necessarily true." This is GRE-speak for looking at the options. You know that Frank could be in space 4, in which case B is true. But Frank could be in space 6, in which case B is false. Therefore, depending on Frank's placement, choice B is "not necessarily true."

15. **D.** From the chart, you know that Frank could be in spaces 4 or 6. If he won't bat next to Karl, he can go only in space 6. Look at the chart to see the only possible order.

16. **A.** Just look at the chart. You'll notice how carefully the question is phrased: Which of these *could* be the correct order of batters? You don't know which one *must* be the order; you have two options, based on Frank and Harold's positions.

17. **B.** First, identify the argument. The argument is that children today are learning less than children did ten years ago. This conclusion is based on evidence that says that teachers spend less time on basics and more time on administrative matters. For this to be true, the author must assume that more teacher time on basics contributes to learning while more teacher time on administrative matters detracts from learning. To strengthen the argument, support this assumption. Choice B does so by stating that time spent on basics does indeed contribute to student learning.

Choice A is a "so what?" How do you know whether 100 hours a year is a larger number of hours or a smaller number than field trips a decade ago? You have no basis of comparison.

Choice C is very, very tempting. Just because teachers are spending less time in the classroom, however, does not mean children are learning less. Maybe the teachers are showing kids more via computers or cable TV shows. There are all sorts of other ways children can learn besides having a teacher in front of them. They could read *scintillatingly* (sparkling, giving off flashes of light) brilliant books like this one, for example.

Choice D doesn't give you enough information. You need to know how many children were flunking at least one class in high school ten years ago before you can support the statement that children are learning less today than they did ten years ago.

Choice E also discusses just one facet of learning. Just because parents are less involved in their children's education does not necessarily mean children are learning less. If my own father, for instance, had been *less* involved in my calculus homework, I'm quite sure I would have learned it faster and a lot less painfully.

18. **C.** In terms of logic, *some* means at least one, making choice C a true statement. The ice works better than the prescription lotions and salves, so at least one treatment is superior. Choice E goes too far, though. You cannot infer anything about over-the-counter medications from the research about ice. Choice B is a tempting wrong answer, but all you know from the stimulus is that prescription lotions and salves aren't very effective. Perhaps some other prescriptions will do wonders. Choice D seems to make a lot of sense. However, it does not deal with the information in the stimulus, which has to do with treatment effectiveness. Choice A is too extreme and most likely false. Physicians may be very good at estimating the severity of a rash but may be incapable of prescribing a lotion or salve to take care of it.

19. **B.** The author makes a couple of giant leaps here. First, there was a correlation between hair color and being a Miss Universe finalist but nothing to prove that being blond caused the women to be finalists. More critically, who is to say that being a finalist in a Miss Universe has anything to do with this author's ability to get a date? Fortunately for those of us who are not Miss Universe, some men are happy with mere mortals.

    Choice A is possibly true and, as such, would mess up the author's reasoning. Nevertheless, it is too indirect to be a good answer. You can't fault the author for not thinking about such a specific possibility — and one that has only a chance of being true.

    Choice B expresses the real problem with what the author is thinking. The author is using a beauty pageant result to make a conclusion about her ability to get a date. What if she has an absolutely abominable personality? Will hair color make a difference? What if the men she is attracted to prefer women of her hair color?

    Choice C does get to the correlation versus causation question, but it is not strong enough. Even though the finalists may not have been picked *solely* because they were blond, the blond hair may have had a lot to do with their selection. Choice C would have been good had it said that the contestants were picked solely for reasons other than hair color.

    You may eliminate choice D the same way you eliminated choice A. In addition, choice D mentions the vague word *attention*. What about getting dates?

    Choice E is close, but the fact may remain that men are attracted to blondes. There could be many reasons why men don't like to date Miss Universe finalists, but hair color may not be one of them.

Questions 20–24

Create a week's calendar right on your scratch paper. Statement I gives info that doesn't fit into the calendar. Put it to the side in case you need it later. "No shots unless check-in." Statement II again has info that doesn't fit neatly onto the calendar. Put a note to the side: "same disease, same day." Statement III finally gives you something to write on the calendar. Put **Emp** on Wednesday, Friday, and Sunday. If you put down Tuesday, scratch it off; the statement tells you that Tuesday is an exception. Statement IV has to be postponed. You don't know when pneumonia patients check in yet. Put a big mark in the margin to remind you to come back to this statement later. Statement V tells you to put **Ec** under Tuesday and Thursday. Statement VI tells you to put **Pn** under Monday, Wednesday, Friday, and Saturday. Sunday is the exception. You always have to be careful to note the exceptions. You may want to circle them in the statements.

Note: Now you can go back to statement IV. You know that emphysema and pneumonia patients check in on Wednesdays and Fridays; put **Ca** for cancer patients in on those days. *Don't forget to go back to statements you skipped earlier.*

Statement VII means that **Cl** (colitis) patients can check in only Saturday, Sunday, Monday, and Tuesday because those are the consecutive days with no cancer patient check-ins. BUT look out for the next statement. Statement VIII won't allow patients to check in on Mondays, which means that Monday and Tuesday disqualify for consecutive days for **Cl** (colitis) patients, who have to settle for Saturday and Sunday. This means that you must remove **Pn** from Monday.

Your final calendar looks like this:

Sun	*Mon*	*Tues*	*Wed*	*Thurs*	*Fri*	*Sat*
Emp			Emp		Emp	
		Ec		Ec		
			Ca		Ca	
Cl						Cl
			Pn		Pn	Pn

A calendar game is one of the easiest games to diagram and one of the quickest to finish. If you're taking the CBT, you may want to invest significant time in this game; it's one of the easiest to get correct. Think of it as a gift from the GRE fairy.

20. **A.** A look at the chart gives you this information.

21. **C.** On Wednesday and Friday, patients with three diseases, emphysema, cancer, and pneumonia, can be admitted.

22. **E.** On Saturday, pneumonia patients are admitted but not cancer patients. On both Wednesday and Friday, both pneumonia and cancer patients are admitted.

23. **D.** On Wednesday and Friday, both cancer and emphysema patients can be admitted.

24. **E.** Every day except Saturday (and Monday, in which no one is admitted) has either eczema or emphysema patients.

Everything, but everything, depends on the chart, graph, or diagram you make. If it is off even a little bit, you are probably going to miss every question. Be the Degas of Diagrams, the Chagall of Charts. Spend your time on the pictures, and then you can zoom through the problems.

Questions 25–29

First, list your pool, using the first letters of the names. Break the pools up into newcomers and veterans:

Newcomers: R, S, T, V, Y

Veterans: H, I, J

Now, go through each of the statements, making notes on its content. Notice that this sort of game does not require you to make a diagram. You are not trying to find the positions or order of the people.

For statement I, jot down H ≠ I because Hank will not serve with Ingrid. This statement also allows you to deduce that, because two veterans are needed, they will be either H + J or J + I. This means that J definitely will be on the board. When you deduce a solid piece of information like this, write it in big letters and circle it. It usually affects the rest of the problem.

For statement II, write two separate comments: T ≠ J, and V ≠ J. Because you deduced just a moment ago that J must be on the board, neither T nor V can be on the board. Because R, S, and Y are the only newcomers left, and because three newcomers must be on the board, they get the job.

Statement III gives you that Y ≠ H. That means that H cannot be on the board because Y must be on the board. Earlier you deduced that the veterans are going to be either H and J or J and I. Eliminating H gives you J and I. your final grouping, therefore, is Newcomers: R, S, Y, and Veterans J and I. Now you're ready to answer any question dumped in your lap.

25. **C.** Take one rule at a time and note the violators. These violators must be included in the answer because the question asks for the options that are *not* possible. There must be three newcomers and two veterans. Option I has only one veteran, so it must be part of the answer, eliminating choice B. The rule that states that neither Tawny nor Virginia will serve with Jack makes option IV impossible, eliminating choice A. Options II and III do not violate any of the rules and are possible, leaving C as the correct answer.

26. **B.** In this case, H can serve. The only thing holding him back was Y's reluctance to serve with him. Putting H back into the game gives you two possible groups:
H + J + R + S + Z and I + J + R + S + Z

When a question introduces a new player or a new member of the pool, it often is very time-consuming. You in effect have to redo the entire game, going through each statement as if you were reading it for the first time with a new group. If you're rushed for time, this is a good question to "guess and go" on. Choose something (because wrong answers are not counted against you on the GRE), but don't waste much time on the question.

27. **A.** You just figured out that the only possible group is J, I, R, S, Y.

28. **A.** With I on the board, the combination must be I + J + R + S + Y. Did you recognize the stupidity of this question? Ingrid must always be on the board in our game. That means that the question doesn't add any new information but is really just asking you to read your original diagram.

29. **A.** This is an easy question if you see the trick. Because Hank will not serve with Ingrid, the Board cannot have three veterans. If you wasted time on this question figuring out the possible groupings of newcomers — well, take solace (comfort) in the fact that you earned some anonymous test maker (okay, me) brownie points with her boss.

30. **C.** The author leaps to his conclusion that Angelica will attend Harvard after saying that Angelica has been accepted to Harvard. This follows only if it is true that acceptance definitely leads to attendance, which is what choice C says. If choice C is not true, it is easy to see how Angelica could attend elsewhere or nowhere at all.

Choice A is very tempting in that it seems to force Angelica to attend Harvard. However, Angelica could decide to stay out of school next year. Choice C is matter of fact and says that students such as Angelica will attend Harvard. Because choice A does not guarantee Angelica's attendance, it is eliminated.

Choices B and E both miss the mark in that they focus on what it takes to qualify for Harvard. Angelica has already been accepted, so she presumably has met Harvard's standards. She may choose, even after fighting so hard to get where she is, not to attend Harvard.

Choice D expresses a reason why many students desire to attend Harvard, but this does not force Angelica to attend. She may decide that, for other reasons, she will attend a different school; prestige may not be important to her.

31. **D.** For a small-group survey to reflect the opinions of a larger population, it must be large enough and, more importantly, have various groups present in the proportion that they appear in the larger group. To take an extreme example, a poll taken at the Republican National Convention would not be valid to predict a presidential election because the percentage of people at the convention who will end up voting for the Democratic candidate in November is far smaller than the percentage of Americans who will vote for the Democrat. Sample size is also important, in that randomly picking a group of five people is more likely to produce, say, 80 percent Republicans than will a random selection of 1,500 people. Choices B and E point to these sampling problems and thus serve as possible explanations for the discrepancy between the polls and the actual election. Eliminate them, remembering that you are looking for something that does *not* explain the discrepancy.

Choices A and C are also plausible explanations. It could be that Truman came on strong in the last two weeks (choice A) or that Dewey didn't collect all the votes the polls indicated he should have gotten because the Dewey faithful didn't show up (choice C).

By the process of elimination, you have choice D. Whether this statement is true or false is not important. What is critical is what the poll participants and voters of 1948 thought. The Truman voters may have thought this way on Election Day, but then why did Truman trail in the polls? Additionally, the choice D statement may have become evident only after Truman left office in January, 1953. This choice does not explain the discrepancy.

32. **B.** Because negatives can be so confusing, try to rewrite the statement in a positive form. If *few* children *don't* love ice cream, *many* children *do* love ice cream. If many children do love ice cream, and Athalie is a child, she probably loves ice cream.

The word *probably* is a great word to buddy up to. It is such a wimp, such a namby-pamby, hedging, *equivocating* (deceptive) word that it can fit into nearly any situation. While few things are *always* true or *never* true, many things are *probably* or *sometimes* true. When I see the word *probably*, I "assume it's guilty until proven innocent." I head straight for it.

Choice A does not follow the argument. If Athalie is a child, there is no reason to assume she is a typical child. Maybe she wants to grow up to take the GRE and is looking forward to the event. How bizarre.

Choice C goes overboard. Just because Athalie is a child and most children love ice cream doesn't mean Athalie pigs out on the stuff. She might love it but not get too much of it because of her nutrition-conscious (that is, spoilsport) parents.

Choice D is totally wrong. If few children don't like ice cream, most do; it's not logical to assume that Athalie is one of the few who doesn't. Be careful: If the question said, "Which may be true . . ." choice D *may* be true. It's not likely, but it is possible. Always note what the question is asking for.

Choice E again is out in left field. We don't know whether most children are or are not allergic to ice cream; we know only that few don't love ice cream.

Questions 33–35

First, write down the various dog's names for the pool: Rover, King, Spot, Lassie, Fido, and Prince. (A lot of original thought went into those names, eh? The pooches may as well be called *Cliché, Banal, Trite,* and *Hackneyed.*)

Next, make two sets of dashes. Put six dashes for the ranking of movie contracts, six more dashes for the ranking of intelligence. Then use the information given in the statements to fill in the spaces.

Statement II tells you to put Spot in the second-to-last (*penultimate,* if you want to use a *pedantic, pretentious* term, and why not?) space. Lassie also goes in the last space of the movie contracts chart.

Statement IV puts Prince in space 4 on the intelligence chart and space 3 on the movie contracts chart.

Statement V puts Rover in the first spot of the intelligence chart and in the third to last space (*antepenultimate*) of the movie contracts chart. You also get the information that Fido must be in the second to last space of the movie contracts list (you already know that Lassie is in the last or ultimate space).

Your final charts should look like the following:

Movie contracts

King	Spot	Prince	Rover	Fido	Lassie
1	2	3	4	5	6

Intelligence

Rover	(Fido or King)	(Fido or King)	Prince	Spot	Lassie
1	2	3	4	5	6

Did you take special notice of the fact that spaces two and three in the intelligence chart could be filled by either Fido or King? When you have a double option like this, you often have a question about it.

33. **C.** Look at the chart, from most intelligent to least intelligent. The question carefully asks which *could be* the order, not which *must be* the order. Spaces 2 and 3 could be filled with Fido and King or King and Fido. Either is okay.

34. **C.** Just look at the charts.

35. **C.** Spot has more movie contracts than Prince. If Rex has fewer movie contracts than Prince, he must also have fewer movie contracts than Spot.

Choice A may or may not be true. Because you don't know of any direct correlation between intelligence and movie contracts, you can't make any assumptions. The same is true for choice B. Choice D is wrong. King has the most movie contracts of all the dogs. You don't know enough about the ranking of friendliness of the dogs to know whether choice E is true or not.

Chapter 21

How to Ruin a Perfectly Good Day, Part II: Practice Exam 2

• •

Are you bloody but unbowed and ready to have another go at it? The following exam consists of three sections. (You were kind enough to laugh at my jokes; I'm kind enough to leave out the experimental section.) There is one section each of verbal, quantitative, and analytical. You are familiar (practically *intimate*) with the question formats by now.

Please take this test under normal exam conditions and approach it as if it were the real test. This is serious stuff here!

1. **Work with your computer when you won't be interrupted (even though you'd probably welcome any distractions).**

2. **Use scratch paper that is free of any prepared notes. (On the actual GRE, you will get blank scratch paper before your test begins. You will have a little time before the clock starts to jot down a few notes and formulas and a series of columns of numbers or letters that you may want to use to help you eliminate answer choices, but you may not whip out a ready-made version of such test-taking aids.)**

3. **Turn off the clock at the beginning of each test section and be very careful on the first five questions. Remember that these earlier questions contribute more to your score than do the later questions.**

4. **If a question is truly impossible for you, guess and move on. You do not have the option of skipping the question and coming back to it. The computer will not let you move on until you mark and confirm an answer.**

5. **Make sure that you get to the end of the test section (30th question for verbal, 28th question for quantitative, and 35th question for analytical). If you have to, make wild guesses to reach the end before time expires. Unanswered questions will hurt your score more than incorrect ones will.**

6. **If you get to the last question before time expires, you have the option of answering it right away and finishing your test early (you can't use the time to go back and check your work) or relaxing for a while and marking your answer shortly before time expires. If you feel pumped up and you're on a roll, do the former. Give yourself the breather if you feel bombarded by the test.**

7. **Do not leave your computer while the clock is running on any one section.**

8. **You will get a one-minute break after the first section and the option to take a ten-minute break after the second section.**

After you finish, check your answers with the answer key. A sample scoring chart is provided at the end of this chapter. Take a few minutes to go over the answer explanations to all the questions, not just the ones you missed. This is your last chance to pick up one more nugget of knowledge, that final bit of information that could put you over the top.

Answer Sheet

Begin with Number 1 for each new section. If any sections have fewer than 50 questions, leave the extra spaces blank.

Section 1	Section 2	Section 3
1. Ⓐ Ⓑ Ⓒ Ⓓ Ⓔ	1. Ⓐ Ⓑ Ⓒ Ⓓ Ⓔ	1. Ⓐ Ⓑ Ⓒ Ⓓ Ⓔ
2. Ⓐ Ⓑ Ⓒ Ⓓ Ⓔ	2. Ⓐ Ⓑ Ⓒ Ⓓ Ⓔ	2. Ⓐ Ⓑ Ⓒ Ⓓ Ⓔ
3. Ⓐ Ⓑ Ⓒ Ⓓ Ⓔ	3. Ⓐ Ⓑ Ⓒ Ⓓ Ⓔ	3. Ⓐ Ⓑ Ⓒ Ⓓ Ⓔ
4. Ⓐ Ⓑ Ⓒ Ⓓ Ⓔ	4. Ⓐ Ⓑ Ⓒ Ⓓ Ⓔ	4. Ⓐ Ⓑ Ⓒ Ⓓ Ⓔ
5. Ⓐ Ⓑ Ⓒ Ⓓ Ⓔ	5. Ⓐ Ⓑ Ⓒ Ⓓ Ⓔ	5. Ⓐ Ⓑ Ⓒ Ⓓ Ⓔ
6. Ⓐ Ⓑ Ⓒ Ⓓ Ⓔ	6. Ⓐ Ⓑ Ⓒ Ⓓ Ⓔ	6. Ⓐ Ⓑ Ⓒ Ⓓ Ⓔ
7. Ⓐ Ⓑ Ⓒ Ⓓ Ⓔ	7. Ⓐ Ⓑ Ⓒ Ⓓ Ⓔ	7. Ⓐ Ⓑ Ⓒ Ⓓ Ⓔ
8. Ⓐ Ⓑ Ⓒ Ⓓ Ⓔ	8. Ⓐ Ⓑ Ⓒ Ⓓ Ⓔ	8. Ⓐ Ⓑ Ⓒ Ⓓ Ⓔ
9. Ⓐ Ⓑ Ⓒ Ⓓ Ⓔ	9. Ⓐ Ⓑ Ⓒ Ⓓ Ⓔ	9. Ⓐ Ⓑ Ⓒ Ⓓ Ⓔ
10. Ⓐ Ⓑ Ⓒ Ⓓ Ⓔ	10. Ⓐ Ⓑ Ⓒ Ⓓ Ⓔ	10. Ⓐ Ⓑ Ⓒ Ⓓ Ⓔ
11. Ⓐ Ⓑ Ⓒ Ⓓ Ⓔ	11. Ⓐ Ⓑ Ⓒ Ⓓ Ⓔ	11. Ⓐ Ⓑ Ⓒ Ⓓ Ⓔ
12. Ⓐ Ⓑ Ⓒ Ⓓ Ⓔ	12. Ⓐ Ⓑ Ⓒ Ⓓ Ⓔ	12. Ⓐ Ⓑ Ⓒ Ⓓ Ⓔ
13. Ⓐ Ⓑ Ⓒ Ⓓ Ⓔ	13. Ⓐ Ⓑ Ⓒ Ⓓ Ⓔ	13. Ⓐ Ⓑ Ⓒ Ⓓ Ⓔ
14. Ⓐ Ⓑ Ⓒ Ⓓ Ⓔ	14. Ⓐ Ⓑ Ⓒ Ⓓ Ⓔ	14. Ⓐ Ⓑ Ⓒ Ⓓ Ⓔ
15. Ⓐ Ⓑ Ⓒ Ⓓ Ⓔ	15. Ⓐ Ⓑ Ⓒ Ⓓ Ⓔ	15. Ⓐ Ⓑ Ⓒ Ⓓ Ⓔ
16. Ⓐ Ⓑ Ⓒ Ⓓ Ⓔ	16. Ⓐ Ⓑ Ⓒ Ⓓ Ⓔ	16. Ⓐ Ⓑ Ⓒ Ⓓ Ⓔ
17. Ⓐ Ⓑ Ⓒ Ⓓ Ⓔ	17. Ⓐ Ⓑ Ⓒ Ⓓ Ⓔ	17. Ⓐ Ⓑ Ⓒ Ⓓ Ⓔ
18. Ⓐ Ⓑ Ⓒ Ⓓ Ⓔ	18. Ⓐ Ⓑ Ⓒ Ⓓ Ⓔ	18. Ⓐ Ⓑ Ⓒ Ⓓ Ⓔ
19. Ⓐ Ⓑ Ⓒ Ⓓ Ⓔ	19. Ⓐ Ⓑ Ⓒ Ⓓ Ⓔ	19. Ⓐ Ⓑ Ⓒ Ⓓ Ⓔ
20. Ⓐ Ⓑ Ⓒ Ⓓ Ⓔ	20. Ⓐ Ⓑ Ⓒ Ⓓ Ⓔ	20. Ⓐ Ⓑ Ⓒ Ⓓ Ⓔ
21. Ⓐ Ⓑ Ⓒ Ⓓ Ⓔ	21. Ⓐ Ⓑ Ⓒ Ⓓ Ⓔ	21. Ⓐ Ⓑ Ⓒ Ⓓ Ⓔ
22. Ⓐ Ⓑ Ⓒ Ⓓ Ⓔ	22. Ⓐ Ⓑ Ⓒ Ⓓ Ⓔ	22. Ⓐ Ⓑ Ⓒ Ⓓ Ⓔ
23. Ⓐ Ⓑ Ⓒ Ⓓ Ⓔ	23. Ⓐ Ⓑ Ⓒ Ⓓ Ⓔ	23. Ⓐ Ⓑ Ⓒ Ⓓ Ⓔ
24. Ⓐ Ⓑ Ⓒ Ⓓ Ⓔ	24. Ⓐ Ⓑ Ⓒ Ⓓ Ⓔ	24. Ⓐ Ⓑ Ⓒ Ⓓ Ⓔ
25. Ⓐ Ⓑ Ⓒ Ⓓ Ⓔ	25. Ⓐ Ⓑ Ⓒ Ⓓ Ⓔ	25. Ⓐ Ⓑ Ⓒ Ⓓ Ⓔ
26. Ⓐ Ⓑ Ⓒ Ⓓ Ⓔ	26. Ⓐ Ⓑ Ⓒ Ⓓ Ⓔ	26. Ⓐ Ⓑ Ⓒ Ⓓ Ⓔ
27. Ⓐ Ⓑ Ⓒ Ⓓ Ⓔ	27. Ⓐ Ⓑ Ⓒ Ⓓ Ⓔ	27. Ⓐ Ⓑ Ⓒ Ⓓ Ⓔ
28. Ⓐ Ⓑ Ⓒ Ⓓ Ⓔ	28. Ⓐ Ⓑ Ⓒ Ⓓ Ⓔ	28. Ⓐ Ⓑ Ⓒ Ⓓ Ⓔ
29. Ⓐ Ⓑ Ⓒ Ⓓ Ⓔ	29. Ⓐ Ⓑ Ⓒ Ⓓ Ⓔ	29. Ⓐ Ⓑ Ⓒ Ⓓ Ⓔ
30. Ⓐ Ⓑ Ⓒ Ⓓ Ⓔ	30. Ⓐ Ⓑ Ⓒ Ⓓ Ⓔ	30. Ⓐ Ⓑ Ⓒ Ⓓ Ⓔ
31. Ⓐ Ⓑ Ⓒ Ⓓ Ⓔ	31. Ⓐ Ⓑ Ⓒ Ⓓ Ⓔ	31. Ⓐ Ⓑ Ⓒ Ⓓ Ⓔ
32. Ⓐ Ⓑ Ⓒ Ⓓ Ⓔ	32. Ⓐ Ⓑ Ⓒ Ⓓ Ⓔ	32. Ⓐ Ⓑ Ⓒ Ⓓ Ⓔ
33. Ⓐ Ⓑ Ⓒ Ⓓ Ⓔ	33. Ⓐ Ⓑ Ⓒ Ⓓ Ⓔ	33. Ⓐ Ⓑ Ⓒ Ⓓ Ⓔ
34. Ⓐ Ⓑ Ⓒ Ⓓ Ⓔ	34. Ⓐ Ⓑ Ⓒ Ⓓ Ⓔ	34. Ⓐ Ⓑ Ⓒ Ⓓ Ⓔ
35. Ⓐ Ⓑ Ⓒ Ⓓ Ⓔ	35. Ⓐ Ⓑ Ⓒ Ⓓ Ⓔ	35. Ⓐ Ⓑ Ⓒ Ⓓ Ⓔ
36. Ⓐ Ⓑ Ⓒ Ⓓ Ⓔ	36. Ⓐ Ⓑ Ⓒ Ⓓ Ⓔ	36. Ⓐ Ⓑ Ⓒ Ⓓ Ⓔ
37. Ⓐ Ⓑ Ⓒ Ⓓ Ⓔ	37. Ⓐ Ⓑ Ⓒ Ⓓ Ⓔ	37. Ⓐ Ⓑ Ⓒ Ⓓ Ⓔ
38. Ⓐ Ⓑ Ⓒ Ⓓ Ⓔ	38. Ⓐ Ⓑ Ⓒ Ⓓ Ⓔ	38. Ⓐ Ⓑ Ⓒ Ⓓ Ⓔ
39. Ⓐ Ⓑ Ⓒ Ⓓ Ⓔ	39. Ⓐ Ⓑ Ⓒ Ⓓ Ⓔ	39. Ⓐ Ⓑ Ⓒ Ⓓ Ⓔ
40. Ⓐ Ⓑ Ⓒ Ⓓ Ⓔ	40. Ⓐ Ⓑ Ⓒ Ⓓ Ⓔ	40. Ⓐ Ⓑ Ⓒ Ⓓ Ⓔ
41. Ⓐ Ⓑ Ⓒ Ⓓ Ⓔ	41. Ⓐ Ⓑ Ⓒ Ⓓ Ⓔ	41. Ⓐ Ⓑ Ⓒ Ⓓ Ⓔ
42. Ⓐ Ⓑ Ⓒ Ⓓ Ⓔ	42. Ⓐ Ⓑ Ⓒ Ⓓ Ⓔ	42. Ⓐ Ⓑ Ⓒ Ⓓ Ⓔ
43. Ⓐ Ⓑ Ⓒ Ⓓ Ⓔ	43. Ⓐ Ⓑ Ⓒ Ⓓ Ⓔ	43. Ⓐ Ⓑ Ⓒ Ⓓ Ⓔ
44. Ⓐ Ⓑ Ⓒ Ⓓ Ⓔ	44. Ⓐ Ⓑ Ⓒ Ⓓ Ⓔ	44. Ⓐ Ⓑ Ⓒ Ⓓ Ⓔ
45. Ⓐ Ⓑ Ⓒ Ⓓ Ⓔ	45. Ⓐ Ⓑ Ⓒ Ⓓ Ⓔ	45. Ⓐ Ⓑ Ⓒ Ⓓ Ⓔ
46. Ⓐ Ⓑ Ⓒ Ⓓ Ⓔ	46. Ⓐ Ⓑ Ⓒ Ⓓ Ⓔ	46. Ⓐ Ⓑ Ⓒ Ⓓ Ⓔ
47. Ⓐ Ⓑ Ⓒ Ⓓ Ⓔ	47. Ⓐ Ⓑ Ⓒ Ⓓ Ⓔ	47. Ⓐ Ⓑ Ⓒ Ⓓ Ⓔ
48. Ⓐ Ⓑ Ⓒ Ⓓ Ⓔ	48. Ⓐ Ⓑ Ⓒ Ⓓ Ⓔ	48. Ⓐ Ⓑ Ⓒ Ⓓ Ⓔ
49. Ⓐ Ⓑ Ⓒ Ⓓ Ⓔ	49. Ⓐ Ⓑ Ⓒ Ⓓ Ⓔ	49. Ⓐ Ⓑ Ⓒ Ⓓ Ⓔ
50. Ⓐ Ⓑ Ⓒ Ⓓ Ⓔ	50. Ⓐ Ⓑ Ⓒ Ⓓ Ⓔ	50. Ⓐ Ⓑ Ⓒ Ⓓ Ⓔ

Verbal Section

> Time: 30 minutes
>
> 30 questions
>
> *Directions:* Choose the answer choice most nearly opposite in meaning to the question word.

1. LUCID
   - (A) turbid
   - (B) vivacious
   - (C) minuscule
   - (D) domineering
   - (E) spicy

2. INDIGENOUS
   - (A) foreign
   - (B) amiable
   - (C) satisfactory
   - (D) lustrous
   - (E) pallid

3. ERUDITE
   - (A) timid
   - (B) rash
   - (C) loquacious
   - (D) uneducated
   - (E) gargantuan

4. HAPLESS
   - (A) saturnine
   - (B) fortunate
   - (C) cacophonous
   - (D) mordant
   - (E) ambiguous

5. BURGEON
   - (A) garble
   - (B) purchase
   - (C) aggravate
   - (D) wither
   - (E) dominate

6. NOXIOUS
   - (A) froward
   - (B) salubrious
   - (C) inane
   - (D) erudite
   - (E) vapid

7. SANGUINE
   - (A) supple
   - (B) stygian
   - (C) doting
   - (D) morose
   - (E) voracious

8. EXTIRPATE
   - (A) abolish
   - (B) exacerbate
   - (C) introduce
   - (D) adulate
   - (E) seethe

Go on to next page

Directions: Each of the following questions features a pair of words or phrases in capital letters, followed by five pairs of words or phrases in lowercase letters. Choose the lowercase pair that most closely expresses the same relationship as that of the uppercase pair.

9. TONSORIAL : HAIR ::
   (A) professorial : job
   (B) medical : disease
   (C) stentorian : throat
   (D) sartorial : apparel
   (E) canine : teeth

10. EUPHORIC : LACHRYMOSE ::
    (A) affluent : destitute
    (B) dexterous : skillful
    (C) lax : casual
    (D) weary : fatigued
    (E) jovial : intelligent

11. GARRULOUS : PROLIX ::
    (A) cantankerous : polite
    (B) intrepid : brave
    (C) pedantic : energetic
    (D) asocial : amiable
    (E) gruesome : diligent

12. HEIRLOOM : ANCESTOR ::
    (A) red herring : magician
    (B) bequest : testator
    (C) instrument : musician
    (D) rules : renegade
    (E) throne : usurper

13. ACRIMONIOUS : SWEET ::
    (A) begrudging : eager
    (B) depraved : possessive
    (C) itinerant : experienced
    (D) lascivious : lustful
    (E) protean : changeable

14. THIN : EMACIATED ::
    (A) immune : impervious
    (B) imperious : regal
    (C) happy : ecstatic
    (D) sarcastic : sardonic
    (E) insulting : demeaning

15. ANGRY : INCENSED ::
    (A) noticeable : flamboyant
    (B) obdurate : stubborn
    (C) ancient : outmoded
    (D) melodious : euphonious
    (E) calm : pacific

16. Although often - - - -, James Michael realized the importance of proceeding slowly with his task and deliberately forced himself to examine all the options available to him before making the decision on the best way to proceed.
    (A) impetuous
    (B) pensive
    (C) uncouth
    (D) dilatory
    (E) unenthusiastic

Directions: Each of the following sentences has one or two blanks indicating that words or phrases are omitted. Choose the answer that best completes the sentence.

17. Although he lacked the - - - - that he would like to have in the field, Dr. Dickstein felt confident enough of his premise to continue arguing - - - - against the physician, whom he considered to be a dangerous quack and a charlatan.
    (A) fidelity . . exhaustively
    (B) grace . . indifferently
    (C) skill . . lackadaisically
    (D) expertise . . vehemently
    (E) ability . . tentatively

Go on to next page

18. The feeling that one is being watched is not always mere paranoia; indeed, the ---- and random viewing of citizens by some governmental bureaus is quite probably more ---- than is commonly known.

    (A) intermittent . . widespread

    (B) haphazard . . ironhanded

    (C) arbitrary . . fly-by-night

    (D) flagrant . . surreptitious

    (E) unauthorized . . banal

19. At the ---- of his career, Ken basks in the kudos and ---- of judges and audiences alike.

    (A) apogee . . plaudits

    (B) lapse . . reproofs

    (C) apex . . fecklessness

    (D) genesis . . effrontery

    (E) nascency . . perjury

20. The ---- her peers the speaker received when she presented her report was but a small sample of the disdain that she had to face daily at the university that was attempting to make her quit despite her tenured position.

    (A) abasement by

    (B) plaudits of

    (C) encomium of

    (D) laudation of

    (E) demise of

21. The ---- look with which the defendant accepted his fate left the jury ---- whether they in fact had done the correct thing in finding him guilty.

    (A) insolent . . inquisitive about

    (B) complacent . . wondering

    (C) plaintive . . ambivalent about

    (D) quiescent . . irresolute over

    (E) giddy . . befuddled by

Directions: Each passage is followed by questions pertaining to that passage. Read the passage and answer the questions based on information stated or implied in that passage.

Community property is a legal concept that is growing in popularity in the United States. A few years ago only the western states had community property laws and few people east of the Mississippi had ever heard the expression "community property." Now several states have adopted or modified laws regarding community property. *(Line) (05)*

Community property is jointly owned by both wife and husband. Generally, the property that was owned by a spouse before the marriage is known as separate or specific property. It remains the property of the original possessor in case of a separation or divorce. Community property is anything gained by the joint effort of the spouses. *(10) (15)*

Gifts specifically bestowed upon only one party, or legacies to only one spouse, are separate property. However, courts often determine that a donor had the intention to give the gift to both parties, even though his words or papers may have indicated otherwise. Community property goes to the surviving partner in case of the death of one spouse. Only that half of the property owned by the testator can be willed away. *(20) (25)*

22. In which of the following instances would a gift to one party become community property?

    I.   When the court determines the intent of the donor was to make a gift to the couple.

    II. When the property is real (land) rather than personal (possessions).

    III. When the court determines that the intent to give the gift was formed by the donor prior to the party's marriage.

    (A) I only

    (B) II only

    (C) I and III only

    (D) II and III only

    (E) I, II, and III

Go on to next page

23. You may infer that the author would most likely agree with which of the following?

    (A) Community property is the fairest settlement concept for marital property.

    (B) Community property laws currently discriminate against the working spouse in favor of the homemaker spouse.

    (C) Community property laws will probably continue to increase in number throughout the U.S.

    (D) Community property laws will be expanded to include all property acquired during the marriage, regardless of its source.

    (E) All inheritances received by one party during the marriage are in theory, if not in fact, community property.

Due to the involuntary, simultaneous con-
Line traction of 15 facial muscles, the upper lip is
      raised, partially uncovering the teeth and effect-
      ing a downward curving of the furrows that
(05) extend from the wings of both nostrils to the cor-
      ners of the mouth. This produces a puffing out of
      the cheeks on the outer side of the furrows.
      Creases also occur under the eyes and may
      become permanent at the side edges of the eye.
(10) The eyes undergo reflex lacrimation and vascular
      engorgement. At the same time, an abrupt strong
      expiration of air is followed by spasmodic con-
      tractions of the chest and diaphragm resulting in
      a series of expiration-inspiration microcycles
(15) with interval pauses. The whole body may be
      thrown backward, shaken, or convulsed due to
      other spasmodic skeletal muscle contractions.
      We call this condition laughter.
      Of all human expressive behaviors, laughter
(20) has proven a most fascinating enigma to philoso-
      phers and scientists alike. Its psychology, neurol-
      ogy, and anthropological origins and purpose are
      only partially defined. But its effects and uses are
      becoming increasingly apparent to health care
(25) professionals.
      Laughter is considered to be an innate
      human response that develops during the first
      few weeks of life. Evidence of the innate quality of
      laughter is seen in its occurrence in deaf and
(30) blind infants and children who are completely
      without visual or auditory clues from their envi-
      ronments. Darwin propounded in his *Principle of
      Antithesis* that laughter develops as the infant's

powerful reward signal of comfort and well-being
to the nurturing adult. This signal is totally anti-   (35)
thetical perceptually to the screams or cries of
distress associated with discomfort. Laughter
seems to play an important role in the promotion
of social unity, production of a sense of well-
being, communication of well-being, and as a   (40)
mechanism for coping with stressful situations.
Physiologically, both reflexive (tickle-response)
and heart-felt (mental response) laughter effect
changes to the human system which may be significant in the treatment and prevention of ill-   (45)
ness. These include laughter's association with
an increase in pulse rate, probably due to
increased levels of circulatory catecholamines
(blood catecholamine levels vary directly with
the intensity of laughter). There is an increase in   (50)
respiration. There is a decrease in blood CO_2
levels. There is a possible increase in secretion of
brain and pituitary endorphins — the body's natural anesthetics which relieve pain, inhibit emotional response to pain, and thus reduce   (55)
suffering. There is a decrease in red blood cell
sedimentation rate ("sed rate" is associated with
the body's level of infection or inflammation).
While it is possible that the effect laughter
and other salutary emotions have is primarily   (60)
one of a placebo, this in no way minimizes the
therapeutic potential for these emotions.
Hippocrates propounded that the mind and body
are one. It may be possible that there is a physical chemistry associated with the will to live.   (65)
Further investigation of the effects of positive
emotions upon health and well-being may give us
the keys to unlocking the power of the life force.

24. The author responds to the possibility that laughter has a placebo effect by

    (A) discounting the benefits of laughter.

    (B) continuing to discuss a link between laughter and health.

    (C) denying that the physiological responses discussed in the previous paragraph are real.

    (D) emphasizing that laughter is a learned response.

    (E) recommending other preventative measures.

Go on to next page ⟹

25. It can be inferred from the passage that an infant unable to laugh would

    (A) be unable to convey to adults when he is distressed.

    (B) never have increased catecholamine levels.

    (C) have certain handicaps in his ability to interact with others.

    (D) be likely to cry more often than an infant who is able to laugh.

    (E) not benefit from any placebo effects.

26. According to the passage, laughter

    (A) is associated with the contraction of many muscles.

    (B) increases blood pressure.

    (C) directly lowers the sed rate.

    (D) increases CO_2 levels in the lungs.

    (E) is essential for pain reduction.

A key study has shown that the organic
Line matter content of a soil can be altered to a depth
of 10 cm or more by intense campfire heat. As
much as 90 percent of the original organic matter
(05) may be oxidized in the top 1.3 cm of soil. In the
surface 10 cm, the loss of organic matter may
reach 50 percent if the soil is dry and the temperature exceeds 250° C. The loss of organic matter
reduces soil fertility and water-holding capacity
(10) and renders the soil more susceptible to compaction and erosion.

Sandy soils attain higher temperatures and
retain heat longer than clay soils under similar
fuel, moisture, and weather conditions. From this
(15) standpoint, it is desirable to locate campgrounds
in an area with loam or clay-loam soil. Sandy soils
are less susceptible to compaction damage, however, and are more desirable for campgrounds
from this standpoint.

(20) A water-repellent layer can be created in a
soil by the heat from the campfire. This condition
was noted only in sandy soils where the temperature remained below 350° C during the campfire
burn. Campfires often produce temperatures
(25) above this level. By comparison, forest fires are a
shorter-duration event, and soil temperatures
produced are more likely to create water repellency-inducing conditions. The greater areal
extent of forest fires makes them a more serious
(30) threat than campfires in terms of causing soil
water repellency.

If the soil remained moist for the duration of
the campfire, the increased heat capacity of the
soil and heat of water vaporization kept the soil
temperature below 100° C. At this temperature, (35)
little loss of organic matter occurred, and no
water repellency was created. For areas where
the soil remains very moist, campfires probably
have little effect on the soil properties.

Studies show that softwood fuels burn faster (40)
and produce less heat flow into the soil than do
hardwood fuels under the same conditions. Elm
and mesquite were the hottest burning and
longest lasting fuels tested. In areas where some
choice of fuels is available, the use of softwood (45)
fuels should be encouraged in an effort to minimize the effect of campfires on soil properties.

The effects of campfires on the soil in a
campground can be lessened by restricting the
fire site to the same area, even if permanent con- (50)
crete fireplaces are not installed. In this manner,
any harmful effects are restricted to a minimum
area. If campfires are allowed to be located at
random by the user, the harmful effects tend to
be spread over a larger part of the campground. (55)
The placement of a stone fire ring in the chosen
location is one way to accomplish the objective.

These data support the decision to install
permanent fireplaces in many areas and to
restrict the use of campfires elsewhere in the (60)
park. This eliminates the harmful effects of campfires on the soil and allows the campground to be
located on sandy soil with low compactibility and
good drainage.

(65)

27. It can be inferred from the passage that campfire users generally

    (A) evaluate the amount of soil damage that can result before they build a campfire.

    (B) are concerned with the possibility that their campfire can cause a forest fire.

    (C) have no regard for the biological conse-quences that result from their camp-fires.

    (D) consider many areas of a campground to be suitable for a campfire.

    (E) favor sandy soil over clay-loam soil as a campfire site.

Go on to next page

28. The main idea of this passage is that

    (A) excessive campfires will eventually make it impossible to grow crops.

    (B) soil temperature affects soil fertility.

    (C) only certain woods allow for high-quality campfires.

    (D) soils must be able to absorb water to sustain organic matter.

    (E) steps can be taken to minimize soil damage from campfires.

29. Long-lasting campfires are more likely than short-lived ones to

    (A) create water repellency-inducing conditions.

    (B) maintain soil fertility.

    (C) occur with softwood fuels.

    (D) restrict damage to the top 1.3 cm of soil.

    (E) produce higher soil temperatures.

30. It can be inferred from the passage that the author would be most likely to agree with which of the following?

    (A) Campfires should be banned as destructive to campfire soil.

    (B) Organic matter decreases soil erosion.

    (C) Clay-loam soil is preferable to sandy soil for campsites.

    (D) The longer the duration of the fire, the higher the resistant soil temperatures.

    (E) Campfires will not burn in areas with moist soil.

STOP You may check your work on this section only.
Do not go on to the next section until you are told to do so.

Quantitative Section

Time: 30 Minutes

30 questions

Notes: All numbers used in this exam are real numbers.

All figures lie in a plane.

Angle measures are positive; points and angles are in the position shown.

The answer choices are:

A if the quantity in Column A is greater.

B if the quantity in Column B is greater.

C if the two quantities are equal.

D if the relationship cannot be determined from the information given.

Column A	*Column B*		*Column A*	*Column B*

1. In Debittown, the roller rink is 10 kilometers from the school, which is 3 kilometers from the coffee shop.

Distance from the roller rink to the coffee shop	13 kilometers

2. $a = \frac{2}{3}b$; $b = \frac{3}{4}c$

Fraction that a is of c	$\frac{1}{3}$

3. | $x^{-y} \times y^{-x}$ | 1 |
|---|---|

4. | $a^{10} \times a^{5} \times \frac{1}{a^{3}}$ | a^{12} |
|---|---|

Area of circle O=36π

5. | Length of arc *NP* | 36π |
|---|---|

6. $-20 \leq x < 0$

Greatest possible value of x^3	0

7. $a * b * c = 3a + 4b - \frac{1}{2}c$

$3 * 6 * 12$	27

8. | The average (arithmetic mean) of 10^2, 11^2, and 12^2 | 11 |
|---|---|

9. | y | 110 |
|---|---|

10. | 300% of 30 | 60% of 15 |
|---|---|

Column A	Column B

11.
$$a \times b = c$$

c	b

12.

20 percent of 120	120 percent of 20

13.

The number of days in four years	The number of years in forty decades

14.

0.5043×10^5	50.43×10^{-2}

15. Rachel and Shayna are looking at a shelf of 84 books at the library. The difference between the number of books that they look at and put back and the number of books that they look at and check out is 20. How many books did they put back? (They put back more books than they took out.)

(A) 24
(B) 32
(C) 35
(D) 52
(E) 64

16. What is the number of square units in the area of parallelogram *ABCD?*

(A) 40
(B) 36
(C) 32
(D) 26
(E) 24

Questions 17–19 are based on the following graph.

17. The amount of money spent on television advertising in 1970 is what percent of that estimated to be spent in the year 2000?

(A) 200
(B) 100
(C) 50
(D) 10
(E) It cannot be determined.

18. In 1970, the money Company X spent on salaries was what percent greater than the money it spent on promotion?

(A) 5
(B) 20
(C) 25
(D) 400
(E) 500

19. The amount of money spent on overhead from 1950 to 1990 inclusive was

(A) $3,500,000
(B) $350,000
(C) $35,000
(D) $400,000
(E) $4,000,000

Go on to next page

20. $\dfrac{6a^{10}b^5c^7}{3a^5b^9c^7}$

    (A) $2a^2b^4c$

    (B) $\dfrac{2a^2b^4}{c}$

    (C) $\dfrac{2a^5b^4}{c}$

    (D) $2a^5b^4$

    (E) $\dfrac{2a^5}{b^4}$

21. A box of candy contains three types of candy: 20 creams, 15 chews, and 12 nuts. Each time LaVonne reaches into the box, she pulls out a piece of candy, takes a bite out of it, and throws it away. She pulls out a cream, a nut, a chew, a nut, a cream, and a chew. What is the probability that on the next reach, she will pull out a nut?

    (A) $^{15}\!/\!_{47}$

    (B) $^{13}\!/\!_{41}$

    (C) $^{10}\!/\!_{41}$

    (D) $^{13}\!/\!_{15}$

    (E) $^{11}\!/\!_{15}$

Use the following graphs to answer questions 22–23.

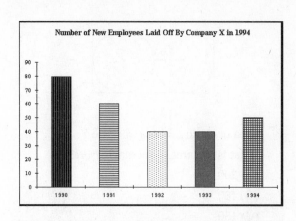

22. From information given, if no additional new employees are hired by Company X in 1994, the number of employees in Company X will be

    (A) 180

    (B) 160

    (C) 140

    (D) 120

    (E) It cannot be determined.

23. From information given, the number of new employees hired by Company X from January through June of 1994 was

    (A) 180

    (B) 160

    (C) 140

    (D) 120

    (E) 100

24. Women's shoes of the following sizes were sold on Saturday: 8, 7½, 6½, 5½, 6, 6½, 8, 7, 6, 8½, 8. What is the difference between the mode and the median?

    (A) 0

    (B) ½

    (C) 1

    (D) 1½

    (E) 2

Go on to next page

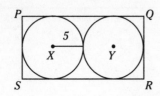

25. Area of circle X = area of circle Y

What is the area of rectangle *PQRS?*

(A) 200

(B) 180

(C) 150

(D) 100

(E) 25

26. $\boxed{\begin{array}{l} \widehat{x} = x + x^2 \text{ for all prime numbers} \\ \widehat{x} = x^2 - x \text{ for all composite numbers} \end{array}}$

$\widehat{4} + \widehat{5} =$

(A) 50

(B) 42

(C) 40

(D) 20

(E) 19

27. Gwendolyn studies from 9:30 a.m. to 12:27 p.m. How long does she study?

(A) 3 hours 57 minutes

(B) 3 hours 27 minutes

(C) 3 hours 3 minutes

(D) 2 hours 57 minutes

(E) 2 hours 27 minutes

28. The longest chord of a circle is two units. What is the area of the circle in square units?

(A) 4π

(B) 2π

(C) 1π

(D) $\frac{1}{2}\pi$

(E) $\frac{1}{4}\pi$

STOP You may check your work on this section only.
Do not go on to the next section until you are told to do so.

Analytical Section

Time: 60 minutes

Questions: 35

Directions: Each question or set of questions is based upon a specific passage or upon a set of conditions. To answer the questions, you may find it useful to draw a diagram or chart. Select the best answer to each question.

1. Cars are safer than planes. Fifty percent of plane accidents result in death, while only one percent of car accidents result in death.

   Which of the following, if true, would most seriously weaken the preceding argument?

   (A) Planes are inspected more often than cars.

   (B) The number of car accidents is several hundred thousand times higher than the number of plane accidents.

   (C) Pilots never fly under the influence of alcohol, while car drivers often do.

   (D) Plane accidents usually involve just one plane while car accidents often involve other vehicles or a pedestrian, increasing the number of potential fatalities.

   (E) The percentage of car accidents that result in death is far higher on roads that allow cars to travel at high speeds.

2. UCLA basketball fan: I am so glad that college basketball changed its rules and put in a shot clock. When there was no shot clock, a team with inferior ability could keep the ball away from the other team by passing the ball around the entire game. The winning team should be the one that is better at shooting baskets, not at playing keep-away.

   North Carolina basketball fan: I disagree. The object of basketball is to win. If playing keep-away is the way for a team to win, it should do so.

   The North Carolina fan's response indicates that he has misunderstood the UCLA fan's remark to mean

   (A) games without a shot clock are boring.

   (B) true basketball does not involve a game of keep-away.

   (C) it is unwise to utilize a keep-away strategy, even when permitted to do so.

   (D) a game with a shot clock is better than a game without one.

   (E) teams with superior ability have a very difficult time winning when a keep-away strategy is used.

3. A passbook savings account is a great investment because it allows one to accumulate a fortune. All people who have become wealthy through their investments have invested in a passbook account.

   Which of the following arguments has a flaw in the reasoning most similar to that found in the preceding statement?

   (A) Calculus is a valuable subject because calculus helps you to master GRE math. All calculus students do well on the math portion of the GRE.

   (B) Penicillin is a useful drug because it cures many diseases. Penicillin kills the bacteria that causes several diseases.

   (C) This rectangle could be a square because rectangles and squares share many properties. All squares are rectangles.

   (D) The run-and-shoot offense is ineffective because teams that use it usually lose. Defensive coaches have devised ways to stop the run-and-shoot offense.

   (E) Training wheels on a bicycle typically do more harm than good because they make it harder for a child to learn to ride a bike. Training wheels provide too much support and thereby make it impossible for a child to develop a sense of balance.

Go on to next page

4. Cancer is less curable now than it was 100 years ago. In 1895, only 5 percent of all deaths were caused by cancer, whereas cancer is responsible for 25 percent of all deaths today.

   Which of the following most weakens the argument?

   (A) Scientists have developed many cures for cancer over the past 100 years.

   (B) Immunizations and other health care measures protect humans from non-cancer diseases that were fatal 100 years ago.

   (C) Heart disease causes a higher percentage of deaths now than it did 10 years ago.

   (D) New technologies produce many cancer-causing agents.

   (E) Modern medicine alleviates the pain that cancer patients endure.

Questions 5-7 are based on the following information:

International Day Camp has two vehicles at its disposal to transport campers to a tour of a dairy. One vehicle is a minivan that can seat seven, including the driver. The other is a sedan that seats five, including the driver. The available counselors are Alban, Brown, and Chen, who must select from the camper roster of Kang, Leon, Madrid, Nguyen, Oliphant, Pascal, Quint, Robinson, Smith, Toorani, Umdekar, and Valdez. The selections of counselors and campers must conform to the following conditions:

I.   Counselors must drive the vehicles.

II. The number of campers on the field trip must not be more than three times the number of counselors.

III. If Alban is selected, Valdez is also selected.

IV. Robinson and Smith may not both be selected.

V.   If Nguyen is selected, Chen will not be selected.

VI. Valdez will not be selected unless Smith is selected.

5. Which of the following groups may go to the dairy?

   (A) Alban, Brown, Chen, Kang, Leon, Madrid, Smith, and Valdez

   (B) Alban, Brown, Leon, Madrid, Quint, Robinson, Toorani, and Umdekar

   (C) Alban, Chen, Madrid, Pascal, Quint, Robinson, Smith, and Valdez

   (D) Brown, Chen, Kang, Madrid, Nguyen, Robinson, Toorani, and Umdekar

   (E) Brown, Chen, Kang, Madrid, Oliphant, Toorani, Umdekar, and Valdez

6. The inclusion of which of the following guarantees that at least one of the vehicles will have empty seats?

   (A) Alban

   (B) Leon

   (C) Nguyen

   (D) Smith

   (E) Quint

7. If Robinson is selected, all the following will be rejected for the trip EXCEPT

   (A) Alban

   (B) Nguyen

   (C) Pascal

   (D) Smith

   (E) Valdez

Questions 8-12 are based on the following information:

A lawn mower repairman is fixing three mowers: one orange, one yellow, and one green. After he has reassembled the mowers, he is unhappy to find that he has parts left over: four nuts, two large bolts, one small bolt, and three washers. He must put the parts back according to the following rules:

I.   If he puts a large bolt on a mower, he must put a washer and a nut on that bolt.

II. If he puts a small bolt on a mower, he must put a nut on that bolt.

III. He may not put a washer on the green mower.

IV. The small bolt goes on the yellow mower.

V.   At least one part must go on each mower.

Go on to next page

8. Which of the following is an acceptable distribution of parts?

    (A) Orange: one nut, large bolt; Yellow: two nuts, large bolt, small bolt, three washers; Green: nut

    (B) Orange: two nuts, two large bolts, two washers; Yellow: two nuts, one bolt, one washer; Green: no parts

    (C) Orange: two nuts, one large bolt, two washers; Yellow: one nut, one small bolt; Green: one nut, one large bolt, one washer

    (D) Orange: one nut, one large bolt, one washer; Yellow: two nuts, one large bolt, one small bolt, two washers; Green: one nut

    (E) Orange: two nuts, one large bolt, one small bolt, two washers; Yellow: one nut, one large bolt, one washer; Green: one nut

9. If both large bolts go on the yellow mower, which of the following must be true?

    (A) The orange mower has more parts than the green mower.

    (B) The yellow mower has an odd number of parts.

    (C) All three washers are on the yellow mower.

    (D) The green mower has two nuts.

    (E) The orange mower has only a washer.

10. Which of the following statements must be false?

    (A) A nut is on the yellow mower.

    (B) There are more washers than large bolts on the yellow mower.

    (C) There are more parts on the yellow mower than on any other mower.

    (D) A washer is on the orange mower.

    (E) There are two parts on the green mower.

11. If only one nut goes on the orange mower, what is the maximum number of parts that can be on the orange mower?

    (A) three

    (B) four

    (C) five

    (D) seven

    (E) eight

12. If the repairman is allowed to put a washer on the green mower and each mower must have fewer than five parts, where do the large bolts go?

    (A) on the orange and green mowers

    (B) on the orange and yellow mowers

    (C) both on the orange mower

    (D) on the yellow and green mowers

    (E) both on the green mower

Questions 13-17 are based on the following information:

An academic team coach must select five players to compete in an upcoming match. To maximize her team's chances of winning, she must include two strong math players, a strong humanities player, and a strong social science player. Her roster includes Ann, Beth, and Carlos, who are strong math players; Damien and Elaine, who are strong humanities players; Fahid, Gail, and Haroon, who are strong social science players; and James.

The coach's selections must conform to the following conditions:

If she selects Carlos, she must select Fahid.

If she selects James, she may not select Fahid.

Elaine is chosen for the team.

The team may not include two or more social science players.

Go on to next page

13. Which of the following is an acceptable group of five players?

    (A) Ann, Beth, Elaine, Gail, Haroon

    (B) Ann, Carlos, Damien, Elaine, Haroon

    (C) Ann, Carlos, Damien, Elaine, Fahid

    (D) Ann, Damien, Elaine, Haroon, James

    (E) Ann, Beth, Carlos, Damien, Fahid

14. If the coach selects James, the team must also include

    (A) Damien

    (B) Beth

    (C) Gail

    (D) Carlos

    (E) Haroon

15. If Damien is chosen and Gail is not, how many different teams are possible?

    (A) one

    (B) two

    (C) three

    (D) four

    (E) five

16. Which of the following is *not* possible?

    (A) Carlos and James are both chosen.

    (B) Damien and Gail are both chosen.

    (C) Carlos is chosen, and Haroon is not chosen.

    (D) Three math players are chosen.

    (E) Ann and Haroon are both chosen.

17. James will be selected if which of the following is/are rejected?

    (A) Ann

    (B) Damien and Gail

    (C) Gail and Haroon

    (D) Damien and Fahid

    (E) Carlos and Fahid

18. A study of National Football League Statistics over the last ten years reveals that the losing team threw more interceptions than did the winning team in 82 percent of games played. This statistic clearly indicates that interceptions contribute greatly to team losses.

    The conclusion in the preceding argument depends on which of the following assumptions?

    (A) Fumbles do not hurt a team's chances of winning games.

    (B) A team's chances of winning games are greatly reduced if it throws any interceptions during a game.

    (C) A team that throws more interceptions than its opponent throws and still wins the game must have superior players.

    (D) Interceptions do not result from a team's falling behind in a game.

    (E) Interceptions are harmful primarily because they make it easy for the other team to score points.

19. Voice training is not necessary for one to become an opera star. A survey of those who went through voice training for more than two years found that only 2 percent of them were singing with opera companies.

    Which of the following, if true, would most effectively undermine the argument?

    (A) Nobody has ever become an opera star without voice training.

    (B) The survey also revealed that 70 percent of survey respondents were singing in musical comedies.

    (C) Many of those surveyed were minors and thereby ineligible to be employed by an opera company.

    (D) Most opera stars are freelance performers who do not belong to an opera company.

    (E) Stephanie Weiss, rising opera star and lead soprano in the Metropolitan Opera House's new production of *Die Fledermaus*, went through ten years of voice training.

Go on to next page

20. The cost for sending a fax outside of your local calling area consists of long-distance charges for the time the phone lines are connected to send the fax. The first fax machines required six minutes to send a two-page document. The resultant cost of sending such a document outside of your calling area was twice that of sending the document by regular mail. Even the slowest fax machine currently in use is four times as fast as the first fax machines. Long-distance phone charges for the first minute and each subsequent minute have not changed since fax machines were first used.

Which of the following is the conclusion to which the author of the above paragraph is leading?

(A) Sending a fax of a two-page document is better than mailing it outside of your calling area.

(B) Sending a fax of a two-page document is cheaper than mailing it outside of your calling area.

(C) Sending any document by fax is now cheaper than sending it by regular mail.

(D) Sending a fax of a two-page document is cheaper than sending the document by mail only when its destination is outside the local calling area.

(E) There are no advantages in sending documents by regular mail rather than sending them by fax.

Questions 21-25 are based on the following information:

In the Derby of Legends, horses Riva Ridge, Secretariat, and Tim Tam finish first, second, and third, but not necessarily in that order. The horses are ridden by jockeys Arcaro, Baeza, and Cordero, in no particular order, and are trained by Jolley, Lukas, and Whittingham, in no particular order.

The following information is known:

The horse ridden by Arcaro finishes ahead of the horse ridden by Cordero.

Lukas trains the horse ridden by Baeza.

The horses trained by Lukas and Jolley do not finish in consecutive order.

Secretariat finishes first.

21. If Jolley trains Secretariat, who trains the horse ridden by Arcaro?

(A) Whittingham

(B) Jolley

(C) Lukas

(D) Riva Ridge's trainer

(E) Tim Tam's trainer

22. If the horse trained by Whittingham finishes ahead of the horse trained by Jolley, which of the following must be false?

(A) Cordero rides Tim Tam.

(B) Lukas trains Cordero's horse.

(C) Riva Ridge is the next horse to finish after Secretariat.

(D) Arcaro rides Tim Tam.

(E) Baeza rides Secretariat.

23. Which of the following is possible?

(A) Tim Tam finished second.

(B) Arcaro's horse finished third.

(C) The horse trained by Jolley finished second.

(D) Lukas trained the horse ridden by Cordero.

(E) Riva Ridge finished first.

24. Which of the following would make it necessary that Cordero ride the horse that finished second?

(A) Riva Ridge finished second.

(B) The horse ridden by Baeza finished first.

(C) The Whittingham-trained horse finished second.

(D) Tim Tam was ridden by Cordero.

(E) The Lukas-trained horse finished third.

Go on to next page

25. Which of the following must be true?

    (A) If Riva Ridge is ridden by Cordero, Riva Ridge finishes second.

    (B) If Secretariat is ridden by Arcaro, the Jolley-trained horse finishes third.

    (C) If Tim Tam is ridden by Cordero, Riva Ridge finishes third.

    (D) If Tim Tam is ridden by Baeza, Riva Ridge finishes second.

    (E) If Tim Tam is trained by Whittingham, Tim Tam finishes third.

Questions 26-29 are based on the following information:

A university chemistry department must circulate a journal among Professors Ewing, Filbig, Geffen, Hurst, Ito, Jenn, Kinoshita, and Ludwig. Professor Ewing, the department chair, receives the journal first. Each professor who receives the journal reads it for one day and passes it to another professor the very next day. The journal is circulated in the following manner:

> Ewing to Filbig or Geffen
>
> Filbig to Kinoshita
>
> Geffen to Hurst
>
> Hurst to Ito or Jenn
>
> Ito to Filbig or Jenn
>
> Jenn to Kinoshita or Ludwig
>
> Kinoshita to Ewing
>
> Ludwig to Kinoshita

A professor may receive the journal more than once. Each time she/he receives it, she/he reads it for a day and passes it on the next day.

26. The journal never stops circulating. If Geffen receives it on January 1, what's the earliest she may receive it again?

    (A) January 4
    (B) January 5
    (C) January 6
    (D) January 7
    (E) January 8

27. Suppose that the journal must be circulated to Ewing, Filbig, Hurst, and Kinoshita, but the other professors need not see it. Who besides Ewing, Filbig, Hurst, and Kinoshita must end up seeing the journal?

    (A) nobody
    (B) Geffen only
    (C) Geffen and Ito
    (D) Geffen and Jenn
    (E) Geffen, Ito, and Jenn

28. What is the minimum number of days required for everyone to see the journal?

    (A) eight
    (B) nine
    (C) ten
    (D) eleven
    (E) twelve

29. If nobody receives the journal twice as it circulates from Ewing to Kinoshita, how many ways are there for the journal to get from Ewing to Kinoshita?

    (A) three
    (B) four
    (C) five
    (D) six
    (E) seven

30. Rock fan: This bootleg tape is definitely a recording of an early Beatles jam session. The choice of chords, the voice timbre, even the bantering is typical of the Beatles.

    The rock fan presupposes which of the following?

    (A) The chords of a song are its most distinctive feature.

    (B) The Beatles bootleg jam sessions are very rare and consequently very valuable.

    (C) Music is the only form of art with characteristics that allow the audience to identify the artist immediately.

    (D) No other musicians used the chords or had the voice timbre and bantering found in the tape.

    (E) The Beatles used chords, voice timbre, and bantering that differed greatly from those of any other group.

Go on to next page

31. Parents frequently criticize schools for not doing their jobs. Most notably, they blame schools for low student achievement scores. Surprisingly, the most frequent and vociferous complaints come from those who live in districts where the achievement scores are high.

    All of the following, considered individually, help to explain the apparent paradox *except*

    (A) parents from districts of high achievers are very involved with the schools and are therefore more likely to make critical comments.

    (B) parents of children who use an inter-district transfer to attend a school in a high-achieving district do not hesitate to complain when they feel their children are being ignored in favor of those students who live in the district.

    (C) high scores cause parents' expectations to rise, leading parents to demand that students achieve even more.

    (D) high-scoring districts contain high-profile students whose parents are very likely to complain when they observe that their children's scores do not match those of children who live nearby.

    (E) most complaints about schools come from political activists, most of whom live in high-achieving districts.

32. You will not take Economics 101C unless you complete Economics 101B. You will take Economics 101B only if you complete Economics 101A. If you complete Economics 101A, you must take Economics 102A.

    Which of the following is inconsistent with the information above?

    (A) You are taking Economics 101C, so you completed Economics 101A.

    (B) You completed Economics 101A but will not take Economics 101B.

    (C) You completed Economics 101A but are not eligible for Economics 101B.

    (D) You completed Economics 101A and 101B, and you will take Economics 101C.

    (E) You will not take Economics 102A, but you did take Economics 101B.

Questions 33-35 are based on the following information:

Gregory is planting four pea plants in his garden. The peas on the plants are characterized by color (yellow or green), shape (round or wrinkled), and size (large or small). Each plant has only one type of pea (that is, one plant won't have both a large pea and a small pea, or a round pea and a wrinkled pea, or a yellow pea and a green pea). Each characteristic is found on at least one of the plants. The following information is known about the peas:

The number of plants with yellow peas does not equal the number of plants with green peas.

Plant number two has large peas.

There are no round yellow peas.

If a plant has round peas, those peas are large.

Plant number four has yellow peas.

33. Which information would allow you to determine all the characteristics of plant number four?

    (A) plant number one is small; plant number three is round

    (B) plant number one is round; plant number three is large

    (C) plant number two is yellow; plant number three is yellow

    (D) plant number two is green; plant number three is wrinkled

    (E) plant number two is green; plant number four is wrinkled

34. If plant number two is the only plant with large peas, which plants(s) must have green peas?

    (A) number one

    (B) number two

    (C) number three

    (D) both number one and number three

    (E) both number two and number three

Go on to next page

35. If the peas on plant number one are small and those on plant number three are round, how many possible combinations are there for the four plants?

    (A) three
    (B) four
    (C) five
    (D) six
    (E) seven

Answer Key for Practice Exam 2

Verbal section	Quantitative section	Analytical section
1. A	1. D	1. B
2. A	2. A	2. C
3. D	3. D	3. A
4. B	4. C	4. B
5. D	5. B	5. A
6. B	6. B	6. C
7. D	7. C	7. C
8. C	8. A	8. D
9. D	9. C	9. E
10. A	10. A	10. E
11. B	11. D	11. B
12. B	12. C	12. A
13. A	13. A	13. C
14. C	14. A	14. B
15. A	15. D	15. D
16. A	16. B	16. A
17. D	17. E	17. D
18. A	18. D	18. D
19. A	19. B	19. A
20. A	20. E	20. B
21. C	21. C	21. B
22. A	22. E	22. B
23. C	23. A	23. A
24. B	24. C	24. E
25. C	25. A	25. D
26. A	26. B	26. C
27. D	27. D	27. B
28. E	28. C	28. B
29. E		29. D
30. B		30. D
		31. B
		32. E
		33. B
		34. B
		35. D

Scoring Worksheet GRE

Here's a quick review of what you learned earlier.

On the GRE, you get one point for every question you answer correctly, and zero points for every omitted answer (anything you leave blank). There is no penalty for incorrect answers.

Verbal

Add the number of questions you answered correctly in sections one and two. Round the sum to the nearest whole number. Check your score on the Verbal score chart.

Verbal raw score: _____

GRE Verbal Score Chart

You calculated a raw score on the worksheet. Look for that score in the following table and then move to the right to find your 200 – 800 score.

Raw	GRE	Raw	GRE	Raw	Gre	Raw	GRE
72–76	800	55	590	38	420	21	270
71	790	54	580	37	410	20	260
70	770	53	570	36	400	19	250
69	760	52	560	35	390	18	240
68	750	51	550	34	380	17	240
67	730	50	540	33	370	16	230
66	720	49	530	32	360	15	220
65	710	48	520	31	360	14	210
64	700	47	510	30	350	13	200
63	690	46	500	29	340	12	200
62	670	45	490	28	330	11	200
61	660	44	470	27	320	10	200
60	650	43	460	26	310	9	200
59	640	42	450	25	300	8	200
58	620	41	440	24	300	7	200
57	610	40	430	23	290	6	200
56	600	39	430	22	280	0–5	200

Math

Add the number of questions you answered correctly in sections four and five. Round the sum to the nearest whole number. Check your score on the Math score chart.

Math raw score: _____

GRE Math Score Chart

You calculated a raw score on the worksheet. Look for that score in the following table and then move to the right to find your 200–800 score.

Raw	GRE	Raw	GRE	Raw	Gre	Raw	GRE
60	800	46	670	32	510	18	340
59	800	45	660	31	500	17	330
58	800	44	650	30	490	16	310
57	790	43	640	29	480	15	300
56	780	42	630	28	470	14	290
55	770	41	620	27	460	13	270
54	760	40	600	26	440	12	250
53	750	39	590	25	430	11	240
52	730	38	580	24	420	10	230
51	720	37	570	23	400	9	220
50	710	36	560	22	400	8	200
49	700	35	550	21	390	7	200
48	690	34	540	20	370	6	200
47	680	33	530	19	360	0–5	200

Analytical

Add the number of questions you answered correctly in sections three and six. Round the sum to the nearest whole number. Check your score on the Analytical score chart.

Analytical raw score: _____

GRE Analytical Score Chart

You calculated a raw score on the worksheet. Look for that score in the following table and then move to the right to find your 200–800 score.

Raw	GRE	Raw	GRE	Raw	Gre
50	800	34	610	19	390
49	800	33	600	18	380
48	800	32	580	17	360
47	790	31	570	16	350
46	760	29	550	14	330
44	750	28	530	13	310
43	730	27	520	12	290
42	710	26	500	11	280
41	700	25	480	10	260
40	690	24	470	9	250
39	680	23	450	8	240
38	670	22	440	7	230
37	660	21	430	6	210
36	640	20	410	0–5	200
35	620				

Chapter 22

Practice Exam 2: Answers and Explanations

Verbal Section

1. **A.** You probably got this question right by the process of elimination. *Lucid* means clear (*luc* means light or clear). A lucid explanation *elucidates,* or makes clear, the material. *Turbid* means thick, cloudy, dense. When you stir up waters that are muddy, they become turbid. If you put ice cubes into a glass of Oozo (Greek wine), the liquid becomes turbid. *Vivacious* means lively, full of life (*vi* means life; *-ous* means full of). *Minuscule* means very small.

   Do not confuse *turbid* with *turgid*. *Turgid* means swollen or distended. A corpse floating in turbid waters after a few days would become turgid. (Where else but in *The GRE For Dummies,* 4th Edition can you read answer explanations that manage to work in both Greek wine and floating corpses?)

2. **A.** *Indigenous* means native to. Monsters are indigenous to the spaces under children's beds. Something not native to an area is *foreign* to it.

   Amiable means friendly (**Hint:** think of *ami*, which is *friend* in French, or *amigo*, which is *friend* in Spanish). *Lustrous* means shiny (*lus* means light or clear). *Pallid* means pale.

3. **D.** *Erudite* means well-educated, scholarly. The opposite is *uneducated. Timid* means shy. *Rash* in this context means overly hasty. *Loquacious* means talkative (*loq* means talk; *-ous* means full of or very). *Gargantuan* means huge. Loquacious, erudite people have gargantuan vocabularies and are not timid about using them.

4. **B.** *Hapless* means unlucky. (*hap* means luck; a mishap is bad luck; *haphazard* means depending on luck or chance; hapless is without luck, unlucky.) Choice A, *saturnine,* means gloomy or morose. Choice C, *cacophonous,* means bad-sounding, raucous. (*caco* means bad; *phon* means sound; *-ous* means full of.) My friends who have to listen to my cacophonous singing voice are saturnine (actually, they become *sanguinary,* which means bloodthirsty, but that's another story). Choice D, *mordant,* means sarcastic, caustic. Choice E, *ambiguous,* means uncertain, able to be interpreted in two or more ways. (*ambi* means both; *-ous* means full of. Ambiguous is "full of both," unclear.) An ambiguous response is often the best answer to a no-win question such as, "Does this outfit make me look fatter than before?"

5. **D.** To *burgeon* is to blossom and grow. The opposite is to *wither*. To *garble* is to distort or jumble. A student may garble her words and mispronounce this question as "surgeon" or even (my favorite) "sturgeon." Pretty hard to find the opposite of sturgeon, wouldn't you say? (To whom do you complain when you get a bad batch of caviar? The sturgeon general!)

6. **B.** *Noxious* means poisonous (*nox* means poison; *-ous* means full of). Choice B, *salubrious,* means healthy or healthful (*sal* means health; *-ous* means full of). Many hard vocabulary words are based on Latin roots. Spanish and French languages are also based on Latin roots. If you don't know a word in English, try pronouncing it with a Spanish or French accent and see whether a lightbulb goes on. *Salud* is Spanish for health.

Choice A, *froward:* If you took Practice Exam one, you should certainly know this word by now. It means stubborn, obstinate, obdurate, recalcitrant, refractory, adamant, intractable. Choice C, *inane,* means ludicrous or ridiculous. It would be inane for you not to know *froward* by now. You are too *erudite* (Choice D), too scholarly and well-educated, not to remember that word. Choice E, *vapid,* means dull, tasteless, or uninteresting.

7. **D.** *Sanguine* means cheerful, optimistic, confident. Do not confuse sanguine with *sanguinary,* meaning blood-thirsty. The opposite is *morose,* which means gloomy, or sullen. Choice A, *supple,* means flexible, lithe. Choice E, *voracious,* means greedy, ravenous. Are you voracious for yet more vocabulary, or has this section sated you?

8. **C.** To *extirpate* means to destroy or remove completely, to abolish. The opposite is to *introduce.* Words have more than one meaning; one of the nastier things the GRE does is to use familiar words in unfamiliar senses. To *introduce,* you probably thought, meant to bring together, as in introducing two friends. To *introduce* can also mean add or incorporate. Choice B, to *exacerbate,* is to make worse. Eating ice cream can exacerbate a toothache. To *adulate,* choice D, is to idolize, to hero-worship.

9. **D.** *Tonsorial* means pertaining to hair. No one really expects you to know this word. Instead, assume that unknown words are synonyms and make your sentence, "Tonsorial is hair." Then you can probably narrow the answers down to the two words you don't know (stentorian and sartorial) and make a quick guess. (If I'm underestimating your genius and your vocabulary, I abjectly apologize.) *Sartorial* means pertaining to clothing or apparel. If you want to get your money's worth out of this book, tell your mother that she is looking sartorially resplendent when she asks how her new outfit looks on her. And to be sure that she gets the message, bellow it in a *stentorian,* or loud, voice. In Homer's poetry, Stentor was a character who "has the voice of 50 men." In other words, he was a loudmouth. (I once had a less-than-erudite boyfriend who pouted when I talked about Homer's poetry, telling me that it wasn't polite to discuss former sweethearts and their love poems in front of him!)

Professorial does not mean pertaining to a job. That word would be *professional,* pertaining to a profession or job. *Professorial* means like a professor. In B, *medical* means pertaining to medicine, not pertaining to a disease. Choice C may have made you pause for a moment. Yes, we have canine teeth, but *canine* actually means pertaining to a dog, not pertaining to teeth. Our canine teeth are called that because they are pointed, like dogs' teeth.

10. **A.** You can get a good idea of the meanings of the difficult words in the questions by using two tips you've been given. First, use your roots. *Eu* means good. If you are *euphoric,* you are extremely happy because life is so good (you will be euphoric when you receive your GRE score). Second, try connecting English words with their equivalents in other languages. In Spanish, *lagrimas* means tears; you learned in Biology class that lachrymal glands produce tears. *Lachrymose* means tearful, sad. The words are antonyms. In choice A, the words are opposites as well: an *affluent,* or rich, person, is not *destitute,* or broke.

Okay, what if you can't figure out the meanings of the words in the question? The vocabulary in the answer choices isn't too bad. Work backwards. In choices B, C, and D, the words are similar in meaning. *Dexterous* means skillful, as in a dexterous magician. *Lax* means casual, such as a lax professor who doesn't bother to collect homework. *Weary* means fatigued. Because you can't have three right answers, they must all be wrong choices. The words in choice E appear to be unconnected. Someone *jovial,* or cheerful, may or may not be intelligent; there is no automatic connection between being cheerful and being intelligent. You have now eliminated all the answers but the correct one, A.

11. **B.** The last word in the set often features difficult words. If you recall that *in-* usually means not and *trep* means fear, you can analyze that *intrepid* means not having fear, or brave. Roots also help you to define *prolix*. *Pro-* means big or much; *lix* means speech or talk. Someone *prolix* has "big or much talk," is talkative. *Garrulous* also means talkative.

    Eliminate choice E: What do gruesome and *diligent* (hard working) have to do with each other? Choice C may be a slight trap. *Ped* can be a root meaning foot; a *pedestrian* is a person who goes on foot (which makes him more energetic than a couch potato like me, who jumps in the car to go to the mailbox). However, *pedantic* means scholarly and has no connection to the foot. Someone *asocial* is not sociable (*a-* means not or without), not very friendly. *Amiable* (*ami* means friend, like *mon ami* in French, or *amigo* in Spanish) means friendly. In choice A, *cantankerous* means grumpy or grouchy.

12. **B.** Now this is a hard question because so many of the answer choices are similar. The best sentence is that an *heirloom* is something left to you by an ancestor. A *bequest* (a gift to an heir) is left to you by a *testator* (one who makes the Last Will and Testament). While a magician may incorporate a *red herring* (something that tries to mislead or trick) into his act, he doesn't leave you one. While a musician uses an instrument, he doesn't leave you one. A *renegade* is a person who breaks the rules, a rebel. He leaves you with nothing. A *usurper* is one who takes without authority or right. He takes the throne; he doesn't leave it to you.

13. **A.** The prefix *acr-* means harsh or bitter. Gin can have an acrid taste; a divorce can be acrimonious. (That's one of the society columnists' favorite clichés: The acrimonious divorce between Mr. X and his third wife. Don't knock clichés. They can help you to define a word from its context.) Therefore, something *acrimonious* would *not* be sweet. Something *begrudging* is given grudgingly, not eagerly. Do you remember the prefix *be-?* It's as useless as your appendix. You can just ignore it — the prefix, not your appendix. Think of begrudging as simply grudging. (To help you remember this prefix, think of a belated birthday card: It's simply late. Ignore the *be-.*)

    Choice B has a sloppy trap in it. If you are *deprived,* you are without something, like deprived of the common sense to look for traps like this. But the word here is not *deprived*, it is *depraved* (people often confuse or misread the two words). If you are *depraved,* you are degenerate, without good moral sense. The people who write traps like this one are degenerate. In choice C, *itinerant* means traveling or wandering. You may be more familiar with the word in another form: itinerary, which is your travel schedule. Therefore, being itinerant has no connection to being experienced. In choice D, *lascivious* means full of lust, lustful. A lascivious glance at the itinerant salesperson will get you a reputation for depravity. In choice E, *protean* means constantly changing. Madonna is a protean star, always changing her hairstyle and appearance to keep the audience interested.

14. **C.** The relationship is lesser to greater, or weaker to stronger. First, you are thin, and then you are overly thin, or *emaciated.* First, you are happy, and then you are overly happy, or *ecstatic.*

    The pair of words in choice A are synonyms. To be *impervious* to something is to be immune to it. A teacher is often impervious to the *blandishments* (flattery) of her students who want to raise their grades. *Imperious* means regal. You may know this word in a more common form, *imperial.* (Think of Imperial margarine, with the crown on the box.) They both mean kingly, somewhat haughty and acting like royalty. *Sarcastic* means sardonic. In choice E, *demeaning* means insulting. The prefix *de-* means down from or away from, and it often precedes a word that means to put down, in the sense of insulting. A demeaning insult puts you down, criticizes you, and insults you.

15. **A.** The relationship is from lesser degree to greater degree. First, you're angry, and then you become *incensed,* which means furious, or burning mad (think of burning incense). Choice A also moves from a lesser to a greater degree. Something may be *noticeable*, like a new haircut; however, when you dye your hair neon green, the hairdo turns from noticeable to *flamboyant,* very noticeable or showy.

The pair of words in choice B are synonyms: *obdurate* means stubborn. You can remember this by pairing obdurate with a more familiar *ob* word, *obstinate* (also meaning stubborn). *Outmoded* means out of fashion. Something ancient may or may not be out of fashion; as the song says, "Everything old is new again." In choice D, *melodious* and *euphonious* are synonyms. You can figure out euphonious with roots: *eu* means good; *phon* means sound; *-ous* means full of. Something *euphonious* is full of good sound, or melodious. Choice E also lets you use your roots: *pac* means calm.

16. **A.** The "although" alerts you to the fact that you want a word the opposite of "proceeding slowly." Because someone *unenthusiastic* probably *would* proceed slowly (how fast do *you* go when you approach a task unenthusiastically?), eliminate it. Scratch off *pensive,* meaning thoughtful, meditative. A pensive person would naturally slow down and examine all aspects of a situation. Eliminate *dilatory,* or slow. A slow person would not have to *force* himself to slow down. You have the answers narrowed down to two. *Uncouth* means unsophisticated or ill-mannered, and has no connection to the sentence. *Impetuous* means hasty, rash, precipitate. An impetuous person would usually rush into things and would have to force himself to slow down and examine the situation more carefully.

17. **D.** Focus on the second blank. If Dr. Dickstein felt that the man against whom he was arguing was dangerous, he would argue pretty strongly against him. Eliminate choice B (*indifferently* means not caring one way or the other), choice C (*lackadaisically* means in a mellow, laid-back, nonenergetic way), and choice E (*tentatively* means hesitantly or uncertainly). The second word in A is possible; *exhaustively* means thoroughly. (It does not mean the same thing as exhausted, although an exhaustive search of the house for your missing car keys may leave you exhausted.) The first word, however, doesn't fit. *Fidelity* means faithfulness , as in fidelity between a loving couple (or Fido the faithful companion). That leaves choice D. *Vehemently* means strongly-felt and powerfully.

Do you know the words *charlatan* and *quack* in the question? A *charlatan* or a *quack* is a fraud or nonexpert. A GRE tutor who tells you that you'll get a 1600 if you stand naked in the light of the full moon and bury a toad in your backyard is a charlatan.

18. **A.** Vocabulary is the key to this sentence. You probably could predict relatively easily what types of words go in the blanks; the trouble is finding the words with those definitions. Start with the second blank. Say: The practice is probably more *common* than realized. *Widespread* means common, spread about everywhere.

Ironhanded means severe, strong. Have you heard the expression "rules with an iron fist"? That type of ruler is ironhanded.

Throughout this book, I have used clichés and expressions common to English, like "rules with an iron fist." If you don't understand those expressions or aren't comfortable with them, get someone to explain them to you. Many vocabulary words on this exam are parts of sayings or proverbs, or *aphorisms* (sayings) or *adages* (sayings). I suggest that you pull out an index card and write the cliché or saying on the card, along with an explanation of how it is used and what words are related to it (such as ironhanded). *Fly-by-night* is another cliché. It means temporary, not permanent. This came from the idea that a less-than-honest company would pack up in the middle of the night and leave town, taking its customers' money with it. It would, in effect, fly away in the middle of the night: fly-by-night.

Surreptitious means secretive, concealed. *Banal* means dull or stale from overuse. A cliché is banal.

Here's the vocabulary for the first blanks. *Intermittent* means off and on, not constant. Don't confuse this word with *interminable,* which means endless, or seemingly endless. A lecture can be interminable; a good lecturer will use jokes intermittently to try to keep the listeners' attention. *Haphazard* means nonsystematic, unplanned. *Arbitrary* means dependent on individual discretion and not fixed by law. You make an arbitrary choice when you buy a grab bag.

19. **A.** Start with the second blank. If Ken is *basking* in something, he is enjoying it immensely; it must be good. You could deduce the same thing by knowing that *kudos* means praise, glory, fame. The second word that goes with *kudos and . . .* must be positive as well. *Plaudits* are praises. An *apogee* is the zenith, the highest point. Winning one night on *Jeopardy!* was the apogee of my television career (don't ask what happened the next night; it was my career *nadir* or low point).

    Choice B, a *lapse,* is a pause or break. I had a brain cell lapse the second night on *Jeopardy!* and was full of self-reproof. *Reproofs* are criticisms or condemnations. (To reprove does not mean to prove again; it means to criticize or condemn. People often misdefine this word.) In choice C, an *apex* is the top point, the zenith, the apogee, such that it would work for the first blank. But the second blank lets you down. *Fecklessness* is feebleness, irresponsibility. In choice D, the *genesis* of something is the beginning. *Effrontery* is audacity, shameless boldness. And finally, choice E, *nascency,* is birth, the process of being brought into existence. *Perjury* is false testimony, lying under oath.

20. **A.** If the university is trying to make the speaker quit, she receives *disdain* (contempt, scorn) daily, and the response to her report was a small sample of that contempt. Predict that the blank requires a negative word. If (and this is a big if, I know!) you know the definitions of the words, you can eliminate choices B, C, and D. *Plaudits, encomium,* and *laudation* all mean praise (think of ap*plaud* for *plaud*its and *laud*). *Demise* means death. The speaker may have planned a million deaths for her ungrateful audience, but it's unlikely her listeners died during the presentation. That leaves only *abasement.* To *abase* is to humble or humiliate.

    In the paper-based test, the last question in a segment often has very difficult vocabulary. If you don't know the words and can't narrow the answers down, make a quick guess and go on. (In the computer-based test, you have no choice. The computer does not present you with the next question until you have answer the current one.). Remember that the GRE has no penalty for wrong answers. It's to your advantage to guess, but guess *quickly.* The only way you can hurt your score on a question like this is to spend a lot of time agonizing over the words.

21. **C.** The second half of the sentence leads you to believe that the jury was having second thoughts. Unfortunately, in this case, that doesn't narrow down the answers because all the second words have to do with being confused or uncertain. *Inquisitive* means curious. *Ambivalent* means unclear or of two minds. (The root *ambi* means both. An ambivalent person could go both ways, take either side of an issue.) *Irresolute* means undetermined, wishy-washy. *Befuddled* means confused.

    If the defendant's actions in accepting his fate gave the jury those second thoughts, he must be acting as if he is innocent. That means he is not *complacent* (unconcerned) or *insolent* (disrespectful). He would not be *quiescent,* which means the same as complacent. And *haughty* means arrogant or conceited. If the defendant were arrogant, chances are the jury would be glad to have convicted him, not worried whether it had done the right thing. That leaves only *plaintive,* which means sorrowful, melancholy. Think of the plaintive look on your dog's face when he realizes you are going to eat all your dinner and not give him any morsels.

22. **A.** The passage states in lines 17–20 that a court may deem a gift community property if the donor's intent was to give it to both parties, even if the donor did not state so specifically. Because statement I is correct, eliminate answers B and D. Statement II is wrong; it brings in the distinction between real and personal property, which was not covered in the passage. (For those of you who have gone through *acrimonious* — bitter — divorces and are all too familiar with the concept of community property, shelf your knowledge while answering these questions. Answer them based only on information stated or implied by the passage.) Statement III is also wrong but very tricky. Nothing in the passage stated that the time of the intent to make the gift was important, only the intent of the donor. If you chose C, you read too much into the question.

23. **C.** The author mentions early in the passage that there used to be just a few community property states, but that the number has been steadily increasing. From this, you may infer that this increase will continue.

Choice A is definitely a judgment call. Who is to say whether the community property concept is fair, not fair, the fairest, or the least fair? Passages (unless they are editorial or opinion types, which are infrequent) rarely give personal opinions or push one person's theories or philosophies.

Choice B is well outside the scope of this passage; nothing was mentioned about homemakers. Choice D goes overboard. Just because the author believes there will be more community property states does not mean states will turn *all* possessions to community property.

You learned in the reading lecture to be wishy-washy, not dramatic. Eliminate answers with "strong" words, such as *all, every, never,* and *none.* Choice E has the same problem: It features the excessive word *all.*

24. **B.** Locate where in the passage the placebo effect is mentioned (the beginning of the last paragraph) and then look at what the author says after this. The author is not fazed by the placebo effect possibility. In the same sentence that mentions placebo effect, the author says that the effect does not minimize the therapeutic potential. The sentences that follow emphasize how laughter is good for health, making choice B a good answer. Eliminate choices A, C, and E, which contradict what the author does in the last paragraph. The author basically says that even if laughter's main benefit starts out in the mind (which is what a placebo effect is), the body has a positive reaction. Choice D refers to the previous paragraph, which claims that laughter is innate. The author does nothing to dispel this notion, allowing you to eliminate choice D.

25. **C.** The third paragraph discusses many social and physiological effects of laughter. Choices B and C both bring up topics discussed in the paragraph, but choice B is too extreme.

Remember: The GRE shies away from dramatic or extreme answers. Moderate or even wishy-washy answers seem to be preferred.

While laughter leads to increased catecholamine levels, nothing in the passage indicates that laughter is the *only* way to increase these levels. Choice C is a safe answer. Lines 31–40 point out several social benefits derived from laughter. These benefits may come about in the absence of laughter, but given laughter's important role in these functions, it's fair to say that someone unable to laugh would be at a disadvantage. Choice A is completely illogical: It would make more sense if the question asked about an infant who is unable to cry, not unable to laugh. Choice D cannot be inferred from the passage. Crying occurs when the infant is distressed. While an infant who is unable to laugh may have more frequent stressful episodes than a normal infant, this is not certain. The best conclusion is that an infant who is unable to laugh won't be able to signal comfort as often as a normal infant does. Choice E is similar to choice B. An infant who is unable to laugh may benefit from placebo effects, just not necessarily those produced by laughter.

26. **A.** Pay careful attention to the language used in these choices. The third paragraph ascribes a possible pain reduction role to laughter via endorphins, but this does not mean that laughter is essential. The body probably has other ways to reduce pain. Eliminate choice E. Cross off choice D, which directly contradicts a point made in the third paragraph: Laughter *increases,* not decreases, the levels. Choice C may have trapped you. The word *directly* should have made you eliminate this answer; the GRE plays down dramatic or emphatic words (GRE answers often hedge their bets, using

lame language such as *may* or *probably* or *suggest*). First, no association between laughter and sed rate has been established. In addition, even if there were such an association, you can't get away with saying that laughter *directly* lowers the sed rate. Laughter very well could lower inflammation, which, in turn, lowers the sed rate. Choice B is not mentioned in the passage. Laughter is associated with increased pulse rate, but the passage says nothing about blood pressure. This leaves only choice A, which is mentioned throughout the first paragraph.

27. **D.** The last two paragraphs of the passage urge measures to restrict campfire location. Without such measures, the author claims that campfires will be built just about everywhere and that soil damage will be widespread. It can be inferred from this that campfire users, when left to their own devices, will build a campfire just about anywhere. This leads to choice D as the answer. Because the opposite of choice A appears to be true, eliminate this choice. Choice B is plausible, but there is no mention of a connection between campfire users and forest fires. Forest fires were discussed briefly in paragraph three in relation to water repellency. Choice C goes overboard. There is no information to indicate whether campfire users favor a certain type of soil, eliminating choice E. The scientific findings discussed in paragraph two point to an advantage of one type or the other, but you can't tell whether the campfire users actually consider this evidence.

28. **E.** This passage contains a lot of dry detail about how certain campfire factors damage soil and its ability to support life. Throughout the passage, the author uses these details to recommend a certain action. The author is concerned that campfires damage soil and wants to minimize this damage. Choice E fits this perfectly. Choice A is too extreme. Choices B and D are true statements, but these are just two of several factors mentioned by the author.

    Just because a statement is true does not mean it is the correct answer; in a main idea question, all five choices may in fact be true. Choice C is also a detail but is wrong primarily because the author is concerned that certain woods will lead to soil damage, not with how well the woods will work with the campfire per se.

29. **E.** Common sense suggests that E is the right answer. Paragraph three helps to confirm this. This paragraph mentions that short-lived forest fires are more likely than campfires to create water repellency-inducing conditions (knocking out choice A). This information implies that campfires last longer. Combine this reasoning with the explicit mention that campfires typically exceed 350 degrees and you've got your answer. Choice C is directly contradicted by paragraph four. Choices B and D don't make sense. The passage often mentions that heat flow into the soil damages it. A long-lasting campfire will produce more heat flow than a short-lived one.

    While you certainly do not need to have any background knowledge to answer Reading Comprehension questions (all information necessary is given or implied in the passage), don't hesitate to use your common sense, especially with science passages. Common sense is a good place to start, but do be sure to check your "logical" answer with the facts given in the passage.

30. **B.** The last sentence of the first paragraph states that the loss of organic matter reduces water-holding capacity and renders the soil more susceptible to erosion.

    Note that this question basically required your truly understanding the whole passage. If you didn't read this passage carefully but just skimmed for specific answers to specific questions, this question would have been a good question just to guess at.

Quantitative Section

1. **D.** Please tell me you didn't fall for this trap. Did you pick up your pencil and start to draw a picture of the roller rink, the school, and the coffee shop? As soon as you have to draw a picture, you should be thinking choice D. The answer *de*pends on how you draw the picture. If you put the roller rink, the school, and the coffee shop all in a straight line in that order, then the coffee shop and the rink are in fact 13 kilometers apart. But (and this is a big but, because whenever you see a C answer, you should be paranoid and double-check it) what if you put the coffee shop three kilometers to the other side of the school, between the rink and the school? Then the distance from the rink to the coffee shop is only 7 kilometers, and now the answer is B. If the answer changes *de*pending on how you draw the figure, choose D.

   Problems that require you to find a distance between places or people are often D because the distance depends on the sequence those places or people are in. When you see a "line 'em up" problem, think D.

2. **A.** Are you a fraction-phobe, like most of us? Then avoid fractions altogether and simply plug in numbers. Work backwards and plug in a number for c that will be divisible by both 4 and 3. Try 12. If , then $b = \frac{3}{4} \times 12 = 9$. If , then $a = \frac{2}{3} \times 9$, or 6. Now $\frac{a}{c} = \frac{6}{12}$, or $\frac{1}{2}$. Because $\frac{1}{2}$ is greater than $\frac{1}{3}$, A is the answer. Although this will work no matter what number you plug in for c, why not make life easy and plug in a nice round number? If you plug in something like 10, then $b = \frac{3}{4} \times 10$ or $\frac{30}{4}$ and that's a pain in the fundament (that portion of your body upon which you are sitting even as we speak).

   If you want to do the problem "the real way," it's not hard. You just have to know that "of" means and multiply the whole shebang. $\frac{2}{3}$ of $\frac{3}{4}$ of $c = \frac{2}{3} \times \frac{3}{4} \times c = \frac{6}{12} \times c = \frac{1}{2} \times c$. It comes out the same.

3. **D.** If you chose C, you fell for the trap. You cannot simply multiply the exponents of two unlike bases. For example, if you were to multiply 5^{-2} $\left(\text{which is } \frac{1}{5}^2 \text{ or } \frac{1}{25}\right) \times 2^{-5}$ $\left(\text{which is } \frac{1}{2}^5, \text{ or } \frac{1}{32}\right)$, the answer would hot be 1. The answer depends on the values of x and y: are they positive? Negative? Fractions? With this many possibilities, the answer is D.

   The more variables you have, the better your chances of getting a D answer. Don't immediately choose D when you see a lot of x and y variables, but you should entertain the possibility that the answer will depend on the numbers you plug in.

   Will the end of the QC's have a lot of D answers like this? Not necessarily. However, because questions go from easier to harder and because the hard or tricky questions often have answer D, don't be surprised if you do have what seems a disproportionate number of D's at the end of the exam.

4. **C.** To multiply like bases, add the exponents. One over is the same as a to the negative third power. Add: to the .

   Did you choose D because you don't know what a is? The value of a here, although unknown and unknowable given the information you have, is irrelevant. , no matter what the value of a. This question is very similar to number ten. If both questions **befuddled** (confused) you, return to Chapter 11.

5. **B.** This problem is rather lengthy *unless* you see the shortcut. Here's the long way first: An arc is a fraction of the circumference of the circle. The circumference is 2π *radius*. Because the area of a circle is , the radius here is 6. The circumference, therefore, is 12π. The arc is the same fraction of the circle that the central angle is of 360. Here, put $\frac{45}{360}$ and reduce it to $\frac{1}{8}$. That means the arc is $\frac{1}{8}$ of the circumference of the circle. $\frac{1}{8}$ of 36π is certainly less than 36π.

Ready for the shortcut? You can cut off the last step entirely. You still have to break down the area to find the radius and then work back up to find the circumference. (You should be so comfortable with formulas that you can do this step without even breathing hard.) You can see by looking at the figure that the arc is not the entire circumference, but only a part of it. That means that the arc is less than 36π, and B is larger. You don't need to — and certainly don't want to — find the exact measure of the arc.

If you're getting brain cramps, go back to the Circles section of Chapter 10 and look under Arcs.

6. **B.** When a negative is cubed, it remains a negative. For example, . Therefore, whatever Column A is, it's negative. Stop right there and don't strain the brain any more.

As you go through the QC questions, keep reminding yourself that the name of the game is Quantitative Comparisons, not Problem Solving. You don't have to solve the problem, more times than not. You work until you see which column is going to be greater, and then you stop. The actual solution is irrelevant and unnecessary. And remember: Every second that you save by not working on the QCs is another second that you can use on the regular multiple-choice problems where you *do* need to do all that drudge work.

7. **C.** This is a symbolism problem. It looks more intimidating and difficult than it actually is. Substitute the numbers for the variables in the "explanation." Use the numbers in the same order as the variables. That is, 3 is in the first position, and *a* is in the first position, so substitute a 3 for an *a*. 6 is in the second position and *b* is in the second position, so substitute a 6 for a *b*. 12 is in the third position, and *c* is in the third position, so substitute a 12 for a *c*. That gives you $3(3) + 4(6) - \frac{1}{2}(12) = 9 + 24 - 6 = 27$.

The more calculations you do, the less surprised you should be when the answer comes out to be choice C. This does not mean that, as soon as you find yourself doing a lot of pencil pushing, you should give up and choose C, hoping for the best. It does mean that if you do no work, and you just think the columns are equal, you've probably fallen for a trap, because you frequently have to perform the actual calculations and prove that the columns are equal.

8. **A.** You didn't fall for the trap and put C, did you? I keep warning you: If your first reaction is that the columns are equal, you need to think again. The average of Column A is approximately , not 11.

Suppose that Column A said , and Column B said *b*. What would your answer be then? It would be D, because everything would depend on the value of the variables. Sure, Column A may still be , and Column B may be *b*. But what if ? The columns are the same. What if ? Then A is bigger. What if $b = \frac{1}{2}$? Then B is bigger. Be very wary of these "obvious" questions.

9. **C.** There are two ways you can approach this problem. The sum of the angles in any triangle is 180 degrees. Because you know two angles are 90 degrees (the box indicates a right or 90-degree angle) and 20 degrees for a sum of 110 degrees, you know the remaining angle must be 70 degrees . That angle and the *y* angle are along a straight line, which means they are supplementary and add up to 180 degrees. Subtract 70 from 180 and you get 110.

There's an even easier way to do this problem. The exterior angle is equal to the sum of the two remote interior angles. In simple speech, that means an angle outside the triangle is the same as the sum of the two angles away from it inside the triangle. In this problem, angle .

Most geometry problems simply require you to know the properties of angles and figures. I can't emphasize enough the importance of memorizing everything you can wrestle your brain cells around in geometry. Learn the rules until you can mutter them in your sleep and they'll return to you in your hour of need.

10. **A.** It's easy to do this problem if you convert the percent to decimals (all right-thinking people despise percentages) and remember that *of* means ×. Column A, therefore, is 3.0 (300 percent is the same as 3, or 3.0) × 30 = 90. Column B is .

Did you fall for the trap and choose C? Don't be *disheartened* (sad); it happens to the best of us. You were thinking of only the numerals and forgetting your decimal places. You could have avoided all this grief by using your brain instead of your yellow #2. You know quickly that 300 percent of 30 is more than 30. You know just as quickly that 60 percent of 15 is less than 15. Because more than 30 is greater than less than 15, Column A is greater. Whenever possible, try to talk the problem through rather than solving it precisely. No one really cares what the answer is.

11. **D.** If you chose A, you fell for the trap. What if and ? Then and the columns are equal. What if and ? Then and A is the answer. If the answer DEEEE-pends on what you plug in, choose D.

12. **C.** Please tell me you didn't actually work out this problem. You know that the word *of* means times, or to multiply. If you were to do this problem as a decimal, you'd have and . Because the number of decimal places is the same, the solution is the same as well.

This problem is very common. However, don't get complacent, see this sort of thing, and immediately choose C. What if Column A said .20 percent rather than 20 percent? That would make the multiplication , a very different answer indeed. Keep a wary eye on the decimal point.

13. **A.** You didn't actually work this out, did you? One of the things the QC questions tests is your knowledge of when to pick up your pencil and when just to guesstimate. This problem is a definite guesstimate. With 365 days per year (366 in a leap year), Column A would be . Don't actually work it out. Column is , because a decade has ten years. You can see at a glance that Column A is much larger.

Although it's not a trap in this particular problem, often a question can getcha if you forget about leap year. For example, if a question asks you how much money Mark makes if he earns $200 a day every single day for four years, your answer will be $200 off unless you remember that one of those years has 366, not 365, days.

If you didn't grow up in the United States, you may be accustomed to different units of measurement, such as metric rather than standard. It's important that you take a few minutes to go back to the Units of Measurement portion of Chapter 12 and make sure that you know, for example, how many inches are in a foot, how many pounds are in a ton.

14. **A.** You know that when you multiply by a power of ten, you move the decimal point that many places. If the power of ten is positive, move the decimal to the right. If the power of ten is negative, move the decimal to the left. In Column A, move the decimal five places to the right, which gives you 50,430. In Column B, move the decimal two places to the left, giving you .5043.

15. **D.** Let *x* be the number of books they check out and make represent the number of books that they put back. The equation now is . Next, . Then . Finally, .

If you chose B, you forgot to answer the question, which wants to know how many books were put back, not how many were checked out. .

You can use a great shortcut to narrow down the answers. You know that more books were put back than were checked out. That means that more than half the books were put back and fewer than half the books were checked out. Half of 84 is 42; more than that must have been put back. Only answers D and E could fit. Instead of working through all the garbage algebra, use those two answers. If 52 books were put back, then 20 less than 52, or 32, were checked out. Does ? Yup, it does, and you've finished the problem. If you want to check, try choice E. If 64 books were put back, 20 fewer than 64, or 44 books were checked out. Does ? Nope. Choice D was right all along.

16. **B.** The area of a parallelogram is simply . The base goes from , a distance of 9 units. The height goes from 1 to 5, a distance of 4 units, and .

The height is not the side of the parallelogram, *CD*. If you solved for that answer, you did unnecessary work. The height is a straight line, going from the tallest point down to the base (a height is always perpendicular to the base), as shown in the preceding figure.

17. **E.** Make my day and tell me that I got you to do a lot of useless calculating on this problem. If you found the total promotion in 1970 and then the promotion in 2000 and figured out the percentage, I gotcha. You know only how much was spent on promotion; you can't break that promotion down to television and other types of media blitzes.

18. **D.** Did you fall for trap answers A or E? In 1970, salaries went from 0 to 25, for a total of 25. Promotion went from 45 to 50, a total of 5. While 25 is 5 times as much as 5, it is only 4 times greater, or 400 percent greater. (This percentage jazz comes up a lot on the exam and was covered in detail in the math review. If you're confused by this problem, go back to the percentages section of Chapter 12 and lock yourself in a room with it until only one of you emerges alive.)

19. **B.** Just add up all the overhead amounts: approximately . But again, this is 35 tens of thousands, or 350,000.

If you chose D or E, you included the 10 that was projected to be spent on overhead in 2000. The question specifically asks for the amount spent from 1950 through 1990. Careless reading could cost you points here.

20. **E.** If you chose A, you fell for a trap. (Are you getting totally sick and tired of hearing that expression? Don't fall for so many traps, and you won't have to hear it.) Dividing like bases means subtracting the exponents. For divided by , subtract: . Divide 6 by 3 and get 2. You know that the first term is , so you can narrow the answers down to C, D, and E.

divided by b^9 is b^{-4}, or $\frac{1}{b^4}$. That result eliminates answers C and D; you can stop now.

Just for fun, though, I'll finish this calculation. divided by is 1. Any number divided by itself is 1. (Or you could think of it as being ; any number to the 0 power is 1.) The answer 1 doesn't change in the multiplication; ignore it.

Answers A and B were traps for people who tried instead of subtracting exponents.

Answers C and D were traps for people who forgot that a negative exponent is in the denominator, not the numerator. ***Remember:*** really is $\frac{1}{2^3}$. If you forgot this, return to the thrilling math review.

21. **C.** You can find the probability by using this formula:

# of possible desired outcomes
# of total possible outcomes

The first thing to do is find the denominator. How many candies will be left after LaVonne has chomped into the others? She starts with 47 candies . You know that she throws some of them away. You can eliminate choice A immediately because the denominator must be less than 47.

She throws away a creme (down to 46), a nut (down to 45), a chew (down to 44), a nut (down to 43), a creme (down to 42), and a chew (down to 41). The denominator for the probability of the next candy that she pulls out will be 41 because she'll have some chance out of 41 of pulling out a nut. That narrows the answers down to B and C.

As a shortcut, subtract 6 (the number of candies that she already pulled out) from 47, the number of candies that originally were in the box. I solved the problem the long way to show you where the 41 really comes from.

Now find the numerator. She starts out with 12 nuts, pulls out one (down to 11), and then pulls out another (down to 10). The probability that her next candy will be a nut is $^{10}/_{41}$. (This type of problem is discussed in the probability section of Chapter 11.)

22. **E.** Did I getcha on this problem? You know from your previous calculations on the preceding problem that the new employees hired from January through June of 1994 sum up to 180. However, that does not mean there are only 180 employees in the entire company. Looking at the second graph gives you the idea that there probably were other employees to begin with. Be careful of assuming too much on a graph.

23. **A.** Simply add up the numbers on the graph: , , , , , and .

The first question after a graph is usually ridiculously simple. It checks that you know how to read the chart. Do not look for tricks or traps built into the first question. Those will come later.

24. **C.** If you're like me, your first response to the question "What's the difference between the mode and the median?" was "Median has more letters." But seriously, folks . . . A mode is the most common number, the one that repeats the most times. In this case, the number 8 is found 3 times. The median is the number in the middle.

The median is not the same as the mean. The mean is the average; add all the terms, and divide by the number of terms. The median is the number in the middle *when the terms are arranged in order* (you can't just look at the problem the way it is and choose the middle term). Just think of the median strip in the middle of the highway. In order, these numbers are 5½, 6, 6, 6½, 6½, 7, 7½, 8, 8, 8, 8½. The middle or median term is 7. .

25. **A.** This problem is easier than it looks. If two circles have the same area, they have the same radius because the area of a . The radius of circle Y is 5 as well. The diameters of the two circles are 10 each because the diameter of a circle is twice its radius. The length of the rectangle is 20, therefore, and the width is 10.

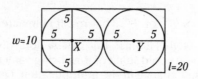

The area of a rectangle is .

26. **B.** Understand what the explanation means. (The explanation is made up for this particular problem. There is no such thing as a "circle" operation in the real world — only in the little universe of the GRE. Lucky you.) The explanation says that you have a number in the circle. If that number in the circle is a prime number (meaning that it can be divided only by itself and 1), you add the number in the circle to the square of the number in the circle.

If the number in the circle is a composite number (one that can be divided by something other than just 1 and itself), you square that number and subtract the number in the circle from the square.

Ugh. You may have to repeat those instructions to yourself a few times. You're really just substituting the number in the circle for the *x* in the appropriate equation.

Because 4 is composite, you use the second line of the explanation. Square 4: . Subtract from that the number in the circle. .

Because 5 is prime, you add it to its square: .

Add the two results: .

This problem has all sorts of trap answers. If you used the first line for both terms, you got 50. If you used the second line for both terms, you got 32. If you confused prime and composite numbers, using the composite rule for 5 and the prime rule for 4, you got 40.

27. **D.** From 9:30 to 12:30 is 3 hours. Gwendolyn studies for 3 minutes less than that, or 2 hours and 57 minutes. Notice that you don't have to go through all the fuss n' bother of converting to minutes, subtracting, and then converting back to hours. Round the study time to three hours, and then subtract three minutes. Don't do more work than you have to; there's no prize for the most equations, you know.

28. **C.** A chord connects any two points on the circumference of a circle. The longest chord in any circle is the diameter. The area of a circle is . A diameter is $2r$; here, , and .

If your answer was 3 or 4, or 9 or 16, you multiplied by or squared π. The problem was worded to avoid having you do so. Note specifically what the problem is asking for, to avoid making this type of careless mistake.

If you didn't know what "the longest chord in a circle" was, you might have wanted a "It cannot be determined from the information given" answer. Well, surprise! There is no such answer among the choices. That's a clue that you *can* solve this problem; think about it a little more. Fill in something, anything. ***Remember:*** There is *no* penalty for a wrong answer.

Analytical Section

1. **B.** The argument concludes that cars are safer than planes. The evidence used to support this conclusion deals with the percentages of accidents that result in fatalities. To justify the conclusion, one must assume that these percentages are the key statistic, that there isn't some other factor that would overcome the supposed 50 to 1 advantage in favor of cars.

   Choice B wipes out the 50 to 1 advantage. One out of every two plane accidents results in fatalities, but for every two plane accidents, there are approximately one million car accidents. One percent of one million is ten thousand. This means that for every one fatal plane accident, there are about ten thousand fatal car accidents. Suddenly, cars don't seem so safe.

   Choices A and C simply indicate that humans make efforts to ensure that planes and flying are as safe as possible. They do not weaken the argument, though, because it still could be the case that many people die in plane accidents.

   Choice D apparently indicates that cars are more dangerous than the one percent figure suggests, but it doesn't affect the picture enough to make this the correct answer. The one percent figure takes everything into account, so even with this information, the fact remains that only one percent of car accidents result in fatalities. The information does indicate that when a car accident results in a fatality, there could be multiple deaths, and this would make cars more dangerous than what is conveyed by the one percent figure. However, consider that the typical plane accident involves more than one hundred people, so choice D doesn't do enough to contradict that argument that cars are safer than planes.

   Choice E simply provides detail on the one percent figure. It is still the case that only one percent of car accidents result in fatalities. The argument does not make the claim that cars are safer than planes no matter what type of road is used, so choice E does not get to the heart of the matter.

2. **C.** The UCLA fan criticizes basketball without a shot clock because he feels that such a rule allows for a game that does not capture the essence of basketball. There is nothing in his statement that criticizes a team's decision to employ a certain strategy. In fact, he implies that a team with inferior talent should play a keep-away game if it is permit-

ted to do so by the rules. He simply says that a team should not be allowed such an option. Nevertheless, the North Carolina fan, by defending the use of a keep-away game, acts as if the UCLA fan said teams shouldn't play such a game. This is what choice C says. For the North Carolina fan to dispute what the UCLA fan said, he should defend the lack of a shot clock, saying something on the order of how such a lack adds intrigue, and so on. Choice A does not really capture the scope of the argument. Neither fan discussed excitement or boredom. The UCLA fan seems to imply that the lack of a shot clock produces a not-so-satisfying game, so if the North Carolina fan thinks choice A, he hasn't misunderstood too much.

A casual reader might be tempted by choice E because the North Carolina fan defends deployment of a keep-away strategy. In addition, this is not what the UCLA fan said. All he said was that a keep-away game could allow a team with inferior ability to win. This does not mean that teams with superior ability could not perfect a keep-away strategy and win many games by using such a strategy. Therefore, choice E qualifies on the criterion of the North Carolina fan's misunderstanding. What makes this choice incorrect is that the response does not address the issue of superior teams. The North Carolina fan would have to say something along the lines of, "The shot clock produced a fair game. Teams with superior talent played superb games of keep-away and won many basketball games."

Choices B and D are implied by the UCLA fan. The North Carolina fan should have picked up on these points. If he had, there would have been less misunderstanding.

3. **A.** The first sentence of the stimulus (the paragraph giving the information) makes a conclusion (passbook accounts are great investments) that follows from some evidence (allows one to accumulate a fortune). The real problem with the argument comes from the next sentence, which backs up the first sentence with some correlational data (wealthy investors have invested in passbooks). What is needed to make this argument convincing is some evidence that shows that it actually was the passbook investments that made these investors wealthy. The second sentence does not accomplish this. It's probable that the investors became wealthy through some other investments. They may have invested in passbooks at one time (perhaps as children), but their wealth arose from something else. Furthermore, it's probable that the majority of passbook investors do not become wealthy, further weakening the connection between passbook accounts and wealth. It could be an underlying cause, such as the realization that money doesn't do good just sitting around or the desire to maintain a balance of safe and risky investments, that leads one to invest in both passbooks and very profitable investments.

In choice A, the second sentence fails to establish that calculus causes high GRE math scores. (Don't panic, don't panic — calculus is *not* required for the GRE; calculus is *not* tested on the GRE. This is just a question.) All you know is that calculus and high GRE math scores go together, but it could very well be that there is an underlying factor, such as a high math aptitude, that causes someone to take calculus *and* to do well on the GRE math. This is the same weakness found in the reasoning of the original statement.

Choice B is incorrect because the second sentence explains how penicillin cures diseases. It explains cause and effect and is therefore more persuasive than the original statement. Choices C, D, and E are weak because the first sentence is not as absolute as what's seen in the last sentence of the original statement. Furthermore, unlike the original statement, the arguments in these choices are pretty logical.

4. **B.** The argument uses the increase in percentage to conclude that cancer is more deadly. To weaken the argument, find a choice that says that the increased percentage reflects something other than an increase in the virulence of cancer.

Choice B is not obvious at first, but what it is saying is that fewer people are dying from diseases other than cancer. Because everyone has to die, if fewer die from something other than cancer, more will have to die from cancer, even if it is not more deadly.

You do not need outside knowledge to answer a question, but what you do know can be helpful. The test makers will not put in a question that is contrary to common sense, history, or general knowledge. One hundred years ago, many children died of such diseases as diphtheria, long before cancer could develop in their bodies. The longer one lives, the better one's chances are of developing cancer. More people die of cancer now, not because it's more deadly but because they live long enough to get the disease.

You may have been tempted to go with choice A because it sounds so direct, but it actually doesn't do the job. Scientists may have developed many cures, but according to the numbers, the cures haven't kept pace with the disease. More cures do not mean that the disease is more curable if the disease increases in virulence. Choice C does not negate that cancer is more deadly. Heart disease may also be more deadly, but that doesn't affect cancer. Choice D *strengthens* the argument by giving a reason why we must be more concerned about cancer today. Choice E would be a candidate if the medicine cured cancer, but all that's discussed is pain relief.

Questions 5–7

The task with this game is to select from a large pool. A good way to keep track of who is selected is to list all the counselors and campers and circle those selected. You can distinguish between the counselors and campers by using capital letters for the counselors and small letters for the campers. Your pool may look like this:

A B C

k l m n o p q r s t u v

Incorporate statement I into this listing by writing "2 or more" by the counselor row.

You must have *at least* two counselors because two drivers are needed, but don't assume that there will be *only* two counselors. The third counselor could go on the trip as a passenger in one of the vehicles.

A B C (2 or more)

k l m n o p q r s t u v

Next, work with the two rules that involve Valdez. (You don't have to go through the rules in any particular order; approach whichever one you think is the easiest to work with.)

Statement III can be summarized as . This rule also means that *not* . This is true because once *v* is out, *A* has to be out because the presence of *A* could bring on *v* and produce a contradiction.

Do not make the mistake of thinking *not* . The presence of *A* guarantees that *v* is included, but *v* could be there even if *A* is not there.

Statement VI says that *s* is necessary for *v*. This means *not* . Think of it this way: *s* is a requirement or a prerequisite for *v*. If *s* fails to show, *v* has to be left home because the requirement was not fulfilled. Therefore, *not* leads to the further deduction of . This means if *v* is there, its requirement, *s,* has to be there.

Combine the third and last rules to get the following:

Statement IV may be summarized as *no* Ⓡⓢ.

The next-to-last (*penultimate*, for those of you with spectacular vocabularies) rule may be summarized as , which allows the deduction of .

Statement II is hard to summarize. Put a mark next to it to ensure that you will remember it and use the information that if only two counselors go, no more than six campers may go on the trip.

Next, make a rough sketch of the number of available seats.

Minivan			Sedan
—	—		—
—			
—	—	—	—
—	—		
—	—		

5. **A.** The most efficient way to answer this question is to take one rule at a time and eliminate any violators. Choice B has Alban but no Valdez, so it is out, as per statement III. Choice C is eliminated because it has Robinson and Smith together, which you learned in statement IV is not possible. Toss out choice D because Chen and Nguyen are together, a violation of the penultimate (next-to-last) rule. Finally, choice E is eliminated because it has Valdez without Smith. According to the last rule, Smith must be there for Valdez to be present. By the process of elimination, choice A is the only combination that works.

6. **C.** Decode this question: Which condition would most limit the number of people included? Because the camper:counselor ratio cannot exceed 3:1, choosing only two counselors would mean that a maximum of only six campers could go on the trip. In other words, only eight people would go on the trip, resulting in four empty seats.

   Choice C would force out one of the counselors because . With counselor *C* out, only two counselors are going on the trip.

   If you are completely stuck on this last question, you can at least eliminate choices B and E. Leon and Quint are not mentioned in any of the rules; therefore, their presence does not restrict anyone else from going on the trip.

7. **C.** Choice C looks promising because Pascal is not mentioned in any of the rules. Someone not mentioned in the rules should be able to go on the trip unless all the spaces are taken. To confirm this, draw the roster and circle *r*.

   A B C

   k l m n o p q (*r*) *s t u v*

   Robinson's inclusion means that *s* is out, which in turn eliminates *v* and *A*.

   A̶ B C

   k l m n o p q (*r*) *s̶ t u v̶*

   After counselor *A* is knocked out, counselors *B* and *C* must be included. Because *C* is in, *n* must be eliminated. You still have plenty of room for Pascal.

Questions 8–12

Did just reading through this game make you think of a Stephen King garden fantasy gone amok? Before going through the answer explanations, keep four things in mind:

1. **This is a very hard game, found in only the most difficult exam. You may not even get something this vile.**

2. **There is no penalty for wrong answers on the GRE. Go ahead and guess.**

3. **Some schools don't put much emphasis on the Analytical Ability score.**

4. **You have friends and family who still love you.**

In this game, you must distribute the parts amongst the mowers. A good way to represent this is to draw three circles for the three mowers. Use letters for the parts and put these in the circles. Here's the initial setup:

Remember to start with the most concrete information. The small bolt (b) goes on the yellow mower.

Another simple rule is that W may not appear in the green circle.

You may combine the second rule (small bolt means put on nut) with your diagram to lead to the following:

Symbolize the first rule to make it easier to remember: works well. This does not mean that . B guarantees but is not necessary for . This means that may be present without B. What you can deduce is that no W and/or no N means no B because to have a B without W and/or N would violate the first rule.

Are you still with me? These games get easier with practice, I promise.

Because N and W aren't in the green circle, B can't be either; you can show that there is no B in the green circle.

Put an asterisk by the last rule to help you to remember it. What does this rule tell you about the green circle? Because there has to be at least one part on each mower, there must be an

N in G. Your final diagram (and you thought the day would never come; o ye of little faith!) and roster are as follows:

```
NNNN
Bbb
WWW
```

Crossed out parts are those that have been used.

After all that work, answering the questions is the easy part.

8. **D.** An effective way to answer this question is to select a rule and eliminate the choice(s) that violate the rule.

   Take the simple third rule (no W on G). Choice C violates it; dump choice C. Look at the fourth rule (small b on Y) and eliminate choice E. Choice B violates the fifth rule. Choice A violates the first rule (by gad, this is a violent exam!) because the orange mower must have a washer to go with the large bolt. Only choice D is left.

9. **E.** This question provides a lot of information, so work with it. Put the two large bolts (which also means two nuts and two washers) in the yellow circle:

   There is only one part left (a W) and because of the fifth rule, it must go in O.

10. **E.** As soon as you find one possibility for a choice, you know that the choice need not be false. Take a look at choice D for number 21, which you know is a possibility that doesn't violate any rules. This shows that choices A, B, C, and D could be true and leaves choice E as the answer. To check, try to make E true:

   Remember that you may not put a W or a B in G. The problem is that the two large bolts must go in O or in Y, but there is only one nut left. A large bolt must have a nut, but this is now impossible for one of the large bolts. Choice E must be false.

11. **B.** First, use common sense and eliminate choice E. You can see from your master diagram that at least three of the ten parts are not in O, which makes eight parts for O impossible.

   Make a quick copy of the diagram and try to put in as many parts as possible into O:

It's easy to put a B and a W with the N (see first rule). Can you add anything to B N W? Forget the other B because , but this question does not allow for a second N. See whether you can add a W.

This is fine because the second B may go in Y along with the final N and the final W:

12. **A.** After you put a B in a circle, you must add . The yellow already has two parts, so adding a B would produce the following unacceptable grouping:

This eliminates choices B and D, which put a large bolt on the yellow mower.

Putting both large bolts on a single mower would produce two B N W combinations, or six parts, on a mower. This eliminates choices C and E. Choice A works. Here is one possibility:

Questions 13–17

Is the room suddenly spinning around? Take heart. A game like this looks harder than it really is. An overview of the stimulus and questions reveals that this is a grouping game in which you must select from various subgroups. In grouping games, be aware that not all of the entities have to be chosen.

A good way to keep track of the information is to list a roster, using a different style of letter (for example, uppercase print, uppercase script, lowercase print, lowercase script) to separate the subgroups. This can be done as follows:

A	B	C	math
d	e		humanities
f	g	h	social sciences
J			

Next, go to the rules. Work first with the rules that are the most concrete and/or easiest to incorporate into the diagram. Start by circling "e" (because Elaine is chosen no matter what). Note how many of the subgroups must be chosen.

A	B	C	2 or more
d	e		1 or more
f	g	h	1 or more
J			0 (doesn't *have* to be chosen)

Work with the remaining rules, using some notations that will help you to remember the rules. Because the team may *not* include two or more social science players, change the notation on *f g h* to .

Whenever possible, try to combine rules. The Carlos/Fahid relationship may be represented as follows: If C, then *f*. This does *not* mean if F, then C. Instead, think of it as "if not Fahid, then not Carlos." If *f* is not present, it's impossible for C to be present because C guarantees the presence of *f*.

Still with me, or packing your bags to be ready when the men in the shiny white coats come? Hang in there. Remember, the hardest part of these games is getting the grouping clear in your mind. After you've done that, you can zip right through the questions. Conversely, if you don't have the groupings clear from the start, you probably won't be able to do any of the questions.

To continue: "If *J*, then no *f*; if *f* then no *J*." You may combine this information with the previous statement that "if C, then *f*" to come up with the conclusion that "if C, then *f* but no *J*" and "if *J*, then no *f* and no C."

In summary:

If C, then *f*

If no *f*, no C

If C, then *f* but no *J*

If *J*, then no *f*

If *f*, no *J*

If *J*, then no *f*, no C

13. **C.** Choose one rule at a time and check the choices for violations. Choice E violates the rule that Elaine must be chosen. A grouping game often has one solid piece of information, that someone must be chosen or must not be chosen. That's a great piece of information to keep uppermost in your mind, as it eliminates answer choices quickly. Choice B is wrong because if Carlos is selected, Fahid must be selected as well. Choice A is wrong because it has two social science players (you can't have more than one); choice D is wrong because it does not include two math players. By the process of elimination, choice C is correct.

14. **B.** Draw a roster:

A	B	C	
d	e		Ⓔ
f	g	h	

            J

If J is chosen, f is out, which also means that C is out.

A	B	C	C̶
d	e		Ⓔ
f	g	h	F̶
J			Ⓙ

Because the coach must select two math players, A and B must be chosen, making B the correct answer.

15. **D.** Draw a roster, incorporating the conditions of this question:

A	B	C	
d	e		Ⓔ
f	g	h	G̶
J			

Remember that the coach must select two from the top row, so try A and B.

A	B	C	Ⓐ Ⓑ C̶
d	e		Ⓓ Ⓔ
f	g	h	G
J			

The coach must select one from the *f g h* row, so she has two options; she can select either *f* or *h*.

If the coach selects A and C, she must also select *f*, because you learned earlier that "if C, then *f*."

A	B	C	Ⓐ Ⓒ B̶
d	e		Ⓓ Ⓔ
f	g	h	Ⓕ G̶
J			

A similar result occurs for B and C, the final way to select two math players.

A	B	C	Ⓑ Ⓒ, A̶
d	e		Ⓓ Ⓔ
f	g	h	Ⓕ G̶
J			

In conclusion, there are four possibilities, choice D.

16. **A.** If you combined the rules as suggested in order to get "if Carlos, then Fahid but not James," you have seen that choice A is impossible. If you are not sure of your choice, check the remaining choices. All you need to do is to show that each choice is possible; if it's possible, eliminate it because the question asks which is *im*possible.

Choice B is possible:

A	B	C	Ⓑ	Ⓒ
d	e		Ⓓ	Ⓔ
f	g	h	Ⓖ	
J				

Keep an eye open for information you already deduced or used in previous problems. You know that answer choice C here was the answer to question 21. This indicates that choice C is possible (C and h need not be together). You may also look at your last diagram for question number 23 to verify this possibility.

Choice D is good:

A	B	C	Ⓐ, B, C
d	e		Ⓔ
f	g	h	Ⓕ
J			

And choice E is also a winner:

A	B	C	Ⓐ	Ⓑ
d	e		Ⓓ	Ⓔ
f	g	h	Ⓗ	
J				

17. **D.** James will be selected if there are only two math players and one humanities player. This means Damien must be rejected, narrowing the field to choices B and D. If you are in a big hurry, take a guess. If you've got time, try one answer. Let's do B:

A	B	C	
d	e	~~D~~	Ⓔ
f	g	h	~~G~~
J			

This still allows A, B, and C to be selected:

A	B	C	Ⓐ	Ⓑ	Ⓒ
d	e		~~D~~	Ⓔ
f	g	h	Ⓕ	G
J				

Note that *J* is not selected. But with answer choice D, there is no way to keep *J* out:

A	B	C	Ⓐ	Ⓑ	~~C~~
d	e		~~D~~	Ⓔ
f	g	h	~~F~~	
J			Ⓙ	

Note: "If no *f*, then no C." There is only one social science player; choose *g* or *h* and then choose *J*.

18. **D.** For all you gridiron-challenged types, don't panic. You don't even need to know the difference between a touchdown and a rubdown to answer this question. The key is to recognize that the second sentence is the conclusion, which states that interceptions are one of the major causes of football game losses. The first sentence provides the evidence for the conclusion, and it says that there is a relationship between the number of interceptions thrown and game losses. Does this establish with certainty that the interceptions have a lot to do with causing the losses? No, for all you know, the

interceptions could come about as a result of a team's losing a game. (Football afi-cionados know that a team that is losing starts throwing more passes and is thereby likely to throw more interceptions.) For the argument to be valid, its author must assume that interceptions are a cause rather than a result of losing. Choice D points to this very thing.

Choice A is out because the stimulus says nothing about fumbles. The argument does not claim that interceptions are the only thing that can hurt a football team. Choice B is too extreme: The author does not have to assume zero interceptions. Choice C is a pos-sible, but hardly definite, inference, as the author doesn't *have* to assume it. The author discusses how interceptions contribute to losses. He is not concerned with how a team can overcome an interception. Perhaps bad officiating allows a team to win despite throwing more interceptions; who knows? Choice E provides one good reason why interceptions might contribute to losing games, but it is not a necessary assump-tion. It could be, for example, that interceptions interfere with a team's ability to score more than they make it easy for the opponent to score.

19. **A.** This argument misses the mark. The conclusion has to do with whether voice train-ing is necessary for operatic stardom, but the evidence runs along the lines of saying that voice training does not guarantee a career in opera. The evidence would be better used to support a conclusion that stated that voice training is not sufficient for one to become an opera star. Even if the evidence stated that only one in a million voice train-ing graduates became an opera star, it still might be the case that the voice training was necessary. A great way to weaken the argument would be to establish that, no matter how difficult it is to become an opera star, it is impossible to become an opera star without voice training. This is pretty much what choice A states.

Choice B would work well if the conclusion stated that voice training is largely unsuc-cessful in helping one land a role as a singer. It does nothing to establish that voice training is necessary to become an opera star.

Choice C suggests that the 2 percent figure will go up after some voice training gradu-ates age. However, it can't be established that voice training is necessary for operatic stardom. It still could be the case that many opera stars made it on raw talent alone.

Choice D suggests that opera company membership is not the place to look for the exis-tence of opera stars, but it does not say anything about whether voice training is neces-sary or not. Maybe all those opera stars had voice training, but maybe they did not.

Choice E provides a single example (typically not a great weakener) of voice training paying off. Voice training may have worked for Stephanie, but maybe she would have made it anyway. What about other stars? Did they go through voice training?

Question 20

Does this game make you think your mental confusion is, uh, terminal? In your opinion, is Alphabet Communications right up there with other Communicable Diseases? Okay, calm down, take a deep breath, and approach this maze one step at a time.

In most mapping games, the actual locations are not important. The games typically reward your ability to keep track of the connections. Put the terminals in a circle (as in Figure 1):

Indicate the connections with arrows. The simplest way to do this is to point the arrows towards the ending point of a connection (see Figure 2). Double-headed arrows indicate that the connections go both ways (for example., B to C and C to B). Be sure to represent the two different systems (system *X* and system *Y*) with different types of lines. Use a legend, as a map does, to remind you of which system is which.

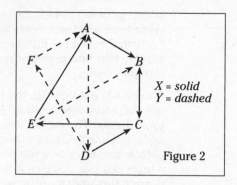

Figure 1   Figure 2

X = solid
Y = dashed

20. **B.** Some simple math will give you the right answer. One piece of information the stimulus gives you is that a six-minute phone connection costs twice what mailing a letter cost when fax machines were first in use. These days you can send a fax in two minutes as opposed to six minutes, which means that sending a fax outside of your calling area will cost you no more than a two-minute call. A two-minute connection costs one-third as much as a six-minute connection; therefore, the charge to send a two-page document by fax is one-third what it was when fax machines were first used. This makes sending documents by fax cheaper than sending them by mail, which is one-half the cost of a fax when fax machines were first used (or even more than one-half if postal rates go up). Whew! Choice B makes sense.

Choice A looks good, but it says "better" rather than "cheaper," making it subjective and incorrect. Who's to say what's better? What if an original is necessary? A fax won't do much good then, no matter how cheap it is. The word *better* goes too far. Choice E can be eliminated by similar reasoning.

Choice C mentions "any" document, pushing it too far as well. What about a 50-page document or a 500-page one? Such a document might occupy the lines for a long time and push the fax charges to the stratospheres.

Choice D is wrong for two reasons. First, the stimulus does not discuss charges that are not outside the local calling area. Second, it is probable that the advantage of a fax over regular mail is even greater inside the local calling area in that such phone line connections are cheaper than long-distance connections, but mail costs are the same inside or outside a local calling area.

Questions 21–25

A good way to keep track of this matching game is to use circles to represent the first-, second-, and third-place finishers. Divide each circle into three parts so that you can "match up" the horse, jockey, and trainer for each position. Here is the basic plan:

Here is the initial diagram.

Horses: R, S, T
Jockeys: a, b, c
Trainers: j, l, w

Fill in the diagram as much as you can, starting with the most concrete information. The last rule can readily be incorporated into the diagram.

Next, work with the second and third rules as they contain a common element, Lukas, which may allow for additional deductions. If Lukas and Jolley are not consecutive, they must be first and third, or vice versa. This also means that Whittingham must be second. Draw both possibilities:

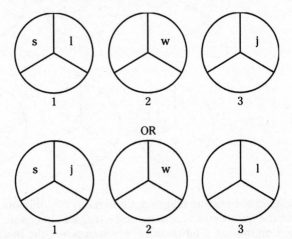

The second rule states that l and b go together, so insert this information into both of the above possibilities. Here is the result:

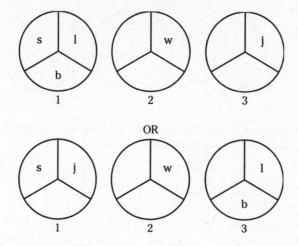

The first rule can now be incorporated into the diagram. (It would not have been so easy had you started with this rule.)

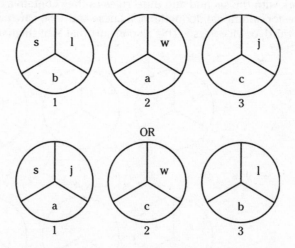

21. **B.** Consult the bottom diagram. Choice B is the only option that fits. A little thinking about the nature of a multiple-choice test would enable you to eliminate choices D and E right off the bat. If either one were an answer, the test maker would have to accept two choices, which won't happen. If, say, choice D were an answer, one of A, B, or C would also be correct because one of these three has to train Rive Ridge.

22. **B.** Only the top diagram allows Whittingham to finish ahead of Jolley. Choice E is definitely out because it has to be true. Choices A, C, and D are all possible. Choice B is the answer because Lukas trains Baeza's horse.

23. **A.** Check each rule, one at a time, and eliminate inconsistent choices until only one choice is left.

    The straightforward, final rule eliminates choice E. The first rule makes choice B impossible. Choice D violates the second rule, and choice C would make it impossible to separate Lukas and Jolley. This leaves choice A as the answer.

24. **E.** What you are trying to do is to determine which choice would force you to go with the bottom options of your two diagrams. Note that it is only this bottom option in which Cordero's horse finished second.

    Choice A works with either option. Choice B works only with the top option. Choice C works with either option, as does choice D. Choice E is the answer because it fits only the bottom option.

25. **D.** The hypothetical nature of the choices requires you to spend some time checking whether each choice is a possibility. Choice A is out because Riva Ridge could finish second or third with Cordero (see the diagrams). Choice B is false: The Jolley-trained horse would be first. Choice C is similar to A. Here, Riva Ridge could finish second or third. Choice D is the answer because only the bottom option can accommodate it. The following results:

Riva Ridge is second. Choice E is false. If Tim Tam is trained by Whittingham, Tim Tam is second.

Questions 26–19

First, make life much easier by changing the professors' names to initials: *E, F, G, H, I, J, K, L.* Map out the connections. *E* is a key figure, so place her near the center and go from there. You don't have to go in order. It's easier to get a chain going by working with common elements. For example, *E→F* links up with *F→K*, which links with *K→E.* This is shown in the following figure:

The completed map is as follows:

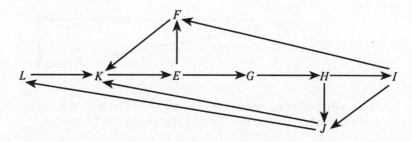

26. **C.** Work backwards. To get the journal back to *G*, it must get to *E*. To get to *E*, it must get to *K*. The shortest route from *G* to *K* is through *H* and *J*. This produces the following route:

If *E* receives the journal on 1/5, *G* will receive it on 1/6.

27. **B.** *G* must see the journal if it is to reach *H* (nobody else connects to *H*). The others can be avoided.

28. **B.** Try the shortest route for both $E \to F$ and $E \to G$. For $E \to F$, it's $E \to F \to K \to E \to G \to H \to I \to J \to L$. That's nine days. For $E \to G$, it's $E \to G \to H \to I \to J \to L \to K \to E \to F$. It's still nine days, so the answer is *B*.

Note that it's crucial to go from $H \to I \to J$. *Going from* $H \to I \to F$ *forces a lot of extra circulating to pick up J. Similarly,* $H \to J \to L$ *forces a lot of extra connections to pick up* I.

29. **D.** Trace out the routes.

If you stopped here, you fell for the trap and chose B. Yes, there are four routes, but the last two routes may be modified by having *J* go to *L* before *K*.

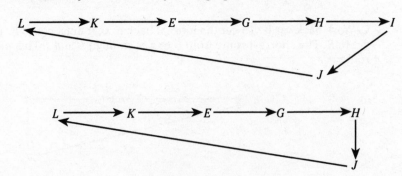

30. **D.** The argument is that the music is recognizable from three characteristics: chords, voice timbre, and banter. The rock fan must be making the assumption, therefore, that the Beatles (and *only* the Beatles) have those three characteristics the way they appear on this tape. If other groups had the same chords, voice timbre, and banter, they would be indistinguishable from the Beatles.

Choice A is too specific. Chords are not necessarily the most distinctive feature of a song; this fan also thinks about voice timbre, for example. Choice B is probably true but is irrelevant to the conclusion that this tape probably comes from the Beatles. If anything, the very rarity of such bootleg tapes argues against this particular tape's being such a Beatles' session. Choice C is way too broad. Nothing is said about any other forms of art. It also flies in the face of common sense. You probably know that people can identify paintings, for example, from characteristics used by the artist (brushstrokes, perspective, use of color, and so on).

Choice E is very tempting. However, the rock fan doesn't assume that the Beatles are the most distinctive group, just that there are means of identifying their distinct characteristics on a tape.

31. **B.** Because of the word *except*, you need to find the one choice that does *not* provide a reason for why those who live in high-achieving districts are likely to complain.

Choice A is very explicit in presenting a factor that accounts for complaints from high-achieving districts.

Choices C and D are especially good at explaining why parents in high-achieving districts are more likely to complain than those in low-achieving districts.

Choice E doesn't focus on how high scores lead to complaints in the way that choices C and D do, but is it still provides an explanation. For all we know, the activists are complaining about low scores in other districts, but the fact remains that they live in a high-achieving district. The complaints are coming from such a district, even though they're not about that district.

Choice B is the credited response for a similar reason that choice E is not the answer. Choice B describes complaints about high-achieving districts, but the complaints are coming from parents who live outside the districts. As such, choice B does not explain so many who live in high-achieving districts complain.

32. **E.** This question is asking for something that is inconsistent with the information, meaning that four of the items will be consistent.

These four consistent items don't necessarily have to be *true*, which makes this type of question trickier than ones that ask for something that is true or false.

Choice A is not only consistent with the information but also has to be true. Economics 101A is a prerequisite for Economics 101B, which is a prerequisite for Economics 101C. If you are taking Economics 101C, you must have completed the prerequisite Economics 101B. To have taken and completed Economics 101B, you must have completed Economics 101A.

Choice B is not necessarily true, but it is consistent with the information. Nothing in the information forces you to take Economics 101B upon the completion of Economics 101A. Completion of the latter course makes you eligible for Economics 101B, but it is not sufficient to guarantee enrollment in Economics 101B.

This necessary/sufficient distinction is very important on the GRE. Economics 101A is necessary for Economics 101B, but it is not sufficient. The connection between Economics 101A and 102A is an example of a sufficient condition. Completion of Economics 101A forces you to take Economics 102A, so 101A is sufficient for 102A. It is not, however, necessary in that you might be eligible for 102A even without taking 101A. The stimulus does not shut off this possibility.

Choice C is tough to eliminate, but it is consistent. Economics 101A is certainly a requirement for Economics 101B, but there may be several other requirements. If you did not fulfill these prerequisites, you are ineligible.

Choice D is not necessarily true because Economics 101A and 101B are necessary, but not sufficient, for Economics 101C, but the choice still presents a situation that is entirely possible. Choice D is consistent, so it is not the answer.

Choice E is impossible. If you will not take Economics 102A, you could not have completed Economics 101A because 101A guarantees 102A. Without taking Economics 101A, you are ineligible for Economics 101B, in direct contradiction to choice E.

Questions 33–35

Your task is to determine which three characteristics belong on each plant. A good way to represent the plants is with a circle divided into three parts. Fill in the information for each plant according to the following scheme:

Start out with four such circles and put L in number two and Y in number four.

The rule prohibiting round yellow peas means that if a pea is yellow, it must be wrinkled, and if a pea is round, it must be green. This may be symbolized as $Y \rightarrow W$; $R \vee G$. Because of this, fill in number four with a W.

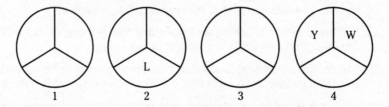

Do not assume that $W \rightarrow Y$. A green wrinkled pea does not violate the rule. In other words, $W \rightarrow Y$ or G. Similarly, don't assume $G \rightarrow R$.

The *penultimate* (next to last) rule can be summarized as $R \rightarrow L$. This does not mean $L \rightarrow R$ (round guarantees large, but a pea can be large without being round). What you do know is $S \rightarrow W$ because if $S \rightarrow R$, there would be a round pea that was not large. Combine $R \rightarrow L$ with $R \rightarrow G$ and write $R \rightarrow$. Round peas are both large and green.

The first rule can be summarized as .

33. **B.** This problem may be a good one to skip for the time being. Little work can be done before looking at the choices. In other words, this turkey is a real time-gobbler.

What you are looking for is the choice that will lead to only one possibility for the size of number four (you already know the color and the shape). If you are really on top of things, you will realize that number four must be small if number one and number three are large (number two is large, so if numbers one, two, and three are all large, number four must be small because the rules tell you that each characteristic is found on at least one of the plants).

Choice A makes number one small and number three large but doesn't restrict the size of number four.

Choice B is what you want. If number one is R, it is also L. Number three is obviously L. This makes number four S because there must be at least one S.

Choice C misses the mark because number three could be small or large. The same is true of choice D. Choice E provides the color for number two, a plant whose size was already known. Being told that number four is wrinkled is redundant; you already knew that.

34. **B.** If number two has the only large pea, numbers one, three, and four must have small peas. Remember that S → W and draw:

A quick look shows that number two must be R (and also G because R → G) because there must be one R.

Number one and number three could both be Y to yield three Y and one G. Neither must be G, so only number two must be G.

35. **D.** Draw a quick diagram, remembering that S → W (number one) and R → (number three).

If number one is Y, number two must also be Y (and W, because Y → W) because . This will give three Y and one G. Number four may be either S or L, so there are two possibilities when number one is Y.

If number one is G, number two is G, but it may be W or R. Number four may still be S or L. In summary, here are the four possibilities when number one is G:

1	2	4
G	G W	S
G	G W	L
G	G R	S
G	G R	L

Add these four to the two possibilities when number one is Y, and you get six.

Part VII
The Part of Tens

In this part . . .

This unit is your reward for surviving the previous 22 chapters. No brainpower is required for these next few chapters. You don't have to work through math problems, don't have to memorize new vocabulary, and don't have to stimulate the synapses at all. These chapters are just for fun, but they do provide invaluable information, such as relaxation techniques to help you get through the GRE. Read on.

Chapter 23

Ten Wrong Rumors about the GRE

● ●

In This Chapter (Remember: These statements are WRONG!)

▶ You can't study for the GRE

▶ Your GRE score will be about the same as your SAT score from high school

▶ The GRE tests IQ

▶ You must pass certain classes to take the GRE

▶ Your score won't improve if you keep retaking the GRE

▶ The GRE has a passing score

▶ You can take the GRE on your own computer at home

▶ You can bring your own laptop to the testing center

▶ Missing the first few questions gives you an easier test and better score

▶ Computer geniuses have an unfair advantage on the GRE

● ●

Sure, you've heard them: the horror stories about the GRE. Rumors abound, growing wilder with each telling: "You have to know calculus!" (Absolutely not.) "It's an open book test this year!" (You *wish!*)

As a test preparation tutor, I get calls all the time from students trying to check out the latest scuttlebutt. Here are ten common stories that make the rounds every year — as dependable as oversleeping the morning of your most important final.

You can't study for the GRE

Why would I be writing this book if that were so? Studying can be done in two ways, each advantageous in its own right. First is the last-minute cram, a review in a few weeks of the types of questions, the approach to each question, the tricks and traps involved in the questions. (Sound familiar? This method is what you've been working on throughout this book.) Second is the long-range study program, in which you learn vocabulary and work on math questions from your freshman year in college on. Obviously, if you've got a year or two to put into this, you should get a dynamite score. Most people, however, benefit greatly from even a few weeks or months of intense study.

Your GRE score will be about the same as your SAT score from high school

Are you the same person you were in high school? You have matured, learned better study habits, and suddenly come to the shocking realization that no one is going to spoon-feed you anymore. You may not have studied much for the SAT, figuring that you could always get into *some* college, somewhere, no matter what your score. You were probably right. But getting into graduate school is not as easy. There aren't as many graduate programs as undergraduate programs, making a more cutthroat competition. Because you realize this, you study harder and study smarter. Besides, your vocabulary almost certainly has improved significantly after four years of college, and vocabulary is usually the most difficult portion of the exam for students.

The GRE tests IQ

Nope. The GRE supposedly tests your ability to do well in graduate school. Some cynics say that all the GRE tests is your ability to take the GRE. Getting into a debate over that point is rather futile because you're stuck with taking the GRE and worrying about it just wastes brainpower you can use for other things. But be reassured that the GRE is not an IQ test. You can learn to improve your GRE score with all sorts of tricks, traps, and techniques; that's *much* harder to do on IQ tests.

Have you ever heard of MENSA, the national high-IQ society? Although the GRE is not a measure of IQ per se, if you do well on the GRE, you can sometimes get automatic membership in MENSA (something that looks great on résumés and impresses the socks off dates' parents). Call the local MENSA chapter to find out what the qualifying score is. Hey, you put the effort into getting the score; scarf up all the benefits from the score that you can get.

You must pass certain classes to take the GRE

Although taking classes like advanced logic or linguistics is useful, let's get real here: Not many people take those courses today. If you are reading this book as a freshman or sopho-more and have the option of taking logic classes, excellent. Doing so will help you with the analytical ability portion of the GRE. But you certainly don't *have* to have a class like that to do well on the GRE. (That's a relief; who has room for that class in an already overcrowded curriculum?) As far as math goes, the GRE tests basic algebra, geometry, and arithmetic. A year of algebra and a year of geometry are sufficient. In short, the GRE has no "required courses" or "prerequisites."

Your score won't improve if you keep retaking the GRE

Although having your score jump hundreds of points is uncommon, it has happened. Your improvement depends on the reason your score was low in the first place and on how much you study before retaking the exam. If your score was low because you didn't understand the format of the exam (for example, you looked at a Quantitative Comparison question and won-dered where the answer choices were!), you can certainly improve that score by taking a few practice exams and becoming more comfortable with the question styles. If your score was low because you fell for all the traps set in the GRE, you can improve your score by going through these materials, learning to recognize those traps, and studying the tips and tricks for avoiding those traps. But it is unrealistic for a slow reader to think that a few weeks of study is going to double her reading speed or for someone who doesn't understand algebra at all to think she can get a year's worth of algebra instruction in an afternoon. You do need *some* basics under your belt.

The study time you put into preparing for the second exam is also important. If you take the exam, get back your scores, register for another exam, and then just a few days before the second exam begin studying again, you may as well forget it. Although experience helps, your score won't soar simply because you've done this before. You have to study for the second test, or you'll repeat the mistakes of the first.

The GRE has a passing score

You can't pass or fail the GRE, but a particular graduate school may have a cutoff score that you must get to be considered for admission. This score is often based on your GPA. A school may decree, for example, that if your GPA is in the 3.0 to 3.5 range, you can get an 1100 (combined verbal and math), but if your GPA is in the 2.5 to 3.0 range, your GRE must be at least a 1200. You will want to find out the GRE ranges considered acceptable by the schools you are considering.

You can take the GRE on your own computer at home

Oh sure, suuuuuuure. You can take the test at home, with your computer, your dictionary, your reference books, and your cousin Morty the Math Genius all standing by, ready to help you! And while we're at it, I'll be glad to come by and stand at your shoulder, pointing out all the traps as well. Sorry. You cannot take the GRE anywhere but at a recognized testing center, usually a Sylvan Learning Center (see information in Chapter 1 about testing sites).

You can bring your own laptop to the testing center

Wouldn't taking your laptop be nice? You could load all sorts of programs into your computer, such as math formulas and algorithms, or pages and pages of vocabulary, and taking the GRE would be a snap. Unfortunately, the GRE people are way ahead of you on this one. Not only do you have to take the exam at a special testing center, but you also have to take it on their computers. The only thing you supply is the brainpower and the Tylenol.

Missing the first few questions gives you an easier test and better score

Right and wrong. The first five questions do indeed determine the difficulty level of the whole exam. For all practical purposes, you start off with a score of 500, right in the middle of the score range (your score can go from 200 to 800). If you get the first question right, you get about +100 and have a 600-level exam going. If you miss the first question, you get about -100 and have a 400-level exam going. The second question is worth about 70 points. If you get it right and you got the first question right, the computer thinks you're smart enough to be working at a 670+ level, and you get a nice hard test. If you miss the second question and you missed the first question, you're working down in the 300s. You'll get an easy test, but you have almost no way to bring your score back up into the 600s. The moral of the story is: The first few questions are that "first impression" the computer gets about you. You never have a second chance to make a first impression.

Computer geniuses have an unfair advantage on the GRE

Computer geniuses have an unfair advantage over all of the rest of us in this age of high-tech; why should the GRE be any different? Let's get real here. Sure, students who are very comfortable with a computer may have a little advantage because they have one less stress factor going into the test, but that's where the advantage ends. The computer skills required for taking the GRE are so minimal that they're almost irrelevant. Hey, if it makes you feel any better, computer geniuses tell me they feel at a disadvantage on this test because of the "annoyingly simplistic technology."

Chapter 24

Ten Dumb Things You Can Do to Mess Up Your GRE

In This Chapter

▶ Losing concentration

▶ Panicking over time

▶ Rubbernecking

▶ Cheating

▶ Worrying about the previous sections

▶ Worrying about the hard problems

▶ Transferring information from problem to problem or section to section

▶ Forgetting to double-check

▶ Looking back and playing "coulda-shoulda"

Throughout this book, you learned techniques for doing your best on the GRE. I'm sorry to say, however, that there are just as many techniques for messing up big time on this test. Take a few minutes to read through them now, to see what dumb things people do to blow the exam totally. By being aware of these catastrophes, you may prevent their happening to you.

And no — no Booby Prize is awarded to the student who makes the greatest number of these mistakes.

Losing concentration

When you're in the middle of an excruciatingly boring Reading Comprehension passage, the worst thing you can do is let your mind drift off to a more pleasant time (last night's date, last weekend's soccer game, the time you stole your rival school's mascot and set it on the john in the dean's private bathroom). Although visualization (picturing yourself doing something relaxing or fun) is a good stress-reduction technique, it stinks when it comes to helping your GRE score. Even if you have to pinch yourself to keep from falling asleep or flaking out, stay focused. The GRE is just a few hours of your life. You've had horrible blind dates that lasted longer than that and you managed to survive them. This too shall pass.

Panicking over time

Every section of the GRE has a specified time limit. On the computer-based test, the time limit is shown by the on-screen clock (which you do have the option of turning off, in case it's driving you crazy). You know going into the test exactly how many questions are in each section and therefore how many minutes you have per question. It's not as if this is some big mystery.

Cheating

Dumb, dumb, *dumb!* Cheating on the GRE is a loser's game — it's just plain stupid. Apart from the legal, moral, and ethical questions, let's talk practicality: You can't predict what types of vocabulary words will show up in the questions; what are you going to do, copy a dictionary on the palm of your hand? All the math formulas you need can't fit onto the bottom of your shoe. Copying everything that you *think* you may need would take more time than just learning it. Besides, the GRE tries very hard to test critical reasoning skills, not just rote memorization. The test never asks a question as straightforward as, "How many degrees in a triangle?" The questions require thinking and reasoning, not just copying down a formula. Short of having a brain transplant, cheating is impractical.

Worrying about the previous sections

Think of the GRE as three separate lifetimes. You are reborn twice and get two more chances to "do it right." Every time the computer prompts you to go to a new section, you get a fresh start. You have one verbal section, one math section, and one analytical section. (I cover the breakdown in much more detail in Chapter 1.) The computer is inexorable. You can't go back to a previous section if you suddenly recall a vocabulary word that had eluded you (such as inexorable, in the previous sentence!) You can't double-check your arithmetic on a math question. Forget one section as soon as you enter the next. Think of this as you would a new boyfriend or girlfriend in your life: Out with the old and in with the new.

Worrying about the hard problems

The GRE contains some incredibly hard problems. If you get the first few questions on the exam correct, the computer assumes that you're a genius and confidently offers you real mind-bogglers later on. If you miss the first few questions, the computer takes it easy on you and gives you a kinder, gentler exam (and, alas, a lower, wimpier score). Suppose that you ace the first few questions and then get some super-hard questions. Of course, you have to answer them because the computer doesn't let you go on until you punch in an answer. But if the question is just way, way beyond you, make a quick guess (emphasis on quick!), go on, and don't fret. A ridiculously few students get total 800s every year. If you get into the 700s or even the 600s, you are in a super-elite club of only a few of the thousands of students who take the GRE annually. Just accept the fact that you can't be sure of your answer on some of the questions and learn to live with your imperfections.

Rushing through the confirm step

When you answer a question, the computer gives you a second chance. Your screen offers you a Confirm button that you have to click on before your answer becomes permanent. Life has so few second chances; take advantage of this one. Sure, you may feel rushed; everyone does, but take those few extra seconds. Keep reminding yourself that the exam is not like a paper-and-pencil test, in which you can come back at the end and double-check for careless mistakes. You make a choice, confirm that choice, and that's all she wrote. Take the few extra seconds before clicking on the Confirm button.

Stressing out over your computer skills (or lack thereof)

The GRE, in and of itself, is stressful enough. The last thing you need to do is add more anxiety to the whole nerve-racking experience of taking the test by worrying about your computer expertise. Can you type, even a little bit, in a one-finger style? If so, you have mastered all of the computer skills that the GRE requires of you. Before you begin taking the test, you complete a very brief tutorial (no, the time spent on that does not count as actual testing time) that refreshes your computer abilities, and you have the Help key available to you at all times during the actual test.

Trying to keep track of the question breakdown

Keeping track of your own (mental, emotional, and psychological) breakdown is a good idea. Keeping track of the question breakdown is not. By "the question breakdown," I mean the number of each type of question. You know that in the verbal portion, for example, you have questions in four formats: Antonyms, Analogies, Sentence Completions, and Reading Comprehension. These questions can be in any order. In other words, don't say to yourself, "Well, I've finished three Sentence Completion questions; I know it's time for Reading Comprehension." The computer makes those decisions, not you. Worrying about which type of question comes next is the high-tech equivalent of flipping forward to see how many pages you have left to read of a novel. All you do is waste your time; you don't shorten the number of pages.

Ignoring the five-minute breaks offered

You are offered a short break (usually 5 minutes) between sections (Verbal, Math, and Analytical). If you don't take those breaks between the sections, you'll be sitting still for hours. I see students often pass on the breaks, especially the first one, wanting to get this whole ordeal over with as soon as possible. Although I sympathize with the desire, I strongly, strongly suggest that you take all the rest breaks that are offered. Even just standing up, swinging your arms, and grumbling a little bit will make you feel better.

Scheduling the test at the same time as your best friend

Depending on the size and availability of the test center, you and your buddy may be able to take the test at the same time. Big mistake. It's only human to try to compare your progress with your friend's. Unfortunately, you and your friend won't get the exact same exam. Your questions will be different. If you see your buddy zooming through the material, a big smile on her face, you may depress yourself unnecessarily. (Maybe she missed the first few questions and now is getting a much easier exam than yours. You never know.) The GRE is one place where the buddy system just doesn't work.

Chapter 25

Ten Relaxation Techniques You Can Try Before and During the GRE

● ●

In This Chapter

▶ Breathe deeply

▶ Rotate your head

▶ Hunch and roll your shoulders

▶ Cross and roll your eyes

▶ Shake out your hands

▶ Extend and push out your legs

▶ Cup your eyes

▶ Rotate your scalp

▶ Curtail negative thoughts

▶ Before the test or during the break, visualize

● ●

Most people are tense before the test, with butterflies dancing in their stomachs. The key is to use relaxation techniques that keep your mind on your test and not on your tummy.

Breathe deeply

Breathing is grossly underrated. Breathing is good. Take a deep breath until your belly expands, hold your breath for a few counts, and then expel the air through your nose. (Be careful not to blow anything but air, especially if your boyfriend/girlfriend is sitting next to you.) Try not to take short, shallow breaths, which could cause you to become even more anxious, as your body is deprived of oxygen. Try breathing in and out deeply while reciting something in your mind, such as your favorite line from a movie, or a totally stupid, mindless rhyme.

Rotate your head

Try to see behind your head. Move your head as far as possible to the right until you feel a tug on the skin on the left side of your neck. Then reverse it and move your head all the way to the left until you feel a tug on the skin on the right. Move your head back, as if you're looking at the ceiling, and then down, as if looking at your feet. You'll be surprised how much tension drains out of you as you do this a few times.

Be careful that you perform this exercise with your eyes closed and make what you're doing obvious. You don't want a suspicious proctor to think you're craning your neck to look at someone else's computer screen.

Hunch and roll your shoulders

While breathing in, scrunch up your shoulders as if you're trying to touch them to your ears. Then roll them back and down, breathing out. Arch your back, sitting up super-straight, as if a string is attached to the top of your head and is being pulled toward the ceiling. Then slump and round out your lower back, pushing it out toward the back of your chair. These exercises relax your upper and lower back. They are especially useful if you develop a kink in your spine.

Cross and roll your eyes

Look down at your desk as you're doing this so that people won't think you're even stranger than they already know you are. Cross your eyes and then look down as far as you can into your lower eyelids. Look to the right and then up into your eyelids and then look to the left. After you repeat this sequence a few times, your eyes should be refreshed.

Shake out your hands

You probably do this automatically to try to get rid of writer's cramp. Do it more consciously and more frequently. Put your hands down at your sides, hanging them below your chair seat, and shake them vigorously. Imagine all the tension and stress going out through your fingers and dropping onto the floor.

Extend and push out your legs

While you're sitting at your desk, straighten your legs out in front of you; think of pushing something away with your heels. Point your toes back toward your knees. You feel a stretch on the backs of your legs. Hold for a count of three and then relax.

Cup your eyes

Cup your hands, fingers together. Put them over your closed eyes, blocking out all the light. You're now in a world of velvety-smooth darkness, which is very soothing. Try not to let your hands actually touch your eyes. (If you see stars or flashes of light, your hands are pushing down on your eyes.)

Rotate your scalp

Put your open hand palm-down on your scalp. Move your hand in small circles. Feel your scalp rotate. Lift your hand and put it down somewhere else on your scalp. Repeat the circular motions. You're giving yourself a very relaxing scalp massage.

Curtail negative thoughts

Any time you feel yourself starting to panic or thinking negative thoughts, make a conscious effort to say to yourself, "*Stop!*" Don't dwell on anything negative; switch over to a positive track. Suppose that you catch yourself thinking, "Why didn't I study this math more? I saw that formula a hundred times but can't remember it now!" Change the script to, "I got most of this math right; if I let my subconscious work on that formula, maybe I'll get it, too. No sense in worrying now. Overall, I think I'm doing great."

Before the test or during a break, visualize

Don't do this *during* the test; you just waste time and lose concentration. Before the exam, however, or at the break, practice visualization. Close your eyes and imagine yourself in the exam room, seeing questions you know the answers to, cheerfully punching the Confirm button. Picture yourself leaving the exam room either dancing in the parking lot because you got your unofficial score right off the computer, or eager to rush home and begin your mailbox vigil, which will end about four to six weeks later with the good news delivered to your door. Think of how proud your parents are of you. Imagine the acceptance letter you get from the graduate school of your dreams. Picture yourself driving a fire-engine-red Ferrari ten years from now, telling the *Time* magazine reporter in the passenger seat that your success started with your excellent GRE scores. The goal is to associate the GRE with good feelings.

Index

• U •

ubiety, 204
ubiquitous, 203
ultimate, 50
uncouth, 254
uneducated, 251
unenthusiastic, 254
unfazed, 51
units of measurement, 124–125
unruly, 204
"unscored" sections, 8
usurper, 253

• V •

vapid, 252
variables
  isolating in equations, 104
  multiplying in parentheses, 105–106
  plugging in numbers for, 144–145, 145–146, 206, 207, 212
  substituting for, in symbolism problems, 101–102
vehemently, 254
veracity, 16, 201
verbal score, 13
verbal score chart, 248
verbs
  in primary purpose questions, 203
  turning into infinitives, in analogies, 21
verdad, 201
vertical angles, 77
vertical axis, 89
vestigial, 54
vi, 251
viable, 41
visage, 51
visualization, practicing before and after the test, 294
vital, 41
vituperative, 205
vivacious, 251
volume
  of any figure, 208, 213
  of a cube, 87
  of a cylinder, 87–88, 208
  of a polygon, 87
  ratio for two similar figures, 80

voracious, 252
votary, 22
vulnerable, 203

• W •

weary, 252
weeks, 125
weighted averages, 115–116
wheedle, 202
whole numbers, 119
widespread, 254
wince, 28
wither, 251
words, looking for the salient features of, 22
work problems, 122–123, 210
wrath, 205

• X •

x, solving for, 104–105
x-axis, 89

• Y •

yards, 124
y-axis, 89
year, 125

• Z •

zealous, 30
zenith, 201
zero, division by, 120
zero angles, 75
zero exponent, 149

Notes

Notes

Notes

Notes

Notes

Notes

Notes

Discover Dummies Online!

The Dummies Web Site is your fun and friendly online resource for the latest information about *For Dummies*® books and your favorite topics. The Web site is the place to communicate with us, exchange ideas with other *For Dummies* readers, chat with authors, and have fun!

Ten Fun and Useful Things You Can Do at www.dummies.com

1. Win free *For Dummies* books and more!

2. Register your book and be entered in a prize drawing.

3. Meet your favorite authors through the IDG Books Worldwide Author Chat Series.

4. Exchange helpful information with other *For Dummies* readers.

5. Discover other great *For Dummies* books you must have!

6. Purchase Dummieswear® exclusively from our Web site.

7. Buy *For Dummies* books online.

8. Talk to us. Make comments, ask questions, get answers!

9. Download free software.

10. Find additional useful resources from authors.

Link directly to these ten fun and useful things at **http://www.dummies.com/10useful**

For other technology titles from IDG Books Worldwide, go to www.idgbooks.com

Not on the Web yet? It's easy to get started with *Dummies 101*®: *The Internet For Windows*® *98* or *The Internet For Dummies*® at local retailers everywhere.

Find other *For Dummies* books on these topics:

Business • Career • Databases • Food & Beverage • Games • Gardening • Graphics • Hardware
Health & Fitness • Internet and the World Wide Web • Networking • Office Suites
Operating Systems • Personal Finance • Pets • Programming • Recreation • Sports
Spreadsheets • Teacher Resources • Test Prep • Word Processing

IDG BOOKS WORLDWIDE BOOK REGISTRATION

Register This Book and Win!

We want to hear from you!

Visit **http://my2cents.dummies.com** to register this book and tell us how you liked it!

- Get entered in our monthly prize giveaway.

- Give us feedback about this book — tell us what you like best, what you like least, or maybe what you'd like to ask the author and us to change!

- Let us know any other *For Dummies®* topics that interest you.

Your feedback helps us determine what books to publish, tells us what coverage to add as we revise our books, and lets us know whether we're meeting your needs as a *For Dummies* reader. You're our most valuable resource, and what you have to say is important to us!

Not on the Web yet? It's easy to get started with *Dummies 101®: The Internet For Windows® 98* or *The Internet For Dummies®* at local retailers everywhere.

Or let us know what you think by sending us a letter at the following address:

For Dummies Book Registration
Dummies Press
10475 Crosspoint Blvd.
Indianapolis, IN 46256

BESTSELLING BOOK SERIES